SKILLS OF MANAGEMENT AND LEADERSHIP

D1460674

Skills of Management and Leadership

Managing People in Organizations

W. David Rees
and
Christine Porter

 palgrave

First published 2015 by
PALGRAVE

Palgrave in the UK is an imprint of Macmillan Publishers Limited, registered in England, company number 785998, of 4 Crinan Street, London N1 9XW

Palgrave Macmillan in the US is a division of St Martin's Press LLC, 175 Fifth Avenue, New York, NY 10010.

Palgrave is a global imprint of the above companies and is represented throughout the world.

Palgrave® and Macmillan® are registered trademarks in the United States, the United Kingdom, Europe and other countries.

ISBN 978–1–137–32561–7

This book is printed on paper suitable for recycling and made from fully managed and sustained forest sources. Logging, pulping and manufacturing processes are expected to conform to the environmental regulations of the country of origin.

A catalogue record for this book is available from the British Library.

A catalog record for this book is available from the Library of Congress.

Typeset by MPS Limited, Chennai, India.

Printed in China

Contents

List of Figures

Acknowledgements

Particular acknowledgement is due to the countless number of management students who in different classes and organizational workshops have allowed us to explain and test out our ideas. Such management students have also contributed their own ideas and given many invaluable illustrative examples about how things work in practice. The classes have been on a wide variety of courses, particularly those run at the University of Westminster's Business School. One of the many insights we have gained is the overlap between the skills needed to work in management and in the diplomatic field. We have also benefited by our involvement with a range of manufacturing organizations, the UK National Health Service, a range of London local authorities and some not-for-profit organizations. Our understanding of the impact of national culture on management has also been developed by a series of overseas management assignments including in China, France, Guyana, India, Indonesia, Malaysia, Romania, and Singapore.

We are also indebted to help from a range of individuals. There are too many for all to be mentioned but they include Hywel Davies, Sarah Dowding, Reece Evans, Robin Evans, Jacqui Gadd, Les Galloway, Denys Groves, Bob Lee, Jonathan Rees, Matthew Rees, Ralph Rees, Angela Rice, Gill Sugden, Fraser Tuddenham and Roger Woodley. Especial thanks are due to Daniel Rees for his help in setting up the manuscript and assembling the companion website. We are also very grateful for the advice, support and encouragement we received from our editor, Ursula Gavin. Heartfelt apologies to others we should have mentioned who are not on this list.

Introduction

Over the years that we have been involved in teaching, writing and consultancy about management we have become fascinated by the way in which people in a wide range of organizations and countries seem to be grappling with similar basic issues and problems. This has enabled us to develop a book that identifies these common key issues and provides practical advice on how to deal with them, within a sound theoretical framework. Most books about management deal with a particular specialized topic. We, however, have anchored our material around the key areas that those with managerial responsibilities are likely to have to deal with. Consequently, we have taken a multi-disciplinary approach as the expertise needed to deal with the key areas we have identified is not confined to a single discipline. In taking this multi-disciplinary approach, though, we have to acknowledge the limits of our own expertise. Whilst we touch on, for example, financial and marketing issues, readers may need to read and/or study further in these specialist areas to meet their own particular developmental needs.

The target audience for the book is those who have or are likely to acquire managerial responsibility. This may include a large number of people who are embarking or plan to embark on a specialist career. In a study we made into the background of those with managerial responsibility we found that 45 out of 50 of those with managerial responsibility had worked as specialists before acquiring such responsibility. Two more had trained as specialists and had been given managerial responsibility in their first job. Only twelve of the group had received prior managerial training and this had not always been effective (see Chapter 1). To the extent that this is likely to be a general pattern it would not be surprising to find that there may often be a managerial gap in organizations. This could mean that insufficient attention is being given to managerial responsibilities and/or that those managerial responsibilities that are undertaken are not always being handled effectively. It is this problem of managerial gap that the book is particularly intended to address.

The specialist route into management is not surprising, given that organizations are normally a collection of specialist departments. The entry point is likely to be as a specialist with people acquiring managerial responsibility as their specialist career develops. An escalator-type progression may then occur which can propel some people into very senior levels within an organization, whether it be private, public or non-profit-making. It creates a strong argument for specialists acquiring some understanding of management and associated expertise. It may be as well for them to acquire some of this knowledge, at least, when receiving their initial specialist or professional training.

The term management has been consistently used, and is defined in the book as 'achieving results through others'. It overlaps with the concept of supervision and it can be difficult at times to distinguish between these two concepts. Supervisors tend to be the first rung of management. Managers tend to have more financial responsibility and strategic involvement – however it can be difficult at times to distinguish between the two concepts. The term management is generally used in the book in a generic way, particularly as much of the content applies to supervisors anyway. It is also necessary to stress that many people will be hybrid managers – that is to say they will combine specialist activity with managerial responsibility. Most management work may in fact be done by people who combine these two activities.

An important related issue is the relationship between management and leadership. The term 'manager', can be relatively easily defined. It is normally an appointed person, fitting into a hierarchy with defined responsibilities and authority. The term 'leader' is much more elastic and much depends on what people mean by the term in a wide variety of situations. It can include people who are responsible to those at the bottom, not the top, of a hierarchy, for example voters. There is also an ongoing debate about whether management is part of leadership or the other way around. In addition management responsibilities and leadership roles may be widely, not narrowly, distributed in organizations. This issue is explored more fully in the book, particularly in Chapter 4 – on managerial and leadership styles. However, the reality is that the material in the book is relevant to those playing managerial or leadership roles, by and large regardless of the definition they come under in particular organizations.

The book is not intended to provide a set of prescriptive remedies. The purpose is to provide readers with a range of relevant key concepts coupled with advice on how these concepts can be applied. Problem diagnosis, though, remains crucial. Appropriate action depends so much on the situation and what can be appropriate in one situation may be quite inappropriate in another. Because of this we have avoided the term 'best practice'. This is because what can be right in one situation may not fit in another. As an aid to the development of diagnostic skills there is a relevant case study at the start of each chapter with guidance notes about the case at the end of the chapter.

Learning outcomes are provided at the start of each chapter with self-assessment questions at the end. Practical illustrations of these concepts are given throughout the book. Where appropriate there are appendices to the chapters to help readers identify and develop relevant skills. Details of further reading are also provided at the end of each chapter to facilitate any necessary further development. References and further reading of particular value are marked with a *. The book itself may also be a good reference for readers before they have to tackle particular activities, such as chairing a meeting.

The consistent feedback that we have received from previous publications, particularly the six editions of *Skills of Management* is that what we write is readable as well as relevant. We have been determined to maintain this style, particularly as we see no point in making issues unnecessarily complicated. The key managerial concepts we have sought to explain are generally not that difficult to understand anyway. The problem comes with application. Unlike purely technical subjects the issue with a text on management and leadership is that it needs to influence people's personal behaviour. This can at times require considerable self-discipline. The recurring issue can be to do what is necessary, not simply what one likes doing.

A specific issue about writing style that needs explaining is the use of the personal pronoun (he or she). We only use these words if they refer to a particular person Language conventions have changed. We have followed the emerging convention of using the term 'they' in a singular as well as a plural context to avoid sexist connotations.

To help readers remember who is who in the case studies at the start of each chapter the initials of the people involved are generally made to correspond with the jobs they have. For example, in one of the cases, Helen Richards is the human resources manager. A Glossary of key management terms used is given at the end of the book. Generally these terms are printed in bold just the first time they appear in the text.

Companion Website

The book's companion website at www.palgrave.com/companion/rees offers a number of resources for both lecturers and students, including 25 original case studies and exercises with accompanying lecturer notes, and PowerPoint lecture slides.

Managers and their Backgrounds

1

Learning outcomes

When you have worked through this chapter you will be able to:

- Identify the key processes involved in managing people
- Explain how people become managers
- Assess the limitations of specialist career structures
- Assess the nature and causes of conflict between specialist and managerial work
- Identify where you are, or someone you know is, on the **managerial escalator**
- Develop a strategy for getting the right balance between specialist and managerial work, for both yourself and others.

Case study

The Player-Manager

Peter Mills was the player-manager of an English League football team. He had stepped down two divisions towards the end of his anticipated football career to accept a job as a player-manager. This was with a view to developing a new career as a football club manager. He found it hard work keeping fit, playing for his team and attending to his new managerial responsibilities. Unfortunately, he broke his leg and could only attend to his managerial duties. For several weeks the team's performance suffered – which he did not find surprising as he had been one of their star players. However, before he was fit enough to resume playing he noticed that the team's performance started improving and eventually their position in the league was higher than when he had become injured. The squad had remained substantially unchanged and he was certain that as a player he had been a significant asset.

Question:

Why might the team's performance have improved?

Introduction

This chapter sets the theme for the whole book. First, the nature of management is examined, then the way in which people become managers. People usually have an escalator-type progression into management. They are likely to have to combine specialist with managerial responsibilities for much of their career and therefore become **managerial hybrids**. To be effective, managers need to be prepared to meet organizational rather than personal priorities. Unfortunately, people may neglect their managerial responsibilities in favour of specialist activity. If this happens, their personal priorities may conflict with organizational priorities. The problem of converting specialists into being managers of other specialists is an international phenomenon, although much, but by no means all, of the material used to illustrate the point in this chapter is British. The four basic causes of poor management are identified, as are remedial strategies for improving the quality of management. The first issue to be developed is the actual nature of management.

The nature of management

The managerial cycle

Management has been defined by Mary Parker Follett[1] (1941) as 'the art of getting things done through people'. An alternative way of describing the process is that it is 'achieving results through others'. The elements involved in the process of management were identified by Henri Fayol[2] (1916) as 'to forecast and plan, organize, command, coordinate and control' (for further explanation see Chapter 3). Synthesizing Fayol's view with later writers, one can identify the basic elements in terms of the managerial cycle as shown in Figure 1.1.

Management in practice

Some writers see the managerial cycle as a simplistic model with too rational a view of the manager. Mintzberg's study of how managers actually operate challenged the concept of the totally rational manager. He observed five American chief executives at work and also reviewed the results of studies of managers at generally lower levels in other Western countries. The overall pattern of managerial work appeared to him to be a hectic and fragmented one with little opportunity for reflective thought. Mintzberg also found that decision-making was often abrupt, intuitive and incremental rather than strategic. It was often influenced by soft information, including internal and external gossip (Mintzberg, 1989).

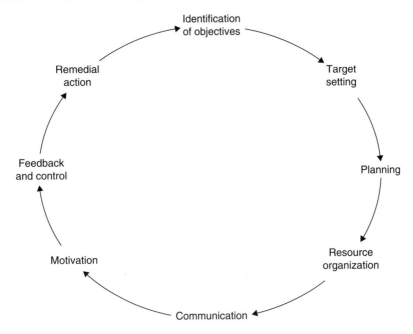

Figure 1.1   The managerial cycle

Another view of the role and skills of the manager was provided by a study of management in local government in the UK (Local Government Management Board, 1993). There is still a general relevance in their observation:

> Management is best defined not as a limited number of 'top' or 'leading' positions, but as a set of competencies, attitudes, and qualities broadly distributed throughout the organization. Management skills are not the property of the few. Effective local authorities will recognize that many jobs which have not conventionally borne the tag 'manager' rely none the less on that bundle of actions – taking charge, securing an outcome, controlling affairs – which amounts to 'managing'. (Local Government Management Board, 1993, p. 8)

The context in which those with managerial responsibilities have to operate is becoming more difficult. As observed in a survey conducted by the Department for Business Innovation & Skills (2012) in the UK:

> The challenges of 21st century leadership and management include working in an environment of constant change and the increasing complexity of organizational structures. Managers must also deal with a

tough economic climate and growing international competition. New technologies, the knowledge economy and the use of social media, greater transparency, rising consumer demands and environmental resource concerns all add to a potent and complex mix of challenges that manages must negotiate to be successful.

How people become managers

Relationship with organizational structure

The structure of organizations is usually such that most employees are engaged in a specialized activity and managers' entries into organizations are usually into a specialized department. The number of general managerial jobs involving, for example, the coordination of the work of a number of different specialist departments tends to be very limited. A specialist background is the pedigree of the vast majority of managers. Early on in their careers, they may have been engaged at a relatively low level on specialized activity. Alternatively, they may have advanced specialist skills that they have acquired either by experience or training or a combination of both. This can be demonstrated by probing into the background of almost anyone you know who has managerial responsibilities. Engineering managers, for example, come from the ranks of specialist engineers. Ward sisters or nursing officers will inevitably have a professional nursing qualification. A head teacher will normally have a teaching qualification. Football managers are invariably former professional players. Small business entrepreneurs are usually running a business based on their initial technical skill, for example in computing, in the building trade or as a motor mechanic.

Managerial responsibilities of the hybrid

The problems of disentangling specialist and managerial work can be demonstrated by identifying the managerial activities in which specialists may become involved, and in which they need to perform both specialist and managerial activities. Managerial activities in which specialists may become involved are:

- Anticipating, planning and allocating work
- Identification of priorities
- Establishing and reviewing work methods
- Quality control
- Management of budgets
- Management of physical resources
- Trouble-shooting
- Supervision of staff (including selection, on-the-job training, appraisal, counselling, motivation, control and grievance handling)

■ Liaison with senior management, colleagues at a similar level and ancillary staff
■ External liaison.

The flattening of many organizational structures has tended to increase the speed at which specialists accumulate managerial responsibilities. Reductions in the numbers of specialist advisers can also lead to a broadening of managerial roles. Conventional specialist and managerial careers and work boundaries often break down so that both specialists and managers have to become multi-skilled. These developments and flexible management structures can also lead to greater lateral movement of employees in organizations.

The managerial escalator

The concept of the managerial escalator is used to explain how specialists become managers. Initially, a specialist may be employed 100 per cent of the time on a specialist activity. This may well be after professional training as an accountant or engineer, or whatever. The competent specialist may gradually acquire minor supervisory responsibilities, perhaps quite informally. For example, this could be helping newcomers with their job. After a certain duration of competent performance (say five years, but it could be as little as one year), it would not be unusual for a specialist to be promoted. Given the structure of organizations, this promotion would usually involve an element of managerial responsibility. An engineer could become a section leader or a sales person a sales manager. The development of the concept of 'team leaders' can lead to specialists acquiring significant management responsibilities despite occupying a junior position.

After a few more years (say five) there could be a further formal promotion, either within the same or another organization. This may have been preceded by a certain amount of accumulated informal managerial responsibility. People tend to be carried along this escalator and may come to the end with most or even all of their time on the managerial side of the axis. The exact course of progress will vary widely from one person to another. However, the escalator-type progression is very common. The managerial activity may well be in a specialist context, but the crucial change is that former specialists may have to spend most of their time managing other specialists, rather than engaging directly in specialist activity themselves.

Figure 1.2 demonstrates, in a simplified form, how specialists can, and often do, become managers. The proportion of time spent on managerial activity by a specialist can be identified by a three-stage process: 1) finding the number of years of employment on the horizontal axis, then 2) reading across to the corresponding % of total activity on the vertical axis, and then 3) subtracting the % of managerial activity from 100% [total activity]. The difference between the amount of time that a person should be spending on managerial activities and the amount of time actually spent is defined as the **managerial gap**.

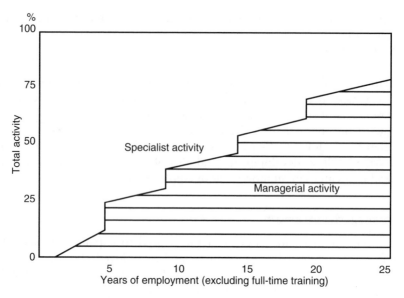

Figure 1.2   The managerial escalator

The conflict between specialist and managerial activity

Nature of the problem

Management does not take place in a vacuum but in a particular set of circumstances – usually requiring specialist knowledge. This knowledge may be necessary so that instructions are sensible, but may also serve to inspire respect in others. The possession of specialist skills is normally an asset and in many cases quite indispensable. If the person who manages in a specialist environment does not understand that environment, they will be under a great, and perhaps insurmountable, handicap. However, the specialist pedigree of most managers is also often at the root of many of the problems that confront them, particularly the danger of getting the wrong balance between specialist and managerial activity.

Some of the problems that are likely to arise may now be obvious. A person may have embarked on a career and acquired specialist skills that they are increasingly less able to use. A person may also have an emotional commitment to their specialist area and a confidence in that area that may be backed up by several years of formal training. Conversely, the commitment to, and training and aptitude for, the managerial side of the job may be low. It would not be unusual for a manager in a specialist environment to have had years of specialist training but only days of management training. This inexorably creates the temptation for managers to adjust the balance of their

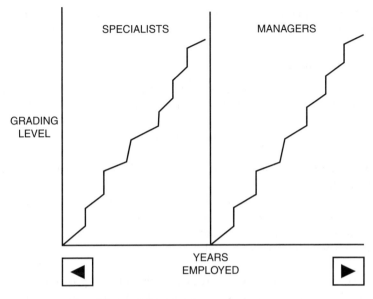

Figure 1.3 Dual careers structures

activity so that they concentrate on what they like doing and what they feel equipped to do, at the expense of the managerial aspects of their job.

Specialist career structures and their limitations

The general problem

The dilemma of the specialist who is forced into management is accentuated by the difficulty that organizations have in providing alternative career progressions. In some cases, it may be possible to get around the dilemma by providing the opportunity for specialist career progression, as illustrated in Figure 1.3. However, the extent to which dual career structures can be created seems to be severely limited in practice, as it frequently proves impractical to separate managerial and specialist duties. Managerial responsibility usually flows from specialist expertise. If a person has to run a specialist unit they are unlikely to be able to do this unless they understand what the employees in their department are doing and can give appropriate guidance about working methods and end results.

Ironically, it may be more feasible to have a person without specialist knowledge at the top of an organization rather than occupying less senior positions. A chief executive can rely on a raft of specialist departmental heads and concentrate on coordinating their work. Even then, however, the chief executive would need a good understanding of the environment in which the organization is operating and of the internal resources and constraints within their organization.

Employee pressures

The pressures for specialist career structures are often employee-driven. Specialists may want to obtain the rewards usually associated with accepting managerial responsibility but without actually accepting such responsibilities. Problems that this can cause for the organization include:

- The demand for highly paid specialist jobs may greatly exceed their availability
- The more highly paid specialists there are, the greater the problems of integrating their work with that of colleagues
- The incentive for and availability of other specialists to accept management responsibilities can be reduced.

The above issues have arisen with regard to the nursing profession in particular. In the National Health Service (NHS) in the UK nursing consultants have been introduced into the career structure. However, their role is essentially to undertake medical work hived off from doctors and they have little in the way of supervisory responsibility. This may well have been a useful innovation because of the need to reduce pressure on medical staff, as well as being a popular development within the nursing profession. However, hospitals are still left with the problem of finding enough capable specialists to undertake crucial managerial responsibilities.

Impact of the labour market

Employers may need to give some attention to how they reward employees and the impact of such rewards on the managerial structure. As explained in Chapter 7, if a particular expertise really is critical to the success of an organization, it may be necessary to pay accordingly, irrespective of management responsibilities. This will help to avoid situations in which workers whose specialist skills are in short supply are promoted to management simply to enable them to achieve a suitable level of reward within the organization. The worst thing to do is to promote people into managerial jobs while letting them think that they need not take their managerial responsibilities seriously. Care needs to be taken that promotion is not done on spurious grounds and that any advantages gained by the organization are greater than the disadvantage of discouraging people from accepting managerial responsibilities.

Experience in the area of information technology

The area of information technology is one in which organizations do recognize that it is sometimes necessary to retain people with commercially important expertise without forcing them to accept management responsibilities. As with other specialist areas, the person with a high level of technical expertise will not automatically make a good manager or have managerial aspirations. However, even in this area a mix of managerial skills and technical expertise is often necessary.

EXAMPLE: Problems in getting the right balance between managerial and specialist work

A Swedish manager commented of a colleague who was both young and brilliant at computer work that he had no interest in paperwork and in engaging with colleagues. As a consequence he had to be relieved of his managerial responsibilities.

The problem of getting the right mix of managerial skills and specialist expertise may be particularly difficult in the information technology area. This is because people may acquire a high level of technical skill at a very early stage in their careers. Management expertise may develop over a much longer timescale. In addition, the patterns of linear thinking that may be the reason for a person's superior technical ability may be quite different from the often more lateral patterns of thought that are needed in management.

Even when information technologists are hired out to other organizations they still need to have the people skills to interact effectively in client organizations. The essential point is that there are limits to the extent to which specialist and managerial activity can be disentangled. This is not to suggest, though, that there should not be experimentation in this area.

The role of administrative support

Sometimes the response to more explicit management pressures has been to give more administrative support to specialist professionals. An example of administrative support being provided is the introduction of partnership administrators or practice managers in professional partnerships, e.g. firms of solicitors, surveyors, general medical practitioners and accountants. A similar development has been to appoint business managers in schools to handle financial issues in particular (Frean, 2008). However, partners, head teachers or governors cannot expect the support staff to determine policy, future strategy and financial priorities, to resolve conflict between partners or to supervise specialists in the professional aspects of their work. More competitive market conditions, including the emergence of more multi-disciplinary partnerships, mean that effective management is bound to become an increasingly important factor in determining success or failure. However, even if appropriate support is given, the dilemma of specialists as managers remains a general problem.

One way of trying to reduce the burden on the person in charge of an organization is effectively to split their job into two. The Secretary General of the United Nations has the twin tasks of being the senior diplomat and the chief administrative officer of the organization. A similar dilemma faces the Vice Chancellors of universities. However, even if it is practical to split such jobs into two, the heads of the organizations may not welcome the idea of hiving off so much of their work to a chief executive because of the authority, responsibility and power that they would lose. There is though at least one example of where such a division of responsibilities does seem to work. In diplomatic missions, the head of mission (the Ambassador or High Commissioner) traditionally concentrates on external representation, leaving much of the internal management to be handled by their deputy.

Reasons for people opting out of managerial responsibilities

Failure to identify the managerial element in a job

One reason why managers sometimes engage in an inappropriate balance of activities may be simply that they have failed to identify that they are doing so. If the general culture in an organization is for over-concentration on specialist activity, an imbalance may not easily be recognized by others, far less be the subject of constructive comment and advice. When a person is experiencing strain in the managerial part of their job, they may seek to avoid this by regressing into their former specialist role. This may provide a temporary refuge, or **comfort zone**, and restore confidence by enabling the person to do what they feel good at. However, like much avoidance behaviour, it is likely to make matters even worse in the long term. A symptom of this may be the eagerness with which a manager insists on **acting down** when an employee is away. This occurs when a boss undertakes tasks that are normally undertaken by their subordinates.

Rewards

The reasons why people strive to obtain positions that they cannot or will not handle properly needs some explaining. A basic cause is that the structure of most organizations is such that this may be the only way for employees to gain promotion with the associated increases in pay, status and authority. Employees may accept promotion without appreciating the shift in emphasis to managerial activity that is required. On other occasions, people may have a calculated strategy of obtaining as many benefits as possible from a job but doing as little as possible of the work involved.

EXAMPLE: An extreme example of opting out

A professor was attracted to the job of head of a college because of the many tangible benefits on offer. However, once he had been appointed he announced that, as he was an academic, he would only undertake academic work. He deemed managerial tasks (or 'administrative work', as he called it) to be beneath his intellectual status. The position then arose that he was not given the only work that he would do (academic), and the only work that he was given was work he would not do (managerial). Needless to say, senior colleagues were very unhappy about this blatant contract violation, particularly as they had to do much of the Head's job for him whilst he enjoyed all the benefits of the position (the Head did, though, at least provide a perfect example of how not to run an organization).

Impact of job titles

The specialist culture that exists in so many organizations is perhaps the biggest single obstacle to effective management. The conflict between specialist and managerial roles can sometimes be revealed by the job titles people use. A management consultant working in the civil engineering industry found that the approach taken by the senior person on site was often indicated by whether they used the title 'site engineer' or 'site manager'. Job titles can be revealing in many other occupations as well, for example, the choice of the term 'buyer' or 'department manager' in a department store. It could also be that the use of the term 'head teacher' indicates a traditional orientation around teaching rather than the management of other teachers. This can be reinforced by a perception that the specialist activity is more important and has more status than managerial activity.

Work preferences

Frequently, managers concentrate unduly on what they simply enjoy doing (particularly their specialization). This can happen in many, if not all, managerial environments. When this was explained to a group of transport managers, they responded by saying that not only did they recognize the phenomenon, but they also had a name for it. Supervisors who insisted on driving, ostensibly to 'keep their hand in', were described by them as being 'cab happy'. Ex-pilots are notorious for this, and the tendency is reinforced by the requirement that a minimum number of hours must be flown to retain a licence. If this type of activity happens only occasionally perhaps one should not worry too much. When it forms a regular pattern, though, there is likely to be a serious problem, since the managerial work could then be neglected.

Another problem can arise with people with a background in a particular management specialism. Like other specialists, they may pay too much attention to their area of historic specialization. Consequently, they may give too much priority in terms of time and decision-making to issues in the area of their management specialism. They may also show favouritism in the allocation of resources.

EXAMPLE: Interpreting a job too much through one's managerial specialism

A cost accountant was promoted into a position as a general manager. Unfortunately, instead of taking a broader view in his new job, he still concentrated on cost control. That was the only area to which he was disposed to allocate extra resources. He neglected the marketing aspects of his job in particular and was reluctant to authorize expenditure that could have generated significant net income. He should instead have concentrated on optimizing the difference between income and expenditure.

Personality factors

The ability or willingness of people to handle managerial activity can be influenced by powerful psychological factors relating to individual personalities. Some people may strive for the power that managerial authority can give, regardless of whether or not they are competent to exercise that authority wisely. Sometimes people may actually be in flight from their specialism, because they are not very good at it or because they have 'burnt out' in that area.

Nevertheless there are perfectly valid reasons why people aspire to positions of greater responsibility. One has sympathy for people who are sucked into management but who are concerned that, if for any reason they lose their jobs, they will have difficulty in returning to their specialist sphere unless they have kept up to date. The point being made, however, is that it is necessary at the selection stage to try to identify the real reasons why a person wants a particular job and to distinguish between valid and invalid reasons.

The fundamental nature of some of the personality factors that may discourage people from applying for managerial positions, or regressing when they are in such jobs, needs examination. One basic possibility is that often extroverts prefer the managerial role and introverts the specialist activity. To appoint or not to appoint just on that basis would be somewhat simplistic. However, the value system that specialists develop in their formative occupational years and their self-image may be much more bound up with specialist rather than managerial activity. This, in turn, may conflict with organizational values.

Personality factors can, in turn, be reinforced by the uncongenial aspects of many managerial roles. This has led Scase and Goffee (1989) to coin the phrase 'reluctant managers', which is also the title of their book. They refer to the 'emotional hardening' that may be necessary to handle managerial roles. They also comment about changing social values and the increasing desire of managers to balance their work and domestic roles.

Pressure from subordinates

The traditions of a particular occupation may influence a manager's behaviour. In teaching, for example, there may be considerable direct and indirect pressure by junior teachers for senior or head teachers to concentrate on teaching. The person in a supervisory position may have to be able to resist the pressures of employees that could lead to them striking the wrong balance. Such a person may also feel that 'they should not give a job to a subordinate that they cannot do themselves' – a popular but dangerous maxim.

There may also be the fear that unless a direct specialist involvement is retained the manager will become out of date and perhaps ultimately unable to manage at all. The problem is that, if a manager responds to these pressures, they may make matters worse. This can happen in two ways: 1) by interfering in the work of employees, and 2) by neglecting the critical managerial aspects of a job. However, employees may quite fail to comprehend the other aspects of a boss's job. Additionally, employees may resent the creaming-off of the more interesting parts of the job by a boss who wants to 'keep their hand in'. This may be particularly annoying if the boss does this on a random basis so that employees never quite know what their job is. Situations where there are 'two cooks in the kitchen' may generate more friction than those in which one cook leaves the other to get on with it and puts up with any adverse comments about their lack of specialist involvement. In some cases, though, employees will be only too well aware of their boss's managerial shortcomings and the pressure will be for the boss to do their managerial job instead of meddling in what was their former job.

Experience in developing countries

The problem of imbalance between specialist and managerial roles is not confined to any one country. Many specialists in developing countries enjoy speedy promotion. This can be caused by the shortage of staff with appropriate skills, the speed with which newly independent countries have had to assume responsibility for managing their own affairs, and the tendency for employees in state and parastatal organizations to be obliged to retire when they reach 55. This early retirement age not only reduces the pool of available talent, but also encourages managers to retain their specialist skills for a post-retirement career. There may also be strong expectations in countries with high **power distance** cultures (see Chapter 4) that the boss will have a detailed knowledge of the technical aspects of their work as well as managerial expertise.

General consequences of opting out

Managers are likely to be judged ultimately by the results they achieve through constructive management of employees – not by possession of specialist knowledge. The specialist knowledge that managers require is that which enables them to supervise others. If employees can do a particular job better than the manager, the manager's skill is in arranging for them to do so. To compete with the subordinate and then fail is hardly to be recommended.

There is a world of difference between a manager having no specialist competence and having adequate specialist knowledge to supervise employees. The latter may be quite sufficient. It would be very nice if all managers knew more about every aspect of the subordinate's job than the subordinate, but it is not very realistic, particularly with changing technology. It may also not do a great deal for the esteem of employees. The manager may have to face up to specialist issues which they cannot deal with. Rather than worry about this, it may be that this is simply an instance when the manager re-routes the subordinate to a source where they may get the right information. The emphasis needs to be on seeing that the specialists maintain and develop their skill base rather than on the manager trying to do this.

A whole host of problems can arise if the weaning process, whereby those with managerial responsibilities get the right balance of specialist and managerial activity, is not satisfactorily accomplished. This is the recurrent theme of this chapter.

Remedial strategies

The remedial strategies needed to deal with the problem of poor managerial performance involve dealing with four basic causes of ineffective performance. These strategies are so important that they are worth being addressed in detail. They are:

1.   Role definition
2.   Managerial selection
3.   Training and development
4.   Monitoring.

Role definition

When managers are reluctant to accept managerial responsibility, a key remedial strategy is to make such responsibilities crystal clear, for example in a job specification and by paying attention to the job title. Accurate role definition is also necessary if the other remedial strategies of selection, training and development, and monitoring are to be effective. This role clarification needs to be an integral part of the basis on which managers are selected. The need to highlight the managerial aspects of a job is necessary for both applicants and those making appointments. This issue is given particular attention in the following section on managerial selection.

Managerial selection

There is a variety of reasons why the wrong people are given managerial responsibility. Two key mistakes are considered in this section: 1) failure to recognize the managerial element in jobs and 2) general selection incompetence. Intervention strategies need to be based on avoiding such mistakes.

Mistake No. 1: Failure to identify and select on the basis of the managerial element in a job

The easiest way to choose a manager is to look at their historical performance and appoint or reject on this basis. The danger in this approach is, however, that there may be critical differences between the duties that a person has performed in the past and those that they may be expected to perform in the future. Unfortunately, this point may not be properly grasped and, in any case, it is so much easier to assess historical performance rather than to speculate about a person's managerial potential. It is, for example, far easier to count the number of international caps that a professional footballer has acquired than to judge whether or not they have the appropriate range of skills to manage a football club. Possession or non-possession of a coaching licence may help to judge technical ability, but not be that helpful in judging any complementary managerial ability or potential that is required.

The likelihood of selection error is increased if selectors view an appointment as a reward for past specialist achievements instead of considering the need to choose the right person for the future. In the police service this sometimes led to sergeants being regarded as 'constables with stripes on their arms'.

The problems that can arise as a result of selecting on the basis of historic performance are satirically and amusingly explained in the book *The Peter Principle* by Laurence and Hull (1970). Their observations contain more than a germ of truth. The basic concept explained in the book is that if one looks backward in time instead of forward when selecting, people will rise up through organizational hierarchies until they pass their 'threshold of competence'. Only when that has happened will there be no basis for appointment at a higher level of responsibility!

The problems of choosing just on the basis of specialist expertise can arise particularly in university appointments. Staff may be appointed merely on the basis of their record of research and publications. This may bring advantages in terms of prestige and research ratings. However, university departments need to be managed effectively just like any other departments. This applies to research units as well and the real need, even in research units, may be to have someone in charge who can facilitate research in the unit as a whole. The unit activity will need to be judged as a whole, not just on the basis of the performance of the head of such a unit.

Mistake No. 2: Incompetent selectors

The appointment of managers may prove to be a fairly random affair. The competence of the selectors may mean that it is often a question of luck as to whether the people with the right mix of skills and potential are appointed in the first place. However, those who find that they have emerged through the selection system as managers need to address themselves to the behaviour that will be appropriate, even if those appointing them did not. A further obstacle to appointment on the basis of suitability to do the job in the UK has, historically at least, been the importance of social class.

The material on selection in Chapter 9 of this book gives practical guidance on how to appoint on the basis of 'fit' with the job. It is crucial that the managerial ability or potential is included in selection criteria. It is also important that those undertaking the selection are competent in the techniques of recruitment and selection, which are also explained in Chapter 9.

Training and development of managers

Whilst management training is a key intervention area, the quantity and quality of training and development has often been neglected. Historically, managers have often received little management training. In a survey of how 50 people (mainly from the UK) became managers by Rees and Porter (2005) it was found that 45 of the 50 had worked as a specialist before acquiring supervisory or managerial responsibility. A further two had trained as specialists before being given supervisory or managerial responsibility in their first appointment. Only twelve had received prior management training and that was not always effective. Many of those interviewed commented on the stresses they experienced when they were first given managerial responsibilities. This fits with the results of a UK-only survey in which it was found that only one in five of UK managers had a management-related qualification There seemed to be a common perception that managerial expertise was something that was simply 'picked up' on the job (Department for Business Innovation & Skills, 2012, p. 6).

There has been some increasing international attention to management training in recent years. This has increased the scale of both qualification training and 'in-house' courses. However, increases in the quantity of management training are one thing – ensuring that training is effective is another. Management training can often be ineffective for a variety of reasons. These include: 1) inaccurate diagnosis of needs, 2) poor selection, 3) unsatisfactory training, and 4) ineffective monitoring. A particular problem with management training is the need for those receiving the training to integrate what they have learnt with their personal behaviour. Sometimes the adjustments that managers need to make in order to manage are effectively beyond them. Also in-house training budgets can be amongst the first casualties in organizations seeking to economize. The problems of providing effective management training are considered further in Chapter 11.

Monitoring

The fourth key strategy is monitoring. This applies whether a manager is managing others or reviewing their own performance. The good work in trying to ensure accurate role definition, selection, and training and development can easily be undone if there is no effective monitoring. A key feature of an effective strategy for correcting imbalance in the job is for those likely to experience the problem to be made more aware of it. They may do this for themselves by learning, perhaps on a trial and error basis. However, training and monitoring of performance can help to ensure that people do not have to learn everything the hard way. Unfortunately, if an organization has too much of a specialist culture, it is particularly likely that those with managerial responsibilities will fail to see the need to monitor and then correct the performance of their employees or themselves.

Managers have a responsibility to see that their own training and development, and that of their staff, fits into an integrated pattern. These are not activities that can be handled just by training departments or by sending people on courses. **Performance management,** on-the-job learning, appraisal, coaching and formal training all need to be integrated. There is a specific responsibility for bosses to see that those who are given managerial responsibilities are also given help through appraisal, counselling and coaching. This is particularly necessary when people make critical moves up the managerial escalator. So often people are 'thrown in at the deep end' by managers who have not handled the transitional problems properly themselves and who blame employees for their shortcomings in a new job.

Summary

The basics of management have been identified in this chapter as a necessary prelude to both the chapter and the book. The essence of management is that it involves achieving results through others. Most managers gradually acquire managerial responsibility and change, in an escalator-like progression, from being specialists to being the managers of specialists. Most managerial activity is probably undertaken by hybrids (i.e. people who combine specialist and managerial activity). Unfortunately, there is often a conflict between the work that those with managerial responsibilities prefer to do and the organization's priorities. Many specialists undertake managerial duties because of the lack of an alternative career structure. There are considerable practical difficulties that prevent organizations arranging specialist career structures.

It is by understanding the above issues that individuals can understand the pressures on them to undertake managerial responsibilities and how they can handle such pressures effectively.

From an organizational point of view the four key remedial strategies are:

1. Accurate definition of managerial roles
2. Effective managerial selection
3. Appropriate and adequate management training and development
4. Effective monitoring of those with management responsibilities.

From an individual's point of view it is particularly important to define one's role accurately, plan appropriate training and development, and develop the means of self-monitoring.

Having identified the need for the proper definition of managerial roles as the first in this sequence of activities both organizationally and individually, it is appropriate that this forms the subject matter of Chapter 2.

Self-assessment questions

1. How did Mary Parker Follett define management?
2. Why are people with managerial responsibilities likely to have a specialist background?
3. Why do organizations find it difficult to provide specialist career structures?
4. Why might those with managerial responsibilities neglect them in favour of specialist activity?
5. Where are you, or someone you know, on the managerial escalator? Where might you be on the escalator in five years?
6. What are the four key areas where attention is needed to ensure that those with managerial responsibilities perform effectively?

Case study notes – The Player-Manager

Learning outcome:

■ To understand the concept of the managerial escalator and see how it might apply both generally in organizations and to oneself

There are likely to be many variables in this case. However, it is quite possible that the club had lost a player but gained a manager. In the situation on which the case is based this was the view of the player-manager and he did not resume playing. It took a broken leg for him to realize that before his injury he had been trying to do two jobs and he needed instead to make management of the club his main priority. The workload on him would have been all the greater because the role of player-manager is wider than the role of player-coach. The combined workload would have been much less had he been a player-coach because much of the managerial work would have been hived off. However, even in that situation it is necessary for a player-coach to identify their priorities properly and not, for example, concentrate too much on activities in their historic comfort zone. This case particularly fits with the concept of the managerial escalator.

Skills development exercise

Approach two people who you know who have managerial responsibility and examine and identify the extent to which their career progression has fitted, and is likely to continue to fit, with the concept of the managerial escalator (Rees and Porter, 2005).

Notes

1. Follett, Mary Parker (1868–1933): An American management writer with ideas well ahead of her time. She had been a social worker and then a management consultant and writer. Although seen as a member of the scientific management school she believed that there needed to be reciprocity in the relationships between employers and employed. She took the people factor into account more than others and was critical of management models that were simply 'top-down'. See the collected works of Mary Parker Follett, 1973, London Pitman.
2. Fayol, Henri (1841–1925): A French mining engineer who became director of a coal mining company at age 19. He could be seen as the father of the classical management school. His writings included *Administration Industrielle et Generale* (1916) His theories included the identification of 14 key principles of management. Key principles included the unity of command and purpose, the scalar chain of command and the division of labour.

References

NB: Works of particular interest are marked with an asterisk.

Department for Business Innovation & Skills (2012), Leadership & Management in the UK: The Key to Sustainable Growth. https://www.gov.uk/government/uploads/

system/uploads/attachment_data/file/32327/12-923-leadership-management-key-to-sustainable-growth-evidence.pdf [accessed 21/10/14].

*Fayol, Henri (1916), *Administration Industrielle et Generale*, Paris: Bulletin de la Societe de l'Industrie Minerale.

*Follett, Mary Parker (1941) (posthumous), *Dynamic Administration.*
    See also the collected works of Mary Parker Follett (1973), London, Pitman.

Frean, Alexandra (2008), *Everyone wants to be a head teacher now someone else looks after the cash, The Times,* 20 October.

Laurence, Peter and Raymond Hull (1970), *The Peter Principle,* Pan. Alternatively, see the Souvenir Press edition, 1969, reissued in 1992.

Local Government Management Board (1993), *Managing Tomorrow,* Panel of Inquiry report.

Mintzberg, H. (1989), *Mintzberg on Management,* The Free Press.

*Rees, W David and Christine Porter (2005), Results of a survey into how people become managers and the management development implications, *Industrial and Commercial Training,* Vol. 37, No. 5, pp. 252–258.
    Research evidence indicating strongly that the route into management is via specialist activity.

Scase, Richard and Robert Goffee (1989), *Reluctant Managers: Their Work and Lifestyles,* Unwin Hyman.

Taking it further

Birkinshaw, Julian (London Business School) (2013), *Becoming a Better Boss – Why Good Management Is so Difficult.* Jossey-Bass.

*Mead, Richard and Tim G. Andrews (2009), *International Management,* Wiley.
    An excellent and detailed account explaining the impact of national culture on management practices.

Porter, Christine and W. David Rees (2012) The Managerial Gap and how coaching can help, *International Coaching and Psychology Review* (The British Psychological Society), Vol. 7, No. 1, pp. 64–71.

Identifying the Manager's Job

2

Learning outcomes

By the end of this chapter you will be able to:

- Distinguish between managerial activity and managerial effectiveness
- Identify appropriate work objectives for yourself
- Prioritize your work using the technique of **role set analysis**
- Manage your time effectively
- Sequence your work effectively
- Explain basic concepts of strategic planning and their importance for you.

Case study

A Managerial Headache

Heather Thomas is the head teacher of an inner city comprehensive school in London with 950 pupils. She has been in the job for three years and is finding the job has not become much easier during that time. Previously she had been head of history in another comprehensive in a more affluent area. She arrives at the school at about 7.45 each morning and rarely leaves before 6 pm. She prides herself on knowing the name of each child and having an 'open door policy' for staff who have problems they wish to discuss with her. She does have a deputy and finds that although that does take some of the load off her shoulders there is often confusion about who is responsible for what.

Much of Heather's time is spent 'fire-fighting', often on issues which, although apparently trivial, can become important if not dealt with. This includes maintenance matters, seeing parents, colleagues, attending staff meetings and discussing matters with the school governors. Unfortunately she often finds that she is the only one willing, able and competent to carry out many of these tasks. She does, though, find that the part-time school bursar is very helpful and supportive. Heather still takes some 6th form history classes once a week, 'to keep her hand in', and to help get the feel of how the school is running. She finds this a relief from many of her other activities. She also has to attend regular governors meetings, though she wishes they could be more productive. Heather spends a significant amount of time before each meeting with the Chair, who she generally gets on with, particularly with a view to ensuring there are no surprises at the meetings. She also often represents the school at outside activities such as educational meetings and conferences and with potential employers. Sadly she finds there is little time left over for curriculum development and other long-term issues that she thinks need attention.

Question:

How might Heather organize her time more effectively?

Introduction

It follows from the previous chapter that the first essential requirement for an effective manager is for the manager to define their job carefully and accurately. Effectiveness depends upon the accomplishment of appropriate objectives rather than just being busy. Consequently, the methodology of objective setting is considered in this chapter. The technique of **role set analysis** is also explained. This can be a very effective way of identifying priorities in a job, and it enables comparisons between 'model' and 'actual' time allocations. The technique can also be used on a departmental or organizational basis. Careful identification of the job is also a necessary foundation for effective time management. The basic elements of time management are explained.

It is not enough for managers to plan just their own work systematically. If they are to be effective, they also need to help develop a rational framework within which others can operate. Consequently, the need for effective strategic planning is also considered. So too are the advantages and disadvantages of setting performance targets.

Activity versus effectiveness

Proactive versus reactive managers

Managers can fall into two groups: 1) those who define what has to be done, get on with it and then go home, and 2) those who create a flurry of physical activity and seek to justify their position by the demonstrable effort they put into a job rather than by the results they achieve. The latter group of managers also tends to be reactive rather than innovative in their responses. The emphasis on effort rather than results tends to combine neatly with a reactive 'management by crisis' approach. There can, perhaps, be some of this in most managers, but it is still useful to make a distinction between the two different approaches.

Sometimes concentrating on effort or activity rather than results can constitute an attempt at self-justification in a combination of humour, pathos and ineffectiveness. This can involve such managerial games as not going home until the chief executive has left, working overtime for the sake of it, and managers seeking to demonstrate to colleagues that they have worked longest and hardest. This is sometimes done simply by **presenteeism** – being physically present without necessarily actually achieving much. Such stratagems may or may not be useful in the short term. It may even be that in some cases they are necessary political ploys, given that there will be political activity in any organization. However, the great danger is that, if managers spend too much time simply justifying themselves, they may actually fail to diagnose what they should be doing and therefore fail to do it. Ultimately, managers are much more likely to be judged by results than by anything else. Activity-centred behaviour is in any case much more likely to spring from incompetence and/or insecurity than from adroit political behaviour. Activity-centred behaviour is also likely to aggravate the position of the manager in the long run rather than improve it.

What is work?

One point that needs to be established at this stage is just how people define work. One view is that it is synonymous with physical activity. This misconception can have most unfortunate consequences, particularly when considering the job of a manager. An example of this misconception can occur when manual workers apply for white-collar jobs. They may find out too late that the mental activity can be far more demanding than the physical activity to which they have been accustomed. The mental activity of a clerk or supervisor simply may not be perceived by a person used to manual work, because such mental activity is not overt.

EXAMPLE: What is work? Activity or effectiveness

A staff nurse working in a hospital noticed that a patient had fallen into a coma. She knew that the patient was on a special diet. Consequently, the staff nurse stopped what she was doing to try to puzzle out if the nurses who would administer drip-feeding to the patient would be aware of his special dietary needs. However, her mental activity was soon interrupted by the ward sister, who brusquely asked her what she thought she was doing just standing there and told her to get on with her work.

1ntl5a01later.

Efficiency versus effectiveness

It is necessary to distinguish between the concepts of efficiency and effectiveness at work. Efficiency can be defined as the extent to which people are working at or near their total capacity. Effectiveness is a different concept. It involves ensuring that people are doing the right things. Ideally employees should be working both efficiently and effectively. However, the two concepts can work against one another.

EXAMPLE: Example of efficiency versus effectiveness

The funding authority for higher education colleges and universities in the UK once introduced a requirement that all academic hours be accounted for. A consequence of this was the generation of activity by some academic staff to demonstrate that they were working to capacity regardless of how effective that activity was. What was really needed, however, was an emphasis on the overall volume and effectiveness of the teaching and related activities such as research.

One source of ineffective activity can be the failure to identify what actually needs to be done. The pressure for activity in some organizations, or for that matter in some people, can be such that activities can be undertaken before the need for them has been properly established. A crucial managerial skill is the need to diagnose both the nature of problems and their underlying causes before action is contemplated. The causes of problems may lie in departments other than those in which problems surface. Consequently an integrated approach may be needed to identify problems and devise appropriate solutions. This topic is considered further in the next chapter. Unfortunately managers all too often adopt prescriptive and often costly solutions before adequate diagnosis has been undertaken. Sometimes prescriptive 'remedies' are brought in from other organizations with little thought as to whether or not they will work within the different circumstances of the organization into which they are imported (Rees and Porter, 2002).

The identification of the manager's job

Perhaps the first thing that any manager needs to do is actually to identify their job. This should be seen as a continuous process rather than a one-off activity. Organizations have to change to survive, and the jobs of managers need to change accordingly. This is why, if a manager has a job description, it should be seen as a starting point for identifying the job, rather than a definitive unalterable document. Job descriptions, whilst being useful, may leave considerable room for interpretation and may also need frequent updating. They suffer too from the deficiency that they usually do not give a clear indication of the priorities in a job. In many cases people may not have the term manager in their job title but may be expected to or need to carry out significant managerial responsibilities.

There are likely to be other ways in which managers identify and adjust their jobs. They are hardly likely to be left completely to their own devices as there will obviously be instructions from more senior managers. In some cases the remit for a manager will be very specific, and the primary problem will be one of doing the job rather than of identifying what needs to be done. In other cases – perhaps where there is significant internal and external change – the manager may need to spend a considerable amount of time defining and redefining what needs to be done. A further guide may be the way the work was performed by a previous job-holder. It would be folly to ignore the way a previous job-holder had performed a job, but perhaps equally foolish not to review their interpretation of a job or not to allow for changed circumstances.

There can be considerable misunderstanding about exactly what is usually being done in a job before one gets to the question of what actually needs to be done. There may be significant surprises when the purpose and content of jobs are clarified. Often the job-holder will find that they are undertaking some tasks of which their boss is unaware. It is also likely that there will be some tasks that they are expected to do of which they themselves are unaware. One of the reasons for such misunderstandings is that the boss may never have fully appreciated the demands of the job. Alternatively, they may have appreciated these demands previously, or even have done the job at one stage, but may be basing their view on what was historically done rather than what is now needed.

Short-term pressures and long-term needs

Much of a manager's time will be devoted simply to responding to pressures and demands from other people. The in-tray tends to dominate the daily pattern of activity. Whatever a manager wants to do in the long term is all very well, but often cannot be contemplated until the short-term pressures have been dealt with. However, there are dangers that a manager will simply react to short-term pressures and not think out what they should be doing from a long-term point of view. This problem can be exacerbated by developments in information technology such as email (key skills involved in using email effectively are considered in Chapter 8). These developments can make a manager too available, whether at work or at home. Managers are less likely than before to have personal secretaries to act as filters or, if they still do, it may be possible for people to bypass the secretary electronically. Consequently, there may be an even greater need for managers to consciously prioritize. Managers may also fall into a particular pattern of responding to certain short-term pressures and ignoring others. It is necessary to periodically review such response patterns to see if they match the needs of the situation.

EXAMPLE: Long-term versus short-term priorities

A freelance TV producer confessed that he only understood the need to identify long-term priorities after conducting a role set analysis in a management development workshop. He explained that on a recent media assignment he had let the executive producer have all the contact with the broadcaster on whom future contracts depended. Partly as a result of that the TV producer found that he was out of work while the executive producer was fully employed as a result of his contact with the broadcaster.

The identification of objectives

As has already been indicated, the reverse of the reactive activity-centred approach of managers is one where objectives are carefully identified and then, hopefully, achieved. A consequential benefit can be that the manager's time is allocated in proportion to the priority of a task. Reactive managers may find, assuming they ever think in these terms, that they have failed to match the time available to the key elements in their jobs. It is all too easy to say what one is doing rather than why. The starting point for identifying the purpose of a job is to identify the objective or objectives. In extreme cases it can emerge that whilst there might have been a historic purpose to a set of objectives this may no longer be the case. It can also emerge that the objective or objectives were never properly identified in the first place as in the following example.

EXAMPLE: Checking job assumptions

The chief legal officer of a local authority in London was asked to explain his various activities during an annual appraisal. He described how he sought to minimize payments to claimants against the council. His technique included ignoring claims for liability the first time they were received. He estimated that this would dispose of 20 per cent of claims. If people persisted with their claims he would next send a complicated and threatening letter. He estimated that that would dispose of a further 20 per cent of claims. The remaining 60 per cent of claims would be contested with a view to paying as little as possible as late as possible. The legal officer was then asked by the chief executive why he resisted all claims and responded that it was to meet his objective of minimizing payments made by the council. The chief executive then made the point that, as the council had a responsibility to the local public, there was a case for simply accepting liability with regard to valid claims. The chief legal officer's response was this option had never occurred to him.

The identification of objectives may overlap with the identification of the key tasks that need to be accomplished for an objective or objectives to be achieved. Humble (1979) advocated that every manager needed to define the six to eight key tasks that needed to be accomplished if the overall job objective was to be achieved. He further argued that if this was done, the residual detail in a job contained for example in a conventional job description would fall into place. He also recommended that the minimum acceptable standards of performance for objectives and key tasks were specified. As part of this approach minimum quantitative and qualitative standards, including cost limits and time deadlines, were to be identified. Humble developed this approach into a formal scheme of **management by objectives.** However, this declined in popularity, partly because, as explained below, it did not address the issue of the potential conflict between employer and employee objectives. It may still be useful for managers to go through this type of exercise on an individual basis. Such a methodological approach anyway needs to form the basis of **performance management,** as the essential first step is to have some criteria for judging what performance should be and then measuring it, either on an individual or collective basis. The concept of performance management and its links with appraisal are dealt with in more detail in Chapter 10.

The identification of objectives can be an integral part of performance management and the establishment of organizational performance indicators. These are increasingly used, especially in the public sector. This has special relevance to the public sector because of the absence of profit or loss criteria. As is explained in the next chapter, there is much more emphasis now on ensuring that public services are customer-orientated. Consequently, key criteria can include measures of customer satisfaction, for example, with regard to service response times and the achievement of appropriate quality standards. A similar approach is for organizations to produce a **mission statement.** This involves defining the purpose of an organization, where it plans to go, and the principles that will enable it to achieve its purpose. A statement of the organizational core values that underpin the mission statement may supplement this. This topic is considered in more detail later in the chapter, in the context of strategic planning.

The definition of objectives can present some problems as also can establishing meaningful mission statements. Key difficulties with the identification of objectives may be:

- Objectives are not be easily defined
- They may not lend themselves to quantification
- They can conflict with one another
- Their relative importance to one another can change
- Organizational objectives may conflict with an individual employee's objectives.

Out of all the difficulties outlined above, it is particularly important to recognize the potential for conflict between organizational and individual objectives. Many managers make the naive assumption that employees will automatically subscribe to organizational objectives, strategies and priorities that are pronounced by senior management. This is in line with a **unitarist** view of organizations, which assumes that what is seen as good for the corporate whole is also good for all the constituent parts. Alan Fox (1965) very lucidly explains how, if one takes the **pluralistic** view of organization, one can see that this is not necessarily the case: individual employee objectives may differ or even conflict with organizational objectives. The potential for such conflict is shown by comparing the two sets of objectives below:

1. **Employer objectives**
   - Cost-effective performance (resulting in low unit labour costs)
   - Control of change
   - The avoidance of stoppages and other sanctions.
2. **Employee objectives**
   - Maintenance of and possible improvement in the terms and conditions of employment
   - Job security
   - Control of change
   - The avoidance of stoppages and other sanctions.

If a comparison is made of the employer and employee objectives above, it will be seen that these objectives can conflict. For example, if the employer wants to maximize cost effective performance by the employees then this will involve having the optimum number of people employed at the optimum level of pay. Meanwhile, the employees will be seeking to ensure job security and current staffing levels and at least maintain or possibly improve their terms and conditions of employment. Additionally both employer and employee will be wanting to control change. The only objective that they have in common is that both employer and employee will be wanting to avoid stoppages of work, the employer because of the impact on productivity, the employee because they will not want to lose pay.

Other conflicts may be less obvious and dramatic, but are nevertheless important. Staff may not, for example, cooperate in reorganizing their work to accommodate new organizational priorities if they conflict with individual priorities. This means that attempts to focus organizational activity so that it is more effective may be limited by the ability of managers to resolve such conflicts. This is particularly difficult if managers, because of a unitarist philosophy, can't see the potential conflict of interests. There may be some opportunity to coerce employees into accepting change, but organizational initiatives usually need active cooperation, not minimalist grudging acceptance, if they are to succeed.

Attempts to refocus organizational activity may be attempted with little or no regard for how to win the active cooperation of the staff. Consequently, many of the statements relating to organizational purpose may just be the rhetorical expression of what senior management hopes will happen, rather than effective planning tools to ensure that aspirations are actually achieved. If formal schemes of **employee engagement** are used it is particularly important to recognize that employer and employee objectives will not automatically be the same. Otherwise employees may become less motivated or 'engaged' if they see that in a clash of objectives the employer objectives always take priority.

Role set analysis

A technique for identifying the priorities in a job or organization is that of role set analysis. The related concept of strategic planning is explained in the final section of this chapter. The definition of role set used in this chapter is that it is those main activities and/or people that take up, or need to take up, most of a person's working time. Role set analysis involves comparing existing activities with current priorities. It can then lead to a consideration or reconsideration of what the end objectives of a job should be.

Potential advantages

The technique of role set analysis has five main advantages. These are:

1. It is easy to apply
2. It is easy to update
3. It can enable managers to ask searching questions of themselves about their priorities and objectives
4. It can also be used on a work group basis to see if the activities of colleagues need to be adjusted
5. It can be used on an individual, departmental or organizational basis to review priorities with regard to resource allocation.

Explanation of the technique

Role set analysis involves using a market research approach to one's job. The raw data consist of the expectations of the main individuals and interest groups with whom one has to interact. Instead of identifying one's job by asking 'what should I be doing?' the starting point is to ask 'what do others expect of me?'. To ask that question one first has to identify just what the main elements in the role set are. The process of identifying the expectations of the members in the role set may be undertaken by analysing data already available and, where appropriate, actually consulting with people about what the expectations are. The next stage is to synthesize this raw data, and the often conflicting pressures, into a coherent form. This is done by presenting the information in chart form.

The key activities, people and groups with whom a manager has to work must be identified. The chart needs to indicate the volume of work (in percentage terms) that is appropriate for each constituent part and also the priorities. It needs to be remembered that there may be some particularly influential members of the role set with whom contact is infrequent but very important. The diagram should be drawn so that the more important members of the role set are located closer to the person at the centre.

The next step is to see that the time and priority allocated to the elements in the role set are in line with what is actually needed. To do this effectively it is best for the person concerned to keep a diary of how they really spend their time over a few representative days. The actual time allocated to the individuals and groups in the role set can then be compared with what is considered desirable (see specimen figures in Figure 2.1).

Actual time spent is shown as a percentage with the model time given in accompanying brackets. Alternatively, time can be shown in hours and minutes. This enables planned reductions or increases in time allocation to be shown.

The example in Figure 2.1 is based on the job of the head of human resource management (HRM) in a professional organization employing approximately

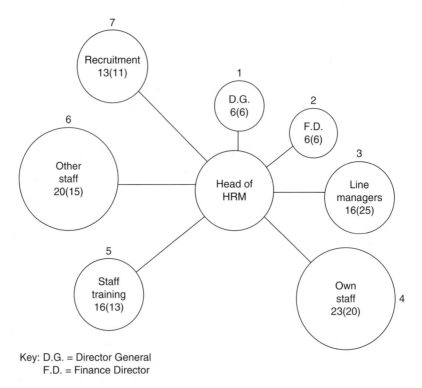

Key: D.G. = Director General
F.D. = Finance Director

Figure 2.1   Role set analysis of the head of human resource (HRM) in a
professional organization

500 people. Two junior HRM officers are also employed. Contact with external visitors has been included under the subject of their visits, mainly recruitment and training. The head of HRM reports to the finance director. The analysis prompted a series of questions, which was the purpose of the exercise. One such question was the appropriateness of the head of HRM reporting to the finance director, and not the chief executive. Others included whether the head of HRM was spending enough time with the line managers and too much with his own and other staff. Proposed adjustments in time allocations are shown in the new model time allocations – in brackets. Time spent working by the head of HRM on his own are allocated according to on whose behalf the work was being done. However, what also emerged was the need for some time to be allocated by the head of HRM for general reflective thought about the job.

Reasons for poor time allocation

There are many reasons why managers fail to identify their priorities and time allocations accurately. Role set analysis rapidly reveals how time can be used more effectively. Reasons for poor use of time may be:

- Accessibility: some people may be both physically and psychologically more accessible than others. There is a danger of ignoring the needs of those who are not so easily available. Managers in turn may be too accessible to some who may take up more time with them than they should.
- Congeniality: it is natural for people to want to spend time with those whose company they enjoy and with whom they share the same values. If this is overdone, however, the activities of individual units within an organization may become lopsided and not integrate well with overall organizational objectives.
- Conflict: people vary in their ability to handle conflict. Most want to avoid it. However, it is often important to air differences of opinion to see if constructive solutions can be found. It may also be important to engage in some maintenance behaviour with colleagues where conflict is particularly likely. This may necessitate talking about non-contentious issues and, if appropriate, social issues so that the relationship is maintained and, if possible, improved. This may help to preserve the working relationship when it is put under pressure by future conflict.
- Work preferences: people may want to concentrate on what they are good and confident at. The tendency for managers with a specialist background to spend too much time on their former specialism was examined at length in Chapter 1. When students study for exams they may need to concentrate most on the subjects where they are weakest and the risks greatest, but where the potential for improvement is most, rather than on the subjects they like most.
- Competence: some important tasks may be very demanding. It is important that people are carefully selected and developed to handle managerial responsibilities in particular.

■ Changing priorities: sometimes people are locked into historic priorities. Shifts in organizational priorities are not always formally announced. Managers need to examine the external pressures on an organization in particular and to develop a 'feel' as to when new priorities have emerged. The pace of change in many organizations is such that managers have to cope with an increasing rate of internal change linked to an increasing rate of external change.

In estimating the amount of time and attention that other individuals or groups require, it is necessary to remember that one can allocate too much time, as well as too little. Employees can feel over-supervised, and those in senior positions may not want to spend too much time with subordinate managers. However, having said this, it is obviously potentially damaging to spend less time with one's boss than the boss deems to be appropriate. It is also necessary to consider what time one needs for oneself, particularly for reflective thought. Diary analyses by managers usually reveal that it is very difficult for them to arrange periods when they can engage in concentrated work or reflective thought without interruption. Such time may, however, be essential if one is to do long-term planning. Appropriate refinements to the role set diagram would be to allow a percentage of time for oneself as well as for those with whom one occasionally interacts who can be classified in the diagram as 'others'.

Job structure

Amongst the benefits that can be obtained from role set analysis is that it may show whether or not a job is viable as currently structured. There may be so many individuals and groups with whom the manager has to interact that the job may be impossible. Alternatively, the manager may be tackling their job in an inappropriate way. One example of this was the manager who, having used this technique, revealed that he was dealing directly with those employees in the tier below his subordinates instead of just with his own immediate subordinates! Whether problems are organizational or of the manager's own making, there may also be health implications if the manager has a pattern of interaction that is just too much to cope with.

EXAMPLE: An overloaded manager

In a management development workshop one participant revealed that he suffered from angina. His role set analysis demonstrated that he was grossly overloaded and that his part of the organization needed restructuring – a factor which cannot have helped his health problems and may even have precipitated them.

Individual priorities

A direct way in which individual managers can identify priorities is to ask themselves 'who is in the position to do me the greatest damage?' The leader of an architectural group, when asked to do a role set analysis on this basis, likened it to the theory of damage limitation. The value of doing this is to see that those who can do the greatest damage are on top of the list in getting their share of the time. As will shortly be explained, it is also of value in working out what to do if one comes under conflicting pressures.

Alternatively, the question can be asked 'who can help the manager most?' and time allocated accordingly, though it is to be hoped that this approach is not used too opportunistically. Establishing the order of importance in the role set is not always that simple. The hierarchy of importance is not always obvious in matrix structures, for agency workers, and with regard to important suppliers or other **stakeholders**. It may not even be obvious in conventional organizations with a hierarchical structure. It is not the most senior person in an organization who is necessarily the first in importance in one's role set. The view senior people have of you may well be important, but it is necessary to work out whose word they take into account when forming their opinion of you.

EXAMPLE: Identifying the wrong key person

One training officer gave an example of how he mistakenly thought the most important member of his role set was the chief executive of a company he was working for. The training officer had numerous differences of opinion with his immediate boss and sought to overcome the bad working relationship by going over the head of his boss, the company secretary, to the chief executive. The company secretary became aware of this and as a countermeasure started giving bad reports about the training officer to the chief executive. Consequently, the more the training officer went to the chief executive the greater the number of bad reports there were made of him. The chief executive, faced with a choice, understandably preferred to accept the view of the more strategically placed company secretary. Ideally, of course, the chief executive should not have allowed the training officer to bypass the company secretary, but that is what actually happened. Eventually the training officer, prompted by good advice from other colleagues, came to realize that the most important person in his role set was the company secretary. In the end he did what he should have done in the first place in his particular case, which was to work on improving his relationship with his immediate boss.

It isn't just people of high status who may be in a position to inflict 'damage' on a manager. Often people in low-status positions, but who control important and perhaps scarce services, can do the same. So too may those who control access to important information or who act as 'gatekeepers' to senior managers. Informal members of role sets may also need to be identified, assessed and handled in terms of their importance. It is also necessary to distinguish between short- and long-term aims in priorities.

Organizational priorities

The emphasis in this section has so far mainly been about working out appropriate time allocations on an individual basis. Role set analysis can also be used to consider how resources should be allocated on an organizational basis. Managers can also review their budget distribution in this way.

EXAMPLE: Prioritization in the police service

An interesting example of establishing organizational priorities is the technique of crime-screening. This is a method of allocating resources for criminal investigative work that is sometimes formalized into a 'points system' by police forces. Offences that might realistically lead to successful detection and conviction are allocated resources in preference to cases in which success is less likely. The amount of available evidence is considered particularly important in allocating points. Consequently, aspects such as the quality of the description of a person, the noting of a car number or the possibility of forensic evidence could be crucial in determining whether a crime is investigated or not. The severity of the crime is another important criterion, as is the estimate of public priorities. Crimes with a low number of points might just be handled on the phone. The technique can also be used to review the allocation of resources between crime detection and crime prevention. The same type of issue arises with medical work in trying to strike the right balance between health cure and health care.

Information and evaluation

There are many ways in which information can be collected about role sets. The technique can be a very useful device for getting people to talk during in-house management workshops about common problems. If syndicates of managers doing similar jobs are arranged, they can critically cross-examine one another about the appropriateness of one another's role set analysis. Workshops can provide a climate in which basic issues, which would not otherwise be discussed, are brought out into the open. The technique of role set analysis can have a powerful catalytic effect in this context. Another method of collecting information is for a manager to take a market research approach and ask colleagues just what their expectations are. Care has to be taken, however, about who is approached and the manner of the approach. One of the potential problems is that expectations are aroused which cannot be met. As a minimum, though, one should reflect on just what the expectations of you are by the other individuals and groups in your role set. This may reveal a variety of misunderstandings about what you expect from others and what they expect from you.

What also may be revealed by role set analysis is that some of the expectations are contradictory. This may happen if the manager is given incompatible tasks or if the sheer volume of work they are expected to do is unrealistic. The most practical way of handling such a dilemma is often for managers to try to judge what the real priorities are amongst the welter of instructions they are given. They also need to be sensitive to changes in organizational priorities. Those senior to a manager may be reluctant to admit that the various expectations are in conflict.

The reality may be that the individual manager has to work out what the real priorities are at a given time. To do this the manager may need to gauge just what the priorities are with others in the role set and the ways in which they may be changing. In an ideal world one would only work in organizations where job demands were compatible and all legitimate expectations could be met. However, as we live in an imperfect world, there needs to be a method for resolving contradictory pressures. One should also recognize that when priorities change it is often politically too difficult for policymakers to say that a certain priority has been abandoned or even downgraded. The most one may get is an admission that a certain objective has been 'put on the back burner'. However, managers ignore these shifts in organizational priority at their peril and need to adjust their pattern of activity to suit the new scale of priorities.

Stress management

The pressures for competitiveness in the private sector and for economy in the public sector are putting managers under increasing stress. Consequently, they usually cannot do all that is expected of them and have to develop some basis for deciding how their own time and the resources under their control are allocated. If everything cannot be done, it seems far more logical to consciously and systematically prioritize rather than do things on a random basis. Individual survival and organizational effectiveness are both likely to be served by conscious prioritization. The best way of coping with managerial stress is to try to reduce it rather than simply deal with the symptoms. Techniques of prioritization can be enormously useful in this context and also in relieving managers of guilt feelings about not meeting what may be impossible demands.

The issue of managerial stress is dealt with further in Chapter 6, and the organizational problems caused by the frequent mismatch between expectations and resources in the public sector in Chapter 3. The issue of individual prioritization is dealt with further in the next section of this chapter.

Individual interpretation and application

What has been explained is a progressively more sophisticated method of gathering data and developing insights about how to identify one's job. After all this has been done, it is up to the manager to evaluate and synthesize the material and stamp their own personality on their job. There is more to identifying a job than working out what those in strategic positions want of you, but it is prudent to take that into account before then adding the essential ingredient – one's own personality.

The concept of role set analysis also stresses the interdependence of managers with others. The importance of the manager's role in creating and energizing teams is examined in the context of organic structures in Chapter 3, with regard to managerial style in Chapter 4 and in handling meetings and team building in Chapter 15.

Time management

When the overall objectives, key tasks and role set have been clarified it may then be appropriate for a manager to consider how effectively their time is used. One view of the manager's job is that the only real resource is their time. There appear to be enormous variations in the ways in which managers either use their time effectively or waste it. Consequently, this topic deserves specific attention. Issues of particular importance are:

- Identification of priorities
- Logical sequencing of work
- Avoidance of fatigue
- Need for managers to avoid wasting other people's time.

Identifying priorities

The reactive or 'grasshopper' (Stewart, 1988) manager's time management may be ineffective, failing to identify the priorities in the job. Perhaps the worst way of prioritizing work is to deal with the last request first, whether it be made in person or be the item just received in the in-tray. Sadly, there are many examples of people who do this regularly. The priorities of a job need to be established quite consciously. To do this it may be necessary to write them down and then either to rank the priorities over a particular time period or to group them into bands of varying urgency. Even well-organized managers find that they have to react to short-term crises and pressures, but they should have as a constant reference point a clear grasp of the priority issues that are accumulating and which merit attention.

Finding the time to think about the job may itself constitute a problem, particularly for managers who are already heavily involved in 'fire-fighting' activities. However, unless they somehow find the time to think their way through to a more rational pattern of activity, managers are unlikely to be effective. One of the problems in organizations is that managers find that they have to cope with so many interruptions that it is difficult to find time to think in a concentrated and systematic way about the job. It may be necessary to do this away from one's normal place of work or to use a secretary or other person as a screen to prevent interruptions. It may also be necessary to have a clear idea of who those people are who make unproductive claims on one's time, with a view to reducing the time spent with them. It is one of the ironies of organizational life that so often the people with the most time to waste are those who insist on spending long periods telling you how busy they are! In such cases it may be particularly necessary to tell people at the start of a discussion how much time you have available for them.

Establishing the priorities in a job may well involve a careful look at the conflict between what a manager prefers to do and what they actually need to do. This is a necessarily recurring issue in this book. The consequences of inappropriate prioritization can even threaten the survival of an organization.

EXAMPLE: Dramatically wrong priorities

A UK company was threatened with a hostile take-over bid. Unfortunately the senior executive responsible for objecting to this failed to attend the government take-over panel meeting that could have blocked the bid. Consequently, the take-over was approved without opposition!

Sequencing work

Two interrelated issues should particularly influence the order in which work is done: 1) priority of importance, and 2) logical sequence. Not all issues need immediate attention. The following checklist may help in identifying the sequence in which work needs to be tackled:

- What needs to be done urgently? This can include minor tasks that have to be completed by an imminent deadline.
- What needs to be done to enable other people to get on with their job?
- What needs to be done when it is convenient, or within a non-urgent time span?
- What can't be done until activities by others have been completed? Such work may be put in a pending tray, though a follow-up system may be necessary to monitor the progress of other people involved in the task.
- What is simply information received which requires no action?
- Which issues can simply be ignored?

EXAMPLE: Route planning

The need for careful sequencing is further illustrated by the following case of two delivery drivers working for the same firm. One driver would look at the first address on his list and drive off and then look at the next address and drive to that and so on. In the course of a day he was likely to retrace his route several times. The other driver would spend about an hour each morning planning his route so that, although he started his deliveries later, he covered his route with the minimum mileage.

Some work may need reflective thought before it is finalized. It is not just the speed at which issues are dealt with that is important, but also the quality of any decisions. The thought may not even need to be conscious, as ideas can suddenly fit into place after subconscious mental activity. Students can also find this when answering examination questions. A difficult question that is put on one side while an easier one is tackled may appear much simpler when it is read for the second time a while later. However, the manager needs to recognize the difference between procrastination and reflection on difficult issues so that an appropriate decision is eventually taken.

Another issue is whether tasks are undertaken consecutively or simultaneously. The answer to this may depend on both personality and national culture. **Monochrones** may prefer to undertake tasks in a linear manner until they are completed. **Polychrones** often prefer to undertake a number of tasks simultaneously. Problems can arise when these two patterns clash, for example, if a monochrone is busily engaged on a task and a polychrone wants something else done immediately. Hall (1987) maintains that these patterns correlate with national culture – for instance, monochronic work patterns are more common in Nordic countries than elsewhere.

Critical path analysis

The concept of logical work sequencing can be developed further by the use of **critical path analysis** (CPA). This is of particular use in planning and controlling tasks where a number of activities need to be carried out simultaneously. The technique has been developed particularly for use on construction projects and in production planning. The benefits of CPA did not live up to early expectations because of unforeseen variables, failures in communication and competing agendas that can affect any project and frustrate **mechanistic** planning systems. If used carefully, however, critical path analysis often is a powerful planning tool and can also be of value for individual work planning. It is often used intuitively by people who have never heard of the term 'critical path analysis', for example a joint of meat is put to roast whilst the rest of the dinner is prepared, because the joint will take longer to cook than

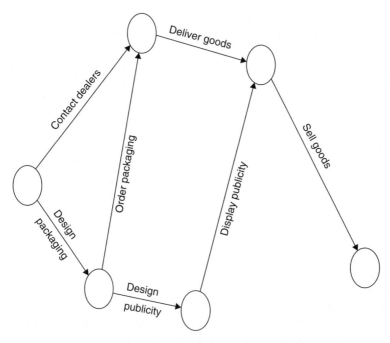

Figure 2.2   Critical path analysis: launching a new product

the vegetables. Alternative titles for CPA are 'network planning' and 'network analysis'.

An example of how CPA can be used in launching a new product is shown in Figure 2.2.

In the launch of the new product, one assumes that the market research and design have been undertaken first. The packaging would then be designed and the dealers contacted at the same time to prepare them for the new product. Once the packaging has been designed it can then be ordered from the supplier. The publicity material can then be created (not before, as one would want to see the packaged product first). When the packaging has been received and orders received from the dealers the product can then be delivered. A further step in the planning can be to show the time period during which each step of the process needs to be completed. Although the example is simple, the written explanation is complicated and difficult to follow. In contrast, the diagram (Figure 2.2) is very clear.

Fatigue

It is necessary for managers to take into account their own physical limitations in planning their workload. Individuals vary considerably in their propensity to fatigue, and fatigue also depends on the commitments a manager has outside the workplace. It can be very tempting to compare oneself to a person with an unusually high degree of energy, but the consequences may be disastrous if the workload is planned on an over-optimistic assessment of what one's physical capabilities really are. If this happens it seems likely that in the long-term the quality and rate of work will suffer and the likelihood of illness increase. A particular danger is that recovery time from fatigue may increase exponentially according to the amount of fatigue. This means that when practicable, one should rest as soon as there are signs of fatigue, otherwise recovery can take much longer. This fits with a British Medical Council study of the impact of increased hours of work in war industries in Britain after the Dunkirk evacuation in 1940. The original working week of 56 hours had to be re-introduced because the longer working week of 69.5 hours had led to the actual hours being worked a week falling to 51 (Reported in Maier, 1955).

Saving other people's time

Managers need to help others use their time productively, as well as organizing their own time management. This can, for example, mean careful preparation for discussions and interviews so that other people's time is not wasted. Prior preparation is particularly important if one has to chair a meeting, as will be explained in more detail in Chapter 15, on meetings, chairing and team building.

EXAMPLE: The time costs of badly planned meetings

At a local government body 23 people from different parts of London were called to a meeting. Many of those invited to the meeting had journeys of an hour or more in heavy traffic or on crowded public transport. The meeting was aborted after less than half hour because it had not been properly planned – the rationale for the meeting had not been clarified in advance and necessary thought had not been given in advance to the decisions that were to be taken. The meeting was postponed to a future occasion necessitating repeat journeys for those attending.

Strategic planning

The need for planning

The concepts explained so far in this chapter have focused mainly on how the individual manager can do their own job more effectively over a relatively short-term period. However, managers also need to take a long-term and corporate perspective. This inevitably means cooperating with other managers to anticipate and, where appropriate, shape the future. If an individual manager can help develop rational long-term policies, this can make their own job easier to perform and may also lead to improvements in other parts of the organization that are even more important. It has already been explained how the techniques of setting objectives and role set analysis can be applied on a departmental or organizational basis as well as on an individual basis.

The essence of strategic planning is that it is the broad means of achieving overall organizational objectives. However, it may also necessitate careful thought about the nature of these objectives. People in commercial organizations often take the view that they are in business to make a particular product or deliver a particular service when the reality is that their overall aim may actually need to be to optimize their return on capital investment. Although the literature on this topic is mainly based on the private sector, the concepts can and need to be adapted for use in the public sector and areas such as **non-governmental organizations** (NGOs), or **non-government entities** (NGEs) as they are sometimes described. There the emphasis is likely to be on the need to provide cost-effective services in a changing environment.

Planning mechanisms

Key concepts and issues involved in strategic planning need to be explained. Even though most managers will not be involved in board-level planning, long-term and strategic planning is also needed at a departmental level. For this to be done, it is necessary to involve the key decision-makers.

The experience of the authors with strategic planning groups from outside the main power structure suggests that these are likely to fail because they do not have the 'clout' or often even the information and expertise with which to fashion long-term policies. The problem that has to be overcome with the key decision-makers is that they are invariably busy people. To complicate matters, such people may be reluctant to commit themselves to long-term strategies, particularly if there are sectional rivalries. Also, even if senior people are given responsibility for strategic planning, if they become distanced from operational reality, their plans may prove to be unrealistic.

The problem of creating time for such strategic planning with key, yet busy, people can be reduced by having a chair who is under less pressure and by the provision of specialist reports for consideration at corporate or long-term planning meetings. It can be inappropriate to include long-term planning with the business discussed at ordinary departmental or board meetings, as this inevitably leads to the short-term issues crowding out the long-term ones. In practice, often the only long-term planning that takes place is that associated with the annual financial budget.

Strategic planning can be a top-down or bottom-up process. In the former, the attempt is made to change the organization in line with a centrally conceived master plan. With bottom-up planning, information is sought from the grass roots to help shape evolutionary development. In practice, there usually needs to be a fusing of these two approaches. Ideally, a long-term plan will be established and short-term plans integrated with it. This may involve 'gap analysis' to establish what has to be done to bring an organization's activities into line with that which is planned. Any long-term plan will, however, need continuous adjustment, especially in turbulent environments. Such ongoing turbulence caused Mintzberg (2009) to view strategy as something that was likely to emerge rather than being determined by conscious planning mechanisms.

The increasing pace of change has caused a reaction against detailed centralized planning because such a process can be too cumbersome to react quickly and effectively. This can lead to a greater need for more organic (flexible) structures. However, this may need to be reconciled with the need for accountability and liability. Key factors that may determine organizational structure and dynamics are considered in the next chapter.

SWOT analysis

A simple model that can be a useful way of undertaking strategic planning is **SWOT Analysis**. The factors analysed using this technique are as follows:

- Factors Internal to the Organization:
  - Strengths
  - Weaknesses
- Factors External to the Organization:
  - Opportunities
  - Threats

If the SWOT approach is used it is important to ensure that the analysis is rigorous. If it is done in a mechanistic and superficial way it may give a false impression of what the strategic options really are (Rees and Porter, 2006, p. 228). At whatever level strategic planning is undertaken, the process needs to be reasonably broadly based – even if the lesson has been learned that one should avoid centralized prescriptive approaches. Many corporate plans revolve just around the financial and marketing dimensions but SWOT necessitates considering the human resource dimension before and not after strategy is determined. The related interconnections between other factors are considered in Chapter 3.

Realistic goals

One of the dangers in strategic planning is that unrealistic goals may be set. Although there may be occasions when the circumstances are right to try and bridge the gap between 'heroic' goals and existing resources, this is not always the case. Whilst organizational capability can be developed, structures changed and cultures altered, there are limits to the change that is achievable. Also, competitors can copy technological achievements. What may be key is the web of working relationships within or even outside an organization and its stock of **intellectual capital**. Incremental improvement may sometimes be the best option.

EXAMPLE: Unrealistic goals

A national UK social work charity embarked on an ambitious programme of expansion by taking over related charitable organizations. Unfortunately the charity did not manage to reap the benefits of synergy which they had been hoping for and instead found that the enlarged scale of the organization brought diseconomies. In particular they did not have the in-house expertise to observe the legal obligations with regard to the employment rights of the employees they acquired. The charity also found that they lacked sufficient managerial capability and it was not long before the organization ran into serious financial difficulties.

Often the difficulties of developing a meaningful and comprehensive corporate plan are so great that it is better to adopt just an incremental plan.

EXAMPLE: Conflict about goals

In a former Communist country in Eastern Europe attempts were made to develop a corporate plan in a national consultative body composed of representatives of employers, trade unions and the government. There were considerable conflicts of interest not just between the different interest groups but also sometimes between members of the same interest group. The logical way forward was to identify those areas where reform was acceptable and could be agreed. This was preferable to perpetual argument and no change at all being implemented (Rees and Porter, 2006, ICT Part 1).

Another example concerns a rural development authority in Southeast Asia. As might be imagined, the job of this agency was to develop rural areas that were in need of economic revitalization. It emerged, however, that there was a major difference of opinion within the development authority about whether its prime function was the prudent development of local industries or the preservation of local communities regardless of cost. Given that there was no immediate prospect of resolving the difference it was necessary to concentrate on areas where organizational reform was practicable (Rees and Porter, 2006, ICT Part 1).

Sometimes mission statements are used as a way of identifying and publicizing the overall aims and values of an organization. This can provide a useful focus both internally and externally. However, there is a danger that such statements degenerate into being 'wish lists' of what organizations believe are acceptable values and realistic aims. For mission statements to be useful they need to be very carefully worked out, with considerable attention being paid to factors such as the possible degree of control of the internal and external environment, the commitment to such documents and the need for its elements to be consistent with one another. Too many mission statements are in practice, to put it kindly, aspirational rather than useful statements of what an organization is and what it hopes to be.

There is a great danger in planning processes that revolve too much around that which is relatively easily quantified. It is also necessary to beware of obstacles to rational debate:

> An assumption about the development of strategy is that those who need to be involved welcome the prospect of open and 'rational' debate. Personality clashes, rivalries, hidden and even ignoble agendas and sensitive developments are some of the factors that can be obstacles to debate. Account may also need to be taken of human frailties such as personal insecurity and individual 'hang-ups'
>
> (Rees and Porter, 2006, ICT Part 1, p. 227).

Targets

The planning and decision-making process in organizations will partly depend on quantitative estimates of what is actually happening, what is expected to happen and what those in charge would like to happen. A problem is that once measures are used as a basis for targets they may get distorted. Distortion is all the more likely if the targets are linked to rewards or penalties. Rewards or penalties may involve the pay of the individuals concerned or future resource allocation to an organization and may even threaten the very survival of an organization (as explained further in both Chapters 3 and 7). These issues can be particularly problematic in the public sector where the measure of commercial profitability is absent, though even that measure is capable of manipulation. What this means is that whilst the use of targets may be necessary, the targets need to be carefully established. The danger is that targets are politically convenient rather than realistic. They can distort organizational activity so that other important activities are ignored, and those involved in meeting targets but not involved in the setting of targets may not be committed to their achievement. Such shortcomings can lead to a range of defensive responses that can involve manipulation so there is just the appearance of target achievement or even downright fraud.

EXAMPLE: Manipulation of record of performance

Growing concern arose in the UK about the possibility that police crime statistics for England and Wales were being manipulated to meet targets and to show that crime was decreasing, when this was not necessarily the case. This could have occurred partly at least because of political pressure. The perceived danger was that some incidents that had actually been reported to the police were not being included and that other incidents were being downgraded. Concern was such that police crime statistics were stripped of their official quality assurance mark by the UK Statistics Authority (*The Times*, 2014). In a subsequent study by a police watchdog it was estimated that 20% of crimes reported to the police went unrecorded (HMIC, 2014).

There is also the danger that targets can be too zealously adhered to. Over emphasis on financial performance targets may well have dangerously under-mined basic standards of patient care in some UK Health Trusts.

EXAMPLE: Over-zealous achievement

Concern about the possible impact of strict adherence to financial targets on patient care at the former Mid Staffordshire NHS Trust led to two inquiries (Francis, 2013; Health Care Commission, 2009). Whilst no statistics of unnecessary deaths were quoted, one press report claimed that between 400 and 1,200 more patients died because of sub-standard care between 2005 and 2008 than would have been expected for the mix of patients admitted (*The Times*, 2009). One of the many criti-cisms of the Trust's managerial performance was that:

> The Trust prioritized its finances and its Foundation Trust application over its quality of care, and failed to put patients at the centre of its work (Francis, 2013, p. 45).

EXAMPLE: The New York Police experience

Rudolph Giuliani (2002) took a very different approach to achieving improvements in organizational performance when he was mayor of New York City. He understood the dangers of targets being manipulated to give only the appearance of progress. He also saw the danger of arousing expectations by target setting and feelings of failure if targets were not met, even if there had been significant improvement. Consequently, instead of developing grand strategies, he adopted a project problem-solving approach to areas of major concern. Whilst other factors may have been at work as well, the murder rate in New York City fell from 1,946 in the year 1993 (the year before he became mayor) to 673 in 2000 (Giuliani, 2002, p. 169). Giuliani also developed the 'broken window' theory. This involved dealing with small issues, such as repairing bro-ken windows in public property, to create a better environment and momentum for improvement. Small issues could be linked to larger issues, for example to criminal behaviour. This in turn could lead to major strategic benefits (Giuliani, 2002, p. 47).

Summary

The importance of identifying realistic job objectives has been stressed in this chapter. Often managers justify themselves by the amount of work they do rather than the results they achieve. Objective setting can be a means of both targeting their activity and assessing their performance. There are many rea-sons why managers may get the balance of their job wrong.

The technique of role set analysis was explained in detail because of its potential to help people organize their work effectively. It can be an easy and effective way of distinguishing between what managers are doing and what they should be doing. Role set analysis can also help managers prioritize, a particularly necessary activity if the managers are overworked. If that is the case, it is better that they consciously decide what is done and what is not done rather than engage in random prioritization, which can lead to important tasks being neglected. Managers also need to distinguish between short-term and long-term objectives. They need to create some time for reflective thought about the future.

Time management was also explained. It includes sequencing work in a logical way. Some account also should be taken of social needs at work. Working too hard can be counterproductive because of the danger of cumulative fatigue.

The need for managers to try and influence the framework in which they operate was explained. Managers should get involved in strategic planning at whatever level possible. This may help prevent their good work being undermined by non-existent or faulty planning elsewhere. Their involvement may also be able to make overall strategic planning more effective.

Self-assessment questions

If you are not in a managerial job you may wish to answer some of the questions with regard to whatever activity you are engaged in. If you wish to check the extent to which your answers to any of the following questions are appropriate, cross-refer to the Table of Contents for Chapter 2.

1. How would you distinguish between managerial activity and managerial effectiveness?
2. Define appropriate work objectives either for yourself or for another person.
3. What are the advantages that role set analysis can have over other methods of identifying work content and priorities?
4. What are the essential elements of effective time management?
5. How would you ensure that you have sequenced your work logically?
6. Why might strategic planning be relevant to you?

Case study notes – A Managerial Headache

Learning outcomes:

■ To identify how the head teacher could organize her time more effectively
■ To enable students to review how effectively they organize their own time

Heather Thomas appears to have a time management problem. She has too much to do and important long-term issues tend to suffer. She may be behaving more like the departmental head she used to be than managing a much bigger operation in possibly a demanding environment. Examples of the activities she may need to give up include knowing every schoolchild's name and regular teaching, even if she does find the teaching therapeutic. She needs to look more pro-actively at the opportunities for delegating to other members of staff. This is likely to include her deputy, secretary and departmental heads. The department heads may be reluctant to undertake more managerial work but there is a limit to what a head teacher can do. There may also be a strong case for either making the position of bursar full-time or for recruiting a further part-time person to help her.

Skills development exercise

Draw a role set diagram either for yourself or another job you know well. Explain the rationale to another person, for example a colleague or fellow student who can critically appraise your work.

References

NB: Works of particular interest are marked with an asterisk.

*Fox, Alan (1965), *Industrial Relations and Industrial Sociology*, Research paper no. 3, Royal Commission on Trade Unions and Employers Associations, London: HMSO.

Francis, Robert QC (2013) *Report of the Mid Staffordshire NHS Foundation Trust Public Inquiry*, www.midstaffspublicinquiry.com.

*Giuliani, Rudolph W. (2002), *Leadership*, Little Brown.
    An interesting and illuminating account of the managerial problems facing the Mayor of New York City and an explanation of how these problems were tackled, which is particularly critical of the use of targets.

Hall, Edward. T. (1987), *Hidden Differences*, Anchor Press/Doubleday.

Health Care Commission (2009), *Investigation into Mid Staffordshire MHS Foundation Trust*, London: HMSO.

Her Majesty's Inspectorate of Constabulary (HMIC) (1 May 2014) *Crime Recording: A Matter of Fact*, London: HMSO.
    An interim report of the inspection of crime data integrity in police forces in England and Wales.

Humble, John (1979), *Management by Objectives in Action*, McGraw-Hill in association with the British Institute of Management.

Maier, Norman, R. F. (1955), *Psychology in Industry*, Harrap, p. 447.

*Mintzberg, Henry (2009), *Managing*, Prentice Hall.

Porter, Michael (1998), *The Competitive Advantage of Nations*, 2nd ed., The Free Press.

*Rees, W. David and Christine Porter (2002), Management by panacea – the training implications, *Industrial and Commercial Training*, Vol. 34, No. 6.
*Rees, W. David and Christine Porter (2006), Corporate strategy development and related management development: the case for the incremental approach, Part 1 – the development of strategy and Part 2 – implications for learning and development. *Industrial and Commercial Training*, Vol. 38, No. 5 and Vol. 39, No. 6.

> *An explanation of why comprehensive strategy development may often be so difficult that the incremental approach may be the only option. This article received a highly commended award by the Emerald Literati Network in 2007. In Part 2 the need for a broad-based approach is explained and also why teaching in the area needs to be multi-disciplinary.*

Stewart, Rosemary (1988), *Managers and Their Jobs*, 2nd ed., Palgrave Macmillan, p. 13.
The Times (2009), *Hundreds die at 'Third World' hospital*, 18 March.
The Times (2014), *Crime figures lose quality mark amid claims of fiddling*, 16 January.

Taking it further

Johnson, Gerry, Kevan Scholes and Richard Whittingham (2011), *Fundamentals of Strategy*, 2nd ed., Pearson.

> *A thorough account of private sector strategy.*

Meredith, Jack R. and Samuel J. Martel (2012), *Project Management – A Managerial Approach*, 8th edn., Wiley.

> *A detailed account of project management techniques, including critical path analysis.*

Porter, Christine and W. David Rees (2012), The Managerial Gap and how coaching can help, *International Coaching and Psychology Review* (The British Psychological Society), Vol. 7.

> *It includes material on role set analysis, the evolution of the concept and its application.*

Rees, W. David (1997), Managerial Stress – Dealing With Causes, Not the Symptoms, *Industrial and Commercial Training*, Vol. 29, No. 2, pp. 25–30.

> *A more detailed explanation and different example of the application of role set analysis and its value in reducing managerial stress.*

The Manager and the Organization

3

Case study

Here We Go

Simon Evans is the chairman and majority shareholder of a European airline. Although new to the airline business, after five years he has expanded his fleet to 30 aircraft, leasing further aircraft on a short-term basis when necessary. His success has been because of his commercial acumen, contacts with banks and other sources of capital and his reputation as a successful **serial entrepreneur**. He also has great energy and enthusiasm, especially for setting up new businesses. Simon is impatient of obstacles and the increasing amount of European Union legislation governing the conduct of airlines and employment of staff. Recently the company has lost two major employment tribunal cases in the UK regarding employment protection, in which Simon had been involved.

When Simon started off in the airline business he hired an old friend, Colin Adams, who had worked for another airline and made him his chief assistant. Colin head-hunted many former colleagues to work for the new company, paying premium rates where necessary. The company was named 'Here we go'. Between them they managed the main functions, which included flight operations, engineering maintenance, reservations, finance, commercial and administration. More than half of the activity is for charter work but the number of scheduled routes has been steadily increasing.

There is not much of a formal organization structure and there is sometimes confusion about who people should go to for direction or advice, Simon or Colin. Simon tends to leave Colin to act as a 'trouble shooter'. Unfortunately Colin recently made a bad mistake when giving advice about maintenance schedules. Additionally, Simon wonders if Colin really has the drive to exploit the good market opportunities that exist for the company. The company now employs 550 people, most of them full-time.

Questions:

1.   How would you assess the organization and operation of the company?
2.   What changes, if any, would you recommend?

Introduction

In this chapter the organizational context in which those with managerial responsibilities have to work is examined. Managers need to appreciate this context and the way in which organizations need to establish structures that are 'fit for purpose'. They may also need to consider how organizational structures and operational methods need to be adapted to take account of changed circumstances and how structure can facilitate or hamper change. Historical and recent theories of organization are explained. Key factors are identified which shape the structure and operation of organizations, particularly **globalization**, competition, information technology (IT), the critical function and national culture. The important concepts of the **flexible organization**, **intellectual capital** and **knowledge management** are also examined. The problems of achieving effective integration of organizational activity are considered and strategies suggested for dealing with this issue. The need to distinguish between role and personality behaviour is necessarily included. The similarities and differences between the private and public sectors are given particular attention as is the nature and increasing importance of non-governmental organizations (NGOs).

Theories of organizations

Scientific and classical management schools

The historical approach to management was that it consisted of a set of principles that were capable of definition and universal application. This was the approach of writers such as Henri Fayol[1] (1916). F.W. Taylor[2] was a member of the scientific management school, which conceptually overlapped with the classical management theorists, including Fayol. Those in the scientific management school concentrated on the effective organization of manual work, production planning and time and motion studies. Taylor advocated the systematic analysis of work, and for management to take over decision-making about which methods of work were used, based on the principle that the average worker preferred a well-defined task and clear-cut standards.

The classical theorists developed the ideas of the scientific management theorists into a framework of organizational principles. The collective view of the classical theorists was that work could be organized so that the objectives of organizations could be accomplished with great efficiency. Organizations were viewed as the product of logical thought concerned largely with coordinating tasks through the use of legitimate authority. Employees were seen as rational beings whose interests coincided with those of the organizations in which they were employed. They were also seen as being capable of working to high levels of efficiency, provided they were properly selected, trained, directed, monitored and supported. Employers would use indoctrination and coercion if necessary to achieve a rational approach. This was presumed to lead to employees behaving exactly as they were told. Great emphasis was also placed on the need for careful and detailed explanation of organizational structure.

Two particularly important concepts that emerged from the classical and scientific management theorists were those of **functional control** and **line and staff relationships**. F.W. Taylor (1972) envisaged organizations based on **functional control**. To the extent that this is practiced nowadays this means that shop floor supervisors are directly responsible to the various functional departments they interact with. Specialists working in these functional departments, such as those responsible for work methods, staff selection and quality inspection will therefore give instructions and not advice to supervisors – even though this means that supervisors do not have **unity of command**. In line and staff relationships, however, specialist (or functional) staff only advise line management and unity of command is preserved. Sometimes in line and staff relationships, the relationship of specialist staff with line managers is described as a **dotted line relationship**. If a functional specialist feels their advice has been ignored in theory their only recourse is to see that the matter is taken up with their line manager's boss.

Whilst the concepts of functional and line and staff relationships are quite separate, in practice the distinction can be blurred. This is particularly because of the potential repercussions of line managers ignoring specialist advice. In addition line managers may find it convenient to let functional specialists take over some of the administrative duties related to a particular function.

Human relations school

Later the limitations of the classical and other writers became apparent, particularly their simplistic approach to understanding how people behave. It was recognized that people did not always do what employers wanted, nor did they always act in a way that employers considered rational (Roethlisberger and Dickson, 1939). The existence of informal networks and working relationships was also observed. This led to the evolution of the human relations school of organizational theory with which Elton Mayo in particular was associated. The Hawthorne experiments conducted at the Western Electric Company in Chicago in the 1920s and 1930s revealed that groups can have a powerful effect on the way organizations work. The work of occupational sociologists has subsequently emphasized the need to view organizations as social entities. As explained in the previous chapter, it is also necessary to recognize that there can be considerable conflict between the objectives of the organization and those of the individuals employed in it. Informal and formal employee organizations, such as organized work groups and trade unions, can also lead to the sharing of power in organizations, such that these are limits to the authority of management.

Systems theory

Another school of thought that has emerged is the systems concept of organizations. This views organizations as dynamic organisms with interconnecting parts. Each part is dependent on integration with related parts if objectives are to be accomplished. Each part, however, has to operate in an environment which influences what the employees in that section want to achieve and are capable of achieving.

EXAMPLE: Disjointed organizational behaviour

In a local evening newspaper, technological developments made it apparently possible to replace the former full-time print production staff by relatively unskilled part-time staff. Whilst this reduced costs in the production department, it dramatically increased problems in the advertising department. This was particularly because of the loss of accumulated knowledge of customers' needs in the production department. There were errors with layout, deadlines and arrangements for repeat advertisements. The consequences of this included the loss of customers and the advertising staff having to spend a significant amount of their time with the remaining customers arranging for rectification work and dealing with customer complaints. This in turn affected the commission payments of advertising staff and caused very high labour turnover in both the production and the advertising departments, thus aggravating the problems. The newspaper depended on advertising for about 80% of its income. Unfortunately the main focus of attention by senior management, who all had a journalistic background, was national and international news. The senior managers, because of their common background, additionally formed a strong social group. This created a specialist culture around news reporting which prevented the crucial issues regarding production and advertising being addressed.

The interrelationship of organizational activities is an important issue, particularly for diagnosing the causes of organizational problems. The approach taken in this book is consistent with the systems theory of organizations. Viewing the organization as a system or set of interrelated parts should enable the manager to identify the cause of a problem even if the cause is not within the department where the problem manifests itself. This theme is considered in more detail later in this chapter in the section on the interrelationship of organizational activity.

A concept that overlaps with systems theory is that of **socio-technical systems**. According to this theory, technical systems need to be effectively integrated with the social organization at work, not simply imposed on it. The concept of socio-technical systems is examined further in Chapter 6, in the context of motivation.

Types of organizational structure and activity

Mechanistic and organic structures

A particularly useful classification of organizational structures is the extent to which they are **mechanistic systems** or **organic systems**. Mechanistic organizations are very often operating in a largely similar way to that identified by the classical theorists and are often found in large-scale organizations operating in stable environments (Burns and Stalker, 1972). This is in contrast to more rapidly changing environments where more adaptive 'organic' systems may be necessary to facilitate quicker decision-making and adaptation. Burns and Stalker also argued that for innovation to be effective there needed to be close liaison, informal or formal, between production and research and development staff so they could appreciate the options available to each other and the constraints they were subject to. There will be organizations that have intermediate stages between the two extremes of mechanistic and organic and which also may have both types of arrangement within the one organization.

Innovation and networking

Some innovation in organizations is likely to occur naturally due to internal discussions and/or external interactions and happens incrementally. There may also be a need to structure external interaction in order to facilitate innovation. A study of Proctor & Gamble's product innovation arrangements revealed that for every internal scientist or engineer there were 200 comparable external ones. This led to the company's Connect and Develop policy which had the aim of seeing that half of their product innovation came from ideas generated outside the organization, including from customers, suppliers and business partners (Huston and Sakkab, 2006).

Matrix structures

An organizational **matrix structure** is a variation of organic arrangements. Essentially, a matrix structure involves setting up more or less permanent project-type groups to which people are allocated from resource centres. The line, or command, structure is retained on the resource group side but the appropriate mix of specialists can then be allocated, full-time or part-time, to product-type teams. This arrangement is very often found to be necessary in high-technology organizations. It is also often found in universities and colleges. It can assist in seeing that clients' needs are properly identified and met. If you have resource groupings only, as is often the case in universities, for example, the danger is that activity is focused on the development of the discipline alone without regard to the needs of clients. A feature of behaviour in many organizations, though, is that in any conflict between project groupings and the line structure it is the latter that usually wins. This is because of the power base of the command structure rather than because it necessarily has the better arguments. However, it is still necessary to see that those who lead project groups are selected and trained properly to increase their chances of success. This can easily be ignored because project leaders may not be seen as conventional managers, despite the responsibilities that they are likely to have (Rees and Porter, 2004).

The flexible organization

An extension of the concept of the organic organization is the flexible organization. An early commentator about this was Atkinson (1985). Flexible organizations were originally particularly evident in Japan, where security of employment was often guaranteed only to a core of permanent employees: other employees being engaged on a temporary basis. Security for the inner-core workers proved more difficult to sustain however when the Japanese economic boom ended in the early 1990s.

The organizational structure of Japanese companies is interesting and relevant because of the impact of their ideas on organizations throughout the world. An aim of Japanese investment in Western Europe was to circumvent protectionism. Japanese interest in the UK continues with more than 1,300 Japanese companies operating in the UK and the creation of 130,000 jobs (*The Telegraph*, 2013).

Interest in Japanese working practices increased in the UK as labour costs soared in the 1970s and organizations became concerned about their ability to be productive in an increasingly competitive global economic environment. Potentially, an organization is more likely to be able to adapt and survive if the outer core can be shed or replaced easily, as in the model of the flexible organization described above. Whilst people usually prefer to work in the inner core, those who are unemployed may regard a job in the outer core as better than no job at all. Employment in the periphery may provide opportunities for promotion to the core, and this can be a very useful way for employers to screen potential core employees. The requirement for some specialist skills may not be on a full-time basis, so cost-savings are made by employing some specialists part-time. These arrangements give the organization **numerical flexibility**. However, this is at the cost of the job security of those who are only used when needed. Also, some of those with specialist skills may prefer to exploit options in the labour market by having non-standard working arrangements, particularly if that gives them tax advantages as well as greater freedom. This may include those who, having taken early retirement, are amenable to the idea of having their skills brought back in, for example, on a consultancy basis. This has led to an increasing number of people having 'work portfolios' rather than working for one employer. Where specialist skills are in short supply, however, employers may prefer to try and lock people with those skills into the organization by employing them in the core.

Technological developments, such as those in electronic data processing, mean that practices such as working at home and subcontracting are possible in entirely new areas. Organizations that can predict their likely pattern of activity may also offer annual hours contracts so that employees' work attendance varies with, for example, the seasonal demand for their products. Employers may also want to employ some people at peak periods of the day only. Such arrangements enable banks, for example, to have their counters fully staffed at lunchtime, thus overcoming the problem of leaving some counters vacant at a peak time so that staff can have their lunch. Numerical flexibility can also be achieved by employing people on short-term contracts, on **zero-hours contracts** and by using agency workers. With zero hours contracts there is no obligation for the employer to provide any work and employees with such contracts are 'on call' in case there is any work. In extreme cases the degree of flexibility can lead to there being a **virtual organization** with a central point coordinating a network of commercial relationships with very few people at the centre.

Another aspect of the flexible organization is the benefits that may be derived in terms of **functional flexibility**. Staff may be contracted to perform a variety of different jobs and even to operate at varying levels of responsibility in accordance with the fluctuating needs of an organization. Japanese companies in particular place much emphasis on multiskilling and generic job descriptions.

Having explained the greater tendency for numerical and functional flexibility within organizations, it is necessary to say also that if taken too far this can create drawbacks. A sizeable core is needed to retain reasonable continuity and generate organizational **synergy**. Some able people may be discouraged from applying to organizations if, for example, only a fixed-term contract is on offer. Not all activities can be neatly packaged up and subcontracted. It is more difficult to develop an integrated organizational approach with a subcontractor who is only paid for what is strictly defined in the contract. Those in the peripheral workforce also need to be strategically managed. Inadequate attention to their supervision, training and integration can easily lead to the alienation of the customers or clients on which the organization depends.

In assessing the nature and importance of any trend towards more flexible working arrangements, it is probably best to view it as a series of **ad hoc** responses to labour market conditions rather than as an attempt to establish a conceptually different structure.

A constraint on the development of the flexible organization in Europe has been the series of European Union (EU) Directives that have significantly increased the employment protection of employees in countries that are members of the EU. These (and other) directives have created a more level playing field with regard to competition within Europe. However, the directives have had the effect of reducing the cost-savings that could be gained by using the distinction between full and temporary and part-time workers and the use of agency workers. Organizations are generally now unable to treat their part-time workers less favourably than their full-time workers, for example by paying them a lower hourly rate of pay. Additionally, restrictions have been placed on the ability of employers to dismiss employees on short-term contracts. However, such increased protections are not worldwide and employers that are based in countries that are members of the EU still have to compete with employers in countries that do not have such employee protections.

A further constraint on flexible working can be the need for management to retain control of the arrangements.

EXAMPLE: Flexibility and loss of control

British Airways had introduced a considerable element of flexible working. Unfortunately the flexibility that was convenient for the employer was not always convenient for the employees and vice versa. Members of staff were allowed to use 'swipe' cards to clock in and out. Informal arrangements for swapping shifts between staff proliferated. Some weak management compounded the problems that were being generated. Eventually the company lost so much control of who was working and when that it had to try and retrieve the situation. This precipitated strike action in 2003 that lost the company £40 million in revenue.

Outsourcing

Outsourcing is a concept that is related to that of the flexible organization. Historically it has been no different from subcontracting. However, developments in IT and globalization have greatly increased the opportunities for outsourcing. In addition the option to outsource internal services that were previously regarded as an integral part of organizational activity is increasingly being considered. An overlapping concept is that of **off-shoring**. This simply involves outsourcing to another country.

The subcontracting or outsourcing of production components is long established. However, globalization has increased both the competitive pressures to outsource component production and the opportunities. In the case of motor vehicle production, for example, it is increasingly difficult to attach a national identity to a car, despite its brand name. The financing, design, assembly location and component production may be done in a variety of countries and may also involve cooperation between a number of different companies on all these aspects. The development of multi-national and **trans-national corporations** is also likely to cause such organizations to keep the location of their various activities continuously under review, with activities being switched from one country to another relatively easily. Developments in transport such as increasing lorry size, the development of motorways and containerization have particularly assisted, for example, in the import of production components.

Off-shoring has been given a huge boost by developments in IT. This has enabled organizations to switch some activities to other countries with lower levels of pay. In some cases it is even possible to take advantage of different time zones so that work can be sent at the end of the working day to an off-shoring country and be completed by the following morning. Work that has proved particularly suitable for this type of off-shoring includes call centre activity, insurance, credit management and 'back office' financial jobs in general. The growing use of English as the language of international commerce has particularly encouraged organizations in English-speaking countries to outsource and also increased the number of countries that can handle off-shoring.

Sometimes though, the process has been reversed because of the lack of local knowledge of those offering advice when they are based in other countries. It has been found, however, that activities such as auditing can be off-shored and even some middle management functions.

Whilst outsourcing and off-shoring may bring considerable benefits to organizations, it is necessary for managers to be aware of the potential disadvantages, even where there appear to be significant financial advantages. This is just like a situation in which, for example, a canteen service is contracted out and the relationship with the sub-contractor has to be actively managed. In this example there may be particular concerns with regard to quality standards, the service provided, reliability of supply, and the legitimacy of any charges that are made to the client organization. When off-shoring is considered it may be necessary to consider the impact on organizational capacity and the preservation of **intellectual property**. A feature that is distinct to off-shoring is the need to also take into account currency fluctuations, which can undermine the economic rationale of such an arrangement. A further issue that has arisen with some off-shoring of call centres is the need for local knowledge about the needs of customers and the communication problems that can arise because of different nuances of languages between customers and call centre workers. The process of bringing back work to the 'parent country' is known as **re-shoring**.

EXAMPLE: Distance no problem

A company operating in Scotland included shellfish in its food products. It decided to send the shellfish to China in refrigerated containers for the shells to be removed and then have the fish returned to the UK. This saved the company £1 million a year but led to the loss of 120 jobs in Scotland (*The Telegraph*, 2006).

There can be a 'Panama type' effect with off-shoring. This term is appropriate as it is based on the tradition of merchant ships operating under flags of convenience, such as that of Panama, to avoid protective labour legislation. Whilst this can bring considerable cost advantages, it can also lead to the unacceptable exploitation of labour with regard to health and safety, below-subsistence wages and the use of child labour. Quite apart from the ethical issues involved, this may adversely affect a company's image.

Another dimension of outsourcing is the impact it can have on organizational structures and patterns of activity. This is considered later in the chapter in the section on the impact of IT on organizations.

Globalization

An underlying but recurrent theme in this chapter in particular is that of globalization. This affects organization structure, patterns of trade and employment and the pace of change. Globalization is taking place in the context of an increasingly interdependent world. Other dimensions of globalization are political, military, social and religious.

EXAMPLE: The English football Premier League

An interesting example of the pace, scale and nature of globalization concerns the organization of association football in England. Football used to be arranged just as a domestic competition. However, dramatic changes have occurred with the Premiership League. This league has become an important international brand. The international labour market for footballers has developed to such an extent that most of the players in the League are from other countries. There have been occasions when leading teams have fielded sides without a single English player in them. In addition, increasingly financial control of premiership clubs has passed to people in other countries, with most Premier League clubs, and even some clubs in the next division down, being owned by overseas interests. Football coaches have also increasingly been appointed from abroad. Domestic competitions are not as important as they once were and on one occasion Manchester United did not even participate in the domestic cup competition because it was competing in a tournament in South America. European competitions are now the most important inter-club competitions. Revenue is increasingly generated by international television deals, sponsorship and merchandise sales. The naming rights of stadiums can also be a source of income. Premiership football is watched on electronic screens in over 200 different countries. The merchandise is about both the club and its star players. The commercial attractiveness of a star player to a club can partly be the sales of merchandise they can generate worldwide. There can also be significant revenue from image rights to whoever owns the economic rights of a particular player. A further source of income can be overseas investment to promote the image of a particular country. All this is a far cry from the days when the main level of support and income was from local spectators.

Factors that determine organizational structure

There are many variables that will affect the structure and operation of an organization. These may be within the organization, outside it or a combination of the two. Managers need to determine which factors in their particular situation are likely to be important. These could include the impact of technology (including IT), the size of their organization, the identification of the critical function at a given time, and national and organizational culture.

Technology

General

Despite the increasing sophistication of IT equipment, costs are falling and general levels of computer literacy are rising. This has led to increasing use of IT often with profound effects on the structure and dynamics of organizations. Rapid information access may increase an organization's ability, as well as its need, to respond quickly to market changes. It may also facilitate meeting individual customer requirements. This may necessitate flexibility in organizational structures, and, especially in commercial organizations, the stakes are rising. The gains to be made by a rapid response may be high, and the penalties for a slow response correspondingly high as well. Many markets are becoming much more 'perfect' as information is more easily obtained and analysed and as the barriers of time and distance are reduced.

These developments mean that product life cycles tend to be shorter, and national and market boundaries less important and more permeable. The greater volatility of markets and knowledge about their behaviour means that customer and brand loyalty is likely to be less. Organizations may find that they have the knowledge and capacity to enter new markets but, conversely, this may mean that they have to face new sources of competition. A particularly important development has been **e-commerce**, which can and does have a dramatic effect on distribution channels by enabling customers to gain direct access to producers or those holding goods, as is the case with Amazon. Another example of alternative sources of distribution created by IT is the growing preference customers have for booking holidays via the Internet as opposed to using travel agents.

Impact of IT on organizational structure

The changes so far identified may precipitate further internal organizational changes. Potential changes include centralization, de-layering and reduced numbers of employees. Organizations can also operate without owning sophisticated IT systems by 'hotelling' at centres that provide those facilities. A combination of new technology and the reduced number of employees that are needed may also make it possible to start up operations very quickly.

Changes in internal relationships

Power relationships in organizations are likely to be affected by who has and who does not have access to particular data, combined with the ability to handle that information. This means that some people in junior positions can acquire considerable influence. This can be an aspect of the **digital divide** between those who can handle the new technology and those who cannot. Younger people who are products of a more computer literate generation can undermine the authority and status of some senior managers. Some frontline jobs may be made much easier by developments in IT. In other cases, ready access to data enables frontline staff to take decisions that would not previously have been thought possible or desirable. The ability of others to maintain power by their control of, and ability to filter, information will be correspondingly reduced. A further impact has been the blurring of traditional distinctions between blue- and white-collar employees, as new skills replace old ones and the shape of an organization changes. The reduced opportunities for face-to-face interaction between staff may be off-set, in part, by devices such as video- and tele-conferencing. However, such facilities will not replace the casual conversations between staff that can result in the priceless exchange of information. A further dimension of organizational change that may be produced is that created by social networking, for example the use of Twitter accounts, instant messaging and Facebook. This may also lead to a greater 'flattening' of organizational structures, at least in the way they actually operate. Whilst greater transparency about organizations may have positive advantages there can also be dangers such as breaches of confidentiality and misinformation.

Constraints and dangers

The constraints of IT also need to be recognized. Whilst there may be general qualitative gains in decision-making and product reliability, the cost and consequence of system and programming errors may be greatly increased. Other constraints or dangers are:

- Sometimes expensive systems are not integrated and are used on top of existing systems rather than instead of them;
- Systems may be acquired that do not do the job any more effectively than previous arrangements, leading to a low or negative return on the investment;
- Costs and potential difficulties involved in establishing computer systems may not be properly anticipated;
- If the right equipment is acquired, a further adaptation that may be necessary is that of shift-working, so that full use is made of the new facilities;
- The dehumanizing impact of IT on certain jobs may also require consideration; for example, the even greater de-personalization of relationships between staff and customers in supermarkets caused by new technology. Thought should be given to what remedial action can be considered in such cases;
- The security aspects of systems may need considerable attention. Dangers include accidental loss of information, system failures, computer viruses, breach of confidential and statutorily protected information, sabotage and espionage;
- The tendency for technology to race ahead of the ability of organizations to identify areas of application. Even when applications are identified, organizations may lack the ability to use them productively. A key need is for organizations to invest in technical support and in the training of managers and others so that they can make good use of the equipment that is available.

EXAMPLE: De-personalization of customer contact

In 2013 a shop assistant working at a check-out in the UK refused to process a customer's grocery purchases while the customer was talking on her mobile phone. The shop assistant apparently felt dehumanized by the customer's behaviour although the supermarket management later apologized to the shopper and said that it was not company policy to refuse to serve a customer while they were using their mobile phones. However in a poll conducted after the event 89% of voters said that they felt the check-out assistant was right and it was the customer who was being rude (*News Shopper*, 2013).

A further aspect is that some organizations and countries are technology rich and others technology poor. This can have the effect of increasing the gap between the 'haves' and the 'have nots'. The issue of the impact of developments in IT on patterns, particularly of organizational and individual communication is examined further in Chapter 8 on communication.

Skills development

The importance of developments in IT makes it essential for organizations to review what new skills need to be acquired by their staff. This involves more than exhortations that everyone become computer literate. A mix of skills is needed, including system design, programming, data inputting and retrieval, the facility to use a keyboard and the ability to make use of the information processes effectively. The acquisition of these skills needs to be matched to individual requirements. The concept of the **learning organization** (considered in Chapter 11) may be particularly appropriate in this context, especially given the speed of IT developments. The individual skills that people may need and the dangers of using IT are also considered in Chapter 8, Communication, in the section on electronic communication.

Size

Another important factor that will affect the structure and operation of an organization is size. You do not need much formality if you are engaged in constructing a small building, as to a large extent people can see for themselves what needs to be done. The mass production of vehicles, for example, requires much more formality because, amongst other things, people may not easily see how they fit into the total operation. The number of variables that has to be coordinated in that situation creates enormous organizational problems. It may well be that these problems increase on an exponential rather than a linear basis. The solution of breaking the units down into manageable sizes may not be an option if the technology adopted dictates that you need a large integrated plant.

Many organizations fail to grow because of their inability to develop a viable structure to cope with increased work. Larger organizations generally need an element of formality, clear reporting lines, delegation, managerial and specialist expertise, and control systems. Small organizations may also actually fail because they do not have the facilities to cope with extra work or the financial resources to wait until payment on large orders is made. A common constraint in family-controlled organizations is the unwillingness of family members to either bring in or make effective use of people with managerial expertise. They may also be very reluctant to bring in outside capital if that threatens their financial control. Very large organizations may need devolved structures so that the centre is not overloaded and too unresponsive to market conditions. This will particularly be the case if they have a wide range of products or services.

Intellectual capital

As explained in Chapter 2, organizations may increasingly depend on their intellectual capital for survival and development rather than just their physical assets. This is because more organizations are becoming both knowledge-based and amorphous. It can be especially important to attract and retain the right mix of people who have the collective expertise and access to information networks to realize an organization's potential. This is all the more so given the rapidity of many technological developments and the potential rewards in the private sector for organizations that are the first to exploit new market opportunities. A further aspect is that established national economies are less and less able to compete for work that has a low **added value**, because of lower wage rates elsewhere. Consequently, such countries need to sustain their economies by an increasing amount of high added value. This in turn means that intellectual capital needs to be an increasingly important part of their economies.

Intellectual capital can be divided into 'hard assets', like patents and copyrights, software and databases, and 'soft assets'. Soft assets can be described as the expertise of the work force (Stewart, 2002). A further distinction is between **explicit knowledge** within the organization and the less easily identified but still important **tacit knowledge** which is akin to the general 'know-how' held within the organization and some of the individuals and groups within it. A related distinction is between the **intellectual property** that is owned by the organization and that which is owned by the individual. This is likely to become an increasingly contentious issue as individuals may not be as prepared, as in the past, to let an organization take over the rights to all their ideas. A factor in this may be the desire of individuals to improve their prospects of getting jobs elsewhere by retaining the rights to what they consider is their own intellectual property. This means that both employers and employees may need to pay particular regard to any contractual clauses regarding the ownership of intellectual property.

EXAMPLE: Acquiring an empty shell

A Portuguese bank (BCP) acquired an investment management company, despite this being against the wishes of the company's employees. As soon as the merger was completed all the staff handed in their notice in order to set up a rival investment company (Brealey and Myers, 1996, p. 917).

The increased importance of the intellectual capital to organizations can also make them particularly dependent on retaining the goodwill of their staff, because of organizational vulnerability. This may need to involve a delicate balance between seeing that knowledge is spread effectively around an organization whilst not jeopardizing the security of commercial secrets. The organic type of organization, described earlier in the chapter, is more likely to facilitate the distribution of expertise than rigid mechanistic structures.

Human capital management overlaps with the concept of knowledge management, but there are differences. Human capital management does not directly involve the management of hard intellectual assets but is very concerned with the attraction, development and retention of staff with the appropriate expertise to ensure that an organization retains competitive advantage. This concept is given further consideration in Chapter 11 in the context of the **learning organization** and in Chapter 14 in relation to human resource management.

Identifying the critical function

Another factor that needs to influence the structure of an organization is the recognition of the critical function at a given time. Joan Woodward (1965) defined commercial success in part as stemming from the ability of those in organizations to identify the area where it was most important to get the correct decisions. If necessary, the views of the management in the critical function need to take precedence over the views of managers in less important areas. The critical function can vary over time, and in mechanistic structures especially such movement of influence from one function to another may be inhibited. The managers in a traditionally powerful function are not likely to take kindly to having a reduced say in major decisions in order to allow a rival function a greater say. The managers in the traditionally powerful function may, in any case, not fully appreciate that the critical focus of decision-making has moved. The success of managers in solving problems may be their very undoing in this respect. If, for example, difficult design problems are overcome, this removes a constraint. The problem then can be how to increase production or sales. However, a 'critical' function is still interdependent with the other functions in an organization.

The need to recognize the critical function is related to the need for private sector organizations to anticipate market trends and recognize where their future lies, which may not always please those responsible for well-established but declining products and services within an organization.

National culture

Another potentially important variable is national culture. The culture of a nation is formed from the set of beliefs, values, customs and views about behaviour specific to a particular society, which characterizes it in relation to other societies. As explained in the next chapter, care has to be used with the term 'national culture', because there are often wide cultural differences within a country. It may be best to refer to the dominant culture within a country and recognize that there may be other important subcultures. However, culture is an increasingly important factor because of globalization and increasing cultural diversity within countries. Even indigenous organizations need to pay attention to the issue if they are to interact effectively with other societies within and outside their own country. Particular attention needs to be paid to this issue by international organizations. Management structures and practices that appear to work well in a particular country may not be exported easily because the environment in which they operate cannot be transplanted. This also applies to the importation of practices from other countries. Local managers need to be able to adapt the structure, policies and procedures of an organization in accordance with local conditions.

Historically, western countries have tended to impose on developing countries organizational structures based on western rather than local needs. This includes an emphasis on large hospitals in health services, western-style universities in the education sector and political systems as well as in commercial organizations. The importing of particular management practices and customs is not going to radically change organizational cultures in the West. However, given the increasing investment in the West by Asian countries they too need to reflect on how well their organizational practices fit in western countries.

An adaptation that some organizations have made is to become transnational. **Transnational organizations** are structured so that they do not have their roots in any one country. The related issue of developing a managerial style, as opposed to organizational structure, to fit the local culture is considered in the next chapter, on managerial style. The impact of national culture on motivation is considered in Chapter 6 and on communication in Chapter 8.

The interrelationship of organizational activity

Departmentalism

As well as considering the nature of the organization they are in and how appropriate that organization is to its environment, managers need to consider how they relate to the other functions within their organization. Organizations may be arranged on neat departmental lines, but many of the problems that have to be dealt with will not conveniently correspond to a departmental structure. Such structures, although usually necessary, are artificial. Problems may contain many different interactive dimensions. Managerial approaches to such problems will need to be integrated if they are to succeed. True, some problems may confine themselves to departmental boundaries, but this will not always be the case.

There are often considerable barriers to lateral contact between departments, especially in mechanistic-type organizations. Rivalries, role conflicts, different values and differing types of expertise may all act as impediments. Staff may prefer the security of contact with like-minded people within their

own department to the often more hostile encounters with other departments. A lop-sided approach to organizational problems may develop as a
result. This may have a detrimental effect on the work of departments. It may
also lead to problems that straddle departmental boundaries being ignored.
It is all too easy for a bunker (or **silo**) mentality to develop in organizations.
Managers may keep a low profile and just deal with what is clearly in their
own area. This tendency may be reinforced by their initial specialist training,
as explained in Chapter 1. Managers may be much more able to identify the
problems caused by issues within their specialism than those outside it.

Internal markets can reinforce the inherent problems of effective lateral
communication. These markets involve purchaser-provider relationships
between departments. Service providers are financially dependent on the
income they generate from internal purchasers. Whilst this can focus attention on the real needs of service users, such arrangements can also have
severe disadvantages. These include an emphasis on either minimizing or
maximizing internal charges according to whether you are a service provider
or service user. This can distract attention from the needs of the organization
as a whole and from the need to encourage competitive rather than collaborative internal relationships. Experience in the National Health Service in the
UK, as well as the railway industry and the BBC, suggests that these arrangements can easily become counter-productive and also generate vast amounts
of paperwork and other costly forms of control. Such arrangements may
also ignore the costs of running down or closing existing internal activities
(Rees and Porter, 2002). The same issues need to be faced with subcontracting. Whilst there is a clear logic for subcontracting ancillary services,
the process can be carried too far. Hiving off core sections of the human
resource function, for example, can ignore the importance of the lateral
advisory and developmental links needed between this function and line
management. Organizations are not the series of discrete functions that some
accountants imagine. Developing an effective organization is rather more
complicated than assembling a permutation of Lego-style building blocks.

The problem of boundary crossing can be particularly acute in the public
sector, and it follows that there are many examples. The attempt to introduce corporate management in local government has been hampered by the
professional orientation of individual departments and officers. The development of a corporate approach necessitates officers at all levels, not just those
in the top tier, taking a wider approach. The legal profession provides an
example of where well-established professional traditions have led to fierce
opposition to suggestions for change in working arrangements. The older and
more established the profession, the greater seems to be the problem of alter-
ing occupational roles and associated training in line with changing organizational and societal needs.

To understand broader problems – particularly those that fall between different departments – managers need to have some understanding of overall
activity in their organizations. Attempts to bring departments together may

be frustrated, however, because of the conflict this can generate. The objectives of departments may not always be complementary, nor will they all operate at the same level of performance. Consequently, much time and effort can go into justifying the activity of a particular department to others rather than developing common problem-solving approaches. The hidden agenda at interdepartmental meetings can be to ensure that no failings in one's own department are to be exposed. However, if everyone takes that approach, the real issues to be discussed simply get lost behind smokescreens. One has only to look at the annual report of a company that has made a loss to see the standard smokescreen that can be put out for public, if not internal, consumption. The list of causes for poor performance is likely to include inappropriate legislation, national and international trading conditions, unfair competition, government policy, failures by suppliers, acts of God, bad luck, trade unions and a deterioration in the standards of society. It might include incompetence by previous executives, but is most unlikely to include admissions of failures that were within the current management's control.

The magnitude of the problem of departmentalism is compounded by the fact that often only an interdepartmental group with complementary skills and expertise can identify the very nature of problems. If the current objectives of an organization, or the major constraints impeding the achievement of those objectives, are to be defined this may be accomplished only by a pooling of knowledge. Even when the nature of a problem is identified, the causes may be far from obvious. One of the traps that people can fall into is to assume that the problems that emerge in particular departments have their causes in those same departments. Productivity levels may be influenced, for example, by production control, organization structure, investment policy and human resource management policies. It may be pointless trying to recruit more and more labour to boost production if the production process or planning is inadequate. In some cases, problems, causes and solutions may all exist in the same department, but it is dangerous to assume that this is always the case. That is why the importance of the systems approach to organizations was stressed earlier in this chapter (Rees and Porter, 2013).

The 'knock-on' effect of decisions

A further issue of which managers need to be aware is the implications of their decisions for other departments.

EXAMPLE: Example of the 'knock on' effect

Sales were increased in a soft drinks company when the sales department lowered the limit on the size of orders that could be accepted. Unfortunately, the extra revenue was not sufficient to cover the additional transport costs involved.

The poet John Donne's observation that 'no man is an island' can be applied to managers. They need to see their experience as something to be shared, to help identify and deal with problems facing the whole organization, rather than simply a means of justifying the activity of their own department. They may not be capable of resolving the problems facing their own department alone anyway.

Remedial strategies

There are preventative strategies which can reduce the problems created by poor inter-departmental liaison. As has previously been indicated, the most important strategy is to have the right fit between organizational structure and purpose. Whatever the formal structure, though, other means can be found to improve cooperation. Broadly based management training may be important. Positive steps can be taken to encourage teamwork by the creation of joint departmental teams or project groups containing staff from a range of departments. Contacts made in this way can help develop informal networks, which are often the glue that holds organizations together and facilitates coherent activity. The geographic arrangement of work can also have an important and constructive impact if this dimension is given attention. Colleagues, especially those who are not in regular contact with one another, may find it very useful to meet in accessible communal areas such as coffee points. Unfortunately, this idea is often missed, with the consequence that work is physically arranged on the 'battery hen' model, with no thought given of the need to promote informal, and sometimes even formal, interaction. Even open-plan offices may be counterproductive as the 'goldfish bowl' environment may discourage relaxed or confidential exchanges.

Whilst informal networks can sometimes work against the objectives of the organization, they can also be an essential supplement to its activity. In some cases they are mechanisms for coping with deficiencies in the formal organization. They may also break new ground in demonstrating what organizational mechanisms need to be encouraged and even formalized.

EXAMPLE: Formalizing informal developments

The housing construction department of a local authority in London laid down concrete pathways on new estates. Unfortunately the residents often found shorter and more convenient routes to follow. This led to mud pathways being created that were used to supplement or replace the concrete pathways. Engineers came to the conclusion that it might be best to not lay any pathways when estates were built but instead to concrete over the mud pathways once it became clear which routes the residents preferred.

One could argue that the process of formalizing informal arrangements is also evident in the way an increasing number of couples in the western world live together before formalizing their established relationships in marriage.

Role behaviour

Personality versus role behaviour

When interacting with colleagues it is important for managers to be able to distinguish between personality behaviour and **role behaviour**. Role behaviour occurs when a person acts in accordance with the requirements of the position that they hold. Managers may meet with opposition from colleagues that can be wrongly attributed to personality factors.

It would be foolish to pretend that personality factors never have an influence on people's behaviour, but it can be all too easy to miss the point that a person may feel obliged to behave in a particular way because of the demands of their job. The danger is that the issue can become personalised. Real role conflicts can thus be exacerbated by personality conflicts. Traditions of hostility can develop and spread through whole departments. It is, unfortunately, so much easier, and often more satisfying, to blame a particular dispute on the actual personality of a protagonist. Sometimes this will even be true – a particular person may clumsily or wrongly interpret a role. It can be very difficult, in the heat of the moment, to reflect that there is nothing personal in the perhaps crucial conflict in which you are involved. The basis of the conflict, however, may be entirely to do with roles, and it may be possible to contain the area of conflict by putting one's case assertively but not aggressively. The concept of **assertiveness** is explained in detail in Chapter 4. It is as well to remember, too, that whilst role conflicts can be incorrectly identified as personality clashes, it is rare for the mistake to be made the other way around. The constant danger is that conflict is wrongly attributed to personalities, rather than the reverse.

Failure to recognize that people's behaviour stems from their roles, rather than their personalities, is particularly likely when the roles are informal. Often people adopt positions because, for example, they have particular information to hand which is not generally available or of a significance that may not be generally appreciated. This may drive them into conflict with others, even though their formal roles appear to be compatible.

Reducing conflict

The reason for distinguishing between role and personality behaviour is the need to contain the area of conflict to the minimum. It is also important to get the diagnosis right if one is attempting to resolve the conflict. If one makes the mistake of assuming that a conflict is personality-based when in reality it is because of roles, the false solution may emerge of changing the personalities involved. Thus, an 'awkward' person may be transferred or dismissed, only for the same 'awkward' behaviour to re-emerge with the next job-holder. The original solution, as well as having been wrong from an organizational point of view, may also constitute a grave injustice to the person who is removed. In some cases it may even be that a person is only doing their job correctly if they are being awkward. Traffic wardens (or 'parking attendants' as they are increasingly called), for example, are frequently seen as awkward people. However, the creation of the job of traffic wardens was partly because of the need to avoid giving police the contradictory role of enforcing parking regulations and developing positive relationships with the general public.

In working out whether behaviour is a product of the role or the person, it is important to ensure that people are given viable roles. If people in managerial positions are expected to issue penalties but no rewards to employees, it is unreasonable to expect them to have an easy working relationship with the same employees. There is an inevitable tendency in organizations for there to be competition for the handing out of rewards – such as wage rises, good news and special privileges – and a great reluctance to get embroiled in, for example, disciplinary matters. A way of making it easier for a manager or supervisor to handle the disciplinary aspects of their job is to allow them also to take the credit for distributing rewards when these are available.

The task of distinguishing between role and personality behaviour can demand considerable intellectual effort and emotional discipline. However, the rewards can be considerable, starting with the more accurate diagnosis of organizational problems. This can in many situations lead to real instead of false solutions. The amount of personal injustice can be reduced and, last but not least, the amount of personal aggravation for oneself diminished (Rees and Porter, 2013).

General organizational developments

It is appropriate at this stage to review some of the major recent developments in organizations. To do this it is necessary to distinguish between the public and private sectors, as well as the not-for-profit sector. The distinctions are, though, sometimes blurred. An example of this blurring has occurred as a result of the trend in the UK as elsewhere for greater contracting out of work from the public to the private sector. It is also not clear in some cases, such as universities, whether they should be classified as part of the public or not-for-profit sectors. In addition, some not-for-profit organizations may receive a significant part of their income from public funds. It is also necessary to consider how the public sector is influenced by private sector practices. There is also often an international dimension, as in the case of multi-national corporations and international non-governmental organizations. However, there are some general trends in the various sectors that merit consideration. It is also necessary to consider the issue of **corporate governance** and how it affects all three sectors. This concept embraces the aim or aims of an organization, key objectives, the main strategies and policies for achieving such aspirations, reward strategy, ethical standards and statutory obligations. Organizational structures will need to provide effective mechanisms for meeting these requirements.

The private sector

Organizational developments relating to long-term and corporate strategy, including the relationship between operational units and the centre, were covered at the end of the previous chapter. Competitive pressures have caused many private sector organizations to downsize and sometimes the concept of being 'lean and mean' has been carried to such an extreme that organizations have become 'anorexic'. There has been a general tendency to move towards semi-autonomous business units with financial performance targets. This has reduced the potential for cross-subsidization within organizations. However, the move to semi-autonomous business units sometimes is contradicted by demands for detailed control information and prior approval on a range of matters large and small. The concept of added value has been prominent, with units and individuals expected to justify themselves more in terms of their profitability. These developments in turn have led to a trend towards much smaller head offices. There has been a reaction, too, to the Taylorist scientific management approach of division of labour, functional control and non-involvement of the workforce (explained at the beginning of this chapter). This has partly been a consequence of more volatile markets. There is more emphasis now on flexibility, multi-tasking and workforce involvement in process, product and service improvement. This in turn has necessitated more emphasis on training and creative human of resource management. The search for new markets and cost reduction opportunities is also causing more collaborative ventures. Another development has been for companies to plan international marketing strategies. As markets have become globalized, so it has become more possible and appropriate to market global or regional, as opposed to national, products.

The public sector

A recurring theme in the section on the public sector is how changes in its framework and operation are creating a much more managerial, as opposed to administrative, culture. This is with a view to getting better 'value for money' with the resources available.

In many countries there has been a systematic attempt to redraw the boundaries between the public and private sectors so that many of the activities that were previously in the public sector could be run privately instead. Rising public expectations and reduced economic growth have forced a rethink of the role of the state in many developed countries, including attempts to reduce the expectations of what the state should do for individuals.

Part of the rationale for reducing the level of state involvement in many economies has been a desire to further increase a culture of 'enterprise', as opposed to 'dependency'. A political advantage for governments in devolving authority within the public sector is that sensitive decisions about prioritization and resource allocation can be removed from central government.

Comparisons between the private and public sectors

As a corollary of reducing state ownership and control there has been a strong trend towards the more effective use of those activities still financed or run by the state. There have been attempts to make the public sector operate more like the private sector. Whilst the public sector has undoubtedly had lessons to learn from the private sector, it would be a mistake to imagine that the differences between the two sectors can be ignored. It would also be a mistake to ignore the considerable variations within the private and public sectors. Public bodies are democratically accountable, have statutory obligations and often have to operate in a sensitive political environment. The process of decision-making may be slower, more complicated and more risk averse than the private sector. The aims of public sector bodies often cannot be easily defined and quantified. Often public sector organizations are very large. Much of the private sector, by contrast, is in small units with clear commercial goals. These differences enable private sector organizations often to behave in ways that would be quite inappropriate in the public sector, particularly with regard to risk-taking. The overall need in the public sector can perhaps best be described as being for the various elements of that sector to become more businesslike without trying to operate as businesses.

Having defined the distinctive nature of the public sector, it is appropriate to examine the way a more commercial approach has been adopted. One way of explaining this is to examine the historic differences between management and administration. This has been done by a British civil servant associated with the Treasury Centre for Administrative Services. The emphasis with management (as opposed to administration) is on results and on taking calculated risks; with administration the emphasis is on procedures, accountability and risk avoidance. These are not complete opposites but rather the ends of a continuum. The general thrust in the public sector has been to shift it more to the managerial end of the continuum. The full list is included as an appendix to this chapter.

Another basic change is that policy and budgeting is now much more finance-led instead of being on a needs or demand basis in the public sector. This in turn has meant that managers have to make the best use of a given level of funding, which may necessitate making deliberate decisions to prioritize, as explained in the previous chapter. Often the level of funding is geared to **key performance indicators** (KPIs). In the UK at least there has been a substantial move to use private sector cash to boost investment in the public sector, for example with major transport projects. Publicly funded organizations are now expected to take less of a custodial approach to their assets and more of a market orientation to matching resources with demand. This is in keeping with greater customer orientation and focus on service delivery. In the UK a number of organizations have been required to guarantee minimum standards of service to the public, and in some cases been obliged to make penalty payments if the standards are not met.

An increasing amount of work is organized on a contract basis, with public sector bodies being partly or totally financially dependent on the winning and retention of contracts, sometimes in competition with the private sector. The practice has now come to be known as 'market testing'. This concept is sometimes applied to employment contracts, especially for senior positions. Renewal is logically likely to depend on performance. Amongst the effects of the structural and operational changes in the public sector is the identification of much more explicit managerial roles than before. This means that there is a much clearer need for those in positions of authority to develop managerial skills.

The evaluation of performance in the public sector has increasingly been on the basis of performance as measured by key performance indicators. Whilst the use of such measures may be necessary, it is also necessary to be aware of the ways in which they can be manipulated. This issue was discussed with regard to organizational targets in Chapter 2. The risk of manipulation of measures and targets is also covered in Chapter 10 in the context of **performance related pay**. Whilst there has been a move to performance-related pay in the public sector, the results have often been disappointing.

Not-for-profit organizations

The not-for-profit sector includes charities and this in turn can be said to include organizations such as churches and trade unions. They can also be described as non-governmental organizations (or entities) (NGOs). The activities of international not-for-profit organizations (INGOs) are increasing; examples of increasingly active international not-for-profit organizations are Amnesty International and OXFAM. As economies become richer, and less is controlled by the state, more income becomes available for the activity of not-for-profit organizations. In turn this may mean that developed countries are more easily able to finance activities abroad either directly or via INGOs.

Decision-making may be convoluted in not-for-profit organizations, particularly where a number of countries are involved. This will be all the more so if a **consensus** is needed for major decisions. This may mean that policy can only be agreed on a lowest common denominator basis. A further problem with decision making by consensus is that each party may in practice have a veto thus delaying decision taking. However, one way of facilitating decision-making can be the use of qualified majority voting on some issues, as happens in the European Union.

There are other problems that are particularly likely to occur in not-for-profit organizations. One is that those in charge may be chosen for their commitment to a particular cause rather than their ability to run an organization. It may also be the case that a professional management structure is not developed. As those in charge may give up a lot of time on a voluntary basis the organization may fail to pay its staff appropriately, feeling that staff should make financial sacrifices in the interests of the organization. If a not-for-profit organization is dependent on a volunteer element to achieve its aims and objectives, they may have to accept volunteer labour on the basis on which it is offered and have relatively little in the way of sanctions if volunteers do not do quite what is expected or required of them.

Corporate governance

A further factor that is likely to shape the structure and nature of organizational activity is corporate governance. Whilst this can be an essential organizational mechanism, good practice cannot be taken for granted. The collapse of the western credit boom in 2007/2008 helped reveal the wave of reckless lending and illegality that had preceded it. This included the collapse of the USA-based Lehman brothers in 2008, setting a new record in the size of the American bankruptcies. Other bankruptcies and illegalities, including cases of huge rogue trading, have included the United Bank of Switzerland Bank (UBS), Society General (France) and the need for massive state banking rescues in the UK. Illegal selling practices that came to light, included mis-selling of insurance policies linked to loans, the mis-selling of payment protection insurance policies, the manipulation of interest rates to the disadvantage of customers and money laundering. Yet another issue was the lack of control of incentive payments with senior banking staff able to benefit from huge bonuses when their banks were losing money and even facing bankruptcy. The negative effect that incentive payment schemes can have is considered further in Chapter 7 (Reward).

Faith in the quality of corporate governance in the UK was further shaken by the exposure of phone hacking by some newspapers and the danger of overly close relationships between some newspapers and some police officers (Leveson, 2012). In addition major problems of governance by the BBC were revealed in their handling of the sexual misconduct of the former TV star Jimmy Savile (Pollard, 2013). This dark side of organizational behaviour can exist and can provide ethical dilemmas for those who come across it. Unfortunately, a related feature for employees can be that compliance rather than competence or ethical behaviour is what some bosses want.

The aftermath of the credit crunch

Poor and even illegal corporate governance in the finance sector in particular has had a number of consequences. These have included economic stagnation, cautious banking practices including significant restrictions in providing credit, resignations of senior staff, and large fines by regulatory bodies. This has led to calls for greater internal and external regulation of the financial services sector with greater control on the level of bonuses in particular. Some shareholder groups have become much more interested and active on this issue, particularly as in some cases companies seemed to be run more in the interests of senior management than shareholders. Such developments have significantly influenced the economic framework in which organizations have to operate.

Control of the chief executive

Problems of corporate governance may arise when too much authority is vested in the hands of the chief executive. A check against this can be to ensure that the chief executive does not also act as chair of the board. However, even then chief executives can and sometimes do accumulate enormous power. This can be done by the control and manipulation of information, control over other executives, influencing appointments to the board and patronage. Also the fact that the chief executive is likely to be a person of ability and is, unlike external board members, employed full-time can further increase their potential power. Sometimes a high concentration of power leads to abuse. This can particularly be the case in the not-for-profit sectors in which organizations are not allowed to pay their governors or trustees, which can reduce the pool of competent trustees who are available and/or the time they can make available. It can also prove difficult to control the activities of an active governor who undertakes tasks that others do not have the time or inclination to do.

Other stakeholders

Some companies are also paying increasing attention to stakeholders in their organization other than shareholders and employees. This may be either because of genuine concern or because of enlightened self-interest or a combination of the two. The growing sensitivity of customers is likely to create commercial pressure on an increasing number of private organizations to demonstrate that they have ethical business practices and that they are behaving responsibly with regard to the local community and the environment. As was explained earlier in this chapter, off-shoring can lead to exploitative labour practices and, apart from the ethical issues involved, this can lead to negative publicity for the companies concerned. Developments such as these have led some companies to develop formal policies of **corporate**

social responsibility. The fairtrade movement is an example of customer pressure for goods where producers in developing countries are paid a reasonable price. However great care may be needed in the evaluation of policy statements of corporate social responsibility. This is to check whether they amount to more than convenient public relations statements. A dimension of this can be statements about organizations' concerns about the environment some of which have been dubbed **greenwash** as opposed to 'whitewash' where they are seen as lacking in genuine concern about the environment. An issue of increasing public concern, especially with regard to multinational and transnational corporations is the extent to which they use aggressive tax avoidance policies to reduce their tax burden.

There are also pressures on public bodies to behave as responsible employers. An interesting development in the USA concerns the use of government purchasing power to influence business behaviour. The federal government has increasingly sought to impose ethical business practices on government contractors.

The issue of corporate governance in developing countries arises particularly when those countries request aid. Increasingly aid is only given if certain conditions are met. These are likely to include the country's record with regard to democracy, human rights and good governance. As explained in Chapter 10 in the context of appraisal, some countries may arrange a **peer audit**, by another developing country, of their corporate governance in order to demonstrate their eligibility to receive aid. The impact of globalization also has to be considered. The rise of multinational and transnational corporations is likely to cause such organizations to identify less with any one particular country and to arrange their tax affairs so that corporation tax payments are minimized rather than geared to where their activities are actually conducted.

Summary

This chapter has attempted to set the scene within which those with managerial responsibilities have to operate. Key organizational theories have been examined. Organizational types that have been described and analyzed include mechanistic and organic structures, matrix arrangements and the flexible organization. Managers need to examine the fit between what is appropriate in terms of organizational design and operation and what actually exists. Key factors that shape organizational structure have been identified. These include the impact of technology, particularly IT; size; the extent to which the organization is dependent on its intellectual capital; the nature of the critical function; and national culture. The importance of the market, and the way it needs to influence organizational structure, was stressed in the examination of key organizational theories.

The dangers of sectional goals conflicting with broad organizational objectives have been examined and suggestions made as to how such conflicts may be handled. These particularly include developing lateral organization links and broadening the base of training so that people can have a broader view of the organization. The need for managers to distinguish between personality and role behaviour has also been covered. This is because of the unnecessary aggravation that can occur if managers fail to analyze the behaviour of colleagues in terms of their role.

There are distinct differences in the nature of the private and public sectors. However, some trends have been common to both sectors. These include pressure for more market- or client-orientated structures with a generally greater devolution of authority for decisions in financial and other matters. Governments are under pressure to secure value for money in the public sector and often find it convenient to devolve authority for sensitive decisions about resource allocation. Whilst public sector organizations need to be run in a businesslike way it is important to remember that they are not businesses as they have constraints, such as democratic accountability, that businesses do not. The rising importance of the not-for-profit sector has meant that managerial issues in this area have also been considered. Finally the issue of corporate governance has been considered as has the reality that good practice cannot be taken for granted. This chapter is an essential prelude to considering the topic covered in the next chapter: managerial and leadership style.

Self-assessment questions

1. Why is it important for managers to have an understanding of the options in organizational design?
2. What are the main factors shaping the structure and operation of an organization with which you are familiar?
3. Why might units within an organization pursue sectional rather than corporate aims? And what can realistically be done to deal with this problem?
4. Why might role behaviour be mistaken for personality behaviour?
5. In what ways might managers need to behave differently in the private sector as compared with not-for-profit organizations?

Case study notes – Here We Go

Learning outcome:

◾ To enable students to draw a basic organization chart in which they relate structure to purpose.

The company is very dependent on the expertise and judgements of Simon Evans, the chief executive who also has financial control of the company.

There is strong central direction but if the expected further expansion takes place it may be that a clearer and more formal organization structure needs to be implemented. Drafting a new organization chart could be a useful exercise. This should include clarification of the responsibilities of Simon Evans and his chief assistant, Charles Adams. The heavy reliance on Simon Evans may be also be a significant risk, particularly if he makes a misjudgement, falls ill or loses interest in the company and wants to build up another entrepreneurial activity instead. What we know about his personality suggests he is somewhat of a risk taker, for example the important employment tribunal cases he has lost.

If Simon makes an important commercial misjudgement, or if the market moves against it, will the company have the resources to cope? There is also the issue that it may be difficult for anybody internally to develop as a natural successor. Simon has not been very tolerant of a mistake by Colin, despite making mistakes himself. Given these factors one option may be to sell the company whilst the going is good.

Skills development exercise

Evaluate the extent to which the structure of an organization with which you are familiar is fit for purpose. (It will help if you identify the extent to which appropriate objectives have been established and organization structure and activity geared to their achievement.)

Appendix

The different characteristics of Administration and Management

	Administration	Management
Objectives	Stated in general terms and reviewed or changed infrequently	Stated as broad strategic aims supported by more detailed short-term goals and targets reviewed frequently
Success criteria	Mistake-avoiding Performance difficult to measure	Success-seeking Performance mostly measurable
Resource use	Secondary task	Primary task
Decision-making	Has to make few decisions but affecting many and can take time over it	Has to make decisions affecting few and has to make them quickly
Structure	Roles defined in terms of areas of responsibility	Shorter hierarchies

(*continued*)

Continued

	Administration	*Management*
	Long hierarchies, limited delegation	Maximum delegation
Roles	Arbitrator	Protagonist
Attitudes	Passive: workload determined outside the system; best people used to solve problems	Active: seeking to influence the environment; best people used to find and exploit opportunities
	Time insensitive	Time sensitive
	Risk-avoiding	Risk-accepting, but minimising it
	Emphasis on procedure	Emphasis on results
	Doing things right	Doing the right things
	Conformity	Local experiments: need for conformity to be proved
	Uniformity	Independence
Skills	Literacy (reports, notes)	Numeracy, statistics, figures

Notes

1. Please refer to Chapter 1, page 20 for a note on Fayol.
2. F.W. Taylor (1856–1917) was a leading figure with regard to 'scientific management' – some would say 'the father'. He worked in the American steel industry, initially as a labourer and later in industrial engineering consultancy. He developed the concept of time and motion study. He also developed the concept of functional management and the associated concept of division of labour. His seminal book was Principles of Scientific Management, first published in 1911. He believed in rewards for hard work and effective selection and training. The implementation of 'Taylorism' did provoke fierce resistance by many trade unions, who unlike Taylor, perceived conflicts of interest arising between some at least of the workers and management. These included treating workers like robots and redundancy fears because of increased productivity.

References

NB: Works of particular interest are marked with an asterisk.

Atkinson, John (1985), *Flexibility, Uncertainty and Manpower Management*, IMS report no. 89, Institute of Manpower Studies.

Brealey, Richard A and Myers, Stewart C (1996), *Principles of Corporate Finance*, 5th ed., McGraw-Hill.

Burns, Tom and G. M. Stalker (1972), *Management of Innovation*, Tavistock Publications, first published 1961.

For a summary of this work, see Honor Croome (1970), Human Problems of Innovation, *Ministry of Technology pamphlet.*

Huston, Larry and Nabbil Sakkab (March 2006), *Connect and Develop – Inside Procter and Gamble's New Model for Innovation,* Harvard Business Review.

Leveson, Lord Justice (2012), *Report into the Culture, Practice and Ethics of the Press,* London: HMSO. www.Levesoninquiry.org.uk.

News Shopper (2013), Shopper's Anger at Crayford Sainsbury's Checkout Mobile Ban, http://www.newsshopper.co.uk/new   s/10520083. *Shopper's_anger_at_Crayford_Sainsbury'_checkout_mobile_phone_ban* [accessed 29/07/13].

Pollard, Nick (2013) *The Savile Inquiry,* BBC. http://www.bbc.co.uk/news/uk-20782889 [accessed 14th February, 2015].

*Rees, W. David and Christine Porter (2002), Management by panacea – the training implications, *Industrial and Commercial Training*, Vol. 34, No. 6.
    The dangers of applying prescriptive solutions without careful problem diagnosis.

*Rees, W. David and Christine Porter (2004), Matrix Structures and the Training Implications, *Industrial and Commercial Training*, Vol. 36, No. 5.
    An explanation of the nature of matrix structures, dual reporting relationships and how they can be made to work effectively.

*Rees, W. David and Christine Porter, (2013), The development of diagnostic skills by management coaching, *International Coaching Psychology Review*, Vol. 8, No. 2.
    An account of how the diagnostic skills of managers can be improved by taking a systems approach. Also elaborates on the need to distinguish between personality and role behaviour.

Roethlisberger, Fritz Jules. J. and Dickson, William J. (1939), *Management and the Worker,* Harvard University Press.
    *For one of several abridged accounts see John Sheldrake (1996). *Management Theories: From Taylorism to Japanization, Chapter 11, Elton Mayo and the Hawthorne Experiments, International Thomson Business Press. See Sheldrake's book also for a very clear and useful account of the thoughts of key earlier management writers.*

*Stewart, Thomas A (2003), *The Wealth of Knowledge: Intellectual Capital and the Twenty-first century Organization,* Crown Business.
    A thorough account of the concept of intellectual capital by one of the leading writers in the field.

The Telegraph (2006), http://www.telegraph.co.uk/news/uknews/1534286/12000-mile-trip-to-have-seafood-shelled.html [accessed 22nd January, 2015].

The Telegraph (2013), Japan tells UK to stay in the EU. http://www.telegraph.co.uk/finance/10193252/Japan-tells-UK-to-stay-in-the-EU.html [accessed 29th July, 2013].

Taylor, Frederick Winslow (1972), *The Principles of Scientific Management,* Greenwood Press, first published 1911.

Woodward, Joan (1965), *Industrial Organization: Theory and Practice,* Oxford University Press. For a summary of this work see Joan Woodward, *Management and Technology* (Ministry of Technology pamphlet, 1970), reprint.

Taking it further

Dick, Penny and Ellis, Steve(2005), *Introduction to Organizational Behaviour,* 3rd edn., McGraw-Hill Education.
    A comprehensive guide to the theory and practice of organizational behaviour, with an emphasis on the psychological dimension.

Fayol, Henri (1967), *General and Industrial Management,* transl. Constance Storrs, Pitman; first French edition published 1916; Storrs' translation first published 1949.

Johnson, Gerry, Kevan Scholes and Richard Whittingham (2011), *Fundamentals of Strategy,* 2nd edn., Pearson.

   A thorough account of private sector strategy.

*Mead, Richard and Tim G. Andrews (2009), *International Management,* 4th edn., Blackwell.

   A first-rate and comprehensive account of how national culture can shape management practice.

*Rees, W. David and Christine Porter (2006), Corporate strategy development and related management development – the case for the incremental approach, Part 2 – implications for learning and development, *Industrial and Commercial Training,* Vol. 38, No. 6.

   This includes an explanation of the dangers of corporate decision-making based on too narrow a range of variables.

Managerial and Leadership Style

4

Case study

The New Broom

Harold Fleming is the head of finance of a company operating a small chain of retail stores. He has recently noticed an unexpected increase in staff turnover in the accounts department. He finds this surprising given the previous stability in the department and the generally friendly atmosphere there has been there. The increase in turnover also does not seem to fit with the fact that the work appears to be have been made easier recently by the introduction of a computerized accounts system.

Initially the new accounts system did have a number of problems. However, due to the energy and perseverance of the newly appointed systems manager, Stephen Middleton, most of these problems have been sorted out in the nine months since Stephen started. Invoicing has been handled much more quickly and this has improved the cash flow of the company. The fact that some of the old established staff left was not initially a problem as they did not need to be replaced. However, the continuing labour turnover is now becoming a problem and is affecting the quality of the service.

Harold has asked Stephen to investigate the problem. Stephen has reported back saying that he has not been able to establish the cause of the reduced morale. The only comment he has picked up is a chance remark by one of the staff who has worked in the department for some years that 'things are not what they were'. Because the accounting system is up and running, Stephen has been able to spend a significant amount of time with individual accounts clerks sorting out problems with them. This has been particularly necessary because the accounts supervisor, Ann Smith, has told staff to pursue any technical problems, however minor, with Stephen.

Harold is tempted to speak to the accounts supervisor himself, particularly as he had a good working relationship with her when she had reported directly to him. During that time she had few problems with her staff and generally seemed to get on with them very well. However, he is reluctant to speak to her as that might undermine the authority of her new boss, Stephen.

Questions:

1. What reasons might there be for the reduced morale in the accounts department?
2. What action may need to be taken and by whom?

Introduction

Managerial style can be defined as 'the way in which results are achieved'. The term managerial style overlaps with the concept of leadership. The range of commonly practised managerial and leadership styles is examined in this chapter. People need to be aware of their own preferred style but also of the need to adapt their style to the needs of the situation (the contingency approach). Trends in management and leadership style are examined, as are key factors such as organizational pressures and national culture that can influence it. A style that is often required is the ability to behave assertively as opposed to being aggressive or non-assertive. This concept is examined, as are the key skills in assertive behaviour.

The topic of handling change is a recurrent one in this book. The opportunity is taken in this chapter to review the key variables and to cross-refer to other parts of the book where the variables are examined in more detail. Finally, the effectiveness of managers and leaders is considered. Managerial and leadership styles need to be a means to an end and not ends in themselves. A questionnaire is included as an appendix to the chapter so that readers can identify their own preferred style. Whatever style or styles is or are used, ultimately people will be judged by the results achieved.

Trends in managerial and leadership style

The concept of management and leadership style

Managerial and leadership styles were defined in the introduction to this chapter as 'the way in which results are achieved'. Management overlaps with the concept of leadership. However, not all leaders are managers. While managers can provide leadership, those in a range of other roles can also be leaders. This is in line with the concept of **distributive leadership**. Managers are appointed and are responsible to those who appoint them. In contrast, leaders are not always appointed. In representative structures, for example a trade union, leaders are responsible to those who have allowed them to become their leader, which may or may not have involved a formal election. Leaders in such situations need to demonstrate that they represent the needs of the group they represent, while the objectives of managers can sometimes conflict with the objectives of the groups they have to manage (refer to unitary and pluralistic perspectives, Chapter 2).

Some writers (beginning with Drucker, 1955) see organizations as led by **heroic leaders**, charismatic figures who devise overall objectives and strategy and drive organizations forward, with managers simply being there to implement their vision. Whilst there may be some such leaders, limitations with this approach include identifying too sharp a distinction between the roles of leaders and managers. However, Mintzberg (2009), for example, does not see such a sharp distinction and sees management as needing to incorporate strategic vision. The notion of organizational leaders as heroic figures also suggests that their personal characteristics will be appropriate to any organizational situation, regardless of the match between the individual's strengths and the situational requirements. Post-heroic leaders put more emphasis on engaging the whole team and on distributive leadership. People in organizations are not divided into 'sheep' who are not leaders and 'goats' who are. For an organization to operate effectively, different leaders may need to take charge at different times.

EXAMPLE: The non-distributive leader

A newly promoted senior manager in a high-tech organization came to grief because he wanted to take the lead in all situations, even though he was new to the organization. He was unwilling or unable to recognize that on some issues there was knowledge and expertise within the group he was leading which he did not have. He was unable to grasp that his role was to optimize the contribution of the group, rather than be the all-knowing leader. Inevitably this pattern of behaviour proved to be unsustainable: the group became demotivated because they felt that there was no recognition of their skills or expertise. In addition, the new policies that the manager initiated were often flawed because they were inappropriate to the needs of the organization. The synergy that could have been created by allowing others to take the lead from time to time where appropriate was also missing.

The issue of distributive leadership is considered again in the context of chairing meetings as discussed in Chapter 15.

Whilst the nature of management can be relatively easily defined, this is not the case with leadership. When the term 'leadership' is used it is usually necessary to probe into what is meant. People with 'leadership' in their job title can range from team leaders of, for example, first line operatives, to chief executives. Often too the tasks that are specified in the job of a leader contain many conventional managerial tasks, with a requirement for key managerial skills. Sometimes the term leadership carries a status connotation associated with heroic strategic activity that is at a higher level than mere management. Whether that is based on reality or optimistic aspiration may be another matter (Rees and Porter, 2008). The concept of leadership is often confused with **charisma**. While charismatic leadership can be appropriate in some situations, this is not always the case. Sometimes charismatic leadership can be the reverse of what is needed, particularly if the person concerned needs to be primarily a facilitator and conciliator. Finally, comparing leaders and mangers, it is often the case that the career paths of managers tend to be clear, which may not be the case for those with the designation or aspiration to be leaders.

The authority of the manager

Managers will normally have a certain amount of formal authority to do their job. Usually this will have been delegated to them by a higher level of management, enabling them to take decisions and commit organizational resources. They will also need to have some authority over their staff in the way of rewards and penalties. The extent of a manager's authority will vary considerably according to their seniority, and from organization to organization. However, a number of factors have tended to limit the authority of individual managers. These factors are identified below.

Organizational developments

Organizations are becoming more complex. This is because of factors such as accelerating change, technological development (particularly in the area of information technology) and **globalization**. Levels of uncertainty are generally rising and knowledge within organizations is often becoming diffuse. Also, the process of management is increasingly becoming the management of **intellectual capital** rather than that of physical resources. The ability of managers to control the flow of information is often greatly reduced due to increased accessibility resulting from advances in IT. The cumulative effect of these changes is often to make the manager more of a facilitator rather than a traditional authority figure.

Legal developments

Increasingly managers are constrained in what they can do by the law. This is particularly so in the area of employment rights, for example unfair dismissal and anti-discrimination law. The ability of managers to hire and fire at will has been considerably curtailed, in western countries in particular.

Social developments

Social trends, such as rising levels of education, have created pressures for people to manage in a more acceptable way. Managers and leaders are often also dependent on their employees for information and expertise. Younger employees, for example, may be more able than their bosses to access and manipulate new information systems.

While there are discernible general trends, the extent to which they have impacted on individual organizations and managers will vary widely. Some managers still rely significantly on their formal authority. Even managers who do not rely too much on their formal authority may need to use it when all else fails. Feelings of insecurity amongst employees may depend very much on their personal individual prospects of alternative employment.

Sapiential authority

As organizations change so managers may be more dependent on their **sapiential authority** rather than their formal authority. Sapiential authority is that which derives from a person's expertise. The sapiential authority of a manager may lie in their specialist area, their organizational facilitating skills, or both. A person other than the manager could become the leader in a situation where they have more expertise in that particular situation than the manager does. In such a situation it is important that the manager reflect on whether it is necessary for them to be the leader at all times, or only at those time when they are the person with the most expertise. There could still be an important facilitating role for the manager to play in such a situation for example making it possible for the group to achieve their objectives by removing any organizational obstacles.

Power and influence

Whereas authority (the right to get something done) is officially sanctioned by the organization, power is distributed throughout organizations and may be invested in people at any level and not just managers. The determinants of power are not simply at the disposal of the organization in the way that authority is. Power can involve the ability to mobilize resources to achieve results. It can be used effectively even if the manager does not actually possess power but the party whom the manager is seeking to influence believes that they do. Power can flow from a person's position (positional power) in the organization or as a result of their personal attributes. Positional power can derive from the following four factors in particular:

1. Legitimacy: this exists when employees feel that the manager has the right to ask for particular tasks to be undertaken.
2. Coercion: this is the ability to discipline or penalize by withholding rewards. This type of power is more effective if used as a perceived threat rather than if penalties have to be imposed.
3. Rewards: these are the tangible benefits that a manager has at their disposal and will include not only salary increases but also other benefits that the employee values. These could include improved work schedules, promotion and formal recognition of a job well done.
4. Information: managers and others, by virtue of their position, often have access to information that people need to carry out their jobs. This information may be acquired in a variety of ways and not just by formal channels.

Changes in the environment can affect the power balance. For example, in times of skills shortages particular employees may possess more power than they do when their skills are available in abundance. This change in power is determined by the state of the labour market and may not be within the organization's control.

Lateral relationships

Managers may need considerable political skills in negotiating their working relationships with other departments. General organizational developments are such that fewer organizations have a traditional bureaucratic structure. The trend is to have more flexible and organic (as opposed to mechanistic) structures, as explained in Chapter 3. In organic structures there will be a need for, and a pattern of, relatively open access to people in other parts of the organization. This in turn can generate a greater need for work arrangements such as project teams and matrix structures. Managers and other employees may find that they often report to more than one boss.

Managers as facilitators

Organizational trends are such that managers and leaders are increasingly likely to be the focal points for assembling the right mix of financial, physical and human resources to undertake specific tasks. This is particularly so in organizations with a high level of intellectual capital, as described in the previous chapter. These developments in turn affect managerial and leadership style.

Managerialism

The notion of managerialism is often associated with the idea of adopting management practices which fit with those often applied in the private sector. This would include striving for organizational effectiveness including regular monitoring which cuts across the professionalism and independence of employees. In a managerialist culture, senior management teams are perceived as instituting inappropriate notions of efficiency. Sometimes such criticisms may be justified. In other cases, though, they may be a necessary and appropriate attempt to achieve more with a diminishing unit of resource.

As will be explained further in the following section of the current chapter, there are options in management and leadership styles. Style is not an end in itself and it is incumbent on each manager to identify the style which is most appropriate for achieving objectives in the culture in which they find themselves working.

Options in managerial and leadership styles

A number of writers have identified options in managerial and leadership style. Styles are generally viewed as being neutral: what matters for organizational achievement of goals is that the style used is effective and to be effective it will need to match the situation. There are a number of theories that explore managerial or leadership styles. Trait theories are examined here, as are the concepts of contingency and management team mix. Transformational and transactional leadership styles are defined and compared. The concepts of **unitary and pluralistic frames of reference** are also relevant.

Trait theories

A traditional way of examining the broader concept of leadership is to identify the personality characteristics that are required by a leader. If this approach is used, one can quickly generate a long list of personality traits. This may include characteristics such as honesty, intelligence, consistency, integrity, firmness, ruthlessness, flexibility, vision, charisma and so on. It would be very difficult to find a person who possessed all these characteristics. Furthermore, many of the characteristics can be the opposite of one another, such as consistency and flexibility.

If any value is to be made of trait theories it is necessary to identify what traits are important in a given situation. The traits that are important in one situation may not be important in another or may even be a handicap. A matching exercise needs to be undertaken when selecting managers to try and ensure that the person appointed has the right critical traits required for a particular job. If the demands of the job change, the person appointed may no longer match the changed requirements. Consequently, it may also be necessary to consider how a manager or leader would be able to adapt to changed circumstances.

There are many examples from the world of politics of leaders not being able to adapt to changed circumstances. Great leaders can be thrown up in times of revolution or war who might otherwise have remained in relative obscurity. This is in keeping with the adage 'cometh the hour, cometh the man'. However, when the revolution or war is over a different style of leadership may be required. Often great revolutionary or war leaders have been unable to adapt to the demands of peacetime. This may because the very qualities that made them great revolutionary or war leaders may be the opposite of what is required in peacetime.

Many successful business people have failed in the political world. Conversely, many politicians have failed in business. A reason for this may be that business people operate in a hierarchical environment with an executive chain of command. Politicians need the skills to develop and retain grassroots support. Successful business people may particularly require financial acumen and politicians the power to impress an audience.

EXAMPLE: Serial entrepreneurs

An interesting way in which some entrepreneurs have coped with the change in behaviour that might be required when they have successfully created one business is to create another business. A particularly good example of a **serial entrepreneur** is Sir Richard Branson. His series of Virgin enterprises includes retail stores, radio, air travel, rail travel and finance.

McGregor's Theories X and Y

McGregor in his seminal book in 1969 distinguishes between managers who manage in a Theory X style and those who manage in a Theory Y style. Assumptions that Theory X managers make about employees are said to include the view that:

- Employees need and respond to close direction and control
- People prefer to avoid work if they can
- Employees do not want to accept responsibility
- Employees have to be coerced to achieve organizational objectives.

The assumptions made by Theory Y managers about employees are said to include the view that:

- Individual and organizational goals can be integrated
- Work is a natural activity

- Employees will respond positively to objectives to which they are committed
- Emotional satisfaction can be achieved at work
- Employees will, under the right conditions, accept responsibility.

The value of this classification is to identify the assumptions of other managers and yourself. On the face of it, the Theory Y style is more enlightened, but the basic point is that the style adopted needs to fit the situation. The danger is that managers may have fairly fixed assumptions and consequently have difficulty in adapting their style to a situation that requires an approach different to their natural one. It is also necessary to distinguish between managers with genuine Theory Y styles and managers whose allegiance to Theory Y is only superficial. Critics of Japanese techniques of employee involvement, which could be interpreted as Theory Y style, simply see these techniques as attempts to create a coerced consensus (Garrahan and Stewart, 1992). The relationship between managerial assumptions about why people work and people's motivation is examined further in Chapter 6.

Transformational versus transactional leaders

Bass and Riggio (2006) have written about the concept of **transformational leaders** who are there to stimulate employees, motivate and inspire by giving a clear vision of organizational goals, provide a role model and give what they call 'individualized consideration' – understanding the strengths and weaknesses of each individual employee while providing them with support to make the best of their capabilities. This is seen as distinct from **transactional leadership,** which is based on the idea that people perform best when there is a clear chain of command, when employees are carefully monitored and when rewards are clear. Transactional leaders reward individuals for appropriate levels of performance; such leaders get things done by making and fulfilling promises of recognition, advancement, or pay increases. Transformational leadership is depicted as a higher form of leadership that aims to bring out the most in individual employees. According to Northouse (2013, p. 185) the concept of transformational leadership includes 'assessing followers' motives, satisfying their needs, and treating them as full human beings.' The difficulty in being a transformational leader arises from the underlying assumption that organizational and individual objectives never conflict. While managers can often construct situations so that organizational and employee objectives can both be met, unfortunately this is not always the case. So while managers may aspire to be transformational leaders, they will need to bear in mind the limitations of the approach. Meanwhile, many employees would be pleased to work for a transactional leader in an environment where the chain of command is clear, and the promise of future rewards are fulfilled. Even then, it may be the case that for understandable organizational reasons, the promised rewards are not forthcoming.

Contingency theories

Several theorists have examined the idea that a chosen leadership style needs to be contingent on key factors in whatever situation requires leadership. This is consistent with Mary Parker Follett's concept of 'the law of the situation', explained in Chapter 1. John Adair (1982) identified three key factors that he believes are important in determining an appropriate leadership style: task, group, and individual needs. He suggested that the effective manager will be the one who gives priority to one of these three overlapping interests according to the needs of the situation. If, for example, there was an emergency, task needs would predominate: there would be no point in having a period of consultation if it was imperative that a task was completed in a short period of time. The importance of the situation is such that one must beware of the concept of 'best practice'. What may be appropriate in one situation may be quite inappropriate in another. Using the term 'good practice' instead of 'best practice' allows for varying responses according to situational demands.

Protagonists of contingency theory point out that it is difficult to accommodate a wide variety of variables into a personal value system. Many managers also have a preferred behavioural style and find it difficult to adapt to new situations. However it remains the case that particular circumstances will require a response that is aligned to the needs of the situation. Those appointing managers will need to bear in mind that different situations will require different managerial styles and that therefore it would be preferable to appoint someone whose preferred management style fits the needs of the situation.

Authentic leadership styles

Authentic leadership theories have developed in the last few years as a response to corporate scandals. Leaders are considered to be authentic if they proactively conduct business in an ethical and socially responsible manner. The emphasis is on people and ethics over profit and share price. Authentic leaders are mission driven and focus on results. There is a useful emphasis on the need to be self-aware and to reflect on one's own style. The concept does not lend itself particularly to training interventions since it is built on the idea of being true to one's own beliefs and values, rather than simply accepting the corporate culture. Just as with transformational leadership, there is a problem with the theory in taking into account conflicting objectives between the organization and employees. For example, the concern about employees said to be associated with this theory could conflict with decisions that have to be made in an organization to promote profits or protect the share price.

Need for complementary styles

There can be occasions when managers and other colleagues need to have complementary styles.

EXAMPLE: Two examples of necessary complementary styles

A former British Royal Air Force officer commented about the relationship between the commanding officer of a unit and their adjutant. In his view it was necessary for the one to take a hard disciplinary line and for the other a much softer line and be psychologically available, so that they could find out what people really felt as well as soothe any hurt feelings. He also maintained that it did not matter who took the hard line and who the soft line as long as each took one role and that they worked as a team. That way effective control, based on reliable information and reasonable morale, could be exercised. If both the commanding officer and the adjutant adopted the same style he argued either there would be an excess of control and lack of reliable information or the reverse. Another example of this would be fee-charging doctors or dentists who will usually leave the potentially embarrassing business of payment to their receptionist, so that it does not interfere with the relationship between the professional and their client.

Organizational factors

While managerial style will be influenced by the individual personality of a manager, a number of external factors are also likely to influence their style and are outlined below.

Values

Organizations will have certain expectations of the way in which their managers behave. Managers may be selected and trained in such a way that these values are reinforced. They may also be rewarded or punished according to whether they conform or not to organizational values. The values of organizations are sometimes enshrined in documents such as **mission statements**. These can be genuine statements about organizational values or statements of how the organization would like to be viewed. In the latter case, managers need to be careful not to confuse the stated values with the real value system that may operate in an organization. It is particularly important that prospective or new managers try and identify the real values in an organization before they commit themselves to joining it or, if they have joined it, to see what adaptations in behaviour they may need to consider.

Nature of the work

The nature of the work may influence the managerial style. Of particular importance will be the knowledge gap between the manager and employees. The nature of the work will largely determine the level of skill needed in employees. The knowledge gap may be high if the work is predictable and routine; it may be small if the work is demanding and varied. The greater the gap, the more appropriate it may be for the manager to behave in an authoritarian way. If there is a small or even reverse gap, the more consultative the manager may need to be.

The time pressures affecting the work are also likely to influence managerial style. Organizations that are capital intensive, for example process-based plants such as oil refineries, may be able to have reasonable staffing ratios. This will reduce the time pressures on managers and enable them to consult more. Organizations in which labour costs are high may have to keep staff to a minimum, which in turn can mean that there is less time for consultation. The consequences of error may also be a factor. If the consequences are small, an authoritarian style may be appropriate. Conversely, if the consequences are high, managers will need to investigate and consult more fully. In emergencies, however, managers may need to behave in an authoritarian way.

Style of the boss

Managers need to take into account the values of their boss as well as those of the organization at large. The boss is usually in a powerful position to put pressure on an employee. While some bosses will be able to see the value of having employees with complementary skills, some may expect them to behave as 'clones'. Consequently, employees will need to work out the values and style of their boss and the extent to which they are expected to model themselves on it. One of the problems that organizations can have is that the 'cloning' process can go on throughout the managerial hierarchy. This may not necessarily be of benefit to the organization, but it can reinforce the pressure on an employee to conform to established values and patterns of behaviour. If one is unlucky enough to work for an incompetent boss at least one can try and learn from their mistakes and not repeat them oneself.

The managerial or leadership style of a boss can greatly influence the way in which issues entrusted to subordinates are handled. A study of the former Wales Gas Board (below) showed how attempts to change managerial style were frustrated by the very style that was meant to be changed.

A study of former Wales Gas Board

The Wales Gas Board had been statutorily obliged to consult with representatives of the employees. Seventeen consultative committees were established, but eight of them collapsed. Ostensibly, this was because the employees stopped nominating representatives to serve on these eight committees. Detailed analysis of consultative committee minutes showed, however, that the managers who had chaired the eight collapsed committees had taken a very reactive approach to discussions.

> They had also often ignored those issues raised by the employee representatives. This contrasted with the productive discussions at the nine other committees. These prospered because the managers who chaired them generally prepared for the meetings, actually raised more items for discussion than the employee representatives, and took the issues raised by the representatives seriously. Ironically, the committees were most successful at those well-run establishments where they seemed to be least needed and vice versa (Rees and Porter, 1998, pp. 165–170).

The impact of national culture

National culture was identified in the previous chapter as one of the factors that determine organizational structure. The term is used instead of 'societal culture' because it is much more generally used and broadly understood. Care has to be used throughout in using the term 'national culture' because of the danger of stereotyping This is all the more so because stereotypes tend to emphasize negative rather than positive characteristics. Also there may be significant minority sub-cultures.

National culture is an increasingly important topic because of growing cultural diversity within countries and globalization. Managers are also more likely to have to work abroad, even if only for short periods, which may require considerable adjustment on their part. It is important that managers avoid taking an **ethnocentric** approach and adapt appropriately to other cultures. The growth of international organizations in both the private and the public sectors means that managers may have to deal with a number of different nationalities simultaneously.

Hofstede's model

The most important study to date on the impact of national culture on work was conducted in 1984 by Hofstede (2001). His research was based on 116,000 IBM employees in 53 countries. Hofstede found that there were wide variations in values and behaviour between countries. Originally, he identified four dimensions for classifying key national differences that affected work behaviour.

1. Power distance: the length of hierarchies varies considerably. Low power distances in hierarchies encourage individualism and high power distances encourage conformity. This is because the fewer the levels in the hierarchy there are, normally the greater the opportunity and need for decision-making at the levels that do exist. High power distances are associated with authoritarian managerial styles. Certain human resource practices such as performance appraisal systems may be more effective in low rather than high power distance cultures.
2. Uncertainty avoidance: some cultures encourage acceptance of ambiguity and uncertainty while others do not. A high need to avoid uncertainty

can generate anxiety and a need to plan carefully to reduce uncertainty levels. Low needs for uncertainty avoidance, such as in Sweden, can lead to low anxiety about uncertainty and a willingness to take risks.

3. Individualism versus collectivism: there are large variations in the extent to which the focus of work and society is the individual, as in the USA, or the group, as in Japan. This has major implications for the way work is organized. The nature of the culture also has implications for payment arrangements, social control and attitudes to innovation. Group-based reward systems, for example, are more likely to fail if transplanted into more individualistic cultures. Attempts at social control may be relatively ineffective in individualistic countries, but individual merit schemes are more likely to be successful and innovation is likely to be higher.

4. Masculinity versus femininity: masculine cultures are characterized by strong gender distinctions and an emphasis on individual achievement and material possessions. Feminine cultures have greater equality between the sexes and a greater concern for people. In feminine cultures, collaboration is also valued more highly in comparison with competition.

Hofstede (2011) later identified two further dimensions, pragmatism and indulgence. The first was seen as particularly evident in societies with a long-term view of societal development. Indulgence was associated with satisfaction in one's personal life. However, the key dimensions appear to be the four he originally identified.

There are dangers in using any model too prescriptively. The research for Hofstede's work was undertaken in the 1970s and only on IBM employees. There are also the obvious dangers of assuming that everyone will conform to a pattern of national characteristics. In addition, Hofstede did not take account of factors such as organizational and industry subcultures. However, the model is, arguably, the most useful one currently available. If nothing else, the dimensions he identified can give managers a checklist of the factors they may need to take into account when working with people from different national cultures.

Local culture

As well as needing to adapt to national culture, managers may need to adapt to a regional or local culture within their own or another country. Sometimes the cultural variations and mutual antagonisms within countries are very high. A related issue is that managers may also have to deal with 'third country nationals', that is employees who have been imported to work from countries other than the manager's. Managers may also need to beware of being too closely associated with a particular cultural group within a country.

Managing diversity

Workforces are increasingly culturally diverse and managers will need to respond to the characteristics of such workforces, whether they are working at home or abroad, if they are to achieve both organizational objectives as well as some element of social justice. Benefits of managing diversity from the organization's point of view include better utilization of talent as well as increased market understanding. Cross-cultural teams may present certain problems in terms of creating a shared understanding of a situation, including language differences and utilizing different systems of communication, but they can also be more creative. To manage diversity effectively, the manager will find it necessary to develop cross-cultural knowledge and understanding. In addition, it will be necessary to develop an organizational climate that focuses on valuing diversity and an organizational culture that is tolerant of some of the differences in values and behaviour.

An organization can be seen as having a moral obligation towards members of all ethnic groups. At the same time, the benefits of managing diversity effectively from the organization's point of view can include reduced labour turnover and absenteeism, improved problem solving and innovation, greater appeal to minority ethnic groups, improved marketability of goods and services, and a better public image. A recent feature of globalization is the development of a growing international group of workers who move from country to country and no longer have their roots in any particular one. Another major issue, though, is that while there are some strong trends towards cultural convergence there are other factors, such as the increased importance of Islam, and in some cases its radicalization, that are leading to increased cultural divergence. The issue of cultural diversity on selection as well as the related concept of equal opportunities is considered further in Chapter 9.

Working abroad

The problems of cultural adjustment are likely to be magnified if a manager has to work abroad. The natural temptation is for managers working abroad to rely on their own national culture as a model and to judge all other cultures by that. Depending on the country in which they are working, they will find that the responses of employees vary according to the culture of the country and the different industrial context.

Ideally, managers should receive some cultural briefing (and a preliminary visit if that is possible) before they go on an international assignment of some length. However, even with good initial briefing, there will be much to learn once the manager starts to work in another country.

EXAMPLE: Speedy expatriate failure

An engineering manager was sent to Singapore on a three-year appointment. He paid no attention to how he might adjust to the habits, beliefs and expectations of his new colleagues. Instead he plunged straight into the technical aspects of his work. After three weeks he was sent back to the UK.

A further danger for managers working abroad is that they may live and socialize in an 'expatriate ghetto'. If managers restrict their social contacts to other expatriates this may reinforce existing prejudices about the local community and inhibit learning about and appreciating the local culture. It may also not be very good public relations to do this. If managers do try and adapt, however, even if they make mistakes, people from the host community may well be understanding of a person who is at least trying to get it right.

Expatriate failure can be costly both for the organizations involved and for the individuals concerned. The main cost to the organization may be the **opportunity cost**. This is the loss incurred by missing the opportunity to have an employee in place who could have moved the organization in an appropriate way. The chances of failure are likely to be considerably reduced if one accounts for the following six factors:

1. Selection: managers need to be carefully selected for overseas missions. As well as having the appropriate job expertise, managers crucially need to have the ability to adapt to working in a different environment. A precondition for selection is to have an accurate understanding of the job that needs doing.
2. Training: as well as needing induction training, managers may need to have training to prepare them for new job responsibilities. As employees often get promoted when they go abroad, this preparation may need to include management training.
3. Domestic arrangements: if a manager plans to take other family members with them, thought needs to be given to how well they are likely to be able to adapt. Key issues will include the career opportunities for any partner and education facilities for any children. Children may suffer from loss of cultural identity if they spend too much time away from their own country.
4. Length of assignment: the longer a manager works abroad, the more successful they are likely to be in adapting to local conditions. However, the more they do this, the more out of touch they may get with what is happening elsewhere in their organization.
5. Organizational adaptability: organizations need to adapt their structure, policies and procedures to meet local conditions. It may help in making appropriate adaptations if local people are considered for senior positions. Unfortunately, many organizations seek to rigidly impose their own arrangements in cultures when actual variation is needed.
6. Repatriation: organizations often fail to consider the issue of the repatriation of a person sent to work abroad. Expatriates can find that it has been a case of 'out of sight and out of mind'. They may also suffer from reverse culture shock when they return to their own country.

EXAMPLE: The wrong job being identified

Expatriate engineers were recruited for a major internationally funded transport project in the Philippines. However, it emerged that there were plenty of local engineers who could have handled the technical aspects of the work. The need instead had been for expatriates with financial expertise and an ability to understand the local politics who could effectively monitor the financial progress of the project.

National culture and ethics

When working abroad, managers may find that there will be differences in the criteria applied in situations where ethical issues have to be considered before decisions are made. What may be seen as unethical in one culture may be acceptable and even necessary in another culture. A common problem concerns what attitude to take towards questionable payments. In some societies it will be common practice for bribes of some description to be paid when awarding contracts or when securing other people's services. Difficult moral and business decisions may have to be taken about the extent to which one adjusts to apparent local customs. The consequences of decisions may also be difficult to predict.

EXAMPLE: Jumping to conclusions about local customs

Two western companies were operating in the same market in Indonesia. One took the policy decision that they would not pay bribes. The other took the opposite decision and tried to bribe its way into the market. The first company found that virtue was rewarded as the company found it could operate perfectly satisfactorily without paying bribes. The second company found that, once it had become known they would pay bribes, the number of people soliciting them proliferated. Although a considerable amount was paid in bribes it brought no apparent benefits. While concepts of 'honesty' (according to western definitions) may not always be the best policy, this example shows the dangers of jumping to conclusions about what is appropriate local practice.

This consideration relating to selecting and organizational support of managers who are to work overseas needs to be integrated with the coverage of selection in Chapter 9 and on management and employee development in Chapter 11.

Aggressive, non-assertive and assertive behaviours

Assertiveness

Although managerial or leadership style needs to fit the situation, there is a strong case for managers developing the skills of **assertiveness**. This is in contrast to being non-assertive or aggressive. While there may be occasions when managers may need to be non-assertive or aggressive, in general being assertive is likely to achieve better results. In any case, managers need to know how to be assertive so that they have the option of using this style.

Assertiveness training was originally particularly associated with developing the confidence and skills of women. However, the skills are equally relevant to both genders and are appropriate for use in work as well as in personal situations (Back and Back, 1999). These skills involve consideration of the rights of the parties involved in a situation. The patterns of behaviour associated with aggressive, non-assertive and assertive behaviour are outlined below.

Aggressive behaviour

If a manager behaves aggressively they may be standing up for their own rights but behaving in such a way that the rights of others are violated. The apparent assumption behind their behaviour is that their needs are more important than those of others, and that only they have something to contribute.

The consequences of aggressive behaviour may be that the manager concerned is able to vent their feelings and get their way. However, this may be at the expense of worsening working relationships, as well as generating stress in the person who is being aggressive. Aggressive behaviour will sometimes generate aggressive responses. It can also lead to a pattern of employees concealing bad news, which can lead to managers taking decisions on inadequate information (See also Chapter 8 on communications).

Aggressive behaviour is often an emotional response to a situation and not one calculated to be effective. Managers may need to find ways of diffusing their anger before dealing with people who are the object of it. One way of doing this is for the manager to write their initial thoughts down and then rip this up with a view to writing, or doing, something that is more rational. If a manager is having to cope with aggressive behaviour by someone else, they will probably need to let them dissipate their anger and only then try and have a rational dialogue. To do this they will need to curb their own anger and remember not to descend to the level of the person behaving aggressively.

Non-assertive behaviour

Non-assertive behaviour is based on the opposite assumption to that involved in aggressive behaviour. It implies that other people's rights are more important than your own. It also implies that the manager has nothing to contribute. Non-assertive behaviour is a way of dealing with situations in the short-term to avoid initial or further conflict. It may also create short-term popularity. However, in the long term, employees may become frustrated because of the lack of direction. Also, while non-assertiveness may sometimes be appropriate, it may be a form of escapism. Managers normally need to face up to problems, whatever they may be. If they do not, they may internalize their anger, which may not do their health or job performance much good. Non-assertiveness can also cause a manager to overreact on subsequent occasions and behave aggressively.

Assertive behaviour

Assertive behaviour involves recognizing both your own rights and those of whoever else is involved. It also involves recognizing the right of all the parties involved to speak in a direct, honest and open way. Employees are therefore encouraged to behave assertively. This enables the identification of issues that need to be addressed. It also has the potential to enable issues to be addressed in a way that is satisfactory to all the parties involved and which develops constructive working relationships between them. Another potential advantage is that it may take much less emotional energy to deal with issues this way.

The skills of behaving assertively

Key aspects of behaving assertively are:

- Concentrating on facts and not feelings
- Concentrating on issues and not personalities
- Questioning technique and the choice of language can be important
- Phrasing statements and questions in a neutral way
- Avoiding leading statements or questions that may discourage people from raising points that are necessary both for themselves and for the manager
- In seeking to behave assertively, managers also need to consider their tone of voice and body language.

Handling change

Nature of organizational change

The handling of change is considered a number of times throughout this book but it is appropriate to pull the threads together in one section, even if this involves a number of cross-references. It is also necessary to distinguish between specific (or 'set piece') change – for example, the introduction of a new operational method – and erratic and continuous change. It is also necessary to make the point that set piece change is likely to be taking place within the context of a greater or lesser amount of continuous change. A particular type of continuous change is that envisaged by the concept of **kaizen**. This involves discussion groups designed to secure improvements in organizational quality and efficiency particularly found in Japanese businesses. Although individual improvements may be small their cumulative effect may be considerable.

Planning

A key aspect of change is ensuring that management planning is properly thought through. Unfortunately this is not always the case. Initiatives can be taken which deal, for example, with the symptoms of problems rather than the root causes. This crucial issue was previously considered in the section on strategic planning in Chapter 2, in the section on the interrelationship of organizational activity in Chapter 3 and is considered further in the section on diagnostic skills in Chapter 14 (see also Rees and Porter, 2002). Organizational change can have many dimensions and unexpected consequences. This means that whoever seeks to initiate major change needs to grasp the scale of what they are planning. This may necessitate opening up the planning process so that there can be inputs from a range of people who can comment on the appropriateness of the change, anticipate the likely effects, and undertake a realistic cost-benefit analysis. Too often it is assumed that there will be only winners from a particular change and that everyone will be as committed to change as the person who is initiating it. An understanding of the concepts of **unitary frames of reference** and **pluralistic frames of reference**, first explained in Chapter 2, can be vital in identifying whether there will be losers as well as winners and how the manager might handle prospective losers. As also explained in Chapter 2, resistance to change can too often be attributed to inertia. Whilst inertia can be a factor, if employees' genuine interests are threatened by change it is appropriate to identify the nature of the threats to see what, if anything, can be done to reduce, or even avoid, such threats.

A major factor causing change, or being used as an agent of change, is information technology. The impact of changes in this area was considered in some detail in Chapter 3.

The impact of any change could also require taking a **socio-technical systems approach**, as previously explained in Chapter 3. The likely impact needs to be anticipated and potentially allowed for in planning, rather than viewed as an unexpected fallout of change. Other key issues that may need to be taken into account in planning organizational change include national culture and the training and development implications (Chapter 11).

Evaluation of a managerial or leadership style

Different managers or leaders may achieve the same results using different means. Despite the differences between management and leadership, evidence about who is likely to emerge as the informal leader of a group may nevertheless help in judging the effectiveness of the style that managers or leaders adopt. In analyzing the research findings of group behaviour, Homans (1975, Ch. 8) identified six factors that were strongly associated with who would emerge as the informal leader. These factors provide a rough and ready way of evaluating the effectiveness of managerial or leadership style. Although this seems to be suggesting that there is a standard effective style, the factors do take into account the requirements of the situation in which leadership is exercised.

Assessment exercise

As a way of assessing managers or leaders and the appropriateness of their style, *identify one or more managers and rank them on the following six-point scale:*

1. Excellent
2. Very good
3. Good
4. Meets the minimum standards
5. Does not meet the minimum standards
6. Should be replaced

The next stage is to compare the rating or ratings on the above scale with the six points identified by Homans as being characteristic of the behaviour of informal group leaders. *Answer yes or no to the following questions:*

1. Does the leader represent what the group finds to be most important in a person at that time?
2. Does the leader make decisions that turn out, by and large, to be correct?
3. Do they keep their word?
4. Do they settle differences between members in a way the group believes to be fair?
5. Do they allow followers to go to them for advice and keep them informed about what is going on?
6. Do they give information to the group in the form of advice, orders, etc. and maintain two-way communication?

When the second part of the assessment is completed it is necessary to compare the number of 'no' responses with the initial rating of effectiveness. Usually this correlates so that the fewer the 'no' responses to Homans's six characteristics of an effective leader, the more likely it is that the manager or leader will receive a high rating in terms of effectiveness. For example, a person who received six 'yes' responses, and therefore zero 'no' responses, would have received a rating of 1 (excellent). Conversely, a person who was given 'no' six times would be rated as 6 (should be replaced).

This method of assessment can act as a means of identifying the reasons for ineffectiveness as well as a means of assessing the level of performance. It can also be used as a method of self-assessment.

Summary

In this chapter the concept of managerial and leadership style has been explained, as have the differences between the overlapping concepts of management and leadership. Managers are appointed but leaders often emerge as popular choices, particularly in representative structures. Managerial and leadership styles are not ends in themselves but means to an end, that is a means of achieving a particular set of objectives.

The range of managerial and leadership styles has been examined. A key distinction is the amount of direction that the leader or manager gives. Examination of the various theories has shown that this is largely determined by the assumptions managers make about why other people work and other variables in the situation. These variables are likely to include the organizational culture, the level of skill of employees and the extent to which their objectives converge with organizational ones. For managerial and leadership styles to be effective they need to match the situation. This may involve selecting people whose style fits a situation or managers adjusting their style to the circumstances.

National culture also does, or needs to, affect management and leadership style. This is an increasingly important issue because of globalization, and cultural diversity within countries and organizations. The work of Hofstede has been examined in this chapter and in particular the four key dimensions he used to differentiate between managerial styles in different countries.

Whatever style is adopted, there is usually a case for managers or leaders behaving assertively rather than aggressively or non-assertively. Assertiveness involves respecting other people's rights to state their case but being prepared to firmly yet politely state one's own case. The associated skills in doing this have also been explained.

A key activity for managers is the effective handling of change. This is ever more important because of the increasing pace of change. Consequently, the way in which significant organizational change needs to be planned was examined and reference made to other parts of the book where relevant concepts are examined in more detail.

Ultimately, managers particularly have to be judged by their effectiveness and not, for example, by their popularity. An exercise was included within this chapter so that readers can assess the managerial effectiveness of other people. A further exercise has been included as an appendix so that readers can examine their own managerial style and see if there is any need for adjustment.

Self-assessment questions

1. How would you define the concept of managerial or leadership style?
2. Identify the main different types of managerial or leadership style.

3. Why does managerial or leadership style need to match the circumstances in which it is used?
4. What organizational factors can influence managerial or leadership style?
5. Identify key ways in which national culture can affect managerial or leadership style.
6. Explain the differences between assertive, aggressive and non-assertive behaviour.
7. How would you ensure that a change you are involved in is properly planned?
8. How would you evaluate the effectiveness of a particular managerial or leadership style?
9. What is your own preferred managerial or leadership style? If you have managerial or other responsibilities, assess the effectiveness of your style.

Questionnaire

If you want to check on your own managerial style, complete the questionnaire in the appendix to this chapter.

Case study notes – The New Broom

Learning outcome:

■ To identify and evaluate the importance of the concept of socio-technical systems.

Question 1: What reasons might there be for reduced morale in the accounts department?

It is noticeable that Stephen Middleton has not been able to work out the reasons for reduced morale. This may well be because he has only seen the technical aspects of the new computerized system and has not understood the concept of socio-technical systems (see the relevant section in Chapter 6). The social system has been significantly changed. The work of the accounts staff may have been de-skilled and that of the accounts supervisor (Ann Smith) highly marginalized. The job of Stephen will also be significantly de-skilled when he is simply required to see that the system runs properly rather than to design it. Ann seems to have opted out but could perhaps have been a key figure in helping facilitate the change and maintaining morale at a difficult time.

Question 2: What action may need to be taken and by whom?

Possible solutions could include the following. When the new system has 'bedded down' one has to ask if there will be a need for both Stephen and Ann. An option might have been to have engaged Stephen as a consultant and to train Ann to supervise the system that Stephen had designed. At present Stephen is giving personal tutorials to accounts staff but ideally Ann would be capable of being trained to do this. If not, it is necessary to ask if she is still needed, especially if Stephen is to remain in post.

It would be necessary to check on what involvement there has been with the staff on the design and operation of the new system. Social interaction at work can play an important part in productivity and it may be useful to see if that needs constructively improving, for example by installing tea or coffee points.

Appendix

Self-assessment exercise for personal development planning:

1. Do you vary your style to match the situation?
2. Do you naturally adopt a Theory X or Theory Y style based on the assumptions that you make about employees?
3. Do your assumptions about conflict in organizations fit with a unitary or pluralistic frame of reference?
4. Are you generally non-assertive, assertive or aggressive?
5. Are you reactive or proactive in your managerial style? (See Chapter 2 on identifying the manager's job.)
6. Is your orientation primarily managerial or specialist? (See Chapter 1 on managers and their backgrounds.)
7. Do you generally get on with tasks yourself or do you generally ensure that they are done by others?
8. When you chair meetings, is your orientation towards process management or substantive contribution? (See Chapter 15 on meetings, chairing and team building.)
9. How effective is your style?
10. In the light of your answers to the above questions do you need to alter any of your managerial behaviour to improve your effectiveness?

References

NB: Works of particular interest are marked with an asterisk.

Adair, John (1982), *Action-Centred Leadership*, Gower Publishing.
*Back, Ken and Kate Back (1999), *Assertiveness at Work: A Practical Guide to Handling Awkward Situations*, 3rd ed., McGraw-Hill.
Bass, Bernard M. and R. E. Riggio (2006), *Transformational Leadership*, 2nd Edition, Routledge.
Drucker, Peter F. (1955), *Practice of Management*, Heinemann.
Garrahan, Philip and Paul Stewart (1992), *The Nissan Enigma – Flexibility at Work in a Local Economy*, Thomson Learning.

Hofstede, Geert (2001), *Culture's Consequences,* 2nd ed., Sage.

Hofstede, Geert (2011), Dimensionalizing cultures: the Hofstede model in context, *International Association for Cross Cultural Psychology.* http://scholarworks.gvsu. edu/orpc/vol2/iss1/8/ [6/11/2014].

Homans, George (1975), *The Human Group,* Routledge and Kegan Paul.

McGregor, Douglas (1969), *The Human Side of Enterprise,* McGraw-Hill.

Mintzberg, Henry (2009), *Managing,* Prentice Hall.

Northouse, Peter (2013), *Leadership – Theory and Practice,* 6th edn., Sage.

*Rees, W. David and Christine Porter (1998), Employee participation and managerial style (the key variable), *Industrial and Commercial Training* (MCB University Press) Vol. 30, No. 5.

*Rees, W. David and Christine Porter (2002), Management by panacea – the training implications. *Industrial and Commercial Training,* Vol. 34, No. 6.

> *An explanation of the diagnostic skills in management and the need to identify the real nature and causes of problems before devising solutions.*

*Rees, W. David and Christine Porter (2008), The re-branding of management development as leadership development – and its dangers, *Industrial and Commercial Training,* Vol. 40, No. 5.

Taking it further

*Belbin, R. Meredith (2010), *Management Teams – Why They Succeed or Fail,* 3rd edn., Butterworth Heinemann.

> *A very useful account about the roles and dynamics in managerial teams.*

Belbin, R. Meredith (2010), *Team Roles at Work,* 2nd edn., Butterworth-Heinemann.

*Fox, Alan (1965), *Industrial Society and Industrial Relations,* Research paper no. 3, Royal Commission on Trade Unions and Employer's Associations, London: HMSO.

Hillary, Peter (1995), Comments reported in Evening Standard (London), 23 August.

Hughes, Mark (2010), *Change Management: A Critical Perspective,* 2nd edn., CIPD.

> *A thorough examination of the assumptions on which change is based and the complexities, particularly in the private sector.*

*Mead, Richard and Tim G. Andrews (2009), *International Management,* Wiley.

> *An excellent and detailed account explaining the impact of national culture on management practices.*

Northouse, Peter (2013), *Leadership – Theory and Practice,* 6th edn., Sage.

> *A comprehensive account of the topic of leadership, including the different styles and situations in which it is needed.*

Storey, John (ed.) (2010), *Leadership in Organizations: Current Issues and Key Trends,* 2nd edn., Routledge.

> *An authoritative and balanced account, including changing theories of leadership, the international dimension, the public sector, and practical implications.*

Trompenaars, Fons and Charles Hampden-Turner (2012), *Riding the Waves of Culture: Understanding Cultural Diversity in Business,* 3rd ed., Nicholas Brealey.

> *A complementary approach to that of Hofstede. Focuses on cross-cultural leadership.*

Delegation

5

Learning outcomes

By the end of this chapter you will be able to:

- Define, understand and apply the concept of delegation
- Identify and evaluate the importance of delegation
- Establish criteria for deciding what should be delegated and what should not be delegated
- Identify and apply the key skills involved in implementing delegation
- Identify the main barriers to effective delegation and take appropriate remedial action
- Understand the differences between delegation and the overlapping concept of **empowerment**.

Case study

Mission of Trouble

Assume that you are the head of the consular department of a diplomatic mission.

The senior executive officer (SEO), in charge of the visa section, who reports to you, tells you of a problem that she has just experienced with one of the clerks. The clerk failed to 'fast track' a priority visa application. When the SEO spoke to the clerk about it he said that he had not appreciated the urgency of the application and that he had been busy on other work. The SEO also explained that this was the second time this had happened in the three months the clerk had been employed at the mission.

Question:

How should the head handle this situation?

Introduction

Management has already been described in Chapter 1 as 'achieving results through others'. It therefore follows that delegation is a part of every manager's job. It involves giving others the authority to act on your behalf. Criteria are given for identifying what might be delegated and what should not be. Associated managerial skills are also identified. These include risk assessment, consideration of the strengths and weaknesses of subordinates, and the establishment of appropriate control mechanisms. Managers also need to be prepared to spend time training their subordinates so that they are able to handle delegated authority.

Unfortunately, although the concepts involved in delegation are relatively easily explained, many managers are very bad at delegating. Consequently, the barriers to effective delegation are examined here. Whilst some of these managerial omissions are because of a lack of understanding of the nature of delegation, others may be of a more deep-seated nature. A particularly difficult barrier is psychological insecurity on the part of some managers. This can make it very difficult for them to give subordinates reasonable freedom to act on their behalf.

The overlapping concept of **empowerment** is also examined. It is important to try and identify what people mean by this term. Sometimes it is used interchangeably with delegation. However, empowerment often focuses on groups rather than individuals. Historically, it was a 'bottom-up' process whereby community groups in the USA took more control over their lives. Latterly, it has become more used in a managerial context as a 'top-down' process.

The nature of delegation

Definition

Delegation may be defined as 'a person giving authority to someone to act on their behalf'. It should not be confused with orders or giving of instructions to subordinates. Although the manager remains accountable for the actions of the subordinate, the essence of delegation is the conferring of authority on the subordinate. Thus, delegation is much more than just passing a task over to be executed. Like all management techniques it is neutral. It can be used to good or bad effect. What matters is that it is used appropriately.

Accountability

When managers delegate they still remain accountable for the actions of their subordinates. Delegation does not involve abdication of responsibility. This has been illustrated by a number of important and well-publicized cases.

EXAMPLE: Accountability cannot be delegated

The owner of the bankrupt Fire, Auto and Marine Insurance Company, Dr. Emile Savundra, was cross-examined in a fraud trial in Britain in 1967 about the contrast between his personal wealth and the state of his former company. He responded by saying that he had practised modern management techniques – including delegation – and that such questions should be addressed instead to his former financial controller. The judge understood management better than that however, and when sentencing Dr Savundra to a lengthy term of imprisonment, commented that whilst authority can be delegated, accountability remained!

The head of the Royal Bank of Scotland's (RBS) Investment Division resigned in 2013 (*The Times*, 2013) because of the lack of corrective action about interest rate 'fixing'. This had been to the disadvantage of customers and had led to the bank being fined £450 million. Although the head of the investment division had been unaware of the manipulations he had been in charge of the relevant division at the time.

Accountability in the public sector

There is an extra dimension to the general concept of accountability in the public sector because of the issue of public accountability. At one stage in the UK it was the practice for government ministers to accept responsibility and resign if there was a serious enough error by one of their subordinates – regardless of whether the minister even knew of the action beforehand. The following examples explain how the concept has developed in the public sector:

EXAMPLE: Public sector examples

In 1955 it was found that land on Crichel Down, which had been compulsorily purchased by the UK government for military use during the Second World War, had been later used for agricultural purposes and then sold to a private buyer. This was despite an earlier assurance to give the original owner the first option of buying the land back. The Minister was obliged to resign, even though he had not been personally involved in the decision and had had no reason to believe that his officials had acted in other than good faith.

The concept of accountability has been modified by a number of cases, particularly in the public sector regarding the predictability of an event.

EXAMPLE: Reasonable forseeability

The Aberfan disaster occurred in 1966 when a waste heap extracted from a coal mine in South Wales slid down a hill because of heavy rain and engulfed a school, killing 144 people, including 116 children (McLean, 1999). The chairman of the UK National Coal Board offered his resignation but this was not accepted on the basis that the event was not 'reasonably foreseeable'.

Norway's police chief resigned in 2012 after an independent commission found that police could have prevented all or part of the killing of 77 people in a bombing and shooting rampage by Anders Breivik at a youth camp in 2011. Although the police chief had only been appointed weeks before the attack, the report found that the attack should have been anticipated and cited a 'failure to face up to police shortcomings in the aftermath' (*The Times*, 2012).

The Prime Minister of South Korea, Chung Hong Wong, resigned in 2014 after a ferry disaster in which over 300 people, mainly school children, were drowned. He referred to a 'deep-seated evil' in the culture that lay behind the disaster. Allegations included over-loading of the ferry, corruption, deception, incompetence and errors in the rescue attempt. He said that 'As prime minister, I certainly had to take responsibility' (*The Times*, 2014b).

The need for delegation

One of the main reasons for delegation is that it is a means whereby a manager can, having decided their priorities, concentrate on the work of greatest importance, leaving the work of lesser importance to be done by others. Ironically, if delegation is set up effectively, the delegated work may, in time, actually be performed better by the subordinates. This also has the advantages of motivating and developing subordinates.

Effective use of time

The time of managers is limited, thus it is important for them to tackle their work in some order of priority so that the most important tasks get the appropriate attention. If at the end of the day some work has not been completed, or has had to be passed on to others, this should be the work of lowest priority. Even if the work of lesser importance is not done, or is not done so well, this is appropriate behaviour for the person in charge. It would not be sensible for a manager to do their own clerical work, for example, because they thought they could do it better than for example their secretary or a clerk. Running the risk of a slightly lower level of performance by a subordinate is a small price to pay for creating time to concentrate on the more important aspects of a job. Although delegation is initially time consuming, managers somehow have to find the time to establish it effectively, even though the need for delegation arises because they are short of time. Like an investment, the return will be in the future rather than immediately.

The lower the level at which a task is performed, the lower the cost of performing that task is therefore likely to be. Cost needs to be considered, not just in terms of the salary of the person undertaking a particular task, but also in terms of opportunity cost: that is, the opportunity that is denied or created for the manager to do other work.

Effective use of employees

Many managers fail to make effective use of their subordinates. This can reduce their own effectiveness and de-motivate their subordinates. In some cases there would be a blatant disregard of the specialist expertise of a subordinate if the boss tried to do the subordinate's job. What would be the point, and the results if, for example, a chief executive tried to run the accounts department despite having a finance manager?

Arising out of this is the need for managers to seek to dovetail their activity with that of their subordinates. Everybody has relative strengths and weaknesses in their work. If a subordinate has particular strengths it may be appropriate to make use of those strengths rather than compete in that area or simply ignore those strengths. What matters is the effectiveness of the team as a whole rather than the direct performance of just the manager.

Further possible advantages of delegation are that the subordinate often has more time and readier access to the appropriate information than the boss. Also, what is routine work to the boss may be challenging to the subordinate, as well as carrying prestige. The more that subordinates are developed, the more they are likely to be able to undertake in the future.

Managers have to think carefully about the balance between managing by systems and through people. Detailed control procedures tend to be statements of lack of trust and can be unnecessary as well as de-motivating if there are capable subordinates. Such systems may also inhibit healthy evolution and act as an organizational straitjacket. In any case, systems tend to be as good or bad as the people who operate them. A director of one civil service agency commented that the best legacy he could leave the agency was to see that the six key jobs under him were staffed by capable people.

EXAMPLE: Developing managers to do less

The chief executive of an organization invested in the management training of those with managerial responsibilities. Jobs that were mainly supervisory or managerial were given the designation 'manager'. Remuneration was also improved for those with managerial responsibilities. However, simultaneously, more detailed central control was introduced and the number of senior managers at the head office was doubled. The newly designated managers became increasingly frustrated with their work. This was because the clarification of their managerial responsibilities and their management development coincided with a considerable reduction in their delegated authority. Their management training made them all the more aware of this contradiction.

Development of subordinates

A further advantage of effective delegation may be that a manager is setting the pattern for their subordinates to then delegate down the line. One adage about managerial assessment is that you judge a manager by the quality of their subordinates. Such delegation can also be important so that subordinates can deal with emergencies.

EXAMPLE: Extreme example of a failure to delegate

King Philip II of Spain was not a believer in delegation. He governed Spain in the 16th century in a manner which created 'apoplexy at the nucleus and paralysis at the periphery'. All state mail was sent to him and his conscientious attention to detail included sending personal letters to each of the families who lost relatives in the unsuccessful Armada attack on England in 1588.

Effective delegation can also help prepare subordinates for promotion. However, it is important that subordinates take advantage of the opportunities that may be presented to them. It may seem that promotion decisions are taken by the manager responsible for making the appointments. In reality, though, it may be much more the case that it is the manager being considered for promotion who decides for themselves whether or not they get it. Managers responsible for appointments do not make decisions in a vacuum. The existing pattern of behaviour of a manager is likely to influence any decision about their promotion. If a manager has got their pattern of delegation right, and because of that gets promotion, the onus may then be upon them to establish a new pattern so that they prepare themselves for even further promotion. The same reasoning can apply to people running small businesses. The expansion or non-expansion of a small business may depend less on external factors than is often imagined. Much may depend on the ability of the person running a small business to identify and concentrate on the key tasks, leaving the less critical, even if more enjoyable, tasks to others.

EXAMPLE: The self-perpetuating nature of a failure to delegate

Two small hospital groups had been merged, partly because of the ineffective management style of the chief executive of one of the groups, who was prematurely retired. He had operated on the classic Theory X assumptions about his subordinates, explained in the previous chapter. The chief executive of the other group now had to administer both groups. He was much more prepared to delegate and, interestingly, had attracted around him a much more capable group of managers than had his retired colleague, despite a common salary structure.

Initially, the chief executive of the merged group tried to cope with his own increased workload by increasing the delegated authority of the managers in the group which he had taken over. One of the unit managers tried to cope with his extra responsibility doing all the extra work as well as the work he had traditionally undertaken. However, this was too much for him and the work he left undone was most of the extra and important work that had been delegated to him. He was quite unable to identify his new priorities and to delegate down the line, as his new boss had delegated to him. Consequently, the chief executive had to take back most of the delegated authority, recognising that the unit manager had reached his limit as far as his capacity to assume responsibility was concerned. Ironically, the chief executive was then able to delegate even more authority to the managers in the other part of the group, as they were used to coping with increased responsibility. The unit manager, who had been relieved of part of his authority, had imposed his own limit. By demonstrating his inability to cope with increased authority and responsibility, he had not only restricted his own job but ruled himself out of consideration for future promotion. In ways such as this, people can set limits on their career without necessarily realising it.

The skills of delegation

The case for delegation is easy to make. However, people may rush into delegating without effective planning. The delegated work may then be mishandled, causing the boss to withdraw the delegated authority without realising that the problem lay in the lack of planning rather than the basic idea. The factors critical to effective planning of delegation need identification and explanation. As part of this process managers may need to have established a structure within their area of responsibility so that they do not have too many people reporting directly to them. This will involve them looking at their immediate **span of control**. A historic convention was that a senior manager should have no more than six executives reporting to them but the growing complexity of organizations is such that often managers will deal directly with more than that number.

Discretionary authority

The first critical factor is the need for clarity about just what has been delegated. A useful concept in this respect is Wilfred (later Lord) Brown's distinction between the **prescribed** and **discretionary** content of a manager's job (1965, p. 123). Prescribed work is that which must be performed in a predetermined manner. The discretionary element of a manager's job is where they are expected to use their own judgement. For example, a human resources officer could be told that they have authority to determine at what point on a given salary scale a recruit to an organization would start. The salary range to be used, however, would be prescribed. Time and care needs to be taken in defining a person's job in this way, particularly, for example, when a person has just started.

The use of discretion by subordinates must be tolerated, within reasonable limits. A subordinate cannot always be expected to perform in exactly the same way as their manager would. If that is the expectation, then the work concerned is prescribed content not discretionary content. If there is discretion, and it is used sensibly, it can be very demoralising for a subordinate to be told 'I wouldn't have done it quite that way'. If the discretion had been used unwisely, this may well reveal a weakness in the way the delegation was set up originally.

The appropriate use of discretionary powers may well involve considerable discussion between manager and subordinate. The access of the subordinate to the manager needs determining. If people are unsure of how to use their delegated powers, they may well act inappropriately or pass things back up to the manager. When tasks are passed up to managers, the managers need to consider whether they should do them or whether they should be passed back to the subordinate with a reminder about the subordinate's discretionary authority. When an appropriate discretionary area has been established, it is up to the manager to see that the subordinate gets on with their job and does not seek to over-involve them. It is important to clarify what the boss does and does not need to know.

Prioritization

Managers need to develop criteria for judging what they do themselves and what they delegate. Useful criteria are:

■ Existing arrangements for the allocation of work;
■ Confidentiality;
■ Complexity;
■ Managers' strengths and weaknesses relative to those of their subordinates;
■ Speed of response required;
■ Availability of people to do a particular task;
■ Reversibility: if a decision can be reversed quickly and easily then it may be appropriate to delegate it and the consequences of error will not be great;

- Repetition: if an issue or problem arises frequently it may be sensible to delegate it. There will be scale economies in investing time in setting up such a delegation;
- Consequences: if the impact of a decision is small, the risks involved in delegating it will be small. The case for delegation will be stronger if no important precedents are being set;
- Future commitment: future commitments can vary in resource implications and the time scale involved. The smaller the commitment and the smaller the time scale the greater the case for delegation;
- Values and image: the impact of decision making on the image of an organization needs to be considered. Representatives of an organization may, for example, need to be much more carefully briefed about how they handle clients or customers, compared with their dealings with colleagues;
- Authority can only be delegated to people who, in the long run, are going to be able to cope with the delegated powers. This may in turn become a criterion in selection, so that one chooses staff who will be able to integrate effectively with the work pattern of their boss.

The use of the above criteria may also help managers to avoid rationalizing about why they need to undertake a particular task. It is all too easy to pretend that a particular task has to be carried out by oneself when that may not really be the case.

Routing of work

Care has to be taken with work that is routed to the manager but which should be done by subordinates. In some cases colleagues and clients will need to have it explained to them that they should go to the subordinates direct. On other occasions it will be entirely appropriate that the work should be routed to a manager, so that the chain of command is not bypassed. If a manager's boss routes something to them, it does not automatically follow that the manager must do the job themselves. The decision as to who does it is one for the manager. In some cases, especially in high power distance cultures, offence could be caused by a manager refusing to handle a request from a colleague or client themselves. In such situations it is probably appropriate for the manager themselves to pass the request 'down the line' for action. They may then want a report back on what has happened or, if necessary, be able to report back directly to the colleague or client concerned on the outcome.

The real pattern of delegation is likely to be set by the way a manager handles routing decisions such as these. The critical question to be asked, before any work is undertaken, is 'whose job is this?' If managers fail to ask this question they can (and frequently do) get sucked into a counter-productive **micro-management** of their area of responsibility. Other dangers are that managers act simply as post-boxes in which case you have to ask what value they add to the decision-making process. A pattern that can be related to this is that of the **rubber desk**. This is where a manager passes work on to others as quickly as possible without scrutinising it when necessary or reflecting enough on who it should really go to.

The danger of established chains of command being short-circuited has been greatly increased by the development of email. This has greatly increased both the temptation for people to inappropriately involve senior staff and for senior staff to get involved in issues in a counter-productive way. This is such an important issue that a section is devoted to it in Chapter 8 (Communication).

Control mechanisms

All delegated authority needs to be accompanied by effective control mechanisms, particularly in view of the accountability of the person delegating. It is difficult to envisage managers being given plenipotentiary powers, that is being allowed to decide crucial issues without reference to anyone. Control mechanisms can take many forms. These include:

- Getting approval on specified issues before taking action
- Reporting back on issues after action has been taken
- Activity sampling by the boss
- Reporting by the subordinate on exceptional issues
- Appraisal systems, both informal and formal
- Visual observation
- Monitoring of results
- Inspection procedures by the boss, a separate inspection function, or both
- Internal and/or external auditing
- Peer observation
- Internal and external complaints procedures
- Performance indicators are increasingly used in the public sector, in particular to monitor the progress of whole organizations.

EXAMPLE: The potential cost of lack of effective control procedures

Lack of effective control procedures were vividly illustrated by excesses in the financial industry starting in 2007/2008. One example amongst many was the loss of nearly 5 billion euros by the rogue trader Jerome Kerviel working for Société Générale in Paris. However, when upholding his three-year prison sentence in 2014 the French Appeal Court also deemed 'flawed management' to be a significant factor (*The Times*, 2014a).

Management of professionally qualified staff

There can be particular difficulties in trying to set up control systems for professionally qualified employees. This is sometimes because such employees see this as a slight on their professional independence. However, if they are funded by an organization they are accountable for the use of those funds. Their activity needs to be integrated with the rest of the organization. The employment relationship is quite different from being in professional practice on one's own. The dangers of specialists indulging in following their own objectives, which may not necessarily be the same as the organization's, were explained in detail in Chapter 1.

A useful distinction is to hold professional employees accountable for end results but to leave it to them as to how they achieve the results. In some cases, it is necessary to set up systems for monitoring the quality of professional work. This is an issue that is of particular concern in hospitals because of the issues of public and legal liability and the potential seriousness of poor quality work. It has led to the concept of **clinical governance**. The need for further controls over the way general medical practitioners operate, in the UK at least, was dramatically emphasized when, in the year 2000, Dr Harold Shipman was convicted of murdering 15 of his patients. However, the total estimate of the patients he killed was a minimum of 250 (Smith, 2005). A system of peer audit has been developed in both medical and university teaching as one way of increasing the quality control of professionals working in these areas. This technique is considered further in Chapter 10.

Use of deputies

Delegation can be achieved by the appointment of a deputy or deputies. However, such arrangements need thinking through or they can be counterproductive. If a person is appointed as a full-time deputy, it begs the question of what the person does whilst the boss is available. It can be something of a luxury to have a permanent understudy available but not necessarily used. Such an arrangement would also be very frustrating for a deputy of any ability. If the arrangement of routing everything through a deputy is used, it raises the question of just what is the value of such a duplication of activity. This can generate rivalry and competition for what may really be only one job.

Normally deputies would carry ongoing responsibilities as well as being asked to **act up** when the boss is not available. However, there needs to be a very clear understanding between the boss and the deputy about the demarcation between their jobs. Other employees also need to know these arrangements so that they are able to route issues to the correct person.

There is a case for avoiding the title deputy because of the confusion it can cause. Instead, a manager may designate who is to act when they are not available. It may be appropriate to ask just one person to act up or to have subordinates act up according to defined areas of responsibility.

Sometime deputies are used to support a manager who is under pressure. However, before such an arrangement is used, thought needs to be given as to whether there are better solutions or not. This may involve other forms of work reorganization or a review of the abilities of the manager under pressure. If the boss is replaced by a more capable person, there may no longer be any need for a deputy. However, the continuing need for a deputy may be a question people forget to ask in such a situation.

Training and development

Delegating authority to others may well be accompanied by a need to train them in the way in which that authority is to be used. It is no good delegating authority to a subordinate unless they know what to do. All too often this stage is omitted and managers exclaim that people won't assume authority. There may be a need to start training well in advance of the delegation. Training needs to combine the substantive knowledge and skills required by the subordinate in their job with a careful definition of just what constitutes their job.

Training can be formal, informal or both. A useful convention is that when people with managerial responsibilities are absent their subordinates act-up. This is as opposed to the manager in charge of the absent person acting down. Acting up from subordinates can leave managers free to concentrate on high priority work, develop subordinates and help identify promotion potential. Unfortunately, sometimes managers are only too keen to act down because it enables them to engage in their historic and preferred specialist activity.

Obstacles to effective delegation

Even when people recognize the advantages of delegation and are aware of the skills involved in planning it effectively, they may still not delegate to the extent they should. There are a number of barriers to effective delegation – usually these are a lot easier to recognize in others than in oneself. Also, these are sometimes not so much barriers as genuine constraints. Sometimes though it can by very difficult to disentangle imagined from real constraints.

Time

Paradoxically, and as previously explained, delegation may initially be time-consuming. In particular, significant time may need to be spent in identifying what is to be delegated. Delegation is like a capital investment; time spent setting it up may achieve substantial dividends – but only in the future. If the manager does not carefully think through the pattern of delegation, it may backfire and discourage them from further attempts.

Lack of training

Many managers are not trained in how to manage. They may either lack formal training or lack the ability to learn and develop on the job under the guidance of managers. Even those managers who have received formal training may not have been trained in delegation. Despite its importance, it is often quite wrongly assumed that delegation does not need to feature in management training programmes.

Factors outside the manager's control

There can be a number of genuine constraints preventing or limiting the ability of managers to delegate. These include:

- Lack of resources, particularly of subordinate staff – shortages of staff can be in terms of quantity, quality or both
- An organizational climate that discourages delegation
- Their own lack of authority
- Lack of work to do anyway
- Jealousy between subordinates
- Over-ambitious subordinates
- Pressures to do particular tasks themselves that it would be counter-productive to resist
- Confidentiality.

Managerial insecurity

Although there can be genuine limits on the extent to which delegation can be implemented, some managers simply do not want to delegate. Often the greatest obstacle to delegation is the psychological insecurity of a manager. If this is the case, attempts to train a manager to delegate, or exhortations to delegate, may simply fail. One of the problems with management training generally is that managers have to integrate good management practice with their own personality.

The indispensable employee

Sometimes people can deliberately seek to make themselves indispensable. This may be a means of managers dealing with their feelings of personal insecurity. A rough guide to the competence of a manager is to see how well things work when they are absent. The effective manager should have developed systems and staff abilities so that people can cope in their absence. This may not be the case with the ineffective manager. The poor manager may even be glad that things have not gone well in their absence and may even publicize that fact. The creation of a state of indispensability may be subconscious or carefully planned.

EXAMPLE: Accidental indispensability

The head of the avionics division of an electronics company managed his division very effectively for 27 years. Unfortunately he became so good at his job that when he retired nobody could be found to replace him. Ironically, had he been less good at his job a management system may have evolved that could have survived his retirement. As it was the division had to be closed down.

Empowerment

Background

The concept of empowerment has become increasingly fashionable in recent years. The term seems to have originated in the USA when Democratic administrations in the 1960s were seeking to build 'The Great Society'. It was a response by government to the need for disadvantaged groups to have more control over their lives with a view to improving them. These groups particularly included ethnic minorities and the physically and mentally challenged. It was a bottom-up process.

Subsequently, the term empowerment was increasingly used in the business world. Authority was often devolved to lower levels of management to help achieve business objectives. However, this was a top-down process. The practice spread to the public sector, partly as a means of devolving the difficult prioritization that was necessary when expectations outstripped available funds. Clearly though it may well be necessary to establish just what people mean when they use the term. For example does it involve the delegation of authority and freedom to commit resources and, if so, to what extent?

Empowerment in practice

Even if people are clear what they mean by the term empowerment it may be implemented poorly or applied in situations where it is inappropriate. Unfortunately, the term is often used very loosely or applied with a messianic zeal as though it were an end in itself, instead of a means of helping to achieve organizational objectives. It is not a concept that should be applied regardless of circumstances. The use of the term in a business context coincided with an increased pace of change because of globalization and the increasing use of new technology. This in turn has often led to down-sizing and de-layering. A related danger is that those seeking to apply it may ignore the potential for conflict between individual or sectional objectives and those of the rest of the organization. This could mean that the concept is applied in circumstances where it is unlikely to succeed. This is not to say that empowerment is doomed to failure but rather that if the motivational and creative energies that it may generate are to be realized it must be applied and implemented carefully.

Summary

Delegation has been defined as 'a person giving authority to someone to act on their behalf'. However, whilst authority can be delegated, as has been explained, the person who delegates remains accountable for the actions of the person to whom they delegate. Delegation frees up time for the manager to concentrate on the key aspects of their job. It can also be used as a means of developing subordinates. Key skills that have been identified include:

- The need to clarify the discretionary authority of subordinates
- Prioritization of work
- Routing work to the right people
- Establishing appropriate control mechanisms
- Selection and training of subordinates.

Initially, implementing delegation takes time, and so it is time-consuming. As with all investments, the potential rewards are not immediate but become evident in the future. The many obstacles to delegation have been examined. Some of them may be legitimate, such as a lack of staff. Unfortunately, the biggest obstacle to delegation can be the personal insecurity of some managers.

Delegation overlaps with the concept of empowerment. A key difference between the two concepts can be that delegation involves conferring authority on groups of people. However, the term is often used very loosely and it is often necessary to find out exactly what people mean when they use it. It is also necessary to recognize the potential for conflict between empowered groups or individuals and overall organizational objectives.

Self-assessment questions

1. How would you define delegation?
2. Why is delegation a core management skill?
3. How would you decide whether a particular task should be delegated or not?
4. What are the key skills associated with delegation?

5. What are the main obstacles in practice to effective delegation?
6. Identify the differences between the concepts of delegation and empowerment.

Case study notes – Mission of Trouble

Learning outcomes:

- To enable students to see that they should not automatically handle work that is routed to them
- To identify training opportunities at work.

Although this appears to be a case study about discipline, and can be used as such (reference Chapter 13, particularly the concept of the **disciplinary pyramid**), the key issue is delegation. Many students, though, take the view that just because the matter has been brought to the attention of the head of the visa section the head must deal with it themselves. However, this ignores a fundamental question of delegation. The head should ask themselves 'whose job is it?' before getting directly involved. If the head takes over responsibility how is the person with supervisory responsibility going to learn how to handle such issues? Also what precedent would the head be setting in getting involved in apparently minor matters. The head needs to know why the SEO cannot handle it themselves, and if necessary, counsel the SEO about how to deal with the issue.

However, if a serious issue emerges, such as possible bribery for giving 'fast track' treatment, the head would need to get involved.

References

Brown, Wilfred (1965), *Exploration in Management*, Pelican.
McLean, Ian. (1999), *Heartless bully who added to the agony of Aberfan*, The *Observer*, 5 January, p. 23.
Smith, Dame Janet (2005), *The Sixth and Final Report*, 27 January, Published by the Shipman Inquiry.
The Times (2012), *Norway's police chief quits over handling of Breivik Case*, 17 August.
The Times (2013), *RBS executive will walk the Libor plank with £ 700,000*, 6 February.
The Times (2014a), *Trader who nearly razed Société Générale heads for prison*, 20 March.
The Times (2014b) *South Korea leader quits over cries of ferry families*, 28 April.

Motivation

6

Learning outcomes

By the end of this chapter you will be able to:

- Assess the reasons why people perform effectively or ineffectively at work
- Evaluate the assumptions people make about why others work and analyse your own assumptions
- Evaluate key motivational theories
- Evaluate the role that money plays in motivation
- Assess strategies for matching individual needs to workplace requirements
- Explain the link between job design and job performance
- Evaluate the motivational problems caused by market turbulence and job insecurity
- Develop strategies for identifying and handling work-related stress.

Case study

Market Reality

Stanley Mitchell is the overseas sales manager of a medium sized but expanding information technology based company. He has a chronic problem of retaining secretaries. He asks the Human Resources (HR) manager if he can upgrade his current secretary to personal assistant and give her a higher salary to prevent her from leaving. Stanley is a forceful and effective manager and something of a workaholic. His current secretary, Samantha, like the previous secretaries, is a graduate with a few years' experience elsewhere and has been with the company for two years.

The HR manager, Helen Richards, knows that Samantha is well paid compared with other secretaries and compared with the external market. She also knows that Samantha is capable and ambitious. From what Stanley has told her, Helen sees the proposed change in job title for Samantha as only a token change with little or no significant change in responsibility.

Question:

If you were Helen Richards how would you handle this situation?

Introduction

In this chapter the variety of reasons why people work are examined. It is important to consider the range of reasons because it is all too easy for incorrect assumptions to be made. If the diagnosis of reasons for poor performance is inappropriate, corrective action may be taken. Behavioural theories concerning motivation and the practical uses that can be made of these theories are considered. The potential impact of national culture on motivation is also covered. The motivational implications of job design are examined, as is the concept of **job distortion**. A key issue is the extent to which job demands and individual needs can be reconciled, particularly if national economies are experiencing little or no growth.

Increasing market turbulence is causing some employers to introduce flexible employment policies. Whilst this can have advantages for employees, it can also cause a reduction in employer commitment whilst expecting an increase in employee commitment. The accelerating pace of change may be one factor causing increasing stress at work, including reduced job security. Managers need to protect both themselves and their subordinates from undue stress. Whilst some attention is given to the role of money as a motivator, it is considered in more detail in Chapter 7. The further related issues of selection and training are dealt with in Chapters 9 and 11.

Work performance

Maximizing work performance can be defined as 'providing the right conditions for people to work effectively'. One aspect of maximizing work performance will involve motivation. Motivation overlaps with the concept of morale, which is a measure of the extent to which employees feel positively or negatively about their work. While levels of performance and morale are usually positively correlated this is not always the case. There can be cases of people performing well under authoritarian but competent managers, perhaps out of fear, but who feel badly about their work. Similarly you can have instances of people doing as they please and enjoying it but not meeting organizational objectives. Ideally what is needed is a good match between the person and the demands of the job. Also, what most people may want is to have a comfortable amount of challenge, a good boss, good pay and security. Unfortunately, this is not always possible. However, often a better match is possible between individual needs and organizational requirements than is actually achieved.

Diagnosis of reasons for poor performance

If people are not working effectively, or in some cases not working at all, it may be the match between job and person that needs to be examined, not just one of those factors. Some people may never work effectively under any circumstances. Some jobs will always pose motivational problems whoever is supposed to be doing them. However, it is also likely that there are circumstances under which most people will work effectively, just as there are circumstances under which the same people will not work effectively. If there is a problem of ineffective performance it is necessary to establish if it is the person, the job or the matching of the two. Remedial action depends on the diagnosis. It may be that, in the short term, neither can be changed. If that is so, attention will need to be paid to either the type of person selected in the future or the job structure, or both, according to the diagnosis of the reasons for poor performance.

The need for accurate diagnosis has been stressed because it is all too easy for the diagnosis of reasons for poor performance to be faulty. It is a subjective area. The very criteria for judging effective work performance may be difficult to establish, as was demonstrated in the section on the definition of work objectives in Chapter 2. It can be vital to analyze situations in role and not personality terms, as was explained in Chapter 3. If the blame is put on the person working ineffectively, then that absolves the boss, who may then fail to see the connection if the next person in the job also performs badly.

Whilst in some cases the fault will be with the person doing the job, it is important not to automatically assume that this is the case. When the fault is not with the job-holder, there may be uncomfortable implications for the boss. The onus may then be on them to examine the job structure or the support given to the job-holder.

The following checklist may be useful in establishing the reasons for poor performance:

- Job design
- Work organization: this can cover a wide range of factors, including lack of appropriate equipment, shortage of raw materials, poor work flow, inadequate support and incompetent management
- Selection: it may be necessary to examine the match between people's abilities and needs with job requirements
- Training: this may be inadequate

■ Expectations: the expectations of both employer and employee may need reviewing and also the extent to which promises have been kept
■ Pay.

Assumptions about why people work

Alternative sets of assumptions that managers may have about why people work were identified in Chapter 4 in the explanation of Douglas McGregor's (1969) concepts of Theory X and Theory Y. The implicit assumptions that managers make, however, may or may not be accurate or appropriate in relation to particular situations. As well as not necessarily knowing why other people work, managers may generalize on the basis of bad experiences with particular individuals which may not even be very representative of the individuals concerned. The faulty generalizations made by managers can result in them either assuming the worst of their employees or assuming that work is being done properly when more direction and control is actually needed.

Checking one's own assumptions

To check your assumptions about why people work, complete the following questionnaire:

Rank the reasons why you think staff who work, or have worked, for you actually do work. If that is not possible, choose another group of people whom you know. You may need to do some averaging to choose your rankings:

Reasons why people work

■ Chance to use initiative at work
■ Good working conditions
■ Good working companions
■ Good boss
■ Steady, safe employment
■ Money
■ Good hours
■ Interest in the work itself
■ Opportunity for advancement
■ Getting credit and recognition.

When you have ranked the above reasons redo the exercise, but this time identify the reasons why *you* work, also ranked in order of importance. When you have done this, compare the two rankings.

What usually happens is that managers rank three factors more highly for themselves than for their staff. The three factors that managers rank highly for themselves are: 1) the chance to use initiative at work, 2) interest in the work itself, and 3) the opportunity for advancement. What also usually happens is that managers rank three different factors more highly for their staff than for themselves. These are: 1) money, 2) steady, safe employment, and 3) security. It may be that your responses do not conform to this general pattern. Even if they do, this may be for perfectly valid reasons. When managers examine their own reasons for working they are in a position to make informed judgements because of their self-knowledge. They may not make similarly informed judgements when they consider why other people work, and consequently they may make uncharitable assumptions about the reasons for others working or not working.

Even if your assumptions are accurate, other managers may make inaccurate assumptions, and this may affect organizational motivational strategies. Sometimes, however, managers may make the reverse mistake. This can easily happen in small businesses. Proprietors may almost completely identify with their business and assume that their employees do, or should do, the same. The point may be missed that whilst the proprietor may make many sacrifices for the business, it is also the proprietor who will reap most of the financial and psychological rewards if the business prospers. It is also necessary to take into account the concept of **job instrumentality**. This can involve employers or employees carefully calculating the least they need to do to secure their objectives and then behaving accordingly.

Managerial strategies

It may be possible to classify managerial strategies for motivation into one of the four following categories:

1. Coercion
2. Calculated compliance
3. Co-operation: this is likely to include a problem-solving approach and some involvement in decision-making
4. Commitment: this can overlap substantially with a co-operative strategy.

Which strategy is used will depend on managerial assumptions about why people work, organizational circumstances or a combination of both.

Theories of motivation

It is necessary to have an understanding of some of the more important theories relating to motivation. Although the theories that will be examined are not particularly new, nor beyond methodological criticism, they are important and do have relevance to current problems and initiatives.

Maslow

Abraham Maslow (1970) provides a very useful theory for examining individual motivation. He suggests that individual needs are arranged in a hierarchy. The lower-level needs must be satisfied before people concern themselves with higher-level needs. Hunger is seen as a basic need, even more important than the safety. When one need is met, people then try and meet their next need. The third level of needs is social, followed by status. The highest level of need is self-actualization, which involves self-development by successfully responding to challenges. It is the next level to be satisfied that acts as a motivator, like a carrot being held in front of a donkey. If threats emerge to a lower-level need that has previously been satisfied, individuals will refocus their activity to protect the lower-level need.

The actual pattern of needs will vary from person to person. There may be trade-offs between meeting needs at different levels. For example, some people may be prepared to take some risks with their safety in order to meet higher-levels needs, such as self-actualization. The level of need can vary from person to person, for example the amount of status satisfaction that is desired. Also, needs are likely to vary over time and according to situational requirements. A person with considerable domestic commitments may not be too concerned with self-actualization in their job. However, if their domestic commitments are met, they may then wish to achieve self-actualization and to accept greater work responsibilities in an attempt to meet that need. According to McClelland (1961), the need to self-actualize may critically depend on social conditioning during childhood.

Despite the qualifications inherent in Maslow's hierarchy, his ideas lend themselves to practical application. It can help to see that people's needs are matched to job requirements. Ways in which this can be done are job design, selection, training and promotion.

Herzberg

The work of Frederick Herzberg (1960) complements that of Maslow. He conducted research into the motivational factors affecting engineers and accountants working in the USA. Herzberg grouped the responses into the factors that caused dissatisfaction. The factors that were found most likely to cause negative feelings (dissatisfiers) were generally claimed to be external to the job. These are:

■ Company policy and administration
■ Supervision
■ Interpersonal relations
■ Status
■ Salary
■ Security
■ Impact of the job on personal life.

In contrast, the factors most likely to cause positive feelings about the job (satisfiers) were intrinsic to the job. These are:

- Sense of achievement
- Recognition of achievement
- Responsibility
- Advancement
- Interesting work
- Possibility of growth.

The absence of dissatisfiers is not enough to cause positive satisfaction. These tend only to operate in a negative way. For example, if office facilities are poor, that could cause strong negative feelings about the job. If the facilities were improved, that could remove a cause of irritation but would not normally be enough to cause positive feelings about the job. Herzberg termed the potential dissatisfiers 'hygiene factors', related to the context in which a job was done. He argued that it is important to pay attention to these issues, but the opportunity for a measure of self-actualization generally needs to be built into the content of a job if positive feelings are to be created. These 'motivators' require people to have the opportunity to be stretched in their jobs, through overcoming challenges. However, if the challenges are too high, this could cause negative feelings because of failure. Also, there is the danger that challenges that are too demanding may interfere with domestic life.

The opportunity for success or failure can arise out of the same set of circumstances, and the dividing line between the two can be very thin.

EXAMPLE: The thin line between success and failure

The Indonesian captain of an oil tanker said that his most positive feelings about his job came when he had successfully and very skilfully navigated his ship through a typhoon off Hong King when many ships had been sunk. His most negative feelings about the job were experienced shortly afterwards when the ship's agent came on board and carefully checked all the damage but neglected to enquire or comment about the risks that had been experienced by the captain and his crew.

The role of money, according to Herzberg, is that it is primarily a hygiene factor. Inadequate salary could generate strong negative feelings and cause a person to leave their job. However, a good salary was found not generally to lead to strong positive feelings about a job. Paying people more money won't increase performance if organizational obstacles prevent them working more effectively. Also, there is a danger that paying people more money will increase frustration levels by increasing the difference between ability levels and job demands. This issue is examined further in the section on job design later in this chapter. Account needs to be taken of variations in people's desire for money, their circumstances and the fact that some jobs may lend themselves to, or require, financial inducements more than others.

The practical implications of Herzberg's work are considerable. The basic message is: don't ignore the hygiene factors but don't stop there. People may want considerable involvement in their job for their own self-development. Employers may find that this is a source of considerable energy that is available. Conversely, underutilized employees may engage in potentially destructive activity.

EXAMPLE: The devil finds work for idle hands

Two South Wales police officers felt obliged to resign after competing to see who could drive the furthest away from their base during a shift. Two other officers, part of a group known as 'the seaside five', were fined 13 days loss of pay. The fifth officer left for unrelated reasons. The trips made included visits over 30 miles from their base. These activities apparently came to light when a patrol car broke down in England outside the police area (*Western Mail*, 2008).

It is necessary to be cautious in generalizing about the relevance of Herzberg's work. There have been methodological criticisms of it, particularly because of his reliance on the critical incident technique, which only established the highs and lows in the attitudes of employees to their jobs. Also his research was conducted some time ago and only with professional-level employees working in the USA. Furthermore, not everyone wants to, or is able to, concentrate on meeting the higher-level need of self-actualization. This can be for a number of reasons, including preoccupation with meeting lower-level needs. National culture can also be important, and the potential importance of this factor is examined in greater detail later in this chapter.

Herzberg's work, however, can provide a very useful framework for trying to match individual needs to job requirements. The distinction between intrinsic job factors relating to the job content, which can cause positive satisfaction, and external factors relating to the job context, which can cause negative job attitudes, is important and can be put to practical effect.

If people want the opportunity for self-development, the most important thing for managers to do may be to set up their work so that it provides a challenge, then help see that challenge is met. Excessive help may be counterproductive. The main pay-off with human relations skills may be to avoid unnecessarily upsetting employees. The control of the manager over work content will vary, but it is something that usually demands close attention. It may be one of the few important factors that managers can influence. Factors such as organization policy, pay and working conditions may be outside the manager's control. One of the problems for a prospective employee is that it is much easier to judge job context – for example salary, fringe benefits and working conditions – rather than more elusive factors such as independence within the job. Consequently, recruits may only find out after they have started a job whether it really has positive motivational features or not.

Expectancy theories

Another perspective that needs to be integrated with the previously explained theories is that provided by the expectancy school of motivational theorists. The expectancy approach attempts to overcome one of the criticisms of other motivational theories by accounting for individual differences. The general thrust of this approach is to examine whether or not whether incentives are in line with employee expectations.

It follows that it is necessary to check whether the reward system in an organization actually works in the way that it is intended to work. It is no good, for example, expecting to motivate people by offering incremental salary increases or promotion on the basis of merit if the reality is that such rewards are based on seniority or some other factor not connected with merit. Employees are likely to make judgements about what reward system really operates by what they believe is actually happening, rather than by statements of organizational policy. Even if rewards are based significantly on merit it is necessary to convince people of that, as motivation is likely to depend on what people perceive to be happening. It is also necessary to review how equitably rewards are distributed. Even if people are inclined to respond to a particular incentive, they may be discouraged from doing so by perceived unfairness in the way in which rewards are distributed. The relationships between the rewards given to different people may therefore need to be examined, as well as the size of the rewards. The gap between intended and actual reward systems can be alarmingly high. As is explained in the next chapter, some reward systems can degenerate into arrangements for restricting rather than increasing performance.

Impact of national culture

When considering theories of motivation and seeking to improve employee motivation via reward structures or redesigned jobs, the potential impact of national culture needs to be taken into account. Most theories of motivation are based on experience in the United States. These theories are usually based on the assumption that employees have the same values as those in American society – high levels of individualism, low power distances, relatively high masculinity and a consequent emphasis on material values. Using Hofstede's (2001) terminology, those working in an individualist culture may value opportunities for individual promotion and growth, while more collectivist cultures value opportunities to belong to an influential group. Employees in collectivist cultures may not be highly motivated by reward systems based on individual effort which undermine the importance of the group. In western societies there is also much more opportunity for self-actualization than in developing countries where, for those struggling for survival, concepts such as self-actualization may be meaningless. Mead and Andrews (2009) point out that as national cultures change, due perhaps to economic development, so value systems may alter. They give the example of changes in Chinese society where it has become apparent that it is acceptable to make money for one's own gratification rather than just in the service of society.

Job design

One of the major implications of the theoretical perspectives discussed in this chapter, particularly Herzberg's, is that considerable attention needs to be given to human needs in job design. The tradition set by the advocates of scientific management such as F. W. Taylor was, however, to simplify work as much as possible. This enabled employees to be selected and trained to undertake repetitive tasks. This approach later became known as **Fordism**. It did, though, ignore factors such as boredom and social needs. The Hawthorne experiments of 1927–1932 demonstrated that social factors could play an important part in motivating employees to achieve high performance. Later approaches are taken into account in the rest of this chapter, particularly the need to reconcile individual needs with job demands to the extent that such reconciliation is possible.

Ergonomics

Ergonomics involves looking at the job and person in relation to one another as a combined unit. This is in contrast to designing a job and then expecting to find someone who will be both willing and able to adapt to its requirements.

EXAMPLE: Making the worker fit the job

Procrustes was a legendary figure in Greek mythology who had a special bed. He was obsessive about guests fitting his bed exactly. If they were too long for the bed, he cut off their feet; if they were too small, he stretched them on a rack until they fitted. Allegedly the Procrustean approach was used in the engineering industry in the design of some capstan lathe machines. This was because some were best operated by people who were 4 feet 6 inches (1.35m) in height but with the arm span of a gorilla!

The use of the concept of ergonomics can be particularly important in the design of capital equipment so that, for example, instrument panels and other signals are arranged so as to minimize the risk of misreading. It can also be of vital importance in the design of high-performance military equipment. Good design can make all the difference in the achievement or non-achievement of objectives. It can also mean the difference between life and death for the personnel using the equipment on operational or even training missions.

Socio-technical systems

This topic is given some attention in Chapter 3 in the context of organizational design but needs further consideration in the context of motivation. Organizations, as well as consisting of technical systems, also have social structures. Social structures and technical systems overlap and interact to produce socio-technical systems. These can have a positive or negative impact on work performance. It is particularly important to take into account the impact of changes in work arrangements on social structures. This issue is a key topic in the case study The New Broom at the start of Chapter 4.

Marketing of jobs

A further key concept to apply to job design is that of marketing. Companies would soon get into financial difficulties if they designed products without regard for customer needs. Similarly with jobs, it is necessary to consider who would want to do them, or how anyone would do them well. If jobs are particularly boring, for example, there may be problems in recruiting, motivating and retaining staff. Options may be to consider if jobs can either be made less boring or be automated out of existence. Jobs also need to have internal coherence and viability. They need to be assessed as a whole and the questions asked as to who would be able to and want to do such a job. Consideration may also need to be given to how long a job will stay in its present form. If it is likely to change significantly, that may affect the required range of skills and adaptability of applicants. The problem of contradictory job demands also needs to be taken into account. This issue is considered in detail in the next section.

Basic job structure

Basic issues in job design include the range of skills required and the compatibility of the tasks. Many jobs contain a large element of routine activity but some demanding work as well. This is true in jobs as diverse as those of skilled manual workers and general medical practitioners. This process is illustrated in Figure 6.1.

A motivational problem for jobs that have a large element of routine work and a small amount of complicated work is that the capable person

Figure 6.1   The skill pyramid

may get bored with the routine work. It may also be unnecessarily expensive in terms of their salary level. The capable person may also spend too much time on the work they find interesting. Conversely, the person who finds the routine work satisfying may not be very good at the complicated work. Unfortunately, some jobs need to be designed like this for safety reasons. Airline pilots, for example, have to be able to cope with emergencies that it is hoped will never happen. A way of reducing the boredom in skilled jobs can be to hive off aspects of the work so that auxiliary staff can undertake them under proper supervision. Examples of this are the use of practice nurses in general medical practices and dental hygienists in dental surgeries.

A related concept is that of skill mix. This involves comparing the skills actually needed to perform a job and those that job-holders actually have. There needs to be an accurate match so that people on the one hand have the skills to do their jobs, but on the other hand are not performing work that could more cheaply and more satisfyingly be performed by others.

Job distortion

Job distortion can occur when a job is rearranged in a way that satisfies the needs of the organization but not the individual. If, for example, a graduate is recruited to perform routine clerical work initially they may be glad to have the job. However, the graduate may rapidly get bored because of the lack of intellectual stimulation. They may then expand the more interesting parts of the job and ignore the less demanding parts. The greater the gap between the demands of the job and the ability level of the job-holder, the more the

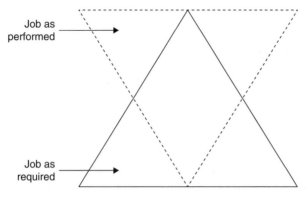

Job as performed

Job as required

Figure 6.2   Job distortion

temptation to try and alter the job. This process is illustrated in Figure 6.2. The continuous lines represent the boundaries of the job that the organization requires to be performed, whilst the broken lines represent the boundaries of the job as it actually is performed.

Another pressure which can create job distortion can be the frustration of a person who considers that they should have a job within the same organization but which is more in line with their ability level. This can particularly happen if a person feels that they have outgrown their job.

EXAMPLE: Too many cooks

Some of the directors in an organization involved with the distribution of public grants were concerned about the lack of career opportunities for capable secretaries. It was proposed to upgrade some of them to positions as personal assistants (PAs) to the directors. Juniors were to be recruited to undertake the more routine aspects of their work. However, it emerged that there was not enough of the more demanding work to justify the PA's having full-time junior assistants. The real solution was to encourage the more capable secretaries to undertake specialist or professional training so that they could apply for genuinely more demanding jobs, either in the same organization or elsewhere.

Job enlargement, job rotation and job enrichment

Job enlargement

Job enlargement is a generic term used to indicate an increase in the number of tasks within a job. This can be achieved by increasing the range of activities, increasing the responsibility level or both. Job rotation and job enrichment can be aspects of job enlargement.

Job rotation

Job rotation involves a horizontal broadening of the job without increasing the level of responsibility. It can be useful in reducing the monotony factor. One example is the rotation of staff working at leisure centres who may move from supervising one sporting activity to another every few hours. A potential disadvantage is this being disruptive of social relationships at work. Also, it does not make jobs inherently more interesting.

Job enrichment

Job enrichment involves a vertical increase in the level of responsibility within a job. Sometimes this can be accomplished informally, for example by a manager delegating more. The practice of having someone act up whilst the boss is away is an example of a temporary form of job enrichment. The ability of managers to delegate varies considerably and this factor is likely to influence the motivation and development of subordinates significantly. The concept of delegation was examined in detail in Chapter 5.

Pay

Sometimes employers respond to the problems of retaining staff to do boring work by increasing their pay. However, a danger of doing this is that the employer then attracts even more able staff who get even more bored with the job even more quickly. This can also happen when employees use their bargaining strength to force up their wages.

EXAMPLE: How bargaining power can increase boredom

Train drivers in the UK are well paid. They are one of the few groups of workers who still have considerable industrial power. This is because of the damage they can inflict by interrupting or closing down train services. However, as signalling systems develop and an increasing number of fail-safe systems are introduced, the job may become less demanding. This can significantly increase job boredom. This is because of the increasing gap between the abilities of the job-holders and the demands placed upon them.

Vulnerability and stress

Corporate involvement and corporate loyalty

Increasing emphasis has been placed by some organizations (and writers) on treating the workforce as a valuable asset whose potential should be fully exploited rather than simply seen as a cost. This idea is in line with the concepts of intellectual capital and knowledge management covered in Chapter 3.

Such initiatives may be reinforced by the social pressures that may be deliberately engineered by employers to obtain compliance with, and commitment to, organizational goals. The concept of the quality of working life is also relevant here. The treatment of the workforce as a valuable asset has the broad aim of bringing together and satisfying both the goals and development of organizations and the needs and development of all their employees. It emphasizes the need to release human potential – which is all the more important given the economic pressures on organizations and rising educational standards within workforces. However, these aspirations may conflict with increasing economic constraints in many organizations and a general lack of growth in many western economies.

The psychological contract

The concept of the **psychological contract** reflects the day-to-day behaviour that management and employees expect from one another. Research shows that where employees believe that management has broken promises or failed to deliver on certain commitments then this has a negative impact on job satisfaction and commitment and, therefore, on the state of the psychological contract (Marchington et al., 2001). Once employees regard this contract as broken it can be difficult to repair it.

Impact on corporate morale

Given the pressures that there are, well intentioned and otherwise, to increase organizational commitment, it is important to recognize the pressures that there are for employees to set limits on their organizational commitment, or even reduce it. A major complication is that the increased psychological commitment by the workforce may be expected at a time when organizations have reduced their commitment to their employees in ways that will now be discussed. The reduced commitment may emerge because of greater competition and reduced funding. It may be expressed by reduced employment security and developments such as the flexible organization (as explained in Chapter 3). A related issue in times of low or no growth is that many people may be obliged to take job that they feel are below their ability level, or remain in jobs they may have outgrown. Unfortunately this can increase the risk of job distortion.

Social trends, including changes in the role of women both in the family and in society generally, also have an impact on the work relationship. The custom of family commitments needing to be subordinated to the primary aim of promoting the career of the man in the home has long been under challenge. In many developed economies the size of the female workforce is approaching half of the total workforce. The pattern of female careers is also changing – women are tending to have children later and to have shorter maternity leave. The growing number of dual-career couples also imposes constraints upon both partners and lessens the dependency on the primary income. In addition a significant number of employees are single parents. However, rising property prices, repayment of student loans and the need for increased pension contributions can force staff to earn whatever they can to meet a scale of liabilities that their parents did not have to meet.

Having explained the constraints that may exist with regard to attempts to improve employee involvement and develop corporate loyalty, it would be foolish to suggest that all attempts are doomed to failure. It is more logical to argue that, given the organizational turbulence that is often inevitable, it is even more important to consider how to try and get the best out of the workforce despite the difficulties. This is more likely to be done effectively if the nature of the difficulties is clearly recognized. It is necessary to consider the human dimension at the time that organizations are being restructured and to build in the direct and intangible costs of change before decisions are finalized. It is also important to have positive and integrated human resource strategies, and the nature of these is considered in Chapter 11 (in relation to training). These developments more than ever increase the importance of competent management.

Stress

The general points have been made that organizations tend to under-utilize and under-involve the human resources available to them but that there is an increasing recognition of the need to correct this. The point has also been made that a variety of factors are causing an increasing number of employees to try and set limits to their work involvement. Consequently, it is probably appropriate for both organizations and employees to consider the optimum level of involvement. This may be particularly necessary given the increasing potential intrusion of work into the home because of developments in information technology. Individuals may need to look carefully at their work in relation to their general lifestyle and periodically conduct an audit on their work-life balance. Whilst the emphasis in the literature on motivation is on under-involvement, over-involvement may present risks for the employer as well as the employee. The dangers of workaholism may include problems of employee replacement, damage to health and the loss of a sense of perspective and good judgement that comes from having other interests as a counterbalance. Workaholics may also seek to establish themselves as role models when they are really self-indulging or engaging in compensatory behaviour.

There is a distinction between pressure and stress. Some managers enjoy high levels of pressure and may perform more effectively when they are put under a certain amount of pressure. The pressure may relate to the volume or responsibility level of work or both. Other managers may react in a different way, and their inability to cope with pressure may result in stress. One could therefore define managerial stress as a symptom of being unable to cope with the workload. Unfortunately, this can precipitate a counter-productive chain reaction with those managers experiencing stress amplifying and transmitting it to those in their immediate circle. Unfortunately some managers may have a habit of amplifying stress when it would be more productive for them to act as **shock absorbers** and within reason protect their employees from some of the pressures and stress they themselves are experiencing.

Stress may be caused by the problems inherent in a particular job, the mismatch between the abilities of an individual and the requirements of a job, or a combination of the two. It is important to diagnose the causes of stress in particular situations because it is only when that is done that one can work out whether the appropriate remedy is to change an individual's behaviour, the pressures they are put under, or both.

It is also important to recognize that work stress is probably on the increase. This is because of the increasing impact of key factors which generate stress. These factors include the rate of change, pressures for cost-effective performance and job insecurity generated by change.

Managers also have responsibility for monitoring the stress under which subordinates are placed. There is also likely to be an increasing need to ensure that managerial styles do not degenerate into harassment and bullying. This is because of rising expectations of the legal duty of care owed by employers to employees (ACAS, 2007).

Whether managers are being submitted or submitting themselves to too much pressure or experiencing stress, the consequent work style may generate an excessive flow of adrenalin within the body. Dependence on physical stimulants such as nicotine and alcohol can prevent an individual from having an appropriate diet and sufficient physical exercise and rest. If the stress is self-induced, it is perhaps just as well to face up to the medical implications in case there is any scope for personal adjustment. There is also the potential benefit that if stress is reduced for oneself, it may also be reduced for those around you.

Doctors and stress consultants may be able to measure stress and advise on how the symptoms are treated, for example by relaxation techniques. However, managerial skills are likely to be needed to deal with the basic causes of managerial stress. The aim of this book is to do just that, by helping managers to define their role and develop the key skills to carry it out effectively.

Summary

The difference between motivation and morale and the wide variety of causes of under-performance have been explained. For effective action to be taken to improve performance, it is necessary to accurately diagnose the reasons for underperformance. If this is not done, corrective action may be ineffective or even counterproductive. One of the mistakes that can be made is for managers to make wrong assumptions about why their subordinates work. Even if there is a problem of low motivation among employees, it is necessary to consider what can be done to improve it. Relevant theories have been examined, particularly the work of Maslow, Herzberg and expectancy theory. According to Herzberg, money is an important hygiene factor but not necessarily an important positive motivator. However, some care has to be taken in generalizing on the basis of Herzberg's research. The impact of national culture on motivation was also considered.

It is important to try and match individual needs and job demands as far as is practicable. This is an issue that needs to be considered when jobs are designed and marketed. One of the consequences of not doing this can be job distortion. Market turbulence and trends towards flexible employment policies can generate job insecurity and this may conflict with employer demands for greater employee commitment. Such factors can also increase the amount of job-related stress. Social trends also often aggravate the conflict between work and domestic commitments. The judgement, effectiveness and health of managers will be at risk if they experience too much stress. They also have a responsibility to see that their employees are not subjected to unreasonable amounts of stress. The development of managerial skills such as prioritization can be an effective way of dealing with the causes of stress. The issue of financial reward is considered further in Chapter 7, which is devoted to that topic.

Self-assessment questions

1. Think of a group of workers you judge to be performing poorly. Identify the reasons for their poor performance.
2. Using the same group as you have used in answer to the first question, what assumptions have you made about why these people work? How accurate are they?
3. Explain any one theory of motivation.
4. What do you believe is the role of money in motivating people?
5. How can a good match be made between individual needs and job demands?
6. Why is it important to take human needs into account when designing jobs?
7. Examine the potential for conflict between employers wishing to increase managerial commitment and managers wishing to redress their work-life balance.
8. How can you try to reduce or avoid work-related stress both for yourself and for others?

Case study notes – Market Reality

Learning outcomes:

- To identify the limitations of pay in motivating staff and explore options in dealing with basic motivational problems
- To anticipate the potential repercussive effects of employee concessions.

The easy thing for Helen Richards to do would be to find a reason for granting the up-grading. However, this could create more problems than it solves. The first problem could be the repercussive claims for upgrading by other secretaries, supported by their bosses. Also, it may not solve the basic problem – Samantha may have outgrown her job and may need to move on. At present she may well be caught in the 'secretary trap' of having no obvious career path. She may need to consider whether she has, or can acquire, sufficient technical skills to aim for a job in line management with the company. An alternative could be to undertake professional training as a route into management. Such options could help develop a career path for Samantha and provide an opportunity for her to develop and improve her motivation rather than do more of the same. This may well not be to Stanley's liking but it may well be in Samantha's interests and would not undermine the pay structure. A problem that can arise in situations such as these is that a few extra responsibilities are given to the secretary who may be less motivated to undertake the routine work that still needs doing. This may fall under the heading of job distortion.

References

NB: Works of particular interest are marked with an asterisk.

Advisory, Conciliation and Arbitration Service [ACAS] (2007) *Bullying and harassment at work – a guide for employees*, London: ACAS. Available at: http://www.acas.org.uk/media/pdf/o/c/Bullying-and-harassment-at-work-a-guide-for-employees.pdf [accessed 9 November, 2014].

Herzberg, Frederick, Bernard Mausner and Barbara Bloch Snyderman (1960), *The Motivation to Work*, Wiley.

Hofstede, G. (2001), *Culture's Consequences*, 2nd ed., Sage.

Marchington, Mick, Adrian Wilkinson and Paul Ackers (2001), *Management Choice and Employee Voice*, Research report, London: CIPD.

Maslow, Abraham Maslow (1970), *Motivation and Personality*, 2nd ed., Harper and Row.

McClelland, David C. (1961), *The Achieving Society*, Van Nostrand.

McGregor, Douglas (1969), *The Human Side of Enterprise*, McGraw-Hill.

*Mead, Richard and Tim G. Andrews (2009), *International Management*, Blackwell.
    A first rate and comprehensive account of how national culture can shape management practice.

Western Mail (2008), *Police officers resign after 'trip to seaside'*, 28 February. [Available at: http://www.thefreelibrary.com/Police+officers+resign+after+%27trip+to+seaside%27.-a0175519337 [accessed 9th November, 2014].

Taking it further

Sheldrake, John (1996), Management Theory from Taylorism to Japanization in *Elton Mayo and the Hawthorne Experiments*, International Thomson Business Press.

Reward

7

Case study

Southern Beers

Southern Beers is an old established brewery company. At one of its plants production workers are given an incentive bonus on top of their basic pay. The bonus formula is very simple – the output of beer each week is divided by the number of production workers. The formula was agreed with the local trade union. The size of the bonus has gradually increased, particularly because of a number of minor improvements in production methods, which have resulted in an increase in the quantities of beer produced. Recently there has been a new development affecting the size of the weekly bonus and that is the reduction in the amount of bottled beer production. Bottled beer production is more labour intensive than beer in barrels. As the employee bonus is calculated according to the total beer production divided by the number of employees involved in its production the bonus goes up even if production stays the same but the number of employees is lower. Local management had initially ignored this but the impact of a reduction in staffing levels had the effect of increasing the weekly bonus by 10%. Now the remaining bottled beer production is to be transferred to another brewery in the group so the size of the bonus based on the old formula will increase by a further 10%. This has caused local management to unilaterally change the bonus formula so that the production workers do not get this further 10% increase in their bonus. Management's reason for doing this is because there has been no change in production methods for those engaged on barrel beer production and the workers formerly engaged on bottled beer production have either left, retired or been redeployed. Without these bonus adjustments the weekly bonus pay would have been one-third of the basic wage. However, the local trade union has complained that this change is in breach of the original agreement between management and trade unions about the calculation of the bonus and is also in breach of the agreement they have with the company that changes in pay structures be the subject of negotiation.

Question:

How would you, as local brewery manager, handle this situation?

Introduction

Having considered the relevance of various behavioural theories of motivation in the previous chapter, it is now necessary to look more explicitly at pay structures. The main factors that do, or should, shape these structures are considered. The issue of internal relativities is examined, as is the way in which job evaluation may assist in establishing and maintaining a rational pay structure. The main types of job evaluation schemes are also explained with their potential advantages and disadvantages. Consideration is given to the European **equal pay** and **equal value** legislation which stipulates that employees should not suffer pay discrimination on the basis of sex.

The advantages and disadvantages of financial incentive schemes and profit-sharing arrangements are also considered. A related key issue is that of pensions, especially given the cost to organizations and the importance to individual employees.

The issue of individual merit pay, especially **performance related pay** (PRP) is deferred until Chapter 10 so that it can be considered in the context of appraisal.

Objectives of pay structures

Pay structures need careful consideration since, to be effective, they need to meet a number of different and sometimes conflicting objectives. The main objectives of pay structures are likely to be:

- Attracting, retaining and motivating employees who are competent in the jobs they are given

- Not paying over-generously, for reasons of cost.
- Establishing internal relativities that minimize feelings of discontent about what other employees are getting.
- Establishing differentials that encourage appropriate employees to apply for promotion.
- Encouraging geographical and functional flexibility for employees where appropriate.
- Reflecting power realities in the organization so that the pay structure is not likely to be easily overturned by groups with strong bargaining power.
- Compliance with any relevant law, particularly European requirements with regard to equal pay and equal value.
- Establishing a structure that is manageable, adaptive and cost effective in administrative expense.
- Having a pay structure that motivates staff.

Trade-offs may be necessary when determining which objectives have higher priority. Pay structures need to be synchronized with other organizational processes such as budgetary control and human resource planning. Such integration is necessary if overall organizational objectives are to be achieved.

Labour market trends

It is appropriate to explain some key changes in the labour market. A general trend is for the range between the lowest paid and the highest paid to be increasing very significantly. Chronic and significant levels of unemployment for those with little skill have tended to depress their market value. Although in the UK statutory minimum pay provides at least some protection against this, it is often seen as a maximum as well as a minimum pay level. This has led to demands for a **living wage**, particularly in areas of relatively high employment and high housing costs. Immigration flows, particularly for example to wealthier countries within the EU, can also depress wages in those wealthier countries. The increase in the supply of labour to wealthier countries is particularly for jobs that do not require a high level of skill and comes from countries where pay is relatively lower. Globalization, including off-shoring, or the threat of such can also depress wage levels. Added to this, as explained in Chapter 3, employers have increasingly been seeing the advantages of having a flexible workforce, and particularly the advantages of **zero-hours contracts**. Consequently, many of the jobs on offer are often for part-time or even occasional work. At the other end of the range globalization can often have the effect of driving up pay for those with scarce skills who can operate in an international market. Added to this weak control by owners of an organization can lead to the **managerial capture** of an organization and lead to senior managers being paid more than the market rate would justify.

In considering the general level of pay, it may need to be increasingly necessary to beware of claims that rates of pay should be such that an organization attracts 'the best' candidates. The danger of this argument is that it can trigger a never-ending spiral of increasing pay rates. This is what has happened in parts of the financial services industry facilitated by the award of large bonuses. As explained in Chapter 3, this has not always increased real profitability but can push up wage costs to high levels with **knock-on effects** across to other areas. By definition not every employer can have 'the best' people and what is actually needed is people who are good enough to do specified jobs at pay rates that are sustainable.

Job evaluation

Job evaluation schemes can provide a useful framework for creating an effective pay structure by establishing a basis for the relationship between the various different types of job in an organization. The determination of wage and salary levels is a process that will take place after such relativities have been established. Job evaluation may also help with the process of salary surveys.

Job evaluation has historically been associated with the determination of administrative and professional pay structures in particular. However, occupational changes, the generally reduced bargaining power of trade unions and, in Europe, equal pay and equal value legislation have all been factors leading to the greater use of job evaluation schemes for manual workers as well.

Even if employees are paid well in comparison with those undertaking similar work in other organizations, there can often be considerable dissatisfaction about perceived internal inequities. Job evaluation can be particularly useful in reducing discontent about this. Even if individuals do not always agree with the results of job evaluation schemes, they may at least accept that the employer has tried to resolve pay issues in a fair and systematic way.

Types of schemes

The process of job evaluation is essentially a systematic way of making a series of judgements about relativities between jobs as a means of explaining pay differentials. In considering the different types of job evaluation schemes, particular attention is paid to important practical problems that are often overlooked in explanations of how schemes are supposed to work as opposed to the ways in which they may work in practice.

A basic distinction between the various types of schemes is between the non-analytical and the analytical ones. Important examples of non-analytical schemes are job classification and job ranking. A recent development has been to evaluate jobs in terms of competencies required or deployed by the person doing a job. This approach may be a factor in an analytical scheme or the basis of a complete scheme.

Non-analytical schemes

Job classification

Using the job classification technique, jobs are looked at as a whole and then grouped into families to which a grade is then allocated. Definitions are sometimes given of the basic characteristics of a classification or grade to help judge where particular jobs should go. Job classification can be a relatively cheap form of job evaluation to install. Job classification also facilitates flexibility in the allocation of tasks, particularly if the range of tasks within a job grade is wide.

Job ranking

Job ranking involves arranging jobs in a hierarchy, and the vertical rank order can be split up into various job grades. This can also be a relatively cheap form of job evaluation.

The basic feature of these non-analytical approaches is that the ultimate grading is achieved by comparison with other jobs rather than by systematically identifying the component elements in each job. Job ranking systems tend to be relatively cheap and easy to operate. However, it can be difficult to defend sex discrimination claims based on European-wide equal value legislation with a non-analytical scheme. This is because it can be argued that the overall judgements contain an element of sex discrimination. Equal pay and equal value legislation is explained later in this chapter.

Analytical schemes

The main analytical schemes, including many of the proprietary schemes offered by consultancy organizations, often involve points rating. A point-rating scheme involves identifying the common factors in jobs (or job demands) and then allocating points to these factors according to the specific demands in each job. An allocation of points, or weights, for each factor is established after systematic internal discussion about the relative importance of the factor to the organization. Each factor in a job is then assessed and a total points score for the job obtained. The total points score indicates what job grade is appropriate. Proprietary schemes are often sophisticated versions of this points rating approach.

The job competence approach

Organizations may use competencies as a basis for part, or even all, of a job evaluation scheme, particularly if **job competencies** are also used for selection and training. The job competence approach is analytical in terms of the processes adopted. It involves a detailed examination of the range and varying levels of skills that can be brought to bear in a job. The job competence approach compares with more traditional approaches where the focus of the evaluation is the job requirements. With job competencies the minimum competencies required in a person to do a job are specified but it is acknowledged that people may perform at a higher level than the minimum. This blurs the more traditional distinction usually made in job evaluation between assessing the needs of the job as opposed to the performance of the individual. The approach recognizes that some individuals can interpret and develop a job more productively than others. The level of competence displayed by a person doing a job can be used to determine the pay grade that they are given.

Choice of scheme

The dilemma for the individual employer is what, if any, scheme to adopt. No one scheme or approach is superior to all others; it is basically a question of choosing the most appropriate scheme for the situation and then operating the chosen scheme in a sensible manner. However refined and sophisticated schemes may appear to be, it must always be remembered that any statistical calculation is built on a basis of subjective judgements of, for example, what factors should be chosen and what weights they should be given. Consequently, one should beware of spurious accuracy and of claims that everything is near perfect because ratings are very consistent. Raters may be consistent in applying a scheme, but as schemes rest on subjective judgements this can lead to consistent error.

Key design factors

The following are the main factors that need to be borne in mind when designing a job evaluation scheme:

Coverage within the organization

Whilst it may seem convenient and fair to have one scheme for the whole of an organization, this is not always practicable. There can be so little in common between, for example, manual, technical and managerial grades that one may have to develop different schemes so that the jobs being compared and evaluated have a reasonable amount in common. There is not much point in having an overall scheme that seeks to assess a chief executive's job in terms of factors such as physical strength, monotony and boredom. However, a counterargument that has emerged in favour of schemes covering all employees is that it may help in defending cases brought under the equal value legislation where comparisons are made between different parts of an employer's pay structure.

Cost

The costs of installing and maintaining a scheme need to be considered. The more sophisticated the scheme, the greater such costs are likely to be.

Another critical cost is the uplift in pay that usually results from the introduction of a scheme. Job evaluation is unlikely to leave the existing pay structure undisturbed, and the holders of jobs that are downgraded normally have their own salary protected. Consequently, an immediate effect of job evaluation is that although no one gets less pay some will get more pay as a result of a scheme being introduced, so the total wage and salary bill will increase. A rule of thumb for major restructuring exercises is that such an uplift will be in the order of three per cent of the total wage bill. However, sometimes the introduction of a job evaluation scheme can get out of hand and the cost increase can be much greater than that.

Size of organization

The investment in a costly scheme for a small group of employees may simply be too great. Also it may be much easier to operate simpler schemes in small organizations because of the knowledge that people have about one another's jobs.

Rate of change

An important factor that often is ignored is the expected rate of change in an organization. Job evaluation schemes are usually introduced on the assumption that the organizational arrangements are fixed. However, the pace of change is such now that one has to evaluate how well schemes will cope with projected change. There is not much point in having an expensive and sophisticated scheme that is soon going to be out of date. This question also needs asking, in a slightly modified form, of existing schemes. It may be that existing schemes, which may historically have been sound, have become irrelevant through not being adjusted, or not being capable of adjustment, in line with organizational change.

EXAMPLE: Dangers of obsolescence

A comprehensive proprietary job evaluation scheme was installed at an engineering factory in London. Unfortunately it became obsolete within four months because of the rapidity of technical and organizational change.

Employee involvement

Trade unions are likely to take more than a passing interest in job evaluation and their involvement in schemes has to be considered. They are likely to see job evaluation as a framework for bargaining. In any case, regardless of whether there is a trade union or not, one needs to consider the issue of employee involvement. If schemes are supposed to incorporate internal views about equity and fairness there needs to be some mechanism for taking employees' views into account with regard to the design and operation of schemes.

If anyone ever did design a perfect system, representatives would still feel obliged to try and bargain about the matter, as what trade union could countenance being told that it had no bargaining role. Unions also often rightly query the basis on which schemes are built and the results they give. Unions may have to distance themselves a little from schemes, however, as otherwise they may seem to be implementing managerial policies. Once a scheme has been established, however, trade unions tend to acknowledge its existence, and use their role to represent anyone who feels that they have a case for upgrading.

Implementation and operation

Job versus person

One of the basic issues to remember is that normally it is the job and not the person that is being evaluated. If a job-holder has outgrown a job, the real answer is for them to be encouraged to seek promotion rather than to distort the pay structure by giving an upgrade that temporarily meets their needs but not the organization's. One must also beware of the danger, explained in the previous chapter, that employees may distort a job to justify an upgrade. In contrast, if a person is not up to a job, it can sometimes be because the job is not graded highly enough to attract people of the right quality.

Choice of factors

Factors in analytical schemes have to be chosen carefully so that they don't overlap. Otherwise a job-holder can benefit twice under such factors as job complexity and education required, which may be different ways of measuring the same requirement. Another complication can arise from the establishment of 'weights' for factors. Apart from the problems of making judgements anyway, there is the statistical problem that the real weights depend not just on, for example, the points allocated for a particular factor, but also on the extent to which those making judgements use the full extent of the scale.

Upgrading claims

There can be misconceptions about the extent to which employees can expect to have a salary increase in return for a change in their duties. Changes in the range of work at a given level do not normally constitute a case for upgrading. Work at a higher level of responsibility may provide a valid basis for upgrading, but even in this case it has to be remembered that job grades normally embrace a range of jobs and, for example, a person's increased responsibility level may not be sufficient to lift them into the next grade. There is a common law requirement for employees to accept reasonable changes in job content and the prudent employer will reinforce this by the use of generic job titles and a flexibility clause in any job description.

Claims for upgrading can also be made on what may turn out to be basic job requirements rather than additional demands. Schemes need to be operated on the basis that there are minimum performance requirements, which justify retention in a given job as opposed to justifying an upgrading.

Down-grading

An almost inevitable consequence of job evaluation is that some jobs will be downgraded. In certain circumstances it may transpire that a jobholder is being over paid in relation to the demands of the job. It may be considered invidious to downgrade the individual so their salary may be 'red-circled' that is to say protected, but other people being recruited into the same job will be paid at the job-evaluated rate. The red-circling may be for a limited amount of time. The pay of the individual might be frozen until the other employees doing similar work catch up to the same rate of pay; subsequently any pay increases can be awarded to all jobholders.

Appeals

Irrespective of whether there is employee involvement in the design of a scheme or not, some sort of appeals mechanism is necessary. Appeals criteria need to be specified, such as a change in duties, and appeals bodies established. These may be managerial panels, or joint management-union panels, or they may involve the use of an outside arbitrator – either sitting alone or chairing a joint panel.

The knock-on effect

A crucial issue in establishing the grading of any job is its effect on the overall equilibrium of the pay structure. Serious inequities obviously should be corrected, but not insubstantial cases for locating jobs in a higher grade. The key issue is not the extra direct costs this would involve but the knock-on effect. The danger is that by solving one person's perceived grievance you can create a host of repercussive claims.

External job market

Another key issue in evaluating jobs concerns the relationship of pay to the external job market. It is no good having pay levels that are out of line with the market. However, markets do not always operate so clearly and systematically that you can dispense with job evaluation. In making comparisons with pay in other organizations, care has to be taken to ensure that you are comparing like with like. The use of job titles alone may be dangerous – for example a title such as 'fitter' can cover a wide range of different jobs in terms of actual duties and responsibility level. Sometimes there can be a marked conflict between internal relativities and the market rate for particular groups for whom there is a strong demand.

The realistic answer in cases like this is not to have a spurious re-evaluation of the staff concerned, but to openly recognize and deal with the problem. It may be necessary to pay a market supplement for such staff or even take them out of the evaluation scheme altogether. This way at least the rest of the pay structure can remain consistent.

Equal pay

A further dimension of pay structures and job evaluation is the law regarding equal pay and pay for work of equal value. Employees in Europe have a broad right not to be discriminated against in terms of pay and conditions of employment on grounds of sex if their work is similar or of equal value to someone of the opposite sex in the same organization. This is a consequence in European Union (EU) member countries of governments being obliged to comply with the requirements of the Treaty of Rome and the Equal Pay Directive of 1975. The right to equal pay is for those engaged on similar or broadly similar work, or on work rated as equivalent under a job evaluation scheme. The right to claim pay of equal value, like the right to claim equal pay, excludes comparisons with employees of the same sex. Equal value claims are usually made by women rather than men, but claims could be made by men if they can argue that their work is valued less than that of female comparators.

The right to equal pay for work of equal value exists where the job demands are the same in categories such as 'effort, skill and decision-making'. This implies a need for some sort of analytical job evaluation if the employer is to try and defend their position. Employers need to be able to provide 'objective' justification for differences in pay between the sexes. If an individual claim succeeds, this may reveal that there is the basis for further claims and if any of these succeed the process may continue. The 'knock-on effect' can lead to the undermining of the whole of an existing pay structure.

For an employer to have a defensible case it may be necessary to review not just a pay structure but the processes by which pay rates and differentials are established. The implications of this for the operation of job evaluation schemes include ensuring that there is a fair cross-representation of any benchmark jobs and that there is adequate representation of both sexes on panels. If a points-rating scheme is used, it is necessary to ensure that the factors and weights used are not discriminatory. The scheme may be designed against a background where the internal 'felt fair' values of the organization represent, for example, those values traditionally associated with males and this may be in conflict with the legal requirement to avoid sex discrimination. Analytical job evaluation fairly applied will help avoid discrimination but not necessarily put a stop to argument. People sometimes think that the use of, for example, sophisticated statistical techniques enables scientifically objective decisions to be made about pay grades. However, what such techniques do is to provide an elaborate means of establishing systematic opinions about job relationships. The judgments about how dissimilar factors, or whole jobs, should relate to one another can be carried out systematically, but the judgments themselves are subjective. It is nevertheless such subjective judgments that may have to be offered as a defence in law and presented as an 'objective' justification for pay differences.

The case law arising out of equal value claims is proving to be a guide as to how the law operates in practice. Important issues have been decided by case law. Case law established in one country is binding on other member countries of the EU. The final judicial authority is the European Court of Justice. The extent to which equal pay and equal value legislation is actually implemented is likely to vary widely within the EU.

Employers have strong financial reasons for appealing against adverse judgements (as do trade unions). Consequently, it can be years before a case is decided. The lessons for employers include taking the basic steps already suggested to avoid obvious discrimination and hoping that they are not targeted for an important test case. If the pay structure is adjusted to take account of possible sex discrimination, the extra pay costs need to be taken into account when any general increase is considered.

Financial incentives

Probably the ideal arrangement for most jobs is that people have interesting work, enlightened supervision and an appropriate basic wage or salary. If the theories of Maslow and Herzberg mean anything at all, such arrangements should lead to effective work performance and satisfied employees. Unfortunately, the achievement of such a happy state of affairs is, needless to say, not always possible. When this cannot be achieved, financial incentives may be appropriate. However, it is most important for managers to ensure that their diagnosis of the reasons for underachievement is correct before they try to improve work performance by the use of financial incentives.

Diagnosis of poor performance

Problems of poor work performance may be due to factors outside the control of the employee. When it would seem that employees could increase output by reasonable increases in effort, it is necessary to ask why the effort is not forthcoming. The structure of jobs and the matching of individuals to jobs may need to be examined. If poor performance is because of poor supervision, it may be that it is the supervision that should be changed and not the arrangements for payment.

It is particularly necessary to examine the standard of supervision, as the long-term effect of incentive schemes can be to diminish the role of the supervisor. Employees operating under incentive schemes may see themselves akin to independent subcontractors, with the supervisor as an external figure who is likely to come into conflict with them over a range of issues concerning the operation of the incentive scheme. Unfortunately, such developments can lead to the continued erosion of first-line supervisors' authority to a point, sometimes, where they act as little more than a conduit for messages between management and the workforce.

Appropriate conditions for output-based schemes

If output based schemes are to be used they are likely to need to meet the following prerequisites:

- The work can be measured and directly attributed to the individual or group; in practice this generally means highly repetitive manual work, as found in mass-production manufacturing
- The pace of work is substantially controlled by the worker rather than by the machine or process they are tending
- Management is capable of maintaining a steady flow of work
- The tasks are not subjected to frequent changes in method, materials or equipment.

Even if the above conditions apply and there is proper monitoring, schemes may become 'slack' because of the cumulative effect of minor production improvements.

A variation on output-based schemes is to pay people commission on sales made. The advantages of this can be that, as is usual in output based schemes, there is an incentive for people to persevere with repetitive work, and the financing of commission by extra sales revenue and sales may be easily measured. However, there can be other factors affecting sales, such as market conditions, and the level of sales commission paid can distort pay structures. In addition it can be difficult at times to identify individual as opposed to group or organizational contribution to sales. Another important issue is the impact of individual incentive schemes on teamwork. The dangers of individual effort having a disruptive impact on teamwork are considered in the final chapter in the section on team building.

Long-term effects

Proposals for introducing incentive schemes and their benefits can seem very convincing. However, managers need to review carefully their diagnosis of

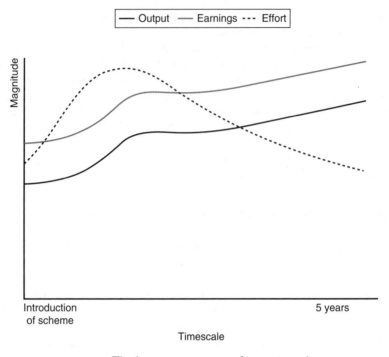

Figure 7.1   The long-term pattern of incentive schemes

the real reasons for poor performance and the possible long-term effects of incentive schemes before committing themselves to this route to higher output. Figure 7.1 shows what can happen in both the short and the long terms if, for example, a payment by results scheme is introduced.

Output may well increase by about one-third after the introduction of a scheme, with earnings going up in relation to output. However, as time goes by even in relatively static production situations there are likely to be improvements in work methods that are not entirely clawed back by the employer in terms of consequential reductions in time allowances. There may also be errors in initial time allowances, and employees can be remarkably ingenious in manipulating schemes to their advantage. The most sophisticated manipulations involve capturing the supervisor and other potential enemies so that the higher levels of management are not aware that ultimately effort may decline whilst output and earnings increase. Schemes can degenerate to such an extent that they actually become arrangements for restricting production – for fear that, if normal effort is resumed, the output achieved would give the whole game away.

Another problem can be the distorting effect that incentive schemes can have on pay structures. If, for whatever reason, the incentive earnings of one group rise, this can create stresses with regard to pay relativities. Sometimes these can be acute and lead to a negative differential on the part of those, for example, who are supposed to supervise them. The introduction of new working methods may be accompanied by fear about the impact of this on earnings and may lead to resistance to the changes or haggling about any consequential adjustments to the incentive scheme. Another problem can be resistance to moving from jobs with slack times to those with 'tight' times. The impact on quality of production or service also has to be examined.

The impact on safety needs to be examined in case employees are actually rewarded for working dangerously. One of the many ways in which this can and does happen concerns some of the 'job and finish' arrangements for lorry drivers. Such schemes may enable drivers to be paid at premium rates for trips done over and above their daily target. As well as encouraging unsafe driving, this may also lead to excessive vehicle wear and fuel consumption.

Group schemes

Most of the comments already made about individual financial incentive schemes also apply to group schemes. However, there are some specific aspects relating to group schemes that also need to be considered. Group schemes seem to work best when the group is no bigger than eight to twelve people, and the task is inherently a group-based task rather than an individual task. If a plant-wide scheme is used, the relationship between individual effort and reward may be too weak for there to be an obvious causal relationship between the effort of the individual and overall output. Individual earnings may move in parallel with total output, but that does not prove that people are working harder because of a group incentive scheme. Employees may perceive that their earnings will be very much the same, however hard or little they work. They may also perceive that many factors other than their effort, or even the effort of themselves and their fellow workers, may affect total output – for example workflow and technological change.

Profit sharing

There are two main types of profit-sharing arrangements – profit-related pay and employee-share option plans. The same issues emerge concerning the weakness of the link between reward and individual performance as are apparent with group bonus schemes; it may be difficult for employees to see the link between the amount of effort that they put into work and the impact on overall company performance. A fallacy about distributing profits in the form of shares is the assumption that once employees have a shareholder role they will forget about their far more important wage-earner role and will simply behave in the best interests of the shareholders. It is when 'weights' are attached to these two roles that it becomes apparent that any link between group performance and group profits may not actually be caused by a profit-sharing incentive. If the roles come into conflict employees may behave in such a way that they protect their wage-earner role and subordinate any shareholder interests to this much greater primary role. Admittedly, often the roles will not be in conflict and there may be a general value in exposing employees to the shareholder perspective. However, variations in profits may in fact have little to do with the supposed motivating effect of a profit-sharing scheme regardless of whether the rewards are in the form of direct payments or shares. Overall company performance may be very dependent on market factors over which employees have little or no control.

Financial incentives and corporate strategy

There are jobs in which the ideal arrangements identified above (i.e interesting job, good supervision, appropriate pay) will simply not always be attainable. There will, for example, be situations in which the structure of jobs is such that they are inherently boring and that, in the short-term at least, output will be best achieved by the use of financial incentive schemes.

The point that it is necessary to stress is that all the potential disadvantages of incentive schemes need to be taken into account before they are adopted. The trouble is that the short-term tangible benefits may be much more obvious than many of the long-term intangible, but nevertheless important, consequences. A policy of choosing 'horses for courses' is appropriate rather than any dogmatic assertion that one should always use incentive schemes or never use them. The matching of pay arrangements to situations can, however, be ill-conceived, or the circumstances in which schemes operate can alter and make them invalid. A common example is when automatic production processes are introduced which predetermine the rate of production, which had previously been determined by operators. If, as a consequence, the speed at which the now-reactive operators work becomes an effect and not a cause of some other variable, it becomes pointless to reward them for something over which they no longer have control. The achievement of high levels of production may be related instead, for example, to ensuring that automatic process equipment is properly maintained and does not break down or operate in such a way that there are quality defects.

The ramifications of incentive schemes are such that considerable thought has to be given, not only to whether they should be used or not, but also as to how they should be managed if they are used. If incentive schemes are used, they may require just as much, or even more, managerial effort to see that performance targets are met, compared with the managerial effort involved when people are paid just a basic wage or salary.

The impact of bonus schemes in the financial services industry has often been particularly dramatic, as has already been explained in Chapter 3. In many organizations the bonus culture has become so strong that it encourages staff to work against the long-term interests of the organization, particularly by mis-selling and in some cases by fraud that could threaten the very survival of an organization. As a counter to concerns about conflicts of interests between staff and customers, some organizations may not only not have financial incentive schemes but will advertise this fact to reassure customers that they are not going to be pushed to buy products or services that do not meet their needs. Development in the financial services industry has been towards commonly deferring part at least of a bonus payment to long-term profitability, the aim being to discourage too much focus on just short term gains.

Pensions

Pensions constitute an important and changing area – both for employers and employees. Cost is an issue for employers, particularly in relation to final salary schemes – because of increased life expectancy, there are now few final salary schemes open to new employees. However, there are strong arguments for an employer having a pension scheme and trying to combine the contradictory pressures of attracting employees and keeping costs under control. In addition, a requirement has been introduced under UK law for employers to provide a pension scheme for workers. This came into effect for large employers in 2012 and it is expected that it will be rolled out to all employers by 2018. The employer will be expected to contribute to the scheme and not induce employees to leave the scheme, although employees themselves can decide to opt out.

Why have an occupational pension scheme?

■ Contributes to an organization's competitive position in the labour market and enhances recruitment and retention
■ Demonstrates that an employer has a genuine belief in investing in people
■ Contributes to a positive employer brand image
■ By sending signals that employees' expectations are important there is potential for impact on motivation, commitment and performance
■ Provides management with the facility of flexing staff numbers through early retirement arrangements.

Occupational pension schemes can be either money purchase schemes or, now more rarely, final salary schemes. Final salary schemes pay benefits that are determined by taking the number of years of employee service and applying them to the final salary on retirement to produce a pensions entitlement. Final salary arrangements therefore provide defined benefits. These schemes are being abandoned by employers, particularly for new entrants to their organizations, because of the open-ended commitment that it places on the employer.

In contrast to final salary schemes, money purchase schemes pay benefits that are determined by the value of a pot of money that is accumulated through employee and/or employer contributions and investment decisions. The pot of money is ring fenced to purchase a pension for the employee. Money purchase arrangements are more attractive to employers because there is a clean financial break with the employee when they retire from the organization. These arrangements also provide employers with an opportunity to reduce the overall level of contribution. Investments made are of course subject to the fluctuations in the stock market making the size of pensions less predictable for employees.

Summary

Employers need to bear in mind the often-conflicting objectives of the pay structures that exist within their organizations. The conflicting pressures on organizational pay arrangements can include the need to pay certain employees more because of market conditions and the need for a pay structure that is, internally within the organization, felt to be fair. Two main frameworks which employers may consider for remunerating their employees, and which may complement one another, are job evaluation and the use of financial incentives.

Job evaluation is a technique that may provide the basis for establishing a rational organizational pay structure and establishing viable internal pay relativities. However, schemes have to be carefully chosen, operated and monitored. A relatively recent innovation has been to grade jobs in part, or even sometimes completely, on the basis of the relevant job competencies that people need.

Despite the European Equal Value regulations, there are strong cost and organizational pressures for schemes to be simpler. The pressures for simpler schemes include the increased rate of organizational change, the desire for broader job banding to achieve greater job flexibility and more emphasis on individual performance in determining pay.

Care needs to be taken before embarking on the use of financial incentive schemes. There are many potential reasons for poor performance, and lack of financial incentive may be only one of them. Even if there is a lack of financial incentive, schemes that link pay to productivity or profitability don't always work. The basic conditions that have to be met for schemes to succeed were identified. Even when the conditions are right for the use of a financial incentive scheme, the right scheme has to be chosen and carefully implemented and operated. A pay issue of increasing importance and complexity that has been covered is pensions. This is because of its cost but also personal implications for employees. The issue of performance related pay is considered in Chapter 10 in the context of appraisal generally.

REWARD **159**

Self-assessment questions

1. What are the main labour market and organizational factors determining the way in which employees get paid?
2. What are the purposes of job evaluation schemes?
3. What are the main operational problems in ensuring that job evaluation schemes remain effective?
4. Under what circumstances might financial incentive schemes be effective?
5. Identify the potential long-term effects of employee financial incentive schemes.

Case study notes – Southern Beers

Learning outcome:

■ To identify the potential negative effects of employee financial incentive schemes.

This case study is a classic example of how incentive payments schemes can get out of control and undermine a pay structure. On the face of it the bonus pay has kept on rising without any apparent extra effort on the part of the production workers. This is because of the random impact of change in production arrangements. Unfortunately the company's attempt to control the increase appears to be in breach of established joint procedures for handling such change. Not only is the scheme causing increased costs but it is likely to be creating tensions about pay differentials within the workforce. The best solution may be some sort of buy-out of the existing incentive scheme to stop the upward spiral. As part of this process it may be necessary to give contractual notice to workers that management wishes to end the existing scheme. The existence of other production sites could threaten continuation of production at the site in question. It would have been better to have started negotiations before the first 10% bonus increase occurred.

Taking it further

NB: Works of particular interest are marked with an asterisk.

*Armstrong, Michael (2012), *Reward Management Practice – Improving Performance through Reward*, 4th edn., Kogan Page.
   A comprehensive and highly practical account and evaluation of reward strategies, and the link to motivation.
Perkins, Stephen and Geoffrey White (2011), *Reward Management, Alternative, Consequences and Context*, 2nd edn., CIPD.

Communication

8

Case study

The Research Merger

Roger Davies is the research director of a pharmaceutical company. The company has grown, particularly by mergers, and the research division employs over 200 research staff, including technicians, with 35 support staff. Roger believes that the time is ripe for some rationalization but that, in the short term at least, this can be done without compulsory redundancies. There are two main departments. In the larger department 120 members of research staff are employed with an emphasis on basic long-term research. This is in line with the traditions of the former owners. The smaller department, which has been part of the group for much longer, employs about 80 staff and has an emphasis on 'research-informed' commercial product development. Roger believes that there is much to be gained by the larger department co-operating more with the smaller one and increasing its emphasis on commercial application. He believes that this will be facilitated by moving both departments into a new purpose-built research building.

Roger has arranged for the staff to visit the new, state of the art, research building and hopes that they will be enthusiastic about the new facilities and future prospects. The new building is on the outskirts of the city, two miles away from the smaller department and four miles from the larger department. To help ensure that the move goes smoothly he has commissioned an employee survey and is rather disappointed by the results. Despite his many written attempts to spell out the exciting prospects for the future, the staff seem more preoccupied with the practical aspects of the move and how it will affect them.

Questions:

1. Why might the result of the staff survey seem so disappointing?
2. What action should Roger take?

Introduction

This Chapter is probably the most important in the whole book. The topic, as well as needing to be covered in its own right, serves as a foundation for much of the rest of the book. It also links back to material covered in previous chapters. This includes the link between organizational structure and the effectiveness of communication, and the growing importance of electronic communication, both covered in Chapter 3. Other phenomena that interrelate with communication are managerial style and culture, topics that are covered in Chapter 4.

This chapter starts with an explanation of why communication is such an important topic. Managers spend most of their time trying to communicate with others. This can be in a variety of ways, particularly talking, listening, writing, reading, attending meetings and electronically. Managers may need to allocate much of their time to allowing others to communicate with them, rather than simply the other way around. If readers are able to develop their communication skills as a result of reading this chapter, they can benefit time and time again. Any benefit may also apply to their life outside work as well.

Unfortunately, managers are often over-optimistic about the effectiveness of the communication process. An understanding of the obstacles is therefore a way of identifying the skills needed for effective communication. Active listening skills can be particularly important. Attention is also paid here to presentational and written skills, including the effective use of email and the relevance of social networking. The impact of national culture is also of growing importance given the rise of globalization. The final topic in this chapter is the role of the mass media. This involves both the interpretation of media messages and presentational skills.

The importance of communication

Managers are likely to spend most of their time engaged directly in some form of communication process. Even when they are working alone – for example, studying or preparing reports – they are relying on other people's attempts to communicate with them or they are preparing to communicate with others. Accuracy in decision-making depends, in particular, on effective communication. If the communication process is faulty, then everything else can be affected.

Experiments, research and sheer personal observation show that most people are far too optimistic about the accuracy of the communication process. This applies not just to communication processes within employing organizations, but to life in general. Even when errors are identified it may be too late, or the inherent faults in the process that will lead to further errors may not be recognized. The effective communication of factual information can be difficult enough, but often attitudes and feelings need to be communicated, and that can be far more complicated. In this chapter practical guidance is given on how managers can identify the communication processes in their organizations with a view to evaluating their effectiveness and improving their own skills.

A problem of communication within organizations is that if it is faulty, everyone else in the communication chain can be misinformed; also, the longer the chain, the greater the chance of further error creeping in. It follows that the need to develop skills for effective communication may be a critical priority for many managers. Regrettably, this need is often not perceived, and managers may neglect the importance of, and the opportunity for, development in this critical area. Communication skills tend to be taken for granted and lack of skill is far more easily recognized in others than in oneself. A consequence of blaming others is that people do not see the need to improve their own skills. It is only when people realize the subtleties concerning effective communication that they may become communication-conscious and start to develop their own skills.

Obstacles to effective communication

Having stressed the importance of the communication process, it is appropriate to develop further the hypothesis that communication in organizations is a great deal worse than most people realize. Explaining the nature of communication processes and the potential for breakdown will do this. Case examples are given to illustrate some of the major points.

Organizational structure

The need for organizational structures to facilitate the accomplishment of organizational objectives was considered in Chapter 3. As part of that process organizations need to be structured so that the right information gets to the necessary people at the right time so that any appropriate action can be taken. Unfortunately, the structure of many organizations does not facilitate communication and therefore the structure is, or has become, 'unfit for purpose'.

There is no single correct model of an organization. Structures should fit the needs of particular situations. Even if the fit between the need for information flows and organizational structure is right, the way in which the organization actually operates may obstruct necessary information flows. Even if the structure is appropriate, the style of individual managers may not be appropriate for the job they are doing. The impact of re-structuring on communication flows may also need careful consideration. The options in managerial style were considered in Chapter 4.

Time

Communication can be time-intensive. This can be because of the need for prior preparation, giving people time to ask questions and the amount of listening that may be required. Time will also be needed to identify potential problems and ways of overcoming them. As managers are usually short of time, and are often not as skilled as they think they are in communicating, insufficient time may be allowed.

Language

Those involved in the communication process may not have a common language. Language differences can occur because of variations in technical understanding, general vocabulary levels and the use of in-house terms that are not familiar to others. This can be aggravated if there are significant differences in ability levels. The complications involved in communicating between different nationalities are dealt with later in this chapter in the section on national culture.

Listening problems

It is appropriate to explain one major misconception about communication at this stage. Communication is usually seen as the need to brief other people. The reality is that most of a manager's time needs to be concerned with *receiving* rather than imparting information and views. The reason for this is simple – in any conversation between two people there is a need to alternate between talking and listening. There is not much point in anyone talking if the intended recipient is not prepared to listen. If the two people involved in a discussion take equal turns talking and listening, they will obviously spend half of their time in the listening role.

As much of the communication in organizations involves face-to-face discussion between more than two people, it follows as a mathematical fact that most managers will need to spend more time listening than talking. There will be exceptions to this, for example when a manager is making a presentation, but the very existence of exceptions such as this reduces the time available for others to do the talking. Admittedly, managers may often need to take the lead in explaining things to their subordinates, but a statistically unequal share of talk in this direction may easily be counterbalanced by the time they have to spend in discussions and meetings involving a number of people when they talk only for a minority of the time. The basic point of this argument is that managers may fail to see that they will normally need to spend more time listening than talking.

Effective listening does not come naturally to all managers, particularly if they do not recognize the importance of it. People who set out to improve the quality of communication in organizations often assume that good communication is synonymous with the imparting of information. House magazines, letters from the chief executive, briefing meetings and training in public speaking are based mainly on the assumption that the problem is in disseminating information. The reality may be that it is more important to unblock the obstructions to information and views flowing in to the key decision-makers. The problem may be that, until such time as communication is effective, managers may not realize that the obstructions are there. In any case, if everyone concentrates on imparting information and views, just who will be left to receive all these messages? It is also easy for people to be distracted from effective listening. They may have other problems on their mind, be physically distracted or simply lack the motivation to listen carefully. The positive skills of active listening are explained later in the chapter.

Bogus feedback

When communication is initiated it is necessary for the initiator to consider both the evidence for assuming that the communication has been effective and the consequences of communication being defective. People can be very aware of their lack of understanding when they are on the receiving end of an instruction. It can be very tempting, however, to create an impression of understanding through silence. The problem is that the initiator may be left with a false impression of their effectiveness. If a message is particularly important it is up to the initiator to search for more positive corroboration than mere silence to confirm that communication has been effective. They will need to consider other forms of feedback and to distinguish between accurate and bogus feedback.

Silence is not the only way in which people give false impressions about having understood explanations. There are occasions when people actually say they have understood when they have not. This commonly occurs, for instance, when someone asks for directions to somewhere but are so confused by the instructions given that they may say that they have understood when they have not. This type of breakdown can happen within organizations and for a variety of reasons. These include fear of embarrassment, inability to understand the person trying to help, politeness and impatience. Often people do not like to show their ignorance to people in positions of authority.

EXAMPLE: Miscommunication

A student nurse was asked to give a patient an air ring. She apparently was not quite sure what to do but guessed that the appropriate interpretation was to move the patient's bed onto the veranda and remove the bedclothes. In actual fact, the nurse had been expected to get an inflatable rubber air ring so that the patient could sit on it and receive a blanket bath. Another student nurse was given the same instruction but with slightly different phraseology – she was told to go and get an air ring. She returned three-quarters of an hour later saying how much she had enjoyed her walk in the hospital grounds!

In the above cases the students' guesswork fortunately just led to comic results. That will not always be the case and such errors in the communication process may be picked up too late or not at all. The errors in the previous examples may be seen as stupidity or feebleness on the part of the student nurses, but such an interpretation misses the point. The fault really lies with the person who gave the instruction for not ensuring that they had made themselves properly understood. Either they needed to make a positive check that the instruction was understood, or they needed to have created a working relationship with the student nurse such that queries could be raised if necessary. The objective with communication should be to ensure that it is effective rather than to ensure that someone else can be blamed if things go wrong.

Nursing examples have been given to illustrate the need to get accurate feedback. However, such problems are likely in almost any organization, particularly if the culture is authoritarian. Sometimes those in authority may go through the motions of obtaining feedback when in fact what they want is simply the pretence and cover that people have had a fair opportunity to raise queries. Rhetorical questions may be used – such as 'Is that clear?' – which do not really invite responses. The technique can be observed with lecturers and after-dinner speakers who leave the opportunity for questions until an impossibly late stage in the proceedings.

Should subordinates nevertheless voice criticisms in situations like those described above, they may have the blame shifted back to them, however unjustly, to discourage further criticism. However, employees can also misperceive the response to their comments or questions. Sometimes it may be necessary and possible for them to raise sensitive issues. In doing this it may be as well to remember the skills of assertiveness explained in Chapter 4.

Resistance to criticism and bad news

It is important to recognize that any manager is going to prefer to hear good news rather than bad news, and to appreciate the temptation for colleagues and subordinates to tell people what they want to hear. In the long term this can be disastrous, and managers and political leaders alike need consciously to recognize the distortion that can occur in channels of communication and beware of succumbing to it.

The chances of blocking out critical or unfavourable news can be greatly reduced if the temptation to do so is consciously recognized and if modern-day equivalents of the ancient Greek tradition of slaying the messenger who brings news of defeat in battle are avoided. Another classical example, discussed below, concerns the Greek mathematician Pythagoras.

EXAMPLE: Extreme example of resistance to criticism

A student of Pythagoras, Hippasus, grasped the concept of irrational numbers (the idea that some numbers can only be expressed in recurring decimal places). Hippasus's theory was contrary to Pythagoras's view that all numbers were rational. However, Pythagoras was unwilling to accept that he was wrong. Sadly Pythagoras had Hippasus drowned as a punishment for identifying this (Singh, 1998).

It is often necessary to make independent checks to evaluate the information that is received. Having said this, it is necessary also to make the point that there are few people, if any, who can cope with the whole truth all the time. Total exposure could be destructive to the individual concerned. What is needed is a realization that the information received in an organization needs careful evaluation, and other information may be needed but has not been passed on. Managers may need to seek out the bad news to the extent that it is necessary and to the extent that they can cope with it. Just as managers get the subordinates they deserve, managers may get the communication they deserve.

Selective perception and bias

In considering barriers to communication, it is also necessary to deal specifically with the problems caused by selective perception and bias. The sheer volume of data that may be available can mean that one has to have some basis for deciding what to look for and what to react to. However, careful judgement is needed in making these decisions. A totally open mind can simply mean that a person is swamped with data. A closed mind can mean that a person doesn't respond to what is under their nose. Particular dangers lie in seeing only what you want to see; making the 'facts' fit what has already been decided, and suppressing unpleasant facts.

As well as having to cope with one's own subjectivity, it must also be recognized that much of the data that is available within organizations is subjective or actually misleading. In Chapter 3 some of the reasons were given as to why department managers might be more concerned with protecting their reputations than with supplying objective data about their performance. Most people working in organizations are likely to be concerned with the pursuit of truth, but people in organizations, as in life generally, are under a variety of pressures to highlight some things and not others. There are also pressures to view events in a particular way. This means that managers need to evaluate carefully the information that is being fed to them.

Selective perception may be particularly likely if the parties involved in the communication process have different objectives. The greater the amount of conflict, the more likely that there are emotional blockages to effective communication. A major problem can be created by the frames of reference of the parties concerned. Managers with a unitary frame of reference may have difficulty in understanding that what is in the interests of an organization as a whole may not necessarily be in the interests of all sections within the organization. The concept of frames of reference is dealt with in detail in Chapter 3.

Gender differences

There may be obstacles of communication when a person is trying to communicate with a member of the opposite sex. It would seem reasonable to assume that just as cultures vary in their masculinity and femininity (Hofstede, 2001) so also there are likely to be variations in the way that members of different sexes communicate, both with one another and with members of the opposite sex. The existence of different national conventions of communication between people of different genders is referred to in the later section in this Chapter on national culture. The extent of the difference is likely to vary according to how much sex equality there is within a particular culture. Whilst there is an obvious danger of unfair stereotyping, the implication of Hofstede's work is that men may tend to be more aggressive and individualistic than women. They may also tend to operate on a low-context basis whilst women may tend to rely more on nonverbal cues, which are high-context (Hall, 1997). Particular difficulties may arise when a person of one sex fails to adapt their style of communication, where appropriate, when communicating with a member of the opposite sex. For example, there may be a lower tolerance level for aggression in communication on the part of many women compared with men. Also the body language and body contact acceptable in communication between men may not always be acceptable in their communication with women.

Skills in effective oral communication

Much of the skill in effective communication lies in recognizing the problem areas that have just been identified. Effective communication is achieved as much as anything by avoiding these traps. One also has to beware of relying on information that is not in the form of original evidence. Groups such as research scientists, historians, medical doctors and lawyers are amongst those who are particularly aware of the danger of distortion – whether deliberate, subconscious or accidental – in evidence that is not received first-hand. It won't always be possible as a manager to rely on direct evidence, but at least the dangers of relying on secondary sources can be recognized. Also, the quality of original or secondary source material provided by managers can be improved by the positive approaches explained in the rest of this section.

Coaxing information

It may be necessary for managers to work hard at coaxing information, particularly if people feel inhibited about discussing a particular issue. The lament, 'Why didn't someone tell me?' can be as much a condemnation of a manager's lack of skill in developing effective channels of communication as a condemnation of others for keeping them in the dark. It can be very hard for those in authority roles to realize the difficulty that others may have in communicating with them. The authority figure may feel totally relaxed and uninhibited and not appreciate that perhaps the very factors that create their security, also create difficulties for others. The proprietor of a business may feel totally self-confident and secure and be amazed to find out, if they ever do, that people who are very dependent on them are reluctant to tell them anything unpleasant. Parents can encounter the same problem with their children. Just as parents may forget what it was like to be a child and may be unaware of many of the thoughts and anxieties that their own children have, so business proprietors and managers may see any suggestion that there are psychological barriers between themselves and their employees as quite preposterous.

Active listening

Adopting a listening role can be harder than taking the lead by talking. The problem with this can be that the more an authority figure prefers to talk rather than listen, the less others may be inclined to give their point of view. There can be a critical moment when people in the subordinate role might just start saying what they really feel, if only the authority figure stays quiet long enough. Once the subordinate has started talking, things may come out with a rush, to the amazement of the authority figure. One useful technique in any such situation can be to count silently, if necessary, to ten before breaking the silence after you have asked a particularly important question.

Once a person has started to talk it can be relatively easy to get them to continue and for any others to join in. The problem is likely to be how to get them started. The authority figure needs to be aware of letting their ignorance, impatience or even their own nervousness prevent such a process starting. Care has to be taken with the timing of invitations for people to open up – it is not only the time and the place that can be important but also the stage in a discussion. It may be necessary to build up rapport gently before the invitation is given.

Thought also needs to be given to the way in which questions are put. Questions such as 'don't you think this is a good idea?' can be leading in nature, and give the impression that all that is required is confirmation of the questioner's views. Alternatively questions can be probing and phrased in such a way as to encourage the respondents to state their own views. One useful distinction, especially important in selection interviewing, is between open questions, which encourage people to talk, and closed questions which limit responses to, for example, 'yes' or 'no'. These issues are examined further in Chapter 9 on selection and Chapter 12 on counselling.

Scene-setting

The choice of time and place to invite people to talk can be critical. There are circumstances in which people may be prepared to 'open up' and circumstances in which they will not. One of the skills of communication is picking up the cues as to whether a person is or is not prepared to talk about a sensitive matter. Even if the place cannot always be chosen, sometimes the geography of a room can be arranged to encourage, or for that matter to discourage, a person from talking. The more status symbols surrounding the authority figure, the less likely a subordinate is to feel free to talk.

EXAMPLE: Example of scene setting

A Human Resources manager who was over 1.9m tall (six foot) always made a point of ensuring that he and the works superintendent were both seated if anything of consequence was to be discussed. The HR manager had learned from experience that the superintendent was self-conscious about being short so he did his best not to emphasize the difference in their respective heights.

Choice of language

Language difficulties can hamper communication between people who have different national languages. Regional dialects can also complicate matters. However, there can be many other and more subtle language problems even between people who are from the same country, region and social class. Technical language, which is beyond the comprehension of some of the participants, may be used in discussion. In any organization there are likely to be abbreviations, words with special connotations, and 'in-terms' whose meaning is taken for granted by those inside the organization. Even when communication is between professionals in the same organization there can be confusion about the meaning of words.

In identifying the appropriate language for communication, attention needs to be given to the possibility of ambiguity. The more serious the consequences of error, the more attention needs to be devoted to avoiding ambiguity. If an illustration is needed to stress this point, it can be provided by the ambiguous use of words which contributed to the world's worst air disaster at Tenerife in the Canary Islands in 1977.

EXAMPLE: Potential consequences of word ambiguity

The Dutch pilot of a KLM jumbo jet, who was ironically also the head of their flight training department, was preparing to take off at Tenerife, in the Canary Islands. He explained that he was ready to the air traffic controllers and in response was told 'OK [pause]. Stand by for take-off. I will call you.' In the pause after the word 'OK' there was radio interference because of a radio query by the captain of an American plane about the intentions of the KLM captain. It seems likely that this caused the KLM captain to assume that the word 'OK' was the complete message. In any event, the KLM captain then took off and collided with the American jumbo jet, killing a total of 583 people. The investigators commissioned by the American Airline Pilots Association concluded that this was the most likely explanation of events (American Airline Pilots Association, 1978).

Body language – general

The expressions, gestures and other body language that people may use without necessarily realizing it can be important cues as to what they really think. Communication is not just imparting information; it often involves, or needs to involve, understanding people's attitudes and feelings, which are not always clearly expressed in words. In some cases people may even feel obliged to say the opposite of what they really think. It is not uncommon, for example, for people to say 'how interesting' in a tone of voice that indicates that they are in fact bored. An adage that makes the point that people some-times accidentally misrepresent themselves is, 'Listen to what I mean, not what I say'.

As words can be an inadequate or a misleading guide to what people really think, it can be important to look for other cues to people's thoughts. A cata-logue could be prepared of what particular physical cues could mean: fidget-ing, that a person has other things on their mind; a glazed expression that a person doesn't understand, or is bored, and so on. Given that such a list could be very long and only be a guide anyway, the point that needs to be stressed is simply to watch for physical cues to a person's real thoughts, espe-cially when it is likely that a person is not able to be, or does not want to be, frank about a particular topic. It can be very tempting to rely just on the words that a person uses, particularly if they give the answer that one wants to hear. To rely on words alone can be quite insufficient.

**EXAMPLE: Contradiction between body language
and other behaviour**

An intriguing example of what might be learnt by studying a person's bodily behaviour concerns an allegation about Nikita Khrushchev's conduct during a famous debate at the General Assembly of the United Nations. Khrushchev interrupted proceedings by banging on the table with his shoe. This was part of his protest about American recon-naissance flights over the USSR in their U2 spy planes, which came to light when the American pilot Gary Powers was captured in 1960. The allegation is that TV cameras revealed Khrushchev had shoes on both feet and that the one he banged on the table just before he left the platform was a third shoe brought into the conference cham-ber expressly for that purpose. If the allegation is true, it reveals that the demonstra-tion was a calculated piece of histrionics and not a spontaneous burst of anger.

The topic of body language is examined again later in this chapter in the context of national culture and also in Chapter 14 in the context of negotiation.

Oral presentation skills

Downward communication

Having emphasized the obstacles to effective communication and in particu-lar the importance of upward communication, it is appropriate to say some-thing about the presentation skills involved in downward communication. At the risk of being repetitive, it is first of all necessary to become aware of the limitations of downward communication, particularly in terms of volume, accuracy and commitment by the person receiving the information to that which is being communicated. There can be a role for devices such as mission statements and team briefings, but only in the context of the appropriate organizational culture and structure, and only if such devices are carefully thought out and competently implemented.

Specific skills

Having commented on the limitations that downward communication can have, it is also necessary to emphasize how effective downward communication can be very important in certain circumstances. Managers have a responsibility to impart information and they need to do this effectively. They need to use time to optimum effect so that they influence the audience in the way they want to without wasting anyone's time. The larger the audience is, the greater the potential for wasted time. If the time available is limited, it is particularly important that the presenter makes good use of it. Crucial decisions can be made as a result of formal presentations, for example, whether or not important business proposals are accepted or not. The reputations of managers may also depend on how effective their presentation skills are, particularly because people will be able to judge how good these skills are. As with teaching, it is no good a person being technically competent if they cannot explain their ideas in such a way that others are motivated to listen and are able to understand. Whatever level of oral presentation skills a person has, it is usually possible to improve it by analysis, preparation and practice. The following checklist may be useful with regard to formal or informal oral presentations.

Issues to consider when making a presentation

- Clarify objectives;
- Identify the target audience;
- Consider what prior publicity may be necessary;
- Geographical and acoustic arrangements;
- Consider structure of presentation;
- Will the opening attract interest?
- To what extent can the audience be involved?
- Motivation and comprehension of the audience;
- Timing (e.g. for dramatic effect), pace and duration;
- Time control (taking into account length of time slot available);
- Beware of reading from notes, as this reduces spontaneity and eye contact – prompt cards or an aide-memoir may be much better;
- Visual aids, e.g. PowerPoint, overhead projector slides, prepared flip chart material, exhibits. PowerPoint should be used as a supplement to presentation and not degenerate to the presenter simply repeating what is on the screen. A useful rule of thumb is to have a limit of seven lines on each slide and seven words a line;

- Clarity of expression and choice of language;
- Eye contact and body language;
- Volume of information – not too little, but beware of presenting too much and losing the audience in the detail;
- Use of humour;
- Pitch and variety of voice;
- Use of examples;
- Rehearsal;
- Opportunity for feedback;
- Back-up notes and sources of further information;
- Evaluation of presentation;
- Modifications for the future.

Written communication

Written communication is a form of one-way communication. Forms of written communication can range from an email to one person to a formal report that will be distributed to a large readership. Websites are also increasingly used to disseminate information. It will be important that writers express themselves clearly, concisely and without ambiguity. Time invested in doing this can avoid error, inappropriate responses, reduce queries and save the time of the reader. If a document is going to a number of people, organizational time can be saved if the distribution list is accurately targeted. The need to invest time in writing was emphasized by the French writer Pascal (1657) when he wrote to a friend: 'I have made this letter longer than usual only because I have not had the time to make it shorter.'

Written language

The language used when writing needs to be convenient to the reader. There are a variety of reasons why writers may use inappropriate language. They may simply use the language that is most convenient to them. However, if this is too full of technical jargon or is unnecessarily complicated the content may not be understood. If the writer wants to communicate and understands their subject, generally it should be possible to explain issues clearly. Written communication that is difficult to follow is often caused more by the deficiencies of the writer than the lack of abilities of the reader.

Sometimes matters have to be expressed in a precise way, and the use of technical language is unavoidable. This can be the case with legal documents, where the only way of achieving the necessary clarity is to use precise legal expressions. However, even when technical language is used there is good and bad practice. There is no benefit in explaining matters in a way that is more complicated than necessary. All too often overly elaborate terms and clumsy expression can result from the writer's desire to impress or a lack of clarity in the actual thinking. Increasingly correspondence is by email, so the skills involved in using this medium effectively are considered later in this chapter in the section on electronic communication.

Report writing

Much of what has already been said in this chapter about written communication applies to reports. Managers are often asked to write reports and these can have an important influence on decision-making. The influence that reports have can, in part, depend on the skill with which they are written. A well-written report can also enhance the profile of the author. Authors need to ensure that they keep to any terms of reference. A key element in the report will be the abstract or executive summary. This will need to include, or be a summary of, the key elements in the report. An abstract is not an introduction emphasizing what is going to be investigated. Rather the emphasis in an abstract should be on what was examined and how and then, crucially, what was found. Hopefully this will motivate potential readers to read the whole report. Recommendations will normally be another key element of an abstract as well as the full report. Reports need to spell out the key issues rather than play them down or hide the message behind too many caveats or qualifications. However, this may need to be balanced against any needs for confidentiality and political sensitivity. Much of the detail may be best put in appendices, which should be referenced in the text. Bear in mind though that appendices are often not read.

Helplines

A growing practice with manufacturers and providers of some services is to give a helpline telephone number or email address. This practice enables clients to engage in two-way communication about the use of the product or service. It may be an important selling point. It may also give the provider of the product or service useful feedback about the quality of any written instructions. Furthermore, it may provide important market research data about customer responses to the product or service itself.

House magazines

Many organizations keep staff informed by way of house magazines or newsletters. This can be very useful, but it has to be remembered that it is an exercise in one-way communication. It is important to devise complementary ways of checking on staff opinion, such as employee representative structures. Readership surveys are a way of judging the reaction to the actual magazines and newsletters. Care, however, needs to be taken about the content of these. Employees may have quite a different perspective on the organization to that of senior managers. It may also be necessary to check that the messages don't have unintended consequences.

EXAMPLE: Potential consequences of publicity

In one national brewing company a copy of the house magazine was produced at a negotiating meeting. The employee representatives wanted to know why the company was only offering a low wage increase when the magazine included details of healthy profits and a major expenditure programme.

National culture

Culture has many dimensions, including class, organization, region and nation. The impact of culture on organizations was necessarily given attention in Chapter 4. The impact of national culture on communications is potentially so great that it is examined separately in this section. That impact is growing for a number of reasons. Globalization, ease of international travel and developments in information technology are making international collaboration in both the private and public sectors much more common. Managers are much more likely to have to deal with people of other nationalities, whether it be in their home country or working abroad.

Some potential obstacles to communication, such as language, are obvious. A feature of language developments is the ever-increasing importance of English as a means of international communication, including between people neither of whom speak English as their first language. There can, however, also be communication differences between those who both apparently speak English as their first language.

EXAMPLE: Misunderstanding within a common language

During the Korean war, the British brigadier in charge of the Gloucestershire Regiment needed reinforcements because he was outnumbered by Chinese soldiers by a ratio of eight to one and was encircled. This was in one of the most famous battles of the war. Unfortunately, he used classic British understatement in reporting his predicament and told his American allies that 'things are a bit sticky'. This was interpreted as the situation simply being a little difficult but not serious enough to need American help. The outcome was that only 39 of the 600 troops in the regiment escaped. The lesson from this example is that people from other cultures may need to beware of missing important nuances of meaning in what, on the face of it, is a common language (*The Guardian*, 2001).

It may be important to use what has become known as 'offshore English' when communicating with people from other countries. This form of English can be defined as that spoken by people whose first language is not English and who have learned the language as adults for practical rather than academic purposes. Other potential obstacles to effective communication may be less obvious but nevertheless important. The very fact that they are not obvious can make them harder to deal with. These obstacles include cultural values and the varying use of body language in different cultures.

National culture can be shaped by many factors. These include history, religion, value systems, geography and climate. These in turn shape the behaviour of people, including the way they communicate with one another. The most important study to date of the impact of national culture on organizations was carried out by Hofstede (2001). This study was examined in some detail in Chapter 4. In high power distance cultures communication is hampered by long hierarchies and associated levels of high social inequality. It may be particularly difficult in such cultures to express views that are contrary to those of people in authority. In cultures where there is high uncertainty avoidance there is an emphasis on formality and on rules and regulations. In collectivist cultures it is difficult for people to express views contrary to the group or organization at large. In contrast to masculine cultures, feminine cultures are characterized by high levels of mutual respect for one another's opinions.

High and low context cultures

A related concept is the distinction between high context and low context communication (Hall, 1987). Some low context cultures, particularly the USA, are characterized by direct and specific expression, often reinforced by written contracts. Other cultures, particularly in Asia, are high context and much more depends on the context in which communication takes place. People in high context cultures will be much more used to interpreting meaning in accordance with factors such as personality, rank and body language. Language itself may be deliberately ambiguous. Demands for greater clarity may be seen as insulting and imply that a person is not to be trusted. The homogeneity, size and social control in a country may be important in determining whether the dominant culture is high or low context. A large country with relatively low social homogeneity and social control will be more likely to be low context. In high context cultures there will be fewer written contracts and this may be why the annual output of lawyers in the USA is equal to the total stock of lawyers in Japan.

Level of feedback

In high power distance and high context cultures, managers may get little genuine feedback on their performance from their employees, particularly if they are not very effective. In such cultures local managers may realize this, but managers originating from low power distance cultures may not realize that they need to look for more discrete indications of employees' views.

EXAMPLE: Dangers of perceived lack of feedback

A British manager was anxious to impose his ideas on a group of Indonesian managers. Unfortunately he mistook silence from the managers for agreement with his suggestions and this led to him pressing his points harder and harder. He had not appreciated the need to carefully evaluate the meaning of silence or the problems the managers would have in directly confronting him. The longer he went on, the greater the resistance he created and the greater the barriers between him and his audience.

Building and maintaining relationships

It may take considerable time to develop working relationships between people of other cultures. It may not be realistic to discuss serious issues until an adequate level of trust is established. The distinction between roles and personalities is not as clear in some cultures as in others. When this is the case, much time may be needed to develop acceptance as a person. Particularly in Asian cultures, considerable care may need to be taken to save people's face as a way of maintaining relationships.

EXAMPLE: Preserving the dignity of others

At a meeting of Indonesian and British managers one of the Indonesian managers made an inappropriate suggestion and everyone including the person who made the suggestion realized its weaknesses. However, so that the standing of this person could be preserved, great efforts were made by all to let him gradually retreat from the idea and to thank him for his initiative. The process took far longer than it would have in many other cultures but this was necessary in the local situation where it was considered important to 'save the face' of the employee.

Body language – cultural

The importance of body language has already been considered because of its general potential importance in communication. However, it is also necessary to specifically consider the cultural aspects. Managers need to pay attention to this, particularly in high context communication cultures. It is also important that they do not assume that particular body language signals have the same meaning in all cultures. The range of body language signals, conscious or otherwise, is great. Illustrative examples of what they might mean are explained below.

Body contact

Conventions about body contact vary considerably between cultures. Germans, for example, are renowned for shaking hands as a form of greeting. However, Indians traditionally clasp their hands together and bow. In France and Russia a traditional greeting is to kiss one another on the cheeks. As well as needing to understand these different conventions, it may be particularly important in certain cultures to take into account potential problems about body contact between people of the opposite sex.

EXAMPLE: Avoidance of inappropriate body contact

When the Chinese head of state visited Iran there was a protocol problem because of the presence of a woman in the Iranian reception party. She could not be seen to be touching the Chinese head of state but had to graciously greet him. The problem was resolved by her presenting him with a red rose which she handed over in such a way that there was no body contact between the two. The visitor expressed delight at the gesture and protocol was preserved.

Eye contact

In low power distance cultures there will be an expectation that people will look you in the eye when talking to you. In high power distance cultures this could be seen as disrespectful on the part of subordinates.

Facial expressions

In high context cultures more of the message may be transmitted by way of facial expression. Conventions may be particularly strict between people of the opposite sex.

EXAMPLE: Misinterpretation of facial expressions

There was a feeling amongst the local female canteen workers in a West London factory that male Indian production workers were unappreciative when served with food because they did not smile when handed their meals. When the Indian workers were made aware of the canteen workers' feelings they were bewildered because in their culture to have smiled in response to receiving food would have been seen as being too familiar. When this story was told to a college receptionist in central London she said she could now understand why she often received broad smiles from some visitors but not often from people from some other cultures.

Spatial relationships

People may have a preferred physical distance between themselves and the person they are talking to. As a generalization, Swedes and Scots tend to prefer a long distance; Arabs and South Americans usually prefer to be closer. According to Argyle (1994) this has led to a Latin American diplomat saying that British diplomats are very good – if only you can catch them!

Electronic communication

The impact of developments in information technology on organizations was examined in Chapter 3. However, the overlapping impact on communication processes also needs to be examined in this chapter. A key skill is that of using email effectively.

Email

The volume of email traffic is such that people can be so swamped by information that they are prevented from getting on with the key aspects of their job. The overuse of email (for example, sending to numerous other people who do not really have to be involved) can lead to managers having to spend much time sifting the important from the unimportant. This also means that managers need to ensure that they in turn do not send out unnecessary emails or unnecessary copies. The whole issue is potentially so important and relatively undocumented that it is appropriate to highlight key features of effective email communication:

- Beware of letting emails sent to you short-circuit existing organization channels. Giving out your email address indiscriminately can encourage this;
- Only copy emails to people who really need to be involved. Beware of 'hostile' copying in particular, e.g. copying critical comments to a colleague's boss;
- Take time to compose an email so that it is to the point. Note too that poor grammar and typing errors betray the fact that you have not spent much time on an issue, which will not endear you to the recipient;
- Controversial, sensitive and confidential issues may be best handled by face-to-face discussion and not by email. 'Screaming' emails are generally to be avoided, e.g. where some of the content is written in block capitals or underlined. Beware of getting involved in email wars or 'flame mail'. It is also necessary to beware of potential data protection liability when sending confidential information;
- When composing an email, give consideration to whether so-called 'text speak' is likely to be acceptable to the recipient or not.

Speed can be a disadvantage as well as an advantage. Email does not give the opportunity for second thoughts. They can also be sent to the wrong person in error or forwarded to others without your knowledge or authority. This can have particularly catastrophic results if large amounts of money are involved, or in situations where secrecy is paramount.

Social networking

It is important to recognize the impact that social networking can have on organizational life. It can greatly increase the amount of shared information and misinformation. Employees may, however, be naïve about the indiscriminate sharing of views and information and may not take into account the potential readership of, for example, blogs and Facebook interchanges. Whilst there can be positive aspects of such communication there can also be negative ones. These include being seen to bring their employer into disrepute, and breaches of confidences. Some employers may also monitor Facebook statements, for example of prospective employees. For their part employers may need to have codes of conduct about what is acceptable and unacceptable behaviour. This may need to include what activities are permissible and what time may be spent on personal use of computer equipment during working hours.

Media communication

General

The amount of time that people spend watching television, other electronic images and listening to the radio justifies a section on the media. Whilst this fits with a general consideration of communication, there may well be specific issues presented in the media that involve people in their role as managers or leaders. The material presented often needs to be carefully evaluated. Managers may also need to use the media to present their views, so consideration is also given to the basic skills of media presentation.

There is an inherent conflict between the responsibility of media reporters and producers to present a fair and balanced programme and pressure on them to attain high viewing or listening figures. The need for speedy reporting can also reduce its accuracy. All this can lead to sensationalized reporting, emphasis on the unusual and camera bias towards dramatic visual images. Presentation on the radio can be more balanced because it does not suffer from camera bias. Newspapers often have clear political affiliations but also offer readers the choice of which sections to read and the pace at which they read them. Although people can decide what programmes they watch on television or listen to on the radio, the content has to be heavily managed because it has to be compressed and contained within a standard format. There cannot be the flexible use that there is with a newspaper.

The implication of the complexities of media presentation and the opportunity for distortion, deliberate or accidental, mean that it is important to evaluate critically what is being presented rather than passively accept it. This is particularly important for managers if the information they receive from the media is likely to influence the managerial decisions they make. It is as well to remember also that a whole range of interest groups are concerned with providing information to the media in order to put over a particular point of view.

Media presentation skills

Given the potential importance of the media it is important that managers know how to present themselves on it effectively if the need arises. The earlier section in this chapter on oral presentation skills may be particularly relevant. However, managers or leaders also need to beware of the potential dangers in dealing with the media. They may have to face unexpected and hostile questions by a person well practised in the art of media interviewing. There is the possibility that they may be confronted by people with an opposing point of view without warning. Pre-recorded interviews can be selectively edited to the organization's disadvantage and/or placed in an unfavourable juxtaposition with other issues and images. Managers may also be misquoted, or have injudicious statements quoted out of context.

Countermeasures that managers may wish to consider in dealing with aggressive or unfair media interviewing include:

- Insisting on a live interview to prevent selective editing;
- Only saying what you want to say – there are no penalties, as there are in exams for example, for not answering questions exactly as an interviewer wishes, apart from whatever conclusions may be drawn by the audience. Politicians can be particularly adept at not answering embarrassing questions;
- Ensuring that when answering questions you use your own words and not ones suggested to you by an interviewer;
- Before replying to a question, considering saying whatever it is you want to say first of all before answering the actual question;
- Recognizing who your real audience is. It will be the viewers or listeners and not those participating in a programme. This may mean that you have to be very clear about your agenda. You may also need to use very clear language, which may differ from that wanted by other people involved in a particular programme;
- If provoked, ensuring that you do not lose your temper. The person who is the most aggressive is the one most likely to lose the sympathy of the audience;
- If you do not want to give an interview, it may be much better to issue a prepared statement rather than simply state 'no comment'.

Managers engaged in potentially newsworthy activities may need to be able to react quickly to put over their point of view. Organizations may need to consider what in-house skills, policies, procedures and facilities they need to handle the media.

Summary

Managers normally spend most of their time trying to communicate with other people. Although the ability to communicate with others is important, it can be even more important to ensure that others can communicate with you. This is particularly so because managers usually need to spend more time receiving than imparting information. Accurate communication is necessary if decision-making is to be appropriate and implementation effective. Unfortunately, communication is often much less accurate than is appreciated. This lack of awareness not only leads to error, but also means that people do not pay sufficient attention to the need to develop their skills in this area. However, communication skills are often easily developed and can lead to important recurring benefits.

Identification of the potential obstacles to effective communication provides a foundation for developing skills in this area. Important obstacles can be poor listening skills, lack of time, lack of a common vocabulary, poor or false feedback and resistance to criticism. A key skill is that of active listening. The way in which oral presentation skills can be improved has also been examined; however, written communication is also important. The ways in which organizational structures can facilitate or hinder communication have been considered. It is also necessary to take into account the problems of communication caused by differences in national culture.

Attention has been paid to the growing importance of electronic communication, including social networking, as well as some of the associated problems. It has also been appropriate to consider the role of the media, including the evaluation of media messages and how to use it to communicate with others. It can be very important for managers to distinguish between their own agenda with regard to media presentation and that of media organizations.

Self-assessment questions

1. Identify six examples of situations necessitating good communication that you have been involved in during the last 24 hours.
2. Taking the examples given in your answer to question 1, identify the main obstacles there have been or might have been to that communication being effective.
3. How could you improve your own interpersonal oral communication?

4. Identify six key skills in effective oral presentation.
5. Identify four key skills in effective written communication.
6. Give examples of how differences in national culture can lead to misunderstanding.
7. Identify good and bad practice in those who communicate with you by email.
8. If you had to give a presentation on radio or television, how would go about it?

Case study notes – The Research Merger

Learning outcome:

■ To enable students to identify the potential limitation of downward communication.

This is a classic case of over-reliance on just downward (written) communication, and lack of opportunity being created by management for staff to communicate. Roger is so pre-occupied with his own agenda that he cannot anticipate the concerns that the staff may have. These are likely to include job security, procedures for appointing people into re-structured jobs, the culture clash between the basic and applied research departments, and the logistics of getting to and from the new building. One has to ask why the managers who report to him have not advised Roger of such staff concerns, which may be shared by those managers. There is a need to activate any existing consultative procedures or to develop new ones. These can be used to address concerns as well as giving Roger an opportunity to explain face-to-face the positive aspects of the change.

References

NB: Works of particular interest are marked with an asterisk.

American Airline Pilots Association (1978), *Aircraft Accident Report: Engineering and Air Safety – Human Factors Report on the Tenerife Accident*, pp. 22–24. *http://www.skybrary.aero/bookshelf/books/35.pdf* [accessed 9th November 2014]
*Argyle, Michael (1994), *The Psychology of Interpersonal Behaviour*, 5th ed., Penguin Books.
    An excellent account of the dynamics of human interaction, including the communication dimension.
Hall, Edward T. (1997), *Beyond Culture*, US: Anchor Books.
Hofstede, Geert (2001), *Culture's Consequences*, 2nd ed., Sage.
Pascal, Blaise (1657), *Lettres Provinciales*. http://books.google.co.uk/books?id=hEVPAQ AAIAAJ&q=shorter&redir_esc=y#v=snippet&q=shorter&f=false [accessed 24/1/2015] Translated by John Evelyn (1658), published by Richard Royston (California, USA).

Singh, Simon (2012), *Fermat's Last Theorem*, Harper Collins UK.
The Guardian (2001), *Needless battle caused by uncommon language*, 14 April, p. 3.

Taking it further

Gowers, Sir Ernest (1986), *Plain Words*, revised by Sidney Greenbaum and Janet
    Whinart, HMSO, also Penguin (1987).
Hurn, Brian and Barry Tomalin (2013), *Cross-Cultural Communication, Theory and
    Practice*, Palgrave Macmillan.
Mead, Richard and Tim G. Andrews (2009), *International Management: Culture and
    Beyond, Ch. 6 Culture and Communication*, 4th edn., Wiley-Blackwell.
        *An excellent account of the implications of the impact of cultural differences in
    communication for the manager.*
Payne, E. Kay (2001), *Different but Equal – Communication between the Sexes*,
    Westport: Praeger.

Recruitment and Selection

9

Learning outcomes

By the end of this chapter you will be able to:

- Establish appropriate selection criteria for a job
- Identify and activate, as appropriate, sources of recruitment
- Assemble relevant and appropriate information about job candidates
- Structure and conduct an effective selection interview
- Assess the rationale for selection panels and their advantages and disadvantages
- Assess the nature and rationale of equal opportunities and diversity policies
- Prepare for and present yourself to the best advantage when applying for a job.

Case study

The Legal Partner

Edward Lawton is the head of the employment law department of a partnership of solicitors. He was promoted to this position after two years working well as a specialist lawyer. He is a non-equity partner, so did not have to put capital into the business when he became a partner. Each of the various departments is headed by a partner – some hold equity others, like Edward, do not.

Edward was promoted when the previous head of department left and his area is seen as offering significant opportunities for growth, not just in employment law, but also the general customer base that this could generate. Unfortunately the expected increase in employment law work has not happened and the department scarcely covers its costs. Neither has the hoped for increase in the customer base. One of the senior partners, Orville Peters, has tried to encourage Edward to take a more proactive approach to promotional work, but with little success. Edward still makes very few claims for entertainment expenses and has not even had his business card altered to show he is now a partner. There has been little attempt by him to exploit contacts with corporate clients, or to develop contacts with bodies such as trade associations, trade unions and colleges. Edward is also very reactive in terms of staff management and development and shows little interest in staff concerns. The quality of Edward's legal work remains high. Orville is aware that competitor partnerships are getting more 'street wise' in the way they promote themselves and wonders what should be done.

Questions:

1. How well was the selection of Edward carried out?
2. What can realistically be done about the problems that have emerged?

Introduction

One of the most critical decisions that managers may have to make is the appointment of their staff. Managers may also be involved in the appointment of staff for other managers – for example, as members of interview panels. It is easier to exercise discretion at the appointment stage than later – it is usually much more difficult to remove staff once they have joined an organization. The abilities of staff can have a critical effect on the performance of the manager concerned. Even though managers may only be involved in appointment decisions relatively infrequently, it is important that the selection decisions they take are the right ones. It is for this reason that a chapter has been devoted to recruitment and staff selection.

One of the crucial issues in maximizing the effectiveness of selection decisions is to adopt a systematic approach. Therefore, topics covered in this chapter are arranged in a particular order according to a systematic approach that managers may wish to consider adopting. This approach includes the need to identify carefully the nature of a job that has to be filled. The long-term aspects of the job have to be considered as well as the immediate requirements. The next step is to identify appropriate selection criteria. Two methods are explained – developing a **person specification** and identifying the necessary job competencies. This leads on to identifying the ways in which suitable people can be encouraged to apply for vacancies. The more accurate the selection criteria the more effective the recruitment process is likely to be. The ways in which information about candidates can be collected are identified. So too are the actual skills involved in selection interviewing, including the skills that may be required at panel interviews. When job criteria are established it may also be appropriate to reflect on the reasons why any previous holders of the job have left. There is no point in simply repeating any selection or managing mistakes that were made about the job in the past.

The chapter includes a section on equal opportunities. This is important, because failure to have effective policies can lead to poor utilization of the human resources available and feelings of inequity. There is an increasing number of legal protections against unjustified discrimination, though these will vary from country to country. In the UK protections are particularly important in the areas of gender, race, age and physical and mental disability. Managers also need to be aware of their organization's policies with regard to equal opportunities, as these policies may be more comprehensive than the statutory protections. The related topic of diversity, which is broader in scope than discrimination and takes a more positive approach to the variations and potential variations in the composition of the workforce than simply avoiding illegal discrimination, is also covered.

Very often specialist expertise will be available from the human resources department to give advice on the process and on relevant legislation. Depending on organizational structure and policies, a human resources department will also be involved in drawing up and placing any advertisements, in attending selection interviews and administering any tests where these form part of the selection process.

The rather different skills that may be required if one is the person being interviewed for a job are also considered. A self-assessment form is included as an appendix to help readers see how they might develop their own, or other people's, selection interviewing skills.

The related topic of choosing people to work abroad and the special issues this can involve was given significant attention in Chapter 4, in the context of the impact of national culture.

Recruitment

A recurring issue is likely to be the extent to which jobs are advertised both internally and externally. It may also be necessary for employers to ensure that their recruitment policies are not in contravention of equal opportunities policies and statutory safeguards. Internal recruitment may be from members of the flexible workforce who merit increased involvement with the organization. Offering internships may be a further way of increasing the labour force. However, if this is done thought will need to be given to the associated training and development of 'interns' and the ethical issue of whether they should be paid or not.

Websites may be an essential way of advertising vacancies and providing information about the organization. Employers may also want to consider the use of recruitment agencies, including head-hunters and media advertising, but will need to bear in mind the cost. Care will also need to be given to the way rejections are handled, particularly as it affects an organization's image and unsuccessful applicants may be successful on a later occasion.

Ironically as prevention can be better than cure, if replacement staff are required it may be appropriate to check why people leave in the first place. Some labour turnover may be both inevitable and healthy for an organization but sometimes people may leave for avoidable reasons. If, for example, people leave because of mismanagement it may well be better to improve managerial practices rather than replace people only to find that the replacements also leave because they have been treated badly. One way of doing this is to see that **exit interviews** are conducted, whether by the line manager or by a human resources officer, or both. Whilst not everyone may be prepared to be open about the reasons why they have left some may provide valuable feedback to their employer. Exit interviews can also help the image of the employer; if a positive note is struck when staff leave then former employees are more likely to speak well of their previous employer than if little or no attention was paid to their departure. Handling departure positively can also make it more likely that a person may re-apply for employment with their former employer in the future, which can and does happen.

Defining the job

Whether a job is new or old, considerable care needs to be taken initially in defining the exact objective and scope of the job. The material in Chapter 2 concerning the identification of objectives and key tasks may be relevant in this context. Even when jobs are well established it is important to remember that the requirements may have changed. The actual tasks that have historically been performed may not be appropriate in changed circumstances. A manager may be unaware of some of the adjustments that have taken place in a job since they perhaps occupied that position. A starting point for identifying the requirements of a job may be to get the existing job-holder to prepare an updated job description. Other information may, however, also be necessary. A job may have been tailored to take account of an individual's strengths and weaknesses. It may be necessary, therefore, to consider the extent to which such tailoring should remain if a new person is being appointed. An account given by an employee of their job may be inaccurate or may reflect what is done rather than what needs to be done. It may even be that the job does not need filling – either because there is no longer any purpose to it or because the individual tasks can more effectively be redistributed amongst other staff.

Sometimes a job may be necessary but not one of the nature originally countenanced.

EXAMPLE: Identifying the job properly

At a panel selection interview, the clear purpose and content of a job was only finalized after all the candidates had been interviewed. The original reasoning about the job in question was inadequate and the questions asked during the interviews led to a more accurate assessment of what was really required. This led to a redefined job being advertised and the whole process of selection being started again. The consolation in this example was that at least the initial error of inadequate assessment of the real job requirements was not compounded by an appointment based on an inadequate job definition.

Short-term and long-term needs

A potential problem area that is often overlooked is the distinction between the short-term and long-term requirements of a position. A person may be recruited to fill a pressing but temporary need. The problem that may then arise is what to do with this person when the need has passed.

The pace of technological and organizational change, in particular, means that the problem of conflict between short-term and long-term needs is likely to occur increasingly in the future. Historically jobs were, and still sometimes are, seen as positions that will remain substantially the same during the working life of the job-holders. This can cause people to try to freeze the activity of an organization so that the demand for their existing skills is perpetuated. Once people join an organization they become part of its political power structure. They are likely to take a lively interest in the prospects for security and promotion of people with their particular range of skills. Academic staff, for example, can take a ferocious interest in seeing that college departments run courses that provide the maximum prospects for maintaining or advancing their particular specialism. This can lead to a conflict between the short-term interests of the individual and the long-term interests of the organization. It may, therefore, be necessary to anticipate the pressures that potential employees will put on the organization to develop in a particular way or remain in a particular mould. In general it may be prudent to at least consider taking on staff with a temperament and range of skills that would make adjustment an easier process compared with applicants who may be over-specialized. Alternative approaches for dealing with short-term problems are to use short-term contracts or buy in consultancy expertise.

EXAMPLE: Conflict between short-term and long-terms needs

Someone with accountancy and computer skills was recruited to establish a computer-based accounts system. When the new system was running smoothly it was found that there was no longer any need for him and he was made redundant. Exactly the same thing happened to him in his next two jobs. Each employer appeared genuinely to think that they needed him for a permanent position. No one had thought through what to do with the person in the medium to long term after the system had been established successfully.

Selection criteria

Having defined a job and balanced short- and long-term needs, the next stage is to identify appropriate selection criteria. The related issues in developing appropriate assessment criteria are explained in the next Chapter (in the context of appraisal). It is necessary to also consider at this stage the main issues in implementing the selection criteria. These are likely to be:

- Validity: are we measuring what we think we are measuring?
- Reliability: are we using a reliable measurement that will produce the same results each time the measurement is made?
- Relevance: are the criteria used relevant to the actual job demands?
- Discrimination: can you distinguish between those who meet the criteria and those who do not?
- Comprehensiveness.
- Assessability.

Two specific approaches for identifying criteria are explained below – establishing a person specification and identifying the required job competencies. Other issues include the relevance of good and bad practice amongst existing job-holders, looking at the job as a whole and the dangers of choosing just on the basis of historic performance. The issues regarding selection of staff required to work in other countries were covered in Chapter 4 (on managerial and leadership style).

Person specification

A person specification identifies the personal attributes that the job-holder needs to have to do a particular job. The establishment of appropriate selection criteria can help with the recruitment and short-listing stages of the selection process. Clear and valid selection criteria encourage those who potentially fit those criteria to apply and may discourage those who do not. The more relevant information that is given about jobs, the more recruitment and selection processes can be assisted by advising potential applicants so that they do not pursue applications that are inappropriate. Clear and appropriate criteria will also facilitate any short-listing process.

It is necessary however to beware of completing a specification in a way that gives a spurious impression of accuracy and certainty. An increasing number of applications are made online. This is increasingly associated with automated decision-making about who to short-list and who to reject. This may particularly create a bias towards that which is easily quantifiable. Whether the 'matching' of applications to criteria is done automatically or by personal scrutiny, at best the accuracy will only be as good as the appropriateness of the selection criteria. Inappropriate criteria can lead to good candidates being rejected and weaker candidates being short-listed or even appointed. Inaccurate criteria may also create a significant administrative burden by encouraging people to apply who are not suited for a job as well as not encouraging people who are. Inaccurate criteria can also contravene organizational equal opportunities policies and make an employer legally vulnerable to claims of illegal discrimination. Existence of clear and accurate selection criteria may also be useful in giving feedback to unsuccessful candidates.

Job competencies

The alternative to drawing up a person specification is a job competencies approach. This sidesteps the issue of personal characteristics and identifies instead the job skills and knowledge that a person needs to have to do a job adequately. Sometimes competencies are split into levels. These can be used to identify the minimum acceptable (threshold) level and the desirable level for a particular job.

An advantage of the job competencies approach is that it may increase pool of likely candidates. However, it can prove complicated and difficult to operate, create too much focus on short-term needs and ignore general issues such as motivation.

Other issues related to selection

The relevance of good and bad practice amongst existing job-holders

A way of identifying appropriate selection criteria may be to consider the extent to which people, satisfactorily performing the same or a similar job, fit the specification or competencies that have been identified. Examples of both good and less appropriate practice in the job may also help.

EXAMPLE: Using standards of good performance to develop selection criteria

A soft drinks company identified the main factors that were linked to good performance in service engineers who maintained and repaired drink dispensers. They found that the key factors were social skills and organizing ability. Customers liked service engineers who were polite and who kept them informed about when they were coming and of any changes in appointments. The company had previously recruited people mainly on the basis of their engineering skills. It found it had over-specified in that direction, particularly as the relevant technical skills could fairly easily be taught in-house. As a result of this investigation, the selection criteria for the job were radically altered.

Motivation

It is necessary to consider what constitutes a good match between a person and a job, as explained in Chapter 6. Someone of high ability may make a poor match for a routine job. In a routine job, a capable person may perform less well than a less able person who does not get bored. The practice of discriminating against people because they are too able may vary, however, according to the organizational philosophy regarding access to jobs.

It may also be necessary to try and identify 'job hoppers', that is to say those people who have a track record of moving quickly from one job to another and not showing commitment to any employer. This can particularly happen with 'trophy' appointments, where an applicant with an apparently prestigious record may be more concerned with promoting their external image than actually doing the job.

Over-reaction to previous failures

A current or former employee may have a particular failing which blinds those responsible for choosing a successor to the other ways in which a person can fail in a job. In their anxiety to avoid choosing someone with such a failing, those responsible for selection may not pay sufficient attention to other inappropriate attributes that candidates may have.

Choosing in one's own image

Particularly with senior positions, what may be needed is a person who complements, rather than replicates, the skills of the other team members. This fits with the findings of Belbin (2010), explained in Chapter 15, on how effective teamwork is achieved.

Emotional intelligence

For some jobs **emotional intelligence** may be particularly necessary. Broadly speaking this is the maturity of an individual. However, it may be the product of innate characteristics as well as acquired behaviour. Most definitions also incorporate the concepts of self-awareness and awareness of others. It is distinct from cognitive reasoning ability. Unfortunately, the possession by an individual of high reasoning ability does not guarantee that they will be able to use it wisely. Emotional intelligence may be particularly important in jobs that are potentially very stressful, such as in management or in conflict situations such as many the military may have to face. What can be critical is the ability of people to use what reasoning ability they have sensibly rather than to simply reason in the abstract. The ability to handle other workers constructively in conditions of stress may be particularly important. Self-control can be a key feature. Whilst emotional intelligence may be an important factor in many jobs, it may not be easy to assess. It may be useful, though, to look for evidence of maturity, or immaturity, particularly in those applying for potentially stressful jobs (Goleman, 2012).

Dangers of selecting on the basis of historic performance

Particular care has to be taken in identifying the differences between someone's previous work experience and the job for which they are applying.

A person who has performed admirably in one job will not necessarily perform well in a different job, particularly if that different job necessitates work at a higher level of responsibility. There is more than a grain of truth in Lawrence Peter's (1970) concept of people passing through their threshold of competence, as previously explained in Chapter 1. His theory is that people are promoted on the basis of having done their last job well until they find themselves in a job which they cannot do, which is when the basis for promotion ceases.

The collection of information about candidates

The identification of realistic and clear selection criteria can be of great value in determining what information is relevant to selection decisions. Information about candidates can be collected from a variety of sources. Scrutiny of job advertisements indicates which employers have worked out the sort of person they want and the information they require and which employers have not. Providing candidates with a well-designed application form can help employers assimilate relevant information in a way that they will find easy to follow. Requesting examples of a candidate's work may help, as may references and testimonials from current or previous employers.

References and testimonials

There is often confusion about the difference between the terms 'reference' and 'testimonial'. A testimonial is an open letter given by an employer to an employee to show to future prospective employers. As it is given to the person who is the subject of the testimonial, the writer may be reluctant to say anything detrimental about the person concerned. On the other hand, the fact that a person is prepared to praise a former employee in an open letter may be because the person deserves it. References, on the other hand, are communications made directly between a former employer and a prospective employer. This may mean that the current or past employer may be more prepared to be frank about the person concerned. However, care has to be taken in the interpretation of written references. Someone writing a reference may feel reluctant to state the shortcomings of a person and mention just their good points. It is often the omissions that are the most important feature of a reference. Also developments in freedom of information legislation may mean that candidates can gain access to written references that former employers have provided about them.

Oral references may be the most accurate, but it is important to beware of the employer just in case they praise an employee they don't want to keep to increase the chance of them leaving. It may be appropriate to approach an employer for which a candidate has worked previously, rather than a current employer, so that the candidate's relationship with their existing employer is not compromised. In evaluating a reference, whether it be good or bad, it needs to be remembered that the information received is about a person's performance in a job which may be significantly different from the job for which they have applied. The past record, although often useful, should only be seen as a guide in making selection decisions.

Accuracy of information

Care often has to be taken in checking the information provided by candidates. Misrepresentation can vary from the gentle massaging of employment histories to outright fraud. Checking for inconsistencies in the information provided, such as dates of previous employment, can help establish if the information provided is accurate. Minor inconsistencies can be signposts for greater misrepresentations. Some organizations ask to see original qualifications and retain copies of these documents.

Internal candidates

If a candidate is applying for a transfer or promotion from within an organization, there may be a wealth of information available about them. Care needs to be taken in evaluating the information, but the quantity and quality of the information may mean that any interview is much less important than may be the case with external appointments. It can have a devastating effect on an organization to promote people who are recognized by colleagues as being incompetent, or to ignore the claims of those who are recognized as being competent. However, practice varies about the extent to which internal reports are admissible. Sometimes the view is taken that it is necessary to rely primarily on performance at selection panel interviews. This issue is considered further in the section on selection panels.

The development of the flexible workforce, explained in Chapter 3, means that people are increasingly likely to want to move from the peripheral to the core workforce or, in some cases, the other way around. Experience of employees in the peripheral workforce, and by them of the organization, can provide invaluable information for both parties if there is ever the prospect of transfer to the core workforce. Another way in which relevant information can be obtained about internal candidates is for promotion is to give them periods of acting up at a more senior level to see how they handle the increased responsibility.

Working interviews

A practice has developed, particularly with office jobs, of sometimes asking candidates to attend for a day or so to undertake a paid 'working interview'. This may particularly fit with the job competence approach in establishing whether or not the candidate has the knowledge and skills to undertake a particular job. However, it is only appropriate if the candidate is able to undertake the tasks they are given without too much briefing and if there are not too many candidates. It may be particularly appropriate for a routine office job where there is only one candidate and the employer wants to check out if they are suitable or not.

Assessment centres

A way of increasing the available information about internal and external applicants is the use of **assessment centres**. These have become increasingly popular in recent years. They can be used both for selection and staff development. The process of assessment often includes group exercises, job-related exercises and psychometric tests. However, more care may be needed with the establishment of assessment centres than is sometimes the case. Even when considerable effort is put in, wrong assumptions about what information is relevant can still undermine the whole process. Conversely, sometimes basic exercises can enhance a conventional selection process. Appropriate case studies, for example, can prove particularly useful as one of the ways of identifying managerial potential.

Psychometric tests

Psychometric tests have also become increasingly popular over recent years, both within the context of assessment centres and independently of them. The term is often used interchangeably with 'psychological testing'. Whilst such tests can provide useful information to facilitate effective selection and development, like any technique they can be misapplied. Dangers include irrelevant tests, incompetent administration, cultural bias, a belief that the test results should determine the decision instead of facilitating decisions made in conjunction with other relevant information, and over-zealous sales promotion.

Data access

There may be some information that employers are required to collect by law. Increasing regulation relating to immigration may mean that proof of eligibility to work in a particular country may be required. In addition details of criminal history may be required if a person is applying for particular jobs, for example relating to sex offences if a person has applied to work with children. In addition there may be legal provisions enabling subject access to data employers have collected. Such access may cover unsuccessful candidates for employment, for example giving them the right to see notes taken during a selection interview.

The selection interview

The selection interview can be much more subjective and unreliable than people realize (Smith and Lister 2008). However, it is often an important – or the only – element in the process. Even if an employer were to dispense with the interview, they would need to consider how they were going to provide the candidates with information and answer their queries, so that the candidates could make decisions about whether or not they should apply for or accept a job. The existence of clear selection criteria does enable an interview to be conducted systematically with the interviewer at least knowing what they are looking for. All too often the information collected at interviews is relatively worthless because the interviewer has not identified clearly enough what they need to know. Even when this has been done, however, a significant amount of skill may be required to obtain the relevant information. Candidates may quite understandably be concerned with emphasizing their strong points and with concealing their weaknesses.

Readers are likely to have noticed the variation in skill demonstrated by people who have interviewed them for jobs. Appropriate training can improve the performance of interviewers with regard to both one-to-one interviews and selection panels.

Planning

Interviewers must have not only established the selection criteria but also studied any relevant information before the interview starts, including organizational policies and procedures regarding selection. They also need to consider what information should be given to a candidate before the interview. The location of an interview needs to be considered, so that it takes place in surroundings that are as congenial as possible for both the interviewer and the candidate. It is also necessary to arrange for the interview to be free from interruptions.

If more than one person is to interview candidates it is necessary to decide whether the interviewing is sequential or joint. Generally, it is easier to coax out information on a one-to-one basis. This may not involve any more organizational time as those involved in single interviewing do not have to sit through the questioning by other people. If more time is needed after the interviews to reconcile a variety of views about candidates this may be well worth the effort because the volume of data may be very valuable. However, the information so obtained may be selectively interpreted and reported and this needs to be borne in mind if this approach is used. The issues involved in joint interviewing are dealt with further in the section on selection panels.

Interviewers should have a good idea of what they want to find out during an interview. They may also want to identify the basic information that they will need to convey to a candidate. Checklists of information to be obtained and imparted can be very useful. It is also prudent to bear in mind that candidates are often understandably nervous and may not absorb much of what they are told. It is necessary to consider the structure and sequence of an interview so that the dialogue can be as effective as possible. If candidates are nervous it may be best to get them speaking as early as possible. It may only be when candidates have settled down that they are capable of absorbing important information.

One way of providing a clear and useful structure to the interview is to undertake a biographical interview. This involves the candidate being asked to explain their educational background and employment history in a chronological sequence. The interviewer can then concentrate on asking any supplementary questions that are needed to fill any gaps. Such supplementary questioning may also need to focus on what the interviewee's actual achievements and skills are. Even if the biographical approach is not used, thought needs to be given to the structure of an interview and the agenda explained to the candidate. All too often interviews are conducted in a 'grasshopper' style, with questions being asked at random with little if any thought being given about how to lead up to sensitive issues. This can be caused not just by lack of skill on the part of the interviewer but also by their nervousness. The development of selection interviewing skills can have the advantage of giving the interviewer sufficient confidence to conduct an interview in a relaxed and effective manner.

Questioning

Considerable thought may need to be given to the way that questions are asked in an interview. To do this, interviewers will normally need to frame their questions in a neutral manner. Even if one were to convert a leading question such as 'Do you work hard?' into a neutral one, it would be fairly obvious what the interviewer was after. It may be more appropriate to ask what the tasks were that most interested a candidate in a previous job and which were the ones which least interested them, and why. It may also be appropriate to ask questions in an open-ended way so that the candidate may open up and talk freely. The more a candidate talks, the more the interviewer is likely to learn. The role of the interviewer may be to guide the interview gently, to look for leads that need to be followed up and to be on the watch for inconsistencies in the candidate's answers. The issues of questioning technique and getting people to talk are both dealt with further in Chapter 12 in the context of counselling.

Listening

One of the most common errors in interviews is for the interviewer to do most of the talking. This reduces the information that can be obtained from the candidate and on which decisions need to be based. A useful rule of thumb is for the interviewer to spend no more than a quarter of the time talking, and to allow for the tendency to underestimate the amount of time that one speaks oneself. Listening carefully can require much more self-discipline and concentration than talking. If answers are unclear to the interviewer, it may be important to clarify just what an interviewee has meant. It may require considerable tact and patience to establish whether one has properly understood the point that a candidate is trying to make.

Interviewer confidence

A hidden agenda in interviews may be that the interviewer, in particular, is frightened of losing control and suffering embarrassment. This may be a reason why interviews are often played far too cautiously, with important issues remaining unexplored. The development of selection interviewing skills may be the most effective way of overcoming this obstacle. This may particularly affect the close of the interview and the explanation to the candidate of just what the position is with regard to their application.

Time allocation between candidates

Many selection decisions turn out to be fairly straightforward. This is most likely to be the case with people who are clearly unsuitable. The greatest time may need to be taken with those candidates who are genuinely marginal and where extra relevant information may justifiably tilt the balance one way or the other. However, time allocation may be constrained by equal opportunities policies, which are considered later in this chapter.

Feedback on interviewing skills

The development of one's interviewing technique may depend not just on practice but on getting feedback on one's performance and adjusting future performance in the light of such feedback. It may be possible for readers to do this for themselves, and for this reason a self-assessment questionnaire on selection interviewing is included as an appendix to this chapter. Readers can complete the questionnaire and identify any of their own weaknesses with a view to seeing if these have been eliminated or reduced when they do their next interview.

Common problems

Freezing

One of the major problems in selection interviews is that both the interviewer and the candidate may freeze into a set pattern of question and answer, with the candidate feeling fairly restricted about the information that they can volunteer. One way of trying to unfreeze both interviewer and interviewee is to show the interviewee around the prospective work area. A dialogue can then develop under much more relaxed circumstances.

When the formal interview discussions have ended, much extra information is often volunteered which should have emerged during the interview but did not. The amount of extra information obtained in this way can some-times be astonishing. It may be appropriate to deliberately build such a 'de-freezing' process into the interview.

Choice of selectors

Ironically, it may well be that the higher up an organization selection deci-sions are taken, the less appropriate they may be. The peer group may often be in the best position to judge, because of their close knowledge of the demands of the job, what is really required in a candidate. It may, therefore, be appropriate to consider whether the observations of the peer group should be sought, including their views on internal candidates. Factors such as sen-iority and length of experience tend to weigh heavily with selection panels in particular. This may be because they do not have the detailed knowledge of candidates and jobs that those closer to the situation have. Consequently, their decisions may be based on very superficial reasoning. More senior man-agers may not have to suffer the direct consequences of an inappropriate appointment. It is an understanding of this issue that has led some university medical schools to include a current student on the selection panels for pro-spective students.

The halo effect

Care also has to be taken to avoid the **halo effect,** where a particular strength in a candidate leads to over-generous assessments of their other attributes. A reverse halo (or horns effect) can also develop where a particular weak-ness leads to a candidate being unnecessarily marked down in all other areas. Obviously, employers also need to be aware of their own subjective views and biases and to allow for such factors in making decisions. A basic point may be not to place undue emphasis on interview performance, whether before a single interviewer or a panel. This can unduly favour the fluent performer, whose subsequent actions on the job may not live up to their interview per-formance. This can be an important issue regarding selection panels. Their role and operation is considered next.

Selection panels

Reasons for panels

Selection panels are such a prominent feature of public sector appointments that they need examination and explanation. The presence of several people on a panel may be necessary because of the various interests that need to be represented at the selection stage. One of the historical reasons for the estab-lishment of selection panels in the public sector was the need to see that jobs were not allocated on the basis of patronage. Subsequently, their structure and operation have often become key features of equal opportunities policies, especially in the public sector. Even when there is no formal requirement for selection panels, there may be a preference by the representatives of an employer to see a candidate together rather than separately. Thus, a line manager and recruitment officer may conduct a joint interview.

If there are clear policies and procedures about how selection panels are to operate, it is incumbent on panel members to understand and respect those policies and procedures. Basic issues concerning panel interviewing will now be explored. This is done to enable readers to understand the dynamics and to assist them with regard to any scope they have in their own organizations for interpreting or designing selection policies and procedures.

The concept of the level playing field

In some organizations there is a strong belief that selection panels should be set up and operated in such a way that they provide a level playing field. This is to ensure that the selection process is operated so as not to favour any particular candidate. In these circumstances the selection decision may be based primarily on interview performance. An alternative approach to providing a level playing field is to rely on the established selection criteria and to allow information from a variety of sources to be tested against those criteria. This will involve making subjective judgements on a wider base of relevant data.

A basic issue is that however much effort is put into attempting to create a level playing field, selection decisions in the end are subjective and the limitations of the objective approach need to be recognized. If, for example, standard questions are asked of each candidate at a panel, subjective judgements still have to be made about what questions are asked, their relevance and the quality and the weighting given to individual responses. Judgements can be influenced by a variety of factors, including hidden interdepartmental rivalries. Questions may rightly or wrongly favour some candidates more than others. If questions are too rigidly standardized it may prevent members from following up leads about strengths and weaknesses that may be relevant to a candidate's application. There is also the danger that standardized questions may be anticipated, particularly by internal candidates, or even that prearranged questions are leaked to a favoured candidate.

Potential problems

The problems of coaxing information out of candidates and probing for their strengths and weaknesses are likely to be much greater at panels compared with single interviewing. The amount of time available to each interviewer is much more restricted and the formality of the situation may inhibit candidates from making fluent responses. Sometimes it is argued that the ability to cope with panel-type situations is a critical aspect of the job. However, this is often not the case and this argument may be used as a rationalization for a selection procedure that has been adopted for quite different reasons. Inappropriate or unlawful discrimination occurs when invalid criteria are used. Follow-up studies may be necessary to determine the validity of the process. If those involved with selection decisions then work with those appointed they will get regular feedback on the appropriateness of their decisions. Problems can arise if panel members make inappropriate decisions and fail to recognize what modifications in selection processes may be needed because of their ignorance of the consequences of past decisions.

The role of the panel chair

The chances of effective decision-making at panels may be improved by careful chairing. If it is not possible to give training to panel members, the person chairing may be able to gently coach members in the skills of interviewing and selection. Where the information obtained by panel interviews is of little value at least it is best to recognize that and use what other valid information is available to panel members as a basis for decision-making.

Equal opportunities

General framework

It is necessary to consider the impact of selection processes in terms of equality of opportunity and the legislative rights which prospective employees and those applying for promotion have to protect them against discriminatory employment practices.

However, the whole purpose of selection is to be discriminatory, in terms of choosing the person best fitted to do a particular job. Anti-discrimination law and policies are designed to prevent discrimination on an antisocial basis, not to oblige employers to choose people at random. Legal and contractual rights may be embraced in overall organizational policies for managing diversity.

The issue of discrimination needs to be viewed not just in the light of the minimum standards set by the law, but as organizational policies. It is sensible for employers to do so anyway: there is no merit or gain for organizations that fail to make use of the talent and potential that is available through unjustified discrimination. A mix of backgrounds can also help with regard to creative thinking within an organization. In addition, as explained in Chapter 3, employers may need to demonstrate that they take the issue of equal opportunities seriously in order, for example, to develop a positive image with their customers and to win public contracts. To do this they will need to look at the range of potentially inappropriate areas of discrimination and not just at staff selection.

Specific areas of potentially inappropriate discrimination

The areas of potential illegal discrimination are increasing. A particularly important piece of legislation in Europe is the EU's Equal Treatment Directive, as is the European Convention of Human Rights. Potential protections exist in the areas of:

■ Sex
■ Race
■ Age
■ Disability
■ Religion
■ Sexual orientation
■ Trade union membership and/or activity.

The above protections in the UK are now subsumed under the Equality Act of 2010. The institution responsible for monitoring compliance in the UK is the Equality and Human Rights Commission. The legislation includes an obligation on employers to actively promote equal treatment between the sexes. The Act also creates a special responsibility on public authorities not to discriminate on the grounds of religion, belief, or sexual orientation in the provision of goods, facilities, services and education.

The concept of **universal inclusion** takes the concept of inappropriate discrimination further. This involves avoiding any discrimination against an employee's personal attributes and which can unreasonably affect employees' treatment and work performance.

It is perhaps easier for employers to fall into the trap of indirect discrimination than direct discrimination. Indirect discrimination occurs when an unnecessary selection criterion is used which has an adverse effect on applicants from a particular sex or group. This can happen, for example, when too much importance is given to experience in job selection which may work against women who have the skills and/or potential to do a job but not have had the same opportunities as men to gain years of experience. The use of job competencies in selection can reduce the chance of such indirect discrimination by focusing on the actual requirements of a job rather than conventional views about what length of experience and qualifications are required.

Remedial action

It may be necessary for employers to demonstrate that they are really complying with legal requirements and not just paying 'lip service' to them. To monitor the situation, it may be necessary for employers to conduct a statistical analysis of their labour force and the reasons for a particular mix. In some cases it may necessary to undertake a pay audit to demonstrate the rationale for the distribution of earnings within an organization. This can be particularly necessary with regard to equal pay or equal value claims, as explained in Chapter 6.

It may be appropriate for employers to take a proactive approach to ensure that any policies they have with regard to equal opportunities are actually working. There is a basic distinction between **positive action** and **positive discrimination**. Positive action involves removing obstacles to equality of opportunity. One example of positive action is giving the option of part-time work, especially to mothers returning from maternity leave. Another example of positive action would be to provide training for individuals to enable them to develop the skills required for more senior jobs. A further example of positive action would be making reasonable adjustments to enable disabled people, who would otherwise be suitable, to take up employment. Positive action may also involve equality targets, but not equality quotas. Positive discrimination involves giving preferential treatment to under-represented groups. In the UK, under the Equality Act of 2010, employers have the option, where candidates are of equal merit, of favouring a person from an under-represented group. The creation of an equal opportunities policy may create dilemmas for some employers. One is the extent to which the policies are applied to subsidiaries in other countries where the law and culture may be very different.

There can be other policy issues that need to influence an organization's approach to what has become known as **diversity management**. These include having public services, such as police services, more representative of the communities they serve. Also more creative energy may be released by having a wider mix of employees compared with an organization with a narrower range of backgrounds and attitudes in their work force. This topic was given some previous attention in Chapter 4, in the context of managerial and leadership style, particularly in the section of managing diversity.

Applying for jobs

This chapter so far has been written from the perspective of the employer selecting candidates for a job. Readers may also be applying for jobs at some stage. It is therefore appropriate to devote some time to considering the selection process from the perspective of the job applicant.

Analysis of the process

As a way of encouraging an employer to make you a job offer it will help to understand the selection process and to get inside the mind of whoever will take the selection decision. It will be necessary to demonstrate the extent to which your application matches any specified selection criteria. This may be particularly important if there is an automated shortlisting procedure. The first stage is to demonstrate that you are worth shortlisting and should be granted an interview. Background research about the organization concerned may be important in framing your approach.

Being interviewed

As first impressions tend to be disproportionately important, dress may need to be on the conservative side. In presenting oneself it is more important to concentrate on the content of what is being said than on peripheral issues like the positioning of one's hands or elimination of gestures. Having said that, prepared responses may sound too mechanistic, so it may be better to make notes on what you think you need to say and even consider leaving the notes at home on the day of the interview, rather than have a scripted response. The questions probably will not come up exactly as envisaged, anyway. You may also need to be aware of important new issues that may arise, such as selection criteria that were not included in any information that you have received, or may not even have been thought of before the interview.

In demonstrating your strengths, clear and interesting responses are to be preferred – convoluted statements may be boring. Samples of work or other relevant evidence may help in presenting your case. Many people undersell themselves by being too deferential to the interviewer(s) or by volunteering weaknesses that may have been better left unmentioned. If you feel that any important aspects have been missed out, you should raise such issues at the end of an interview. This may be made easier if you are asked if there is anything else you want to say. Steering the interviewer(s) to cover the key issues may cause them to be relaxed and feel that they have conducted a good interview.

Account also needs to be taken of the stress that can be present in job interviews. The stress inherent in such situations can be aggravated by problems involved in finding the location, being left waiting, changes in the arrangements and errors by the employer. The ability to cope with such stress before and during the interview can have a critical effect on the outcome. Particular reactions to avoid are talking too quickly and being aggressive. If testing questions are asked or sensitive issues raised these need to be dealt with diplomatically. Interviewers are more likely to appoint people with whom they feel at ease and with whom they think their colleagues will get along. The relevant topics of aggressive, assertive and non-assertive behaviour were covered in some detail in Chapter 4.

Potential bargaining issues

It may be counterproductive to concentrate only on how to persuade an employer to offer you a job if it leads to you being offered a job that you cannot do, starting a job you find you do not want or accepting an offer on unfavourable terms. Consequently, the interviewee, as well as planning how to present themselves, needs to plan to extract the information that they need to enable them to determine whether a job is worth having or to find out if there are any areas where bargaining can be conducted. It may be useful to bear in mind that you can at least ask for time to make your mind up if you are unsure whether or not to accept an offer. Also, the time when your bargaining position will be strongest is when the employer has made an offer and you have not given your decision. If the offer is subject to conditions, such as a medical report or examination or satisfactory references, you may wish to delay resigning from a current job until it is confirmed that these conditions have been met.

Lessons for next time

If you are unsuccessful it may be appropriate to reflect on whether or not it was because there was a candidate who was better than you, or some other reason. In the last analysis, all you can hope to do is to present yourself as well as possible. If one application fails there are likely to be other opportunities where one can successfully demonstrate that you provide the best match with an employer's selection criteria. If you have a run of rejections it is important not to let it lead to you going into interviews with a defeatist attitude and thus under-selling yourself.

You may want to ask for feedback from the organization as to why you did not get a job, but often unsuccessful candidates are too demoralized to do this. If you are perplexed as to why you have not been offered jobs you feel you should have been, one further piece of preparation may be to ask a friend to give you a simulated interview and feedback on your performance. If this can be done with the aid of closed-circuit television so that you can see how you perform, so much the better.

Summary

As with most things, the key to effective recruitment and selection is systematic and careful preparation. This is all the more so as selection decisions can critically affect the performance (or non-performance) of an organization. It may also critically impact on whether one meets one's own work objectives. Knowledge of likely cost-effective recruitment sources is also necessary. It is particularly important to work out the nature of a job and not to rely simply on historic and short-term needs. It is only when this is done that appropriate selection criteria can be identified. An alternative approach is to draw up a list of required job competencies. This is potentially a more rigorous approach but can be time-consuming and difficult for people not familiar with this method to handle accurately.

Selection is likely to be assisted by the careful collection and examination of information about candidates prior to an interview. It is also important to identify what information candidates need to have. Working to sensible selection criteria with the appropriate information available creates a framework for an effective interview. However, interviewers need to develop interviewing skills, which particularly involve good questioning and active listening.

The advantages and disadvantages of selection panels were also considered. These may form part of an equal opportunities policy. The volume of related law has steadily increased in many countries to ensure that the job selection process reduces or eliminates anti-social discrimination. These may be supplemented by further protections provided by individual employers. In addition employers are increasingly embracing the concept of diversity management to make use of the potential advantages of differences in the make-up of their workforce.

This chapter contained a final section on the skills of being interviewed, which have as a starting point an understanding of the selection process from the employer's perspective. An assessment questionnaire is attached as an appendix to this chapter to enable readers to review their own performance as an interviewer.

Self-assessment questions

1. What criteria would you use for selecting a person for a particular job that you know about?
2. What recruitment channels would you recommend be activated to get people to apply for a job you know about?
3. In the example given in question 1, what information would you try and collect about candidates in advance of the interview and how would you go about it?
4. How would you prepare for a job selection interview that you have to conduct?
5. What are the main potential advantages and disadvantages of selection panels?
6. What are the main areas of legal protection against illegal selection discrimination, in your circumstances?
7. What basic steps would you take to ensure that you presented yourself effectively at a job interview?

Case study notes – The Legal Partner

Learning outcome:

■ The main learning outcome is the need to identify and take into account the managerial expertise or potential of a person appointed to a position with significant managerial responsibilities.

1. The problems are easier to identify than the appropriate action. The case is a classic instance of promoting a person just on the basis of their historic performance. Little account was taken of how Edward would tackle the promotional and managerial aspects of his job as head of department. Unfortunately four years has been a long time for him to have been failing to do his new job properly.

2. The pressure on Edward needs to be increased, particularly if there is a danger that his department may become loss making. Targets may need to be set and his continuation with the partnership be put under review. Particular care may be needed in handling Edward because he is, after all, a competent employment lawyer. Reference may also need to be made to the partnership agreement that he would have signed. There does not appear to be enough work to justify employing a new head of department as well as retaining Edward. Unfortunately training may not be answer as Edward has not been prepared to accept the sensible advice he has been given about promotional activities. There is also a lesson in the case for how other appointments are made in the partnership.

Appendix

Interview assessment form

When making your judgements try to relate these to specific acts or omissions on your part. Be sure you understand why you rate each item as you do.

++ Very good
+   Largely satisfactory
0   Not so bad, could have been better
—   Not so good

	++	+	0	—
1. *Preparation:* were you well prepared? Did you have clear and appropriate selection criteria? Were you aware of relevant organizational procedures and policies? Did you have a plan?				
2. *The opening:* how successful were you in opening the interview?				
3. *Putting the subject at ease:* was the subject very nervous? Could they talk freely?				
4. *Facts:* did you collect the relevant facts? Did you find out why and how as well as what?				
5. *Attitudes/feelings:* did you manage to discover these as well as the facts (if appropriate)?				
6. *Questions:* did you ask open-ended questions and probe where necessary? Did you ask leading questions or answer your own questions?				

(*continued*)

Continued

	++	+	0	−

7. *Listening:* did you listen enough? Did you talk too much?
8. *Giving information:* did you give all the information the candidate needed in a way that they could understand?
9. *Manner:* were you courteous, factual, tactful? Were you tense, abrupt, argumentative? Did you make value judgements?
10. *Discrimination:* was there any invalid or illegal discrimination?
11. *Closing:* in what frame of mind did the interviewee leave?

References

NB: Works of particular interest are marked with an asterisk.

Belbin, R. Meredith (2010), *Management Teams – Why They Succeed or Fail*, 3rd edn., Butterworth Heinemann.

Goleman, Daniel (2012), *Emotional Intelligence, Why it matters more than IQ*, Random House.

Peter, Lawrence and Raymond Hull (1970), *The Peter Principle*, Pan.
    Alternatively, see the Souvenir Press edition (1969) reissued in 1992.

*Smith, Paul and Julie Lister (2008), Recruitment and Selection, in Porter, Christine, Cecilie Bingham and David Simmonds (2008), *Exploring Human Resource Management*, Ch. 7, McGraw Hill.
    A useful and systematic account of recruitment and selection, including the use of psychometric tests and the strategic dimension of the area.

Taking it further

Advisory, Conciliation and Arbitration Service (ACAS) (2014), *Asking and responding to questions of discrimination in the work place.* Acas guidance for job applicants, employers and others about discrimination related to the Equality Act 2010.

Daniels, Kathy and Lynda Macdonald (2005), *Equality, Diversity and Discrimination – A Student Text.* UK: Chartered Institute of Personnel and Development.
    A useful account of the key issues in diversity management.

Roberts, Gareth (2005), *Recruitment and Selection*, 2nd edn., UK: Chartered Institute of Personnel and Development.
    A practical and comprehensive guide to the basics of the topic.

Appraisal and Performance Management

10

Learning outcomes

By the end of this chapter you will be able to:

- Identify the range of purposes for which employee appraisal may be used
- Identify and assess the reasons for success and failure of employee appraisal schemes
- Handle employee appraisal situations, formal and/or informal
- Understand and evaluate the concept of **performance management**
- Evaluate the potential advantages and disadvantages of **performance related pay**.

Case study

Performance Appraisal

Brian Hedges has been the head of a service unit in a charity for eighteen months. He has responsibility for providing help and assistance to members of the public. He also runs some fundraising activities to help pay for these services. His recently appointed boss, Carol Edwards, the chief executive meets him to conduct his annual appraisal. During their discussions she explains that she is very concerned about the small net contribution of his fundraising activities, once the costs of running them have been deducted. Bernard had not realized his department was such a drain on the diminishing resources of the charity and checks on the figures both for the current and previous year.

After much investigation Bernard, with reluctant co-operation from the accountant, establishes the following facts:

- The charge for overheads for his income generating activities had increased by 20% over the last year, for no apparent reason
- No financial credit had been given for periods in either year when vacancies had been unfilled
- There was a significant charge for hospitality that Bernard was unaware of having undertaken or even having the authority to undertake
- Some of the income for fee paying activities appears to have been credited to other units which Bernard suspects are running at a loss.

The accountant explains to Bernard that he had to find a way of sourcing activities and balancing the books.

Questions:

1. What should Bernard Hedges do next?
2. What does the case tell you about the appraisal process?

Introduction

In this Chapter the various objectives of appraisal are identified and the point made that this is an area with many potential difficulties. One common problem is that, if schemes are not thought out properly, they may contain conflicting objectives. Another potential difficulty is the high level of interpersonal skills that managers need in appraisal situations. National cultural factors may also need to affect the way that schemes are designed and operated. Consideration of the likely pitfalls is necessary in order to decide whether a formal appraisal scheme should be used or not. This is particularly necessary because of the high failure rate of such schemes. This means that if formal schemes are to be used knowledge of the potential problems is essential. One important distinction is between informal ongoing appraisal and formal appraisal. Ideally these two processes should complement one another.

After the general issue of employee appraisal has been covered, attention is given in this chapter to performance management. Sometimes individual performance appraisal is part of a formal system of performance management. Performance may be improved both by focusing on corporate and individual objectives and the development of key job competencies. Hopefully performance problems can be dealt with constructively. However, if they can't be it is as well to be aware of the procedural and legal requirements for dealing with consistent poor performers explained in Chapter 13 in the context of discipline and dismissal. Although a person who is performing poorly may not necessarily be guilty of indiscipline their future with an organization may need to be reviewed. Sometimes performance related pay is used to maintain or improve performance. As with appraisal, considerable care is needed with the design, implementation and monitoring of performance related pay schemes. It also needs to be remembered that pay is only one of the factors that determine the level of performance.

Objectives of employee appraisal schemes

There is a variety of reasons why managers may need to appraise their employees. The main reasons for carrying out formal appraisals are likely to be:

- Probationary review
- Performance review
- The identification of training needs
- Review of duties
- Pay review
- To determine upgrading
- Determining promotion
- Identifying potential and succession planning.

The distinction between upgrading and promotion is that upgrading is normally because the demands of the job have increased to such a degree that they now relate to a higher level of responsibility. This will be related to the existing job but requiring some extra skills. Promotion, on the other hand, normally involves the employee transferring to a different job that is at a significantly higher level of responsibility. **Talent management** is a longer term and less precise activity than determining promotion.

Potential problems with formal schemes

In an ideal world there would be many potential benefits of conducting an appraisal, giving a formal opportunity for managers and employees to discuss work in a reflective environment. Unfortunately, there are many factors that militate against the full potential of appraisal being achieved. Understanding these problems is necessary in order to decide whether or not to use a scheme and how a scheme might be designed. Appraisal can use up significant organizational time, so it is important that schemes are designed to maximize the benefits and, in some cases, to minimize the damage that they can cause.

The failure rate of schemes

Fletcher (1993, p. 34) refers to a study where 80 per cent of respondents were dissatisfied with their appraisal schemes – mainly because of the multiplicity of objectives. This fits with substantial anecdotal evidence about how managers view their own organizational schemes (such as the case study for this chapter and examples given in the text).

Further evidence about the potential problems is given in Coens and Jenkins (2000). They claim that formal schemes are used in 80 per cent of workplaces in the USA but that 90 per cent of both the appraisers and appraisees involved are dissatisfied with these schemes.

Unclear or conflicting objectives

The objectives of formal appraisal schemes need to be clearly defined. There is little point in appraising just for the sake of it or because it is fashionable. This may not only be a waste of time but may actually be counterproductive. If judgements are made and communicated for no apparent purpose, the people who are judged may rightly feel resentful. Unfortunately, there is a great temptation for people in organizations, as in life in general, to make judgements about other people simply because they like doing so. Superficiality in the judgements and tactlessness in the way any views are communicated may compound any resentment that may have been generated by the process.

The compatibility of appraising with different but simultaneous objectives in mind also needs to be considered. Often this point is overlooked and organizations adopt formal multipurpose appraisal schemes not realizing that some of the objectives set for the scheme may be contradictory. Some employers even carry this to the extreme of formally including the maintenance of discipline as one of the objectives of a multipurpose scheme. Including such an objective would be likely to discredit the rest of a scheme. This is because of the negative connotations of discipline. Also, if a person being appraised sees their level of pay or future promotion influenced by the outcome of the exercise, they may be eager to demonstrate how good they are at their job and play down any shortcomings in their performance or training requirements. If the objectives of appraisal conflict in this way, it is much better to pursue the various objectives at different times rather than have the employee push in a single interview to achieve the objective they have singled out as being the most important.

The compatibility of appraisal with other organizational objectives also has to be considered. It may for example be counterproductive to introduce initiatives emphasizing group performance alongside an individual performance scheme that stresses and may also reward people based on their individual performance.

Over-optimism

Organizations may underestimate the resources needed for a scheme to operate effectively. The key operating cost of any appraisal scheme is managerial time, but those being appraised also need to invest time, and the administrative expenses may also be significant. One of the reasons why multipurpose schemes with conflicting objectives are often established is to save on resources. Organizations may also be over-optimistic about the ability of their managers to handle a formal appraisal scheme. If the managerial structure and associated skills are undeveloped, appraisal may simply be too sophisticated to handle. In such circumstances, improvement in these other areas may need to be a higher priority anyway.

Explanations in textbooks about appraisal tend to suggest that formal schemes can be relatively easily implemented. Unfortunately this is often not the case. What is lacking in the literature is an appraisal of appraisal schemes explaining what actually happens in practice. A badly thought out scheme, or one introduced in the wrong circumstances, can do much more harm than good.

Conflict in appraisal situations

Considerable conflict can be built into appraisal situations, particularly performance appraisal. An employee will not automatically accept that the criteria by which they are being judged are appropriate, or that the judgements made about their level of performance are accurate. This may be because of misperception by the employee of what is appropriate or because, in some cases, the employee has the best appreciation of what is required. The deployment of people in organizations cannot reach that level of perfection where the manager is always more competent than the employee. There is the additional problem that an employee may appreciate what is required as far as the organization is concerned but recognize that this is not necessarily in the employee's own best interests. This was a point that was raised in Chapter 2 when considering management by objectives, and is sufficiently important to need reinforcing here. Organizational and personal objectives do not always neatly coincide. This can mean that at an appraisal interview employees find themselves under pressure to do what they do not want to do. This could involve developing the job in a way they find inappropriate, or making cost savings that could affect their status, promotion prospects or even job security. The delicacy of these and the other issues that can arise during appraisal is such that the manager may require considerable skill and sensitivity to handle the situation.

Confrontation

A danger of formal appraisal schemes is that managers may be precipitated into confrontations with their employees that they cannot handle. The simplistic answer to this is to train managers in appraisal interviewing, but the reality is that many managers, however good they may be in other aspects of their job, may never have the interpersonal skills to handle sensitive appraisal interviews effectively. Many managers, in some cases wisely, just pay lip service to formal appraisal and simply complete any necessary forms with as little embarrassment as possible. Others may simply upset their employees, often without realizing it. Silence by the employee may be taken to mean agreement when the reality may be that the employee may just be managing to avoid losing their temper. Recognition of these problems does at least give the manager a chance of handling appraisal constructively, or of seeing when it is best to leave an issue alone. Sometimes confrontations may be quite unnecessary.

EXAMPLE: An appraisal ritual with no purpose

A government agency in the UK inherited a Civil Service practice of requiring employees to be assessed as suitable for promotion potential before a general promotion board could interview them. The practice of having general promotion boards was then stopped and employees were expected to apply for specific jobs if they wanted promotion. Although there was no longer any formal need to assess whether employees were fit for promotion in advance of them ever applying for a more senior post, the practice still continued. Approximately half of the employees were stigmatized each year by being classified as not fit for promotion when there was no longer any purpose in such an assessment.

Over-generous assessment

As well as there being dangers of unproductive confrontation in appraisal schemes, there can also be the danger that there is a lack of critical comment.

EXAMPLE: Too much praise

A very senior civil servant in a Gulf state was in the habit of giving all his direct employees excellent performance ratings. He came to realize that these ratings were seen as meaningless and after that only gave excellent or good ratings if they were justified. After this change staff felt that the ratings he gave reflected his true opinions. Excellent or good ratings then became something to strive for. The previous practice had actually had the opposite effect and had been demotivating for the employees.

Lack of on-going dialogue

In many organizations managers are required to undertake appraisal of employees in their department as part of a formal scheme. However, whether or not there is a formal scheme, managers need to have an ongoing dialogue with their employees. A formal scheme should supplement and not replace this.

Illegal discrimination

It is necessary to monitor appraisal systems to ensure that they do not involve illegal discrimination. The criteria used in appraisal schemes need to be examined to see if they directly or indirectly unfairly discriminate. Performance, merit, payment or promotion criteria could, for example, place an unnecessary premium on aspects that disadvantage a particular group. This could happen, for example, if numbers of years experience was excessively weighted compared with the actual ability to do a job. This could disadvantage those women who have taken time out to have children.

Non-standard contracts

Consideration also needs to be given to need to appraise staff who are not employed on standard full-time contracts. This may include part-time staff, temporary workers and in some cases agency staff.

National variations

Particular care may be needed in using performance appraisal schemes in international organizations. Schemes designed in one country but used in another need as a minimum to be adapted to take into account local conditions. The very concept of appraisal, giving feedback and encouraging employees to respond to that feedback may be much less acceptable in some countries than others, especially where power distances between managers and employees are high. The process of appraisal may also be complicated by tensions between different ethnic groups. Account also needs to be taken of whether the focus in a particular society is the individual or the group. Individually focused performance appraisal may be much more suited, for example, to North American organizations than those in Japan, where the focus is much more on the work group. Managers may also need to take into account the different cultural backgrounds of people working in their own country.

Other potential problems

One of the other dangers to avoid is the halo effect, a concept familiar from the discussion of selection issues in Chapter 9. A halo effect happens where there is a spin-off from one desirable quality in an employee that causes over-generous ratings in respect of other factors. The reverse halo (or horns) effect occurs when an undesirable quality causes other factors to be marked too harshly. Other common dangers are inconsistent ratings, paying too much attention to that which is easily quantifiable, and inconsistency by an individual appraiser from one employee to another, or between the judgements made by different appraisers.

Strategies for handling appraisal effectively

The rest of this section on appraisal is intended to show how schemes might be made to work effectively. The next chapter on training is also relevant. Effective training necessitates accurate diagnosis of training needs, and appraisal may play a critical part in the identification of these needs. Whatever purpose appraisal is used for and whether it be formal, informal or both, counselling skills are required by the managers handling the process. The skills involved in effective counselling are explained in Chapter 12.

Establishing the rationale and structure of a scheme

The need for clear and compatible objectives for appraisal schemes has already been stressed. What also needs to be stressed is that it is not enough to select one or more objectives and to assume that the logic of a scheme is self-evident. Care has to be taken to ensure that any objectives are realistically attainable and that the actual scheme devised will facilitate the achievement of objectives. It will be no good, for example, deciding to have a performance appraisal scheme that is based on unreliable, inconsistent and irrelevant judgements. Whatever the scheme, a considerable amount of intellectual effort is likely to be needed in identifying its precise objectives and the operational detail that is required if the objectives are to be accomplished. Specific objectives, and the circumstances in which schemes have to operate, are likely to vary widely from one organization to another. It is unlikely that one can simply buy an off the shelf scheme or copy someone else's. This may not stop people doing just that, which is no doubt one of the reasons why there can be so much criticism of appraisal schemes. If schemes are to succeed, much patient effort is needed in developing appropriate in-house arrangements. The stages in the process include identifying and agreeing the objectives of a scheme with appropriate managers, the preparation of appropriate forms and briefing notes, and pilot runs to test the system. It is only then that the next essential step of training line managers in how to operate a system should be undertaken.

Another issue that has to be resolved is whether or not appraisal reports are shown to the employees who have been appraised. One consequence of having open systems is that, not surprisingly, they are likely to lead to only mild criticisms being made by the manager. Employees may have rights of access to what is kept on file, particularly in Europe under the provisions of the European Data Protection Directive.

Balanced score cards

Sometimes organizations, especially private sector companies, use the **balanced score card** method to assess managers (Kaplan and Norton, 1992). This involves identifying the four or so key factors that are necessary for overall organizational success. The factors used could include performance in the following areas:

- Financial
- Customer satisfaction
- Operational
- Innovation.

The key factors chosen would need to fit the needs of the organization concerned. One of the potential advantages of the balance scorecard method is that the managers so assessed consider their performance in key areas and do not concentrate too much on issues of lesser organizational importance. There may be advantages in such a system where the assessment requirements are similar for a significant number of managers. However, there is a danger of applying such a template where there are significant variations in the key performance requirements between managers. In addition, as ever, there is the danger that assessment and discussion is too skewed around quantitative measures and ignores important intangible factors.

Appraisal interview preparation

One of the critical contributions that line managers need to make in operating an appraisal scheme is spending an adequate amount of time in preparing for and conducting interviews. Their preparation needs to include a thorough understanding of a scheme and also being clear about what they want to get from an interview. All the managers involved require this commitment. The boss's boss (the organizational grandparent) may also need to be involved, and there may need to be inputs from other people with whom the appraisee interacts.

Preparation prior to an interview involves more than simply understanding the paperwork associated with a scheme. All relevant information should be assembled prior to an interview. There is no point in making judgements about, for example, levels of output or attendance patterns if objective data is available giving exact details. Judgement may be appropriate about the reason for a particular level of output or attendance pattern – but not to establish what the figures actually are. Care will be needed in deciding what judgements are relevant. Criteria also need to be established to ensure that the judgements are made systematically. Other relevant documentation that will need to be assembled includes details of any previous relevant appraisals – and particularly of any follow-up action that was planned. The job description and original selection criteria are also likely to be needed.

The process should be seen as a two-way discussion, and the appraisee given due notice of any interview and its purpose. A certain amount of tension and anxiety should also be anticipated which may affect both appraiser and appraisee. The appraiser may need to consider what adjustments they need to make, either in their own behaviour or in organizational support, to help the appraisee accomplish their legitimate objectives. It is all too easy to see appraisal interviews as situations where adjustment has to be made only by the employee, but such a view is profoundly misconceived. A further way of endeavouring to secure a constructive outcome is to ensure that recent achievements by the appraisee are clearly acknowledged. All this means that a manager should not try and conduct too many appraisal interviews in one day. The interviews, as well as being likely to be time-consuming, may also be emotionally demanding. Time also has to be allowed for writing up and planning any appropriate action.

EXAMPLE: Pre-determining the outcome

One appraisal interview started badly when it emerged that the more senior manager conducting the interview had already completed the section of the form identifying the future objectives of the person being appraised. This was despite the manager having been on a training course where it had been explained that this should only be completed after and not before the appraisal had taken place.

Feedback

It is crucial for managers to understand the nature of feedback. An extremely dangerous fallacy is that employees always want to know exactly where they stand and will always welcome feedback about their performance. The reality is that most people make a sharp distinction between receiving praise and receiving adverse criticism. Praise is invariably acceptable, but the extent to which people are prepared to accept criticism is limited.

EXAMPLE: Counterproductive feedback

A principal nursing officer failed to distinguish between a senior nursing officer's capacity for receiving praise and her willingness to hear constructive criticism. This led to considerable friction during the formal appraisal of the senior nursing officer by the principal nursing officer. As a consequence the two people spoke to one another as little as possible after the interview thus endangering the smooth running of the hospital.

When feedback does have to be given, in decide what information should be given and in what way, it may help to consider the following checklist of ideas:

- Present data rather than judgments
- Be specific

■ Consider the needs of the person being appraised
■ Praise strengths and achievements
■ Offer appropriate support and recognize the need for appropriate adjustment by yourself as well as the appraisee
■ Generally only give feedback to people about issues that they can do something about by taking into account their own personality.

Self-appraisal

If one is to embark on the performance appraisal of employees, whether formally or informally, it is likely that the best results will be achieved by encouraging the employee, as far as possible, to engage in self-appraisal. This may necessitate the use of counselling techniques, which are explained in Chapter 12. Self-appraisal involves asking the employee to identify the appropriate criteria, the extent to which they have met the criteria and areas of possible improvement. Employees may welcome the involvement this opportunity offers and may be more prepared to criticize themselves than have this done by others. People often tend to be their own harshest critics; employees may also tend to over-criticize themselves for fear of seeming immodest. If this approach is taken, the manager may ironically find that they are in the position of telling employees that they are being too harsh on themselves and explaining that the manager's assessment is more favourable. However, there may be aspects of an employee's performance where the employee does not appreciate the need to change their behaviour. The manager is in a far stronger position, psychologically, to try to draw such aspects tactfully to the attention of the employee if they have previously been building them up than if they had made such observations cold, without making any positive statements earlier in the interview.

Careful judgment has to be made about the extent to which an employee is able to benefit from criticism. If a person is simply going to reject it there may be little point in pursuing discussion. Often, however, someone may be able to take a certain amount of adverse comment – the skill lies in recognizing how much the individual can take. If someone has volunteered three ways in which they will try to improve their performance and is able to accept direct comment about one out of the three areas in which they need to improve, it may be best simply to forget about the other two areas. If their attention is drawn to these other areas, they may become so defensive and demoralized that they refuse to accept the case for any improvement whatsoever. However, there may be occasions when appraisers judge it to be necessary to put on record that parts of a job are not being undertaken satisfactorily even if employees disagree. A way of processing this can be to ask the employee concerned to at least agree the record of discussions, even if there is disagreement about the quality of their performance. It will then be up to the manager to decide what further action may be necessary.

Informal guidance

The general philosophy of self-appraisal (described above) can be used when giving people informal guidance about how to improve their performance. The timing of discussion can be critical with the manager needing to distinguish between the right time to help people improve and when such advice will be resisted. Often this will be best handled as and when problems actually occur. One of the further dangers of formal schemes is that they may be seen as a mechanism for bringing up old issues that are best forgotten. This practice has led some people to refer to the 'annual reprisal interview' (sic). When problems do arise, a counselling technique may still be appropriate. If an employee has a problem, it may be best to start by asking how *they* think it should be handled. Not only may this give the required result, it may also develop the employee's capacity to work things out for themselves. Even if there is a formal appraisal between the manager and an employee, this should not contain many surprises; rather the interview should review the ongoing dialogue that has taken place since the last formal meeting.

Developments in formal appraisal

Peer audit

A development related to self-appraisal is that of peer audit. This involves colleagues being assessed by each other. This has been used particularly in medicine and university teaching. The main benefit is that it can create a formal structure for critical self-appraisal and discussion where none existed before. It may also be more politically acceptable to professionals who often prefer to see themselves more as independent subcontractors than managed employees. Colleagues may be left to choose their partners. Alternatively, some people may be designated as auditors and employees choose which auditor evaluates their performance. This could involve some people carrying out several audits and others none. In the case of university lecturers, the audit would normally include sitting in on a teaching session with the person being audited. The technique is particularly appropriate for performance appraisal, maintaining quality standards and identifying training needs.

The technique of peer audit has interestingly been developed to assess the economic performance of countries. Examples are the African Peer Review Mechanism (APRM) and use within the Organization for Economic Cooperation and Development (OECD). A peer audit by one African country of another can be a useful mechanism in assessing a case for development and/or inward investment by an outside organization. It may also be more politically acceptable to have the review done by another African country that may have a better understanding of the local economic and political situation than auditors from a country outside Africa.

360-degree appraisal

The concept of 360-degree appraisal has increasingly attracted interest. It involves the assessment of a person's performance by all the parties particularly affected by it. The assessors may include not just the immediate boss but also other managers, close colleagues, internal and even external clients or customers. Sometimes information is collected by questionnaire. The theory is that this method will give a much more rounded assessment of a person's performance. Colleagues, for example, often have critical insights and information about a person's strengths and weaknesses that the manager's boss does not have. However, although this form of appraisal has the potential to give a very thorough assessment, there can be considerable practical difficulties in implementing it. More traditional forms of appraisal can be difficult enough but particular attention has to be paid in 360-degree appraisal to the following:

- The time and resource investment required
- Colleagues may be in competition with one another for promotion or other rewards and this may distort the feedback
- It may be inappropriate to ask even internal clients to formally assess a person's performance
- A manager's ability to control and, where necessary, discipline staff may be undermined if they also are under pressure to get good appraisal ratings from them.

Upward appraisal

The related concept of **upward appraisal** is often used to gain feedback about the performance, for example of lecturers and trainers. Forms are completed anonymously and analysed either just by the person involved, by their boss or by the client organization as well. This can provide a useful source of information relatively easily. It is important, though, to carefully evaluate what has been reported. In the case of lecturers and trainers, it may be necessary to focus both on the responsibilities of the person who has taken a session, and also on those who have been receiving instruction, who may need to apply the knowledge that they hopefully have acquired.

Performance management

In the context of performance management it is necessary to examine appraisal in relation to setting objectives, key competencies and performance related pay. The term 'performance management', which originated in the USA, has become increasingly fashionable, and it is important to identify its meaning. It involves the systematic maintenance and improvement of work standards in both individuals and the organization as a whole.

Identifying training needs and appropriate pay arrangements are usually an integral part of the performance management process. An integral part of performance management may be setting performance standards. However, as explained in Chapter 2, this can lead to undue emphasis being placed on quantifiable measures of performance. Also performance statistics may be manipulated to show as favourable a picture as possible. If an organization wishes to demonstrate that someone's performance is up to standard it has to be established that the figures are based on reality and not on convenience. For example, a school's performance standards could be used to judge the head teacher, but the school may use a covert means of selection in order to have the best available pupils to teach so as to maintain or boost the school's performance standards. Similarly, the chief executive of a hospital may be judged on the length of time patients are on hospital waiting lists but these lists may have been reduced by giving a higher priority to minor conditions instead of more severe and resource-consuming treatments. In other words, performance criteria have to be selected carefully and performance results closely examined.

Whatever the problems may be in operating performance management, however, the concept is vital to the success of any organization. The emphasis on aspects such as organizational objectives, integration of activities and employee development are critical ingredients for success under whatever banner they feature.

Criteria for effective performance management

The process of improving performance by trying to integrate individual employee objectives with the organization's strategic plan can be achieved via the appraisal process. To try and do this it is essential to have clear and preferably agreed criteria for judging performance. A methodology for doing this was explained in the context of management by objectives in Chapter 2. Performance management has many similarities with management by objectives. However, performance management is a looser term than management by objectives and is not a brand name associated with one particular firm of consultants.

Setting objectives

Objectives in performance management schemes may be best specified in accordance with the SMART acronym:

- Specific
- Measurable
- Achievable

- Realistic
- Time-related.

Ideally objectives and any specific targets should be established at the start of the appraisal period. There should, however, be periodic dialogue about this. This is necessary because of any changes in circumstances. Also, if corrective action is necessary, it needs to be taken as soon as is practicable and not at the end of the appraisal period, when it may be far too late. Even if everything is going smoothly, job-holders need to be told this rather than being left guessing about whether they are seen to be performing effectively or not. When performance is assessed it is important to distinguish between work behaviour and personalities. There is no point in making judgements about people unless such judgements are a necessary part of the assessment of performance. Any shortfall needs to be identified in objective terms relating to job demands and rather than in terms of personal failings.

The person who is normally best able to assess performance is the immediate supervisor or manager. It is prudent, though, to have someone review the assessment by the person making the appraisal. However, in the event of disagreement, care needs to be taken not to override the judgement of the immediate boss, who may be best placed to assess performance. In the event of an appeal against a performance assessment, those who hear the appeal must also be wary about imposing their own judgement. They may be well advised to concentrate on verifying that the appropriate procedures were carried out. A way of handling performance appraisal is for the person conducting the appraisal to show draft reports to both the person being appraised and their own boss before the appraisal process is completed. This offers an opportunity to eliminate or minimize any disagreement by discussion before the process is finalized.

Related training and development needs

A key element in performance management may be the identification and meeting of training and development needs. One of the ways in which such needs can and perhaps should be identified is via the appraisal process. Other ways in which such needs could be identified are considered in Chapter 11 on training and development.

Performance related pay

Consideration of performance related pay (PRP) was held over from Chapter 7 on payment systems because of the need for such schemes to be grounded in an effective appraisal scheme. The distinction between general performance appraisal and performance related pay is that with the latter there is a formal link between performance and pay. Merit payment can be viewed as a generic term that subsumes performance related pay.

There are a number of reasons why performance related pay has become popular in many organizations. These are:

- Budgetary pressures combined with low inflation – this has caused some employers to question whether they should give both annual pay increases and automatic incremental increases within salary scales;
- An attempt to create more of a performance culture, especially in the public sector, because of economy drives;
- A greater stress on individual as opposed to collective terms of employment, particularly with regard to pay;
- Greater fluidity and flexibility in jobs, which has made the nature of many jobs more personalized;
- Greater use of job competencies so that people are encouraged to develop their competencies within a job.

As with most management schemes, careful analysis is needed about both the wisdom of having performance related pay schemes and the way in which such schemes are actually operated. Important issues to consider are:

- The need for a management structure and culture that is strong enough to operate a performance related pay scheme – these schemes place considerable responsibility on line managers;
- The need for clear and defensible criteria for awarding differential pay increases to people doing the same or comparable jobs;
- A sound appraisal scheme;
- Whether increases should be given to the majority or a minority. Rewarding just the minority can have the effect of also punishing the majority. This can be exacerbated if the fixed distribution method for allocating increases is used, particularly in small departments;
- Whether or not there should be a fixed budget for performance increases. If there is, this can have the effect of only giving increases to those who increase their performance most, whatever the overall increase in performance may be;
- Whether increases are 'one-off' or permanent increases. Also, whether increases are to be consolidated into the basic salary or not;
- Whether the introduction of a scheme is to be preceded by a pilot scheme;
- Identification of linkages with training needs and promotion;
- Mechanisms for dealing with market shortages of particular skills. Schemes can be easily distorted by using them to increase the pay for people with skills that are in short supply;
- The danger that staff will give too much priority to securing a pay increase at the expense of other necessary objectives such as long-term aims and individual and organizational development;

■ If increases are few they act not as motivators but ironically act as de-motivators for those who do not get them;

■ Attention needs to be paid between the relationship between individual and group effort.

The decision as to whether or not a person is to receive an increase, and how much, needs to be taken in private after an informed discussion between the manager and employee. The discussion itself, or the subsequent communication of the decision, should not be allowed to degenerate into a bargaining session about payment. Performance related pay is not a substitute for effective management but an aid to it. As explained in the context of performance appraisal appeals, procedures need to be worked out, but one needs to beware of removing ultimate pay decisions from the immediate manager. The judgement of others remote from the situation could easily be less accurate.

Trade unions tend to be unhappy about performance related pay because of its emphasis on the individual employment contract as opposed to collective negotiation, and the potential for divisiveness within a workforce. However, they may not actually be in a position to prevent their members from having an opportunity to receive more money.

The use of performance related pay involves risks as well as opportunities. It is likely to sharpen the interest in discussions about performance. Also, the case for trying to improve performance in organizations is self-evident. However, schemes need careful monitoring as well as careful design and implementation. The increasing volume of evidence is that initiatives to introduce performance related pay in the public sector in the UK have generally not been very successful. A key factor accounting for failure is organizational culture. Success criteria are often not easy to define. The concept of generating surplus or profit is also alien to many public-sector employees. Additionally management structures and management skills in the public sector are often not as well developed or as acceptable as they are in much of the private sector.

Whilst performance related pay schemes can work, and in some cases are very necessary, there is a danger that employers concentrate exclusively or put too much emphasis on the pay element regarding performance. As explained in Chapter 6 in the context of motivation, there can be many reasons for poor performance. What is needed is an integrated and strategic approach to performance improvement that may or may not include performance related pay. A further and potentially very large danger is that if performance related pay increases are related to objectives or targets these may be set too easily, encourage behaviour that meets individual not organizational objectives or are subject to variables over which the manager may have little or no control. The devastating effects that this can have were particularly evident in the financial services industry, as explained in Chapter 7. Such factors are also likely to have contributed to the huge rises in executive pay in many organizations.

Summary

Employee appraisal occurs for a variety of purposes. Unfortunately, despite the need for effective appraisal arrangements, the failure rate of formal schemes is high. Reasons include having conflicting objectives in schemes, the level of resourcing needed and the problems of giving constructive criticism as opposed to praise to those being appraised. Formal schemes need to be designed realistically and operated effectively. They also need to be supplemented by regular informal discussion and not be a substitute for an ongoing dialogue between a manger and an employee.

The way in which individual performance appraisal may be incorporated into an organizational strategy for performance management was examined. Performance management schemes increasingly involve focusing on employee development and organizational processes as well as achieving objectives and targets. Performance related pay might be part of a performance management scheme. However, remuneration is only one variable affecting performance and the other variables need to be examined as well.

Self-assessment questions

1. For what main purposes are employee appraisal schemes used?
2. Why do formal employee appraisal schemes often fail?
3. How would you prepare for an informal appraisal interview that you need to initiate? (If necessary choose a situation outside of work.)
4. What do you understand by the concept of performance management?
5. What basic conditions need to be met for performance related pay to be likely to succeed?

Case study notes – Performance Appraisal

Learning outcomes:

- To be able to establish valid criteria for assessing people's work performance
- To identify how policy is decided in an organization and evaluate how appropriate any such arrangements are.

Question 1: Bernard needs to try and explain to the chief executive (Carol) the way the information has been manipulated. He needs to be judged on actual performance and work towards appropriate objectives that are measured against accurate and not distorted information.

Question 2: Worryingly major policy decisions seem to have been taken by the accountant in isolation, which needs to be changed. The accounts lack transparency. The accountant has had too much freedom in allocating income and expenditure. Carol Edwards has not done her homework and has accepted misleading information before conducting the appraisal. If remuneration is linked to performance Bernard may feel particularly aggrieved. Sometimes objectives may be too easy rather than too hard. Managers may have a vested interest in seeing that any targets are easily achieved, especially if their pay is linked to achieving targets. Targets may also be very subjective and depend on general assumptions about what should be achieved and how it is measured.

References

Coens, Tom and Mary Jenkins (2000), *Abolishing Performance Appraisals – Why They Backfire and What to Do Instead,* San Francisco: Barrett-Koehler Publishers, Inc.

Fletcher, Clive (1993), *An Idea Whose Time Has Gone,* Personnel Management.

Kaplan, Robert S. and David E. Norton (1992), *The Balanced Scorecard – Measures that Drive up Performance,* Harvard Business Review, January–February.

Taking it further

NB: Works of particular interest are marked with an asterisk.

Huggett, Marianne (1998), 360-degree feedback – great expectations, *Industrial and Commercial Training* (MCB University Press), Vol. 30, No. 4.

Hunt, Nigel, (2010) *Setting up and Running Effective Staff Appraisals and Feedback Reviews,* 7th edn. UK: Chartered Institute of Personnel and Development.

*Hutchinson, Sue (2013), *Performance Management, Theory and Practice,* CIPD.
    A comprehensive balanced account of the topic, including case examples, and covering the private and public sectors; also with an international dimension.

Training and Development

11

Learning outcomes

By the end of this chapter you will be able to:

- Diagnose your own training and development needs and those of others
- Assess the main ways in which training and development needs can be met
- Assess developments in training and development
- Assess the need for and ways in which managers can be trained and developed
- Conduct a basic evaluation of the effectiveness of a training activity
- Establish a career plan for yourself for the next five years
- Establish a **personal development plan** for yourself for the next year.

Case study

The Training and Development Dilemma

Charles Evans has become increasingly concerned about the trading position of the finance company to which he has recently been appointed as chief executive. Particular worries are attracting suitable borrowers and the quality of the managers. The departmental heads, who report directly to him, have frequently complained about the quality of the junior managers who report to them. However, nobody, including the training officer, seems to be taking any initiatives to improve the quality of management. Consequently, Charles makes a direct approach to an experienced training consultant he knows to ask about tackling this problem. This leads to a two-day residential workshop being arranged for all the managers from junior managers upwards, held on a Friday and Saturday. Charles attends the opening session and explains how important he thinks this activity is. Twenty-five managers are scheduled to attend. He is a little surprised to see that two of the five Departmental Heads have not turned up and finds out that they have sent their apologies for absence to the training officer, citing pressure of work.

Charles has concerns about how seriously his departmental heads are taking the training and development initiative and decides to call in for the final session. He finds that for this session none of the departmental heads are present and that two of the three who attended the opening session left immediately after that session. The other head did however seem to have a genuine reason for not attending the final session, because of a sudden domestic emergency and had attended up until the Saturday lunchtime. Charles becomes even more concerned at the comments some of the junior managers make during the final session. The general thrust is that, while the inputs of the two training consultants involved were helpful, the participants felt that the training consultants were addressing the wrong audience. Many examples were diplomatically given of basic managerial failings by the departmental heads. These include lack of delegation, unnecessary countermanding of decisions made by junior managers, emphasis on sales rather than profitability, lack of team work by the departmental heads and the over-statement by some of them of their trading performance. Charles could see that there was merit in many of these comments but that there was also a wide disparity in managerial expertise amongst the junior managers.

Question:

What should Charles do next?

Introduction

It is becoming increasingly important to have a well-trained and developed work force. The key reasons for this include the increased pace of change and greater competition in the private sector. In the public and non-governmental sectors there is the chronic pressure to do more with less and therefore it is essential that each employee is developed to fulfil their job role effectively. The various ways in which training and development needs can contribute to organizational effectiveness are covered in this chapter. These include performance assessment, staff appraisal, ongoing supervision and management, analysis of changes in the external environment, including the law, the identification of the training implications of organizational change and identification of problem areas where training might secure an improvement.

The term training relates to specific needs and activities. It may be formally planned or take place informally on the job. The overlapping concept of development is a wider one which involves exposing people to situations and giving them responsibilities where they can develop their work skills in a much more general and often more fundamental way.

After a consideration of how training and development needs are identified, attention is given in this chapter to the effective implementation of planned training or development. This involves considering the ways in which people learn and the options in the delivery of training and development. This includes coaching and mentoring. There has been a shift to identifying training needs in particular in terms of required outcomes or job competencies rather than inputs. This can help ensure that training is effectively targeted and monitored. The job competencies approach is having an increasingly important impact on the whole range of occupational and professional training and on the education provided in schools, colleges and universities. Another important development is the concept of the **learning organization**. Whilst this can be more of a general aspiration than a solid achievement, it is increasingly necessary for organizations to compete on the basis of their **intellectual capital**. This involves ensuring that organizations are open and flexible enough to adapt and adopt new ideas. The concept is also appropriate for considering in the context of the public and not-for-profit sectors as a way of ensuring that as far as possible organizations in these sectors address the needs of the communities they serve in the most appropriate way.

Specific attention is paid in this chapter to the need for effective management training and development. The potential obstacles to effectiveness in this area are identified, with a view to ensuring that activity is effective. The ways in which activities in this area can be evaluated are also considered. The key element in this is to try and identify what changes in behaviour have occurred as a result of training and to assess how appropriate they are. Individuals need increasingly to take responsibility for their own training and development needs. The pace of economic, organizational and technological change is such that many people will face unexpected and significant changes in their career plans and prospects. Whilst organizations may be able to help with some of this adjustment, it cannot be taken for granted that any particular organization will continue to exist in its present form or even at all. Consequently, the final section of this chapter is about career planning and personal development plans. Readers of this book may also need to pay particular attention to the need to develop their managerial expertise because of the likelihood of them being propelled up the **managerial escalator**, as explained in Chapter 1. The related concept of team building is dealt with in Chapter 15, on meetings, chairing and team building.

Identification of training and development needs

Importance of training and development

Training and development has always been an issue that organizations need to take seriously and, if organized effectively, should be viewed as an essential investment and not an avoidable cost. The return on the investment involved should be such that as a result of the training employees reach an acceptable standard of performance more quickly than would otherwise have been the case. It is also a way of ensuring that employees perform to approved standards and avoid bad working practices. The standards achieved if training and development are properly organized are also likely to be higher than in organizations where training is neglected. Training and development have become even more important as a result of recent developments such as the accelerating rate of change and increased competitive pressures brought about by factors such as globalization and the increasing development and application of information technology. The very ability of commercial organizations strategically to position themselves in the marketplace is likely to depend on them having the right permutation of often very sophisticated expertise to meet market needs. The existence of expertise, or the potential to develop it, can also create strategic options.

Public sector and non-governmental organizations have to take the identification of training needs seriously too. They are increasingly expected to learn from commercial organizations and to obtain value for money in their operations. They also need to be able to interact effectively with other organizations by, for example, being abreast of recent developments in information technology. Related developments include the concepts of continuous learning and the learning organization. Both of these issues are examined later in this Chapter. Another important factor is the increasing amount of capital equipment at the disposal of employees. There is little point in buying expensive equipment and then not having it used properly because employees do not have the skills to operate it. An even greater danger is that employees will misuse equipment or facilities so that expensive mistakes are made. Another basic issue is that the willingness, and the ability, of employees to cooperate in implementing change may be considerably influenced by the extent to which they have been equipped to handle such change.

The cumulative effect of the above developments is that both individuals and organizations have to increase their investment in training, including retraining, in order to remain effective. For this to happen it is crucial that managers regularly review their own training needs and those of their staff. Increasingly individuals may need to take responsibility for identifying their own needs. The rate of technological change and the reduced predictability of career paths make it increasingly difficult to judge what the needs are and individual employees may increasingly be the ones best placed to make an informed guess about the nature of their own training and development needs. This may involve them in identifying how they retain or develop their marketability in case they lose their jobs, for example in a restructuring exercise.

Methodology

There are a variety of ways in which training needs can be identified. The methods used may overlap with one another. Key methods are:

■ Establishing the training needs of newcomers to an organization. Newcomers will normally need some induction training so that they are made aware of the context in which they work. Consideration may also need to be given to the remedial training that they may need to be able to perform the basic tasks in their job.

■ Identifying the gap between actual and potential performance. This may be done by a process of formal performance appraisal and/or ongoing informal managerial assessment of how training might improve performance. Such activities may be conducted on an individual or departmental basis or both.

■ Training needs analysis. Again this may be by a formal process of appraisal and/or ongoing informal managerial assessment of training needs. The focus may include the long-term developmental needs of individuals and groups to prepare them for the future. This may include preparing people for promotion and for being able to be able to handle future organizational changes. Sometimes assessment centres are used as an element in this process. The way in which assessment centres operate was explained in Chapter 9 in the context of selection.

■ Self-assessment. Given the increasing pace of change, individuals may be far better placed than their organizations to map the career paths that may be available to them and the direction in which they want to go. They may also need to demonstrate that they are developing their knowledge and skills to retain membership of a professional body.

■ **Peer audit.** Professional level employees may be dependent on colleagues rather than managers for constructive comment about how they can develop their specialist skills. Such comment may also be more acceptable from peers, especially if the professionals concerned are resistant to a managerial culture.

■ Identification of problem areas. Problems often centre around low levels of throughput and failure to meet quality standards. Many of these problem areas may be susceptible to training.

■ Identifying the training implications of organizational change. Any organizational change has potential training implications that need to be identified. The greater the pace of change, the greater the potential training need. Such needs may arise from organizational restructuring, specific initiatives, new working arrangements, including the introduction of new equipment, and changes in the law. Unfortunately, training needs are often overlooked or inadequately met.

EXAMPLE: Missing the training implications of change

A national bank in the UK launched a major advertising campaign for a new financial product. However, many front-line staff did not have the details explained, or properly explained, to them. Consequently, many potential accounts were lost because staff did not handle enquiries generated by the advertising campaign effectively.

Great care has to be taken to ensure that training needs are realistically identified. The need for training can all too easily be used as a spurious alibi for explaining all shortcomings in performance. Furthermore, performance problems are not always the fault of the individual concerned. What at first sight may seem to be a training requirement may, on closer examination, prove to be a case for changing work arrangements, amending policy or even buying in particular skills. The problems of diagnosing the real issues can sometimes be so complex that the initial diagnosis has to be changed. Organizational weaknesses may emerge that need correction instead of, or as well as, having a training intervention. Even if there is a training intervention, it may need to be with a different group of people.

EXAMPLE: Ignoring a supervisory training need

It was decided to arrange training in employment law for employee representatives at a food processing plant in the UK. The training was to be particularly about some revised disciplinary and dismissal procedures that had been introduced in the organization. The question was then asked about the need to train the supervisors who would have to implement the revised procedures. It was then realized that it was necessary to train the supervisors before the employee representatives so that the 'employee reps' wouldn't be in a more knowledgeable position than the supervisors.

Realism has to be used in judging whether a particular person will benefit from training: some individuals have a remarkable talent for emerging unscathed after the most rigorous of training. Training is not always about the acquisition of new knowledge or skills. Sometimes changes in attitude are needed. However, realism may also be needed in this area, as employees may need to be convinced of both the need for and the personal advantage to them of developing a different attitude. There may also be limits to the extent to which people can change.

EXAMPLE: An unrealistic training and development assignment

A departmental head working in local government in London had poor working relationships with the other members of his management team. His director decided that a training workshop on teamwork, involving all the members of the management team, might improve matters. Unfortunately, it soon emerged that the abrasive management style of the department head was so entrenched that no significant improvement was possible. If anything, the workshop made matters worse by making the head even more defensive and dashing the hopes of the rest of the management team that the workshop would have positive results. The realistic options were for the director to move the head out of his job; for the people concerned, including the director, to come to terms with the head's managerial style; or for people to leave.

Development of the flexible organization means that it is increasingly important to consider the training and development needs of the peripheral workforce. Cost issues that need to be worked out include the marginal costs of releasing an employee, the other things the employee could be doing in that time (known as opportunity cost) and the time it will take for there to be a return on the training investment. Training should be geared to the major problems and issues facing an organization; that way it is more likely to be seen as a necessary investment rather than an expendable cost. It also needs to be recognized that some needs can disappear, for example when skills are transferred from production operators and are handled automatically by new equipment.

Meeting training and development needs

Resource options

There are a variety of ways in which training and developmental needs can be met. These include on-the-job coaching and planned job rotation and progression. Formal training arranged either externally or internally may also be appropriate. The better managers are likely to systematically identify opportunities to help subordinates improve themselves. If they do this managers may find that, when the performance of those subordinates is assessed, there is often relatively little need for further improvement.

The manager as coach

Managers vary widely in their ability and willingness to undertake a coaching role. However, given the need for generally greater training investment, it is increasingly necessary for them to play this role. Sometimes it may be more effective for managers to coach an employee on the job than for such training to be provided off the job. Coaching may be necessary not just because of the need for staff to develop, but also to enable a manager to delegate.

The role of the coach also needs to be considered in the context of managerial and leadership style. Some managers may have a working relationship with their staff such that staff are encouraged to discuss work problems with their manager and in that way learn from them. The managers may also be able to treat many mistakes as learning opportunities rather than occasions for censure. As explained below it is necessary for managers to see that formal training dovetails with on-the-job learning and is not an unrelated activity. The topic of coaching people so that they develop their managerial expertise is considered later in this chapter in the section on management training and development. The related concept of mentoring is also dealt with later in this chapter.

Formal training

Sometimes managers see training as something to be handled entirely by external providers, including an organization's training department. However, there is only so much that can be handled externally, and even that may not be appropriate. Whilst it would be a dangerously parochial view to ignore what external training providers can offer, one must also be clear about the potential conflict of interests between an organization selling training services and an organization considering buying those services. Standardized packages may be inappropriate for particular buyers, as can consultancy services generally. Also one has to beware of entering into dependency relationships with outside organizations that discourage client organizations from working out their own strategies for salvation. Other problems include the lack of responsibility of consultants for implementation and the lack of ownership of their recommendations by the client organization. Care has to be taken too about buying in programmes that are related to the latest fashion rather than the needs of an organization. One sales technique can be to 'bounce' a senior manager into a commitment before those with the internal expertise to judge the appropriateness of what is on offer have had an opportunity to comment. However, external providers may have useful or even vital access to expertise and resources. Potential customers simply need to beware that what is on offer is not always aligned to their needs.

Employees sometimes offer themselves for training that is not related to their needs. This can be for a variety of reasons, including an inflated view of the level at which they require training. A person may opt for a seminar on corporate strategy when their needs may be much more basic, such as the need to develop supervisory skills. External training may also be sought because of its prestige, enjoyment or the prospects it offers for getting a job with a competitor. Not all external training is well handled anyway.

One way of checking the relevance of the training courses on offer is to examine the objectives, or intended outcomes, and to compare these with the actual, as opposed to imagined, needs of subordinates. If the objectives or outcomes of a training course are not clearly stated, that in itself may tell you something about the care with which the course has been designed. The statement of objectives or outcomes can also help in checking if a person has benefited from a course. It is this, rather than just asking a person what they thought about a particular course, that is the acid test. When external training is appropriate the manager may need to help staff apply any relevant lessons, rather than let them suffer the frustration of learning what needs to be done but being unable to do anything about it. A disciplined approach such as this should enable a judgement to be made as to whether the training activity has resulted in a worthwhile return on the investment made.

Strategies for effective learning

Whatever method of learning is used, it is necessary to consider the ways in which people actually learn. This may vary from person to person and also according to the nature of the knowledge to be acquired or skill to be developed. There may also be cultural differences in learning. People from authoritarian and collectivist countries may be more comfortable with prescriptive approaches whilst those from individualistic cultures may prefer to have a significant amount of experiential learning where they work things out for themselves. Whoever is responsible for organizing learning for others needs to examine the fit between their training style and the learning style of the people concerned. This is illustrated by the following example.

**EXAMPLE: Mismatch between training delivery
and student needs**

For a whole academic year a newly appointed lecturer conscientiously prepared his lecture material for the sessions that he took. Towards the end of the year, one of his students, who had attended regularly, explained that he would not be taking the examination. The lecturer was surprised at this as he felt that the student had been thoroughly prepared for the examination. After considerable private discussion the student eventually explained that it was because he had hardly understood a word the lecturer had said all year! This did, however, cause the lecturer to pay serious attention to his teaching methods in the future so that at least he learned from the error of his ways. It also caused him to question whether the term 'lecturer' was a helpful one, as it carried an implication that the primary way in which people learn is from lectures.

The previous example illustrates the need for checks to be made about the effectiveness of training whilst it is in progress. The example also demonstrates the dangers of assuming that information that is imparted is actually absorbed, as was explained in Chapter 8 on communication. If the learning process is ineffective, remedial action needs to be taken quickly. Early feedback on performance is necessary both for the instructor as well as for those receiving training. Unfortunately, the authority system in many learning relationships is such that the blame for failure is automatically placed on those receiving the training.

EXAMPLE: 'It's all the students' fault'

A student on a master's programme in the UK who had had teaching experience complained about the lack of any obvious learning strategies for those studying on the programme. The response she got from the teaching staff was that the institution had a policy of 'high ability intake' and those who could not cope with the programme as it was had no business being on it!

Care needs to be taken to ensure that the explanation of theory is at a level and pace in line with the ability of people to absorb it. Checks need to be taken on the effectiveness of the process. Theory may need to be interspersed with opportunities for practical application, which may also create theoretical insights.

EXAMPLE: The need for regular feedback on progress

A lecturer in photography used to give students feedback on their performance after every few photographs they took. However, it was found administratively convenient to get the students to do their 'field work' over much longer periods. Unfortunately this had the effect of each student often repeating basic errors in a hundred or more photographs instead of being shown how to correct these errors early on.

The link between theory and practice and the timing of feedback on performance are issues that may need to be addressed in many programmes. Consideration may also need to be given to the sequence in which theoretical explanation and practical application take place. The traditional approach is to explain the theory and then give those being trained the opportunity to apply it. However, this does not always work.

Sometimes therefore it may be appropriate to reverse the process of theoretical explanation followed by practical application. This is because some people learn more after exposure to practical issues. This reversed sequence may be particularly suitable for some subject areas and is often appropriate in management training.

EXAMPLE: Where practice needed to come before theory

A series of courses were run on disciplinary handling in a large manufacturing company in the UK. Relevant law was carefully explained in as clear and as interesting a way as possible. However, when the managers were asked to apply the law to a case study they were generally unable to apply even basic concepts. This was because they had not absorbed the legal information in a meaningful way. Consequently, the sequence was reversed and the case study given first. This focused the managers' minds on what was really relevant and motivated them to ask appropriate questions of the tutor during syndicate discussions. They were also more receptive to a presentation of basic legal issues after the case study exercise. The reversal of sequence also made it a much more interesting experience for them.

Some training may involve changing attitudes. This may be more difficult than the development of new skills. Trainees may need to be convinced of the legitimacy of the recommended attitudes before reviewing their own. The problems in doing this are often underestimated when attempts are made to change organizational culture, particularly if the benefits of the change to the actual employees are not obvious. Attitude change may be more easily accomplished in countries that have a high power distance and collectivist orientation such as Japan, than in low power distance and individualistic national cultures such as the UK and Australia. However, such training may be much more likely to be effective if it involves group discussion and not just exhortation. This is because it will give the people concerned more chance to reason through the issues and develop a sense of involvement and commitment.

Consideration needs to be given to organizational support and the reinforcement of learning. Good training practice needs to be reinforced by actual working practices within the organization and not undermined by them.

Effectiveness of training departments

An issue that managers may need carefully to consider is the competence of their own training department, if they have one. Effective training is literally disturbing, as the whole point of it is to alter existing patterns of behaviour. Some training departments help identify and facilitate such change, whilst others either opt out of mainstream activity or are never allowed near it. This can result in the activity of a training department being anaesthetized.

An indication of this phenomenon is the preoccupation of a training department with 'soft' options that do not contain a workshop element. Training may instead be focused on prescriptive packages involving skills, such as report writing and time management, that may be marginally useful to some of the individuals attending courses. A further feature may be that such activities are easily administered. However, such options are not likely to be part of a coherent strategy to address the key issues facing the organization that require significant changes in individual behaviour. Other indications are whether the training department is working in relative isolation from line management and engaging in training that is merely fashionable, random or token – or perhaps all three. Hopefully, managers who want a genuine contribution from their training department will encourage them to become involved with real issues that are relevant to the needs of the organization and not connive in their relegation to dealing only with peripheral issues. Genuine training and development also involves those in senior positions considering what adjustments they may need to make in their behaviour and support.

The learning organization

A number of developments have led to the concept of the learning organization. One way of describing a learning organization is that such an organization is continuously open to new ideas and the need for consequential change. The concept overlaps with the concept of individual continuous development. However, it can be difficult to distinguish between good intentions and practical achievement. Some of the factors that have contributed to the practical and theoretical development of the concept have already been examined. These include the increasing rate of change and the greater need for flexible organization structures. The concept of the learning organization overlaps with that of intellectual capital, which was explained in Chapter 3. If organizations are to survive by the high value-added content in their products and services, they need to develop processes whereby their intellectual capital is developed and maintained. The concept of knowledge management, covered in Chapter 3, also has increasing relevance to that of the learning organization.

The objective of a learning organization is to enable those involved in such an organization to learn and thereby adapt in line with external changes and internal developments. This is meant to involve structuring the whole organization so that such learning is facilitated, particularly in an experiential manner. This makes the approach qualitatively different from discrete 'bolted-on' training activities. The process ideally involves all key stakeholders, including customers and suppliers. The successful creation of a learning organization is seen as the key to organizational survival and development. Other features of learning organizations include the importance of learning from those engaged in other functions so that a 'holistic' approach can be developed. Human resources are seen as 'elastic' and in need of effective motivation and development. A learning organization also creates a learning climate that in turn creates and is reinforced by a social system that values and encourages learning.

The learning organization needs to fit with organizational culture and managerial style. It is much more likely to flourish in organic adaptive organizations than in mechanistic bureaucratic ones. Another basic requirement is that managers have an open style of management and are receptive to new ideas rather than adopt a prescriptive and secretive style.

The objectives of the learning organization are praiseworthy. However, it is important that its practical implementation is thought through rather than create a climate where 'anything goes'. Not all development opportunities can or should be followed up – otherwise organizational activity may lack coherence. There is the danger too that individuals may assume that personal developmental opportunities are automatically beneficial for the organization. Employers need to be clear what the benefits of developmental activities are to the organization as well as to the individuals concerned. In stable situations, or ones where risks need to be carefully controlled, strong central direction may be entirely appropriate. It may also be very difficult to create an experiential learning climate when an organization is restructuring or 'downsizing'.

Other developments

Learning contracts

An adaptation of the competence approach is that of **learning contracts**. Under this arrangement the trainer and trainee or trainees agree what learning outcomes are expected of the trainee. What is also agreed are the inputs that the trainer will give. This should create both more involvement and commitment by trainees and also any necessary re-examination of what it is appropriate to expect from trainees and the support that they need.

Technological developments

Developments in technology have helped with the delivery of training. This has been fortunate because of the greater amount of information that mangers have to be able to access as economies develop. Within the EU, for example, employers in member countries also have to comply with increased regulation in the form of European detailed minimum standards and protections with regard to consumers, the public, the environment and employees. This increase in regulation has often coincided with a reduction in the number of specialist advisers available because of organizational de-layering. A way for managers to cope with the extra responsibilities placed on them is by having access to packages and Internet services explaining government regulations and how to comply with them.

Some developments in technology as an aid to learning have been described as **e-learning**. For this to be effective it may be necessary to allocate time for staff to familiarize themselves with material that is electronically available. This may need to be done away from the work station. It may also be necessary to provide training so that staff know how to use the electronic processes that can be so useful them. E-learning can be particularly useful in organizations where the staff are dispersed in time and place, such as airlines.

Continuous professional development

The concept of continuous professional development (CPD) is being gradually but unevenly applied to membership and training arrangements by professional bodies. Some bodies now make CPD a condition of continuing membership. This involves members being able to demonstrate that they are maintaining and developing their skills, particularly in core areas. A coherent strategy for self-development (also known as personal development planning) is also required. There is also a need for educational institutions to place increasing emphasis on teaching people to 'learn how to learn' and to help them manage such ongoing development. The pace of change is such that on formal programmes a significant amount of material covered early on may be out of date even before the programme is completed. Judgements about learning priorities and access to reference material are increasingly important because of the ongoing explosion in the quantity of information.

Investors in People (IIP)

A national development in the UK has been the development of the **Investors in People** (IIP) scheme. To gain accreditation under this scheme employers must demonstrate that they have a coherent training policy and plan which is adequately resourced and which delivers appropriate results. Organizations must also have an explicit commitment to equal employment opportunities. To retain accreditation employers need either to have an annual external audit or reapply every three years. Ideally organizations use the scheme as a framework for identifying and meeting important training needs and not simply as a public relations kite mark to help attract more customers or clients. The IIP framework is best integrated with existing training arrangements, not as a separate set of policies and procedures.

Management training and development

Its importance

As explained in Chapter 1, the effectiveness of organizations can critically depend on their level of managerial expertise. As also explained in that chapter, often the biggest problem facing organizations is the preference of those with managerial responsibilities to neglect these duties in favour of specialist activity. Effective management training and development can do much to rectify this. However, it is necessary to recognize and avoid the ways in which such activity can be undermined.

Potential obstacles to effective management training and development

The list below identifies some of the potential obstacles to effective management development. A key feature of this chapter is consideration of the extent to which these problems can be overcome. Obstacles to effective management development include the following:

■ Management training and development can be costly and the results difficult to verify. When there is pressure on budgets, long-term and speculative investments like management training are not likely to receive favour and training and development budgets are particularly vulnerable when short-term economies are required. However, if management training is carefully planned and targeted it is likely to be seen much more as an essential investment than an avoidable cost. Also some interventions, like senior managers taking responsibility for coaching junior managers, may not be that costly;

■ Investment in management training and development may fail because people lacking managerial potential have been appointed as managers and because of their lack of potential are unlikely to benefit from development or training;

■ Training and development is not geared to organizational needs and developments;

■ The organizational culture is not supportive of training and development;

■ Inadequate attention is paid to both organizational and national culture. These factors may affect the environment in which people have to operate and the ways in which they learn;

■ Training and development may be offered too early or too late in people's careers for them to make effective use of it;

■ The diagnosis of needs may be correct but the training delivery may be ineffective. Many training contractors, for example, provide programmes that are based around standard prescriptive packages, not around carefully diagnosed organizational needs;

■ A wide range of topics can be passed off as falling within the definition of management education and training. Training can switch to being about management instead of being for managers, and be taught as a set of unrelated theoretical disciplines which can aggravate the problem of the over-compartmentalization of management activity;

■ Undergraduate and other pre-experience management training needs to be reinforced by further training once those concerned have had greater exposure to management problems. Such exposure is likely to lead to an increased awareness of what the problems really are and the concepts and skills that may assist in their resolution;

■ The expectations of what management training can do are often unrealistic. Sponsors and managers may believe that there are prescriptive solutions to most management problems that can easily be learned and applied. Development in managerial expertise is often much more complicated than that;

■ The skills of effective teaching are sophisticated and in short supply and the effectiveness of teaching in this area is difficult to validate;

■ Management training and development, unlike purely technical training, has to be integrated with personal behaviour. This is a particularly sensitive area and egos can easily get bruised if people feel that their job performance is being criticized. Consequently, lessons that people need to learn may be 'blocked' because they are too personally threatening. Also the mere acquisition of knowledge does not mean that people become better managers unless they are willing and able to apply that knowledge;

■ Even if training is effective, one needs to ensure that the result has been achieved in the most cost-effective way.

EXAMPLE: Example of an effective management development programme

It emerged at a London local authority that whilst senior officers were generally well qualified technically there was a need to develop their managerial expertise. Consequently, a series of management development workshops were arranged within each directorate and run by an external consultant and each director. Tailor-made teaching material was prepared, particularly case studies. The workshops were designed to identify and address management problems and this was combined with relevant inputs by the external consultant on relevant management topics. The workshops concluded with action plans being drawn up both for the individuals who attended and for each directorate. A feature of this approach was that there was a culture change within each directorate with regard to the need for and development of managerial expertise. The fact that each directorate was involved in this process meant that the effect of the workshops was reinforced throughout the authority.

Management coaching

It has previously been explained in this chapter, that managers need to accept responsibility for the development of their subordinates. This may be particularly appropriate for the development of managerial expertise. Coaching is usually about the development of specific areas of expertise and the improvement of performance. It normally involves feedback from the person giving the coaching. In some cases this may be an external person who has the appropriate expertise combined with the skills of imparting it. Whilst not all senior managers give their coaching role a high priority, the following is an example of one who did, at least for newly appointed executives.

EXAMPLE: Example of effective management coaching

The chief executive of a London engineering factory told newly appointed senior executives to make a note each day of the issues they would like to discuss with him. He then arranged to see them at the end of the day and spent an hour discussing their queries and related issues with them. After a few weeks he began to reduce the length of the sessions until they stopped completely. After that he expected to spend the same amount of time discussing matters with the new executives as he did with the more established managers, although this could vary according to job demands.

Mentoring

The concept of mentoring has become increasingly popular. Mentoring is a one-to-one relationship with a more long-term focus than coaching. It is designed to help the individual manage their own career development. Whilst some mentoring may be conducted by the immediate boss, formal mentoring involves the appointment of an experienced manager in a different, possibly related, department. The organizational distance this creates can reduce the political problems in the relationship. It can also bring detachment to the role and widen the experience of the person being mentored. Much though will depend on the enthusiasm of the parties and the process skills of the mentor.

Sometimes it may be appropriate to appoint an external mentor (Rees, 1992, pp. 20–21). Although this will normally cost more, it can bring several advantages, which may include:

- Increasing the pool of possible mentors;
- An external mentor need not be involved in internal organizational politics;
- A suitable internal mentor may not be available. The more senior the manager, the more this is likely to be the case;
- Appointment of an external mentor may enable an employee to be developed when they cannot be released from their job;
- An external mentor may be able develop a more confidential relationship with the person they are mentoring than would be possible with an internal mentor. This can assist with the development of a constructive counselling relationship. The skills of workplace counselling are covered in the next Chapter.

A concept related to that of mentoring is **shadowing** (Rees, 1992). This involves development by the programmed observation of a more senior manager in your own organization. It can also be effected by observing the behaviour of a manager doing a similar job to the 'shadower' in another organization

Talent management

Some organizations take the issue of attracting developing and retaining talent so seriously that they create a formal policy to underpin it. A key element is to identify those individuals who can be critical to the success of an organization. It is likely to affect those who have, or are likely to acquire, significant managerial responsibilities. This can involve career management, developmental opportunities and remuneration policies that develop potential and encourage talented individuals to stay with an organization. It may be necessary, however, to ensure that this does not conflict with equal opportunities policies and procedures for the development of other talented people in an organization who may not have been identified as being in the 'talent pool'. Care may also need to be taken to see that the potential shows signs of being realized.

Evaluation

Cost-benefit analysis

Whatever pattern of training and development is adopted in an organization, it is important that it be monitored to ensure that it is meeting the appropriate needs and giving value for money. The identification of training needs in terms of objectives and/or expected outcomes makes it easier to judge whether training has been worthwhile. Cost-benefit analysis is not just an activity that should be undertaken at the end of a learning activity – interim evaluation may be needed so that adjustments can be made in time for those on a programme to benefit before the activity is completed. Follow-up studies may also be needed as well to estimate the long-term impact of training particularly in areas such as management development. The results of such studies can be very useful as a means of improving future activity. The studies may also need to consider alternative ways of achieving required results. Line managers need to be involved in evaluation and follow-up activity to ensure that money spent on their behalf is achieving the desired results. Ways of doing this include interviewing people after they have completed formal programmes to discuss what can be applied in the workplace and reviewing the effectiveness of training during formal appraisal interviews.

Training costs may be relatively easily identified, for example by aggregating the costs of releasing a person with the cost of the training provision. This can then be compared with the benefits, i.e. the effect of the training on actual performance, which may be more difficult to calculate. However, this can provide the framework for a cost-benefit analysis to assess whether or not there has been a net benefit to the organization. It can be particularly difficult to undertake a cost benefit analysis with management training and development. The opportunity cost of releasing managers has to be considered. Also it may be particularly difficult to measure changes in performance and to isolate those changes that have resulted from training. Estimates of whether a person is likely to stay, or be needed, in an organization may also be necessary. Feedback forms can be used to obtain the views of those who have participated in training activities. However, the key issue is to find out what significant changes in behaviour have occurred as a result of the training activity.

Follow-up analysis

One way of trying to overcome some of the above problems is to build into the design of a training programme a follow-up session in the training activity. This may be particularly appropriate with management training. As well as asking people to comment on what has happened as a result of their training, they may also be asked to report on a project designed to demonstrate the application of their learning. As well as helping assess the effectiveness of training this can also have considerable learning value. It may also further motivate people to apply their learning. Participants may also learn from one another's presentations at a follow-up event. However, one methodological problem is disentangling what people have done as a result of the training they have received and what they might have achieved anyway. The follow-up of formal training activities may also reveal that people vary widely in their ability to benefit from the same programme. In some cases the methodological problems of assessing what benefits have derived from training and development activities may be insuperable. However, it may also be the case that activities such as management training and development are too important to be ignored and some investment is necessary as an act of faith.

EXAMPLE: Evaluation of a management development programme at a national oil company

In the national oil company of a developing country an attempt was made to evaluate the effectiveness of a major management programme, spread over some years. The company's activities included oil and gas exploration, production and distribution of oil and gas and increasingly the production of petrochemical products. There were so many variables, imponderable issues and methodological problems that the conclusion was reached that it was not possible to make a valid assessment of the programme's effectiveness. However, given the increasing sophistication and competitiveness of the markets in which the company was operating, and the political need to develop local expertise, the only option was to continue to try and develop local managerial talent sensibly and hope that this was effective.

Retention of trained staff

It may also be necessary to check on the extent to which organizations retain the people that they have trained and developed. This is more necessary in countries such as the UK where job mobility is generally higher than in countries such as Japan. Sometimes organizations make the mistake of making a considerable training investment in employees whom they then lose to other employers because the current employer has not provided the employee with adequate opportunities to use their newfound skills. This can also happen if pay levels get out of line with organizations that are competing for the same skills. It may be particularly necessary to review both the opportunities and pay levels in comparison with 'poacher' organizations who invest little in training themselves but rely instead on recruiting people who have been trained elsewhere.

Responsibility for one's own development

As explained in the earlier section on the identification of training and development needs, individuals need increasingly to take responsibility for managing their own training and development. An individual may be the best person to judge their own needs anyway. In addition, however, they can hardly expect their employer to take a keen interest in helping them to develop if their objective is to move to another organization. As has previously been explained in this chapter, continuing membership of professional bodies may also depend on individuals demonstrating that they have made adequate attempts to maintain and develop their expertise.

Managing one's own career

The management of one's own career is made increasingly difficult by the pace of economic and organizational change. Even if one stays within the same occupation there may be fundamental changes in the knowledge and skills required to meet a changing pattern of job demands. This means that however carefully one plans one's own career it will be necessary to build in an element of flexibility to account for significant and unexpected change. Individuals will normally want to develop employment security as well as to have work that they find interesting. The best form of security may be to try to ensure that you have expertise that is going to be in demand in the marketplace whoever the employer may be.

Personal development plans (PDPs)

Having stated that flexibility needs to be built into one's career plans, a sensible first step in career planning is to try to identify the progression that is realistically available over the next few years. This may identify a gap in skills and expertise that you need to fill. This leads on to the next step – how you propose to fill that gap. This methodology can be applied both to students who have not yet had a full-time job and to people already in jobs. Closing the gap means combining what organizational assistance you can get with arrangements that you may need to make for yourself. For people in jobs this may involve going on external courses even if this is not with the blessing of an employer. In addition, it will be necessary to see that you keep up to date with any current job that you have, so that your expertise does not get out of date. Keeping up to date with your current expertise may also reduce the prospects of your work being declared unnecessary. A recurring theme of this book is that you also need to consider where you plan to be on the managerial escalator.

Constructing a personal development plan (PDP) may necessitate recording achievements, identifying strengths and weaknesses, setting goals and action plans and reviewing progress. People in management or supervisory positions may want to encourage their employees to use PDPs as well as considering using them for themselves. It is suggested in the self-assessment questions at the end of this chapter that readers complete a PDP for the coming year.

Summary

The increasing importance of training and development has been explained in this Chapter. Factors accounting for this increasing importance include the accelerating rate of change, growing competitive pressures, partly because of globalization and the greater capital intensive nature of much employment. Consequently, increased organizational resources need to be spent in identifying and meeting training and development needs. Developments in information technology generate new training needs and provide new ways of meeting them. Developments that have been examined include an emphasis on learning outcomes and the development of specific competencies.

Traditional career paths are often disappearing and individuals need to maintain and develop their expertise so that they retain their marketability. They may also need to be able to demonstrate their continuous professional development if they are to retain membership of a professional organization. The construction of a personal development plan can aid the individual in managing their own career.

The concept of the learning organization is important because of the need for organizations to adjust their stock of human capital to market and community needs. This overlaps with the concepts of intellectual capital and knowledge management.

Management training and development is particularly important because of the need for managers capable of exploiting the potential opportunities for an organization. This is likely to be particularly important for readers of this book, especially in ensuring they get the right balance between specialist and management activities as they move up the managerial escalator.

Another important area is the evaluation of training and development. The establishment of clear learning outcomes can create a logical framework both for the implementation and for the evaluation of training. Follow-up studies can also be instructive in helping determine if the training investment has been worthwhile.

It is important that readers apply the lessons of this Chapter to themselves, as well as others. This is particularly so with regard to their own career planning and personal development plans.

Self-assessment questions

- How would you assess the training needs of an employee, known to yourself, in an organization?
- What are the main ways in which job training needs can be met?
- Why has there been a trend to organize training around outcomes rather than inputs?
- Identify and comment on the ways in which those with managerial responsibilities can be trained and developed;

■ How would you evaluate the effectiveness of a training activity?

■ Identify your own likely career path over the next five years;

■ Construct your own personal development plan to cover the coming year.

Case study notes – The Training and Development Dilemma

Learning outcomes:

■ To evaluate the quality of management in the finance company concerned

■ To develop a strategy and means of improving the quality of management.

One of the many difficulties facing Charles is that some of his departmental heads may not be very good managers. Others might have potential if managed properly, by Charles, and if they are developed effectively. The attitude to workshop attendance has been disrespectful and the alleged manipulation of performance figures is worrying. The management of the departmental heads would seem to need to be tighter. If the heads cannot benefit from joint development activities with junior managers they may need to have group activities for heads and some individual coaching. Appraisal and performance management may need to be important techniques for inclusion.

Some of the junior managers may have promotion potential but others may need to improve. Managerial potential may need a much higher priority at the selection or promotion stage. At least the workshop has enabled Charles to identify potential key problems that need addressing.

Charles has demonstrated the importance of training as a means of improving performance but will need to follow through on this, particularly in discussions with the Departmental Heads. They will need to reflect on how they can improve their own performance, including by training. They will also need to do the same with their subordinate managers. It is also important that the Departmental Heads pay attention to the constructive suggestions that some, at least, of their subordinate managers have made about necessary and potential improvements. Charles is likely to have to stress these issues in the appraisals that he needs to conduct.

References

Rees, W. David (1992), *Someone to Watch Over Me – An Experiment in Mentoring in Hackney,* Local Government, Autumn.

Taking it further

Beevers, Kathy and Andrew Rae (2013), *Learning and Development Practice,* UK: CIPD.

Caplan, Janice (2013), *Strategic Talent Development: Developing and Engaging All Your people for Business Success,* 2nd edn., Kogan Page.

Clutterbuck, David (2007), *Coaching the Team at Work,* Nicholas Brearley Publishing.

Connor, Mary and Julia B. Pokora (2012), *Coaching and Mentoring at Work – Developing Effective Practice,* 2nd edn., McGraw Hill – Open University Press.

Cottrell, Stella (2003), *Skills for Success: The Personal Development Planning Handbook,* Palgrave Macmillan.

Megginson, David and Vivien Whitaker (2007), *Continuing Professional Development,* UK: CIPD.

Mumford, Alan (2010), *Leadership and Management Development,* UK: CIPD.

Porter, Christine and Rees, W. David (2012), The Managerial Gap and how coaching can help, *International Coaching Psychology Review* (British [& Australian] Psychological Society), Vol., 7, No. 1, March.

Rigg, Claire and Jim Stewart (2011), *Leadership and Talent Development,* UK: CIPD.

Workplace Counselling

12

Case study

What to Do?

Oliver Adams is an office assistant employed in the environmental health department of some local government offices. It is the only full-time job he has had and he has been with the Council for the three years since he left school at age 16. His duties include photocopying, distributing documents and filing. He did reasonably well at school but is on the shy side although he gets on well with his colleagues. There is no obvious promotion path for him in his directorate, where in any case there may have to be some staff cuts. His boss, Edward Higgins, learns that there is a council-wide administrative trainee scheme and thinks perhaps it is a good idea if Oliver goes on it. Consequently, he calls Oliver in to his office to discuss it.

At the meeting Oliver is told about the scheme – which includes job rotation around various directorates and lasts for ten weeks. It is explained that whilst it is intended for school leavers Oliver might be eligible for it. His boss, Edward, explains that he will try and see that Oliver's salary is protected and adds that whilst there is no guarantee of a job at the end of the training it should provide the opportunity for Oliver to find something that has more of a future in it. When Oliver asks if his existing job would still be available at the end of the training Edward says that he would have to find a temporary replacement.

Edward hears nothing more from Oliver about whether or not he wants to apply for the trainee scheme but gathers on the **grapevine** that Oliver is quite distressed about the suggestion and does not know what to do. In the meant time the standard of Oliver's work has deteriorated. Edward decides that he had better have another discussion with Oliver.

Question:

How should Edward handle the next discussion?

Introduction

Some reference was made to the need for counselling in the previous chapter on appraisal. It is now appropriate to deal with the subject in greater detail. The nature of counselling is explained, as is the range of work situations in which these skills may be needed. These situations include discussing work-related problems, personal problems that affect work, handling grievances and some disciplinary situations. The skills may be needed with colleagues, subordinates and customers. The basic skills of workplace counselling are explained. These include recognizing the various stages of counselling, identification of the actual problem and active listening. Counselling in this context particularly involves helping people work out their own solutions to problems rather than telling them what to do. This can be very time-consuming and managers may need to take a conscious decision over whether they wish to or should get involved in particular situations. Workplace counselling skills can be particularly useful and necessary when handling grievances and dealing with some disciplinary situations. Consequently, specific sections on these areas are included in this Chapter.

The nature of and need for workplace counselling

The nature of workplace counselling

Workplace counselling can be defined as a purposeful relationship in which one person helps another to help themselves. It is a way of relating and responding to another person so that the person is helped to explore their thoughts, feelings and behaviour with the aim of reaching a clearer understanding. The clearer understanding may be of themselves or of a problem, or of the one in relation to the other. The point of all this is to enable people to work out how they will handle issues, problems or decisions that have to be made, for themselves. The technique is necessary because it may be that it is only by this process that an issue can be understood and/or the commitment created that will lead to an appropriate course of action being taken by the person concerned.

The need for workplace counselling

The need for workplace counselling can arise in a wide range of situations. Appraisal has already been mentioned, and the requirement for these skills in grievance and some disciplinary situations is explained later in this chapter. Counselling may also be particularly necessary, when employees are experiencing work-related stress (see Chapter 6). The need for counselling skills can arise whenever a subordinate or colleague has a work-related problem. Sometimes it may be necessary to use these skills with clients as well. As well as managers needing workplace counselling skills themselves, they also have to consider the extent to which their staff need these skills. It may be particularly important that any employee who has direct contact with clients or the public is trained in how to handle such contacts.

Given that managers spend most of their time in some form of communication and that much of it is oral communication, as explained in Chapter 8, the need for workplace counselling techniques can arise very frequently. The skills may not have the glamour of more high-status management activities, but can nevertheless be one of the most critical of all management skills. The skills may also constructively be applied in one's personal life.

Usually, counselling discussions are initiated by the person who needs the help. However, there will be occasions when managers need to take the initiative and encourage employees to face up to issues that are having an adverse effect on their work. Whoever initiates discussion, some interpretation of an employee's responses will be necessary. Care needs to be taken about the level of discussion and analysis that is attempted. In-depth Freudian probing and analysis, for example, is better handled by those qualified to do it than by amateur psychiatrists. The requirement for counselling in work situations is usually for work-related rather than personal problems anyway. Obviously, personal problems can affect behaviour at work, and counselling may be given by one person to another in the capacity of personal friend. There may well be situations, though, where it is not appropriate for a manager to get involved or where the best help that can be given is to refer a person to an appropriate agency or service.

Specific skills

Having explained the general nature and purpose of workplace counselling, it is now appropriate to explain the skills in more detail. A particular feature of counselling is that managers will often have no advance notice of when they are going to need them. Consequently, if they are to act as counsellors they need to have sufficient mastery of the skills involved to be able to deploy them at a moment's notice.

Choice of counsellor

The choice of who counsels and when is much more in the hands of the person wanting this type of help than with the potential counsellor. A person may choose not to speak about their problems to some people and may refuse offers of help that are made. The opportunity for counselling is likely to be determined by the person wanting help, but it is up to the manager, if invited, to decide whether or not to respond. The counselling that is required may be easily dealt with in a few moments or may involve several lengthy discussions. Those who have the opportunity to provide this type of help have to judge whether it is appropriate for them to give it and to assess whether they are really likely to help, if they have the time to spare and whether there are other more appropriate ways of helping. A complication is that decisions on whether or not to counsel may have to be taken very quickly. If a person is rebuffed they may not ask again or, if counselling-type help is offered, it may be very difficult to stop once it has started.

Stages in the process

There are normally several stages in a counselling interview. Part of the skill of counselling effectively is to identify the pattern an interview may take. The main stages are likely to be:

- Identification of the problem
- Collection and exchange of information
- Checking that all the necessary statements have been made
- Establishing the criteria for a satisfactory solution
- Deciding on the appropriate solution
- Subsequently checking whether or not the solution has worked
- Evaluating any outstanding problems.

The issue of the different stages in a counselling interview is not quite the same as the different styles of counselling. Each person who counsels may have their own style, which may vary from that of other people involved in terms of decision to intervene (or not) and the specific skills that are used. However, whatever basic style is used, it will need to be varied according to the personality of the subject, the issue under discussion and the stage of the counselling process.

Identification of the problem

The problem that a person raises may just be a lead-in or a pretext for going on to discuss much more serious issues. Often the stated problem is rather like the tip of an iceberg. The subject may want to check that they are going to get a sympathetic response before being prepared to reveal the next part of a problem. Sometimes a person may not even be aware that the problem is much deeper than that indicated by them initially. This shows the danger of trying to deal with just the tip. The help that a person may need is help to reason through the whole of a problem in such a way that they can cope with it, allowing for their own personality. It may be that there are also issues of which they are aware but which they deliberately keep secret. This is yet another reason for the counsellor to beware of seeking to impose a solution, as it may be based on an incomplete knowledge of the facts.

To discover the rest of the iceberg and to get the person to speak freely, the counsellor will find it useful to pay attention to their own questioning technique. Open questions (i.e. those that start with an interrogative such as 'how', 'what', 'why', 'where') are more likely than closed questions to help widen the conversation and explore the issues involved than closed questions. Closed questions are often phrased in such a way that they start with a verb: for example 'Do you enjoy your work?' If the interviewee is reluctant to talk, the 'yes' or 'no' given in answer to such a question may only help in a marginal way. There will, though, be situations when a straight 'yes' or 'no' answer is what is appropriate. Other skills that may be useful in building up rapport and encouraging the employee to talk include the processes of summarizing, clarifying and reflecting back saying, for example, 'So that made you feel rather annoyed?'. However, premature intervention by the counsellor can prevent further disclosure by the subject.

Active listening

Appearance of counsellor

Active listening skills, which are necessary in a counselling situation, involve two aspects. The first is to be listening as well as actually hearing what is being said. Non-verbal skills in this situation include eye contact, leaning forward, not shuffling papers or making notes. The counsellor needs to be aware of the need for eye contact when appropriate throughout a counselling interview. That is not to say that they should spend all their time staring at the subject, but eye contact can be helpful in showing that the counsellor is taking an interest in what is being said. It is also necessary to be aware of signals that are being given by a person's body language. This concept has already, and necessarily, had some explanation in Chapter 8 (Communication).

Barriers to communication

The second aspect of listening which is important includes being aware of the source of barriers to hearing exactly what is being said. These barriers include some obvious ones like language differences, day-dreaming and environmental noise. There is also selective perception (hearing what we want to hear), self-consciousness (the counsellor is too aware of the impression they are making) and behaviour rehearsal (the counsellor is busy working out what they are going to say next). There may also be a barrier when the counsellor has problems of their own which occupy their thoughts or where the content of what the employee is saying arouses anger or hostility in the counsellor. In many instances, simply being aware of the likely barriers can help the counsellor to make a conscious effort to eradicate them. These points on listening skills will also be relevant in other types of interview, as will the idea of open and closed questions. Some further points on questioning technique were made in Chapter 9 (regarding selection). The pressure that people are often under before they speak needs to be kept in mind.

EXAMPLE: The build up of pressure

An apocryphal story demonstrates how worked-up people can get before they speak: the story concerns someone who had moved into a new house and knocked at a neighbour's front door to ask if they could borrow the neighbour's lawn mower. The newcomer had worked himself up into such a state of apprehension about the legitimacy of his request to someone he hadn't yet met that when the neighbour opened the door he shouted 'you can keep your lawn-mower – I know you won't lend it to me!' before the neighbour even had a chance to speak.

Level of direction

The amount of direction given by the counsellor will vary according to the situation and the personalities involved. It is the essence of counselling, though, that the person is helped to work out the problem for themselves. Not only may value judgements be inappropriate if made by the counsellor but, if they vary from the value judgements of the person requiring help, that person may see the counsellor as unsympathetic and consequently terminate any discussion. Nevertheless, even given all this, there can be a range of counselling styles (see the appendix to this chapter). At the one extreme a person may be totally non-directive and just give sufficient response, perhaps by way of grunts, to let the other person know that they are actually listening. In other cases it may be appropriate for the counsellor to be rather more interventionist, whilst at the same time avoiding imposing their own views. This can be done in a neutral but friendly manner by positively encouraging a person to elaborate on an issue. Further interventions can be made to clarify what has been said and questions can be asked that are designed to get the person to talk more.

It may be necessary for the counsellor to add information in such a way that the person being counselled feels free to make use of the information or ignore it. This represents a further stage in counselling intervention without sacrificing the neutrality of the counsellor. Another stage is to help the person concerned identify the options available to them – the critical point being that the choice has to be made by the person being counselled and not by the counsellor. This can involve a person taking a decision that is not necessarily in the interests of the organization – for example, to leave the organization (or in some cases to not leave). There is little point, however, in the counsellor seeking to impose the decision that is in the organization's interests, as the person would probably ignore it. If someone is going to decide to leave, it may be just as well to help them come to that decision relatively quickly rather than to let the issue drag on. One problem may lead to another, and perhaps much bigger, area and the counsellor needs to be aware that the closing of discussion on a particular topic is by no means necessarily the end of a counselling interview.

EXAMPLE: The use of non-directive counselling

A newly qualified human resources officer was appointed to his first job. Unfortunately, his formal training had not included counselling. Line managers and others, however, frequently asked his advice about human relations problems. Anxious to help, he made all sorts of suggestions about how these problems might be handled. However, he invariably found that for some reason his ideas were not practicable or acceptable. After a while he realized that the problem was that he was being too directive. He then encouraged people to talk through their problems with him. This enabled colleagues to frame solutions that took account not only of the facts that they had not disclosed and but also of their own personality. He found that colleagues were also more committed to the solutions that they themselves developed. The human resources officer then found that people were often thanking him for his help in solving problems that he sometimes had not even understood, far less had a solution for.

Confidentiality

Normally, the whole basis on which counselling takes place is one of complete confidence. Sometimes, however, the counsellor will need to warn the subject that information that may emerge, or already has emerged, cannot be treated confidentially. If an accountant for example, is told that their cashier has been systematically embezzling money it is hardly likely that they can, or should want to, keep this a private matter between the parties.

Grievance handling

A grievance can be about an action that has already been taken, is proposed or is merely feared. Grievances may be raised by colleagues, subordinates, clients or members of the public. Commercial organizations increasingly promote customer complaints (or grievance) procedures in order to demonstrate their concern for their customers. An increasing volume of statutory protection and provisions for processing complaints reinforces this. Grievance and complaints procedures can provide very useful corrective mechanisms for organizations. There is a danger that, if grievances and complaints are not taken seriously, such procedures will decay.

Counselling may be needed in handling grievance situations. Before we look at the specific skills involved it is necessary to look at the framework within which grievances need to be handled.

Rights of those raising grievances

Employers need to give details of their grievance procedure to employees in the employees' written statement of terms of employment. This needs to include details of any appeal procedure against the outcome of a grievance hearing. In designing and operating such a procedure they need to have regard in the UK to the ACAS Code of Practice on Disciplinary and Grievance Procedures (2009). Failure to follow the Code can be taken into account in any subsequent employment tribunal proceedings. There is also a requirement for employees to try and resolve grievances internally before taking them to an employment tribunal. It may also, as explained in the next chapter on disciplinary handling, be appropriate to use a grievance procedure as an appeals mechanism against minor disciplinary warnings.

Other parties may also have contractual or statutory rights to raise grievances with organizations. Such rights can derive from commercial contracts, consumer protection legislation, or legislation protecting the public. In some cases there is the right of appeal to an ombudsman, either appointed voluntarily or by statute. Trading standards departments are increasingly active in responding to complaints by aggrieved customers. The increase in grievance and complaints procedures has been reinforced by the growth of a litigation culture so that people are more likely to use these procedures. A related development is the promotion of 'no win, no fee' legal services.

Levels for handling grievances

Counselling skills may be most useful in handling informal grievances, which constitute the great majority of grievances. Most issues should be settled at the informal level, and the chances of this happening are increased if front-line staff are selected and trained to handle grievances effectively. With formal procedures the various stages will be specified. Normally the first stage will be informal discussion but, if this stage is inappropriate, the further stages will involve increasingly senior levels of management. These will be used if there is no resolution at an earlier stage.

It is important to examine carefully what is said when grievances are raised and consider whether there is any aspect of the grievance that can be addressed immediately. If this is not done, it can mean that the grievance festers and may become larger as time goes on. Other grievances can then arise and become linked to the original grievance.

Identification of who needs grievance handling skills

Grievance handling skills may be needed by many levels of people within an organization. It is not enough for managers to have the skills to handle grievances effectively themselves. They need to ensure that those people who work for them and who also need the skills are effective in this area. An audit may be needed of those who need grievance handling skills. This may include all those with managerial or supervisory responsibilities, sales staff and other front-line staff such as receptionists and switchboard operators. Airline staff, traditionally at least, compared more favourably with railway staff in their customer handling. This was because of the effort put into customer handling including dealing with grievances. The same soft drinks company referred to Chapter 9, for example, came to recognize that their delivery drivers needed to be selected and trained to act as ambassadors for the company and not just as people who delivered goods. Often aggrieved clients or customers vent their frustrations on the first representative of an organization with whom they come into contact. In fairness to the front-line staff and those making complaints, representatives of the organization need to be trained in how to handle such situations. Such training needs to include details of organizational policies and procedures so that representatives of an organization are well briefed, which in turn helps to develop their confidence when dealing with employee grievances or customer complaints.

The fallibility of grievance procedures

Unfortunately, the formal stages of grievance procedures covering employees tend to be little used, as the immediate boss is usually designated for the task of hearing the grievance but is often also the cause of it! Consequently, the grievance procedure may only have a cosmetic effect.

EXAMPLE: A cosmetic procedure

One group of new recruits to the Royal Air Force in the UK were told of the existence of a grievance procedure. However its existence was explained to them in such a way as to discourage its use: after the stages in the procedure had been explained the new recruits were told that the last person to use the procedure could be observed undertaking punishment drill at unsocial hours!

People are generally averse to receiving no response whatsoever if they have raised a grievance. It would seem better, even if the answer is negative from the employee's or customer's point of view, to have the courtesy to at least tell them that. The problem with ineffective grievance or complaints procedures is that the opportunity is not taken to see if corrective action is necessary, both from the point of the person who may have been aggrieved and the organization which may be failing in a particular respect.

EXAMPLE: The need for a grievance to be addressed

A local government officer asked for two years why he was not being paid an acting up allowance. After receiving no reply during that period, he resorted to using the formal grievance procedure. Unfortunately, by the time the grievance was heard, relationships had deteriorated so much that he ended up being sacked and he instituted proceedings against the organization for unfair dismissal. Even if the employer felt justified in not paying the allowance, a patient explanation of the reasons at the outset may have prevented this breakdown in working relationships.

A misconception that some managers have is that they must support their junior managers. However, if this is done automatically there is no point in having a grievance procedure. There needs to be a sensible balance between the merits of the respective cases. If the employee's complaint is justified, the cause of the grievance needs to be rectified with the employer taking corrective action in perhaps such a way that those responsible lose as little face as is possible. Even if this does cause some embarrassment, at least the grievances should not recur. It is also necessary, though, to make sure that the management or supervisory case is properly heard.

EXAMPLE: The need to hear evidence from the parties involved at the appropriate level

In some organizations there is a failure to hear both the complaint and that of the person being complained about. In one organization the chief executive would deal with grievances himself if they were addressed to him. He regularly failed to check whether or not it would have been appropriate to have grievances dealt with at a lower level. This created a pattern of complaints being raised directly with him. The problem was sometimes compounded by him not ensuring that subordinate managers were given the opportunity to state their side of the case before the outcome was decided.

The role of counselling in grievance handling

There can be a variety of ways of handling grievances, including having a first-class row, ignoring it, referring it to someone else or giving the person what they want. Often grievances cannot, and should not, be ignored. It may be that a person has a perfectly justifiable grievance, but nothing concrete can be done about it. It is in situations like this that counselling may be not only desirable, but is the only course of action that can be taken. This makes it all the more important that those who are likely to handle grievances are given some basic instruction in the skills of counselling. In some grievance situations the answer may be simply to let people talk themselves out of their fury. Their frustration may require an outlet, and counselling techniques may enable them gradually to dissipate their anger.

At the end of the discussion, an aggrieved person may actually thank the person at whom they have directed their anger for their help and go away reconciled to the situation. The dilemma for the person who has to handle the grievance is that, if they openly agree with the complaints, they may compromise their employer, but if they rebut the complaints, they may infuriate the complainant. Neutral yet sympathetic listening in many cases is not merely the only option but may be a complete answer. It may even be appropriate for the person at the receiving end of the grievance to take the initiative as the anger subsides and probe to see if there is any more anger that needs ventilation.

Sometimes the counselling of a person with a grievance will simply mark the end of the first stage of the discussion. It may then be necessary to see what, if anything, can be done about the person's complaint. It may be that a decision has to be deferred or the answer given that, whilst you are sympathetic, nothing can be done. It is crucial, however, that where feelings run high, this is only attempted after the counselling stage has been completed. It may only be then that a person with the grievance can participate in a rational discussion of what can or cannot be done. Even if they still expect some action, a hearing of their case may have gone some way, if not the whole way, to providing psychological restitution. It may also emerge that their anger has prevented them from properly explaining their grievance and that the cause of their dissatisfaction is rather different from that which first seemed to be the case. Clarification of the nature of the grievance may be crucial, as otherwise decisions cannot be sensibly taken about what action should, or should not, follow – yet sometimes it may only be at a relatively late stage in the proceedings that this is possible.

When customers complain, organizations can sometimes seize the initiative by empowering front-line staff to make routine decisions regarding compensation and thus convert dissatisfied customers into people who praise the organization instead. Enlightened organizations will also see that taking employee grievances and customer complaints seriously can be essential parts of good employee relations, quality control and good customer relations. Sometimes organizations take a more proactive approach and conduct surveys of staff and customers.

The processes described above can be very necessary in confrontations between managers and union representatives, or with other special interest groups for that matter. It may be impossible to communicate effectively with representatives until they have ventilated their feelings about a particular issue. It may only be then that representatives are able to listen to the organizational side of a case. The problem for whoever is chairing such joint meetings is to prevent anyone on the organization's side from retaliating and so inflaming a situation. This may be particularly necessary as the opposing interest group may actually have moderated their position after having had time to say their piece.

In the event of there being an appeal against the outcome of a grievance hearing it will be particularly important for the person hearing the appeal to check that 'due process' has been followed. If it has been followed they may then need to consider if the decision made was within the 'range of reasonable options' rather than just impose what they would have done. This is an issue that is explained further in the context of disciplinary and/or dismissal appeals, in Chapter 13.

Counselling in disciplinary situations

Counselling may also be applicable in disciplinary situations. As with grievance handling, counselling can be a necessary first stage and sometimes the only stage in resolving disciplinary problems. The best form of discipline is usually self-discipline, and an attempt to impose a pattern of behaviour on an employee should normally only be considered if the employee is unable to show the appropriate self-discipline. If it is appropriate for them to change their behaviour, one should normally seek to do this with the minimum amount of pressure consistent with that objective. If an employee's performance or conduct is inappropriate, it would generally seem sensible to encourage the employee to see this and work out for themselves the required change in their behaviour. As was explained in the context of performance appraisal in Chapter 10, people can often be their own harshest critics. It would seem far better, therefore, for the line manager to give an employee the opportunity to mend their ways voluntarily rather than to try to impose one's authority. Apart from the greater commitment that this may create, it may also save the employee's face if they are allowed to work out their own salvation. Again, as with grievance handling, even if counselling does not prove to be a complete answer, it may clear the way for appropriate action on any residual disagreement. The counselling stage may also be necessary to clarify the exact nature of the shortcomings, if indeed there are any. One of the problems of disciplinary handling is that there may need to be a considerable amount of discussion before it can be clarified whether there is a disciplinary problem or not. Counselling may, however, be just the first stage in the disciplinary process. The handling of further stages in that process is the subject of the next chapter.

Summary

Managers may often need or be invited to counsel other people about their problems. These may be work-related or personal ones that may affect work. Many will be about minor operational issues that are dealt with quite informally. The essence of counselling is helping people work out their own solution to a problem rather than simply telling them what to do. Counselling techniques may be particularly necessary when appraising staff or dealing with grievances, customer complaints or many disciplinary issues. As managers often get little or no notice of when they may need to use counselling skills, they need to master the basic skills so that they can deploy them immediately if necessary. However, they will also need to judge when it is appropriate for them to get involved in counselling situations and what style of behaviour to adopt at any particular point in the proceedings.

It is also necessary to consider which subordinate staff and colleagues also need to have basic counselling skills. It is likely to be particularly important that front-line staff in direct contact with customers or members of the public have basic counselling skills so that complaints are dealt with promptly and effectively. Even when counselling is not the complete answer, it can help further discussion by defusing a situation and clarifying what the options are.

Effective grievance-handling strategies are important as ways of identifying when corrective action needs to be taken with regard to the person who is aggrieved and with a view to ensuring that an organization is functioning effectively. They are also increasingly important because of increased employee and customer rights. Counselling may also be important as a technique for helping employees change their behaviour in disciplinary situations.

Self-assessment questions

1. What do you understand by the term 'workplace counselling'?
2. In what work situations might workplace counselling be appropriate?
3. What are the key skills involved in workplace counselling?

4. How might counselling be of use in dealing with grievances, whether in the workplace or in another relevant situation?
5. How might counselling be of use in dealing with disciplinary problems, whether in the workplace or another relevant situation?

Case study notes – What to Do?

Learning outcomes will enable you to:

- Understand and evaluate what is meant by the term 'workplace counselling'
- Identify and evaluate key obstacles to effective communication by a person with a workplace problem
- Identify the key skills necessary for effective workplace counselling with a view to applying them.

Oliver has a lot to consider and the most appropriate next step would appear to be for his boss, Edward Higgins, to counsel him. Even if Oliver has understood all that he has been told there are many issues that he has to consider. Uncertainties include whether or not there will be a job at the end of the training and whether or not his pay will be protected during the training, or afterwards. The planned cut-backs in his own department may have introduced more uncertainty about whether his old job will still be available at the end of the training. In addition Oliver would have to fit in with a significantly younger group whilst on the training, should he get on the scheme. A move would also mean giving up a job where he feels settled and secure.

Edward will need to take more account of the genuine concerns that Oliver has when he sees him next than he did before. This will involve using basic counselling skills, as explained in this Chapter.

This case can also be handled as a role-play. A further teaching technique would be to ask course participants to think themselves into Oliver's situation and ask how they would react to Edwards's suggestions. Whatever technique is used the appendix to Chapter 12 headed 'Continuum of Workplace Counselling Styles' should help develop understanding and practical application of key counselling skills.

Appendix

Continuum of workplace counselling styles

The following diagram shows the range of styles that may be appropriate workplace counselling behaviour. The skilful counsellor may need to operate over a range of the continuum at one time and another, and will decide which kind of behaviour will be most effective in each phase of any counselling situation.

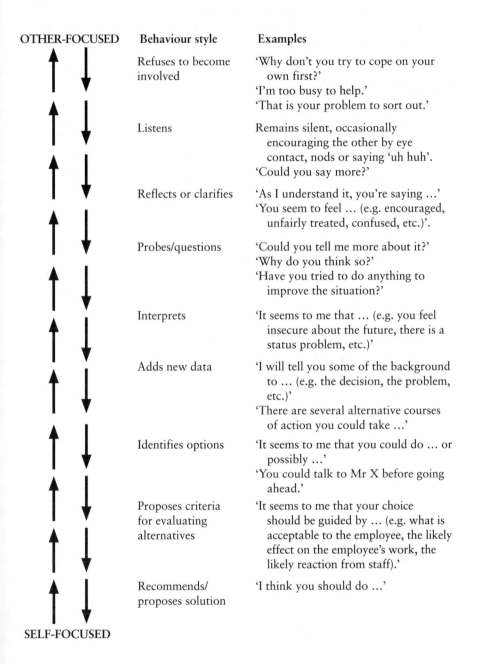

OTHER-FOCUSED	Behaviour style	Examples
	Refuses to become involved	'Why don't you try to cope on your own first?' 'I'm too busy to help.' 'That is your problem to sort out.'
	Listens	Remains silent, occasionally encouraging the other by eye contact, nods or saying 'uh huh'. 'Could you say more?'
	Reflects or clarifies	'As I understand it, you're saying ...' 'You seem to feel ... (e.g. encouraged, unfairly treated, confused, etc.)'.
	Probes/questions	'Could you tell me more about it?' 'Why do you think so?' 'Have you tried to do anything to improve the situation?'
	Interprets	'It seems to me that ... (e.g. you feel insecure about the future, there is a status problem, etc.)'
	Adds new data	'I will tell you some of the background to ... (e.g. the decision, the problem, etc.)' 'There are several alternative courses of action you could take ...'
	Identifies options	'It seems to me that you could do ... or possibly ...' 'You could talk to Mr X before going ahead.'
	Proposes criteria for evaluating alternatives	'It seems to me that your choice should be guided by ... (e.g. what is acceptable to the employee, the likely effect on the employee's work, the likely reaction from staff).'
	Recommends/ proposes solution	'I think you should do ...'
SELF-FOCUSED		

References

NB: Works of particular interest are marked with an asterisk.

*ACAS (2009), *Discipline and grievances at work, Code of Practice.*
   Particularly important for its treatment of grievance handling and related statutory rights in the UK – for web access see http//www.acas.org.uk.

Taking it further

Coles, Adrian (2003), *Counselling in the Workplace (Counselling in Context)*, McGraw Hill Education.
*Franklin, Loretta (2003), *An Introduction to Workplace Counselling – A Practitioner's Guide*, Palgrave Macmillan.
   A practical, readable guide particularly for workplace counselling.

Disciplinary Handling and Dismissal

13

Case study

The Nursery Care Incident

Nesta Morgan is the manager of a local council-run nursery. One fine day she decided to go on a visit to a nearby park with one of her staff and with eight children. This was particularly convenient as her office was being redecorated. Because the nursery was short-staffed, Nesta needed to do the work of one of the nursery staff. Towards the end of the trip Nesta received an urgent call from her boss, Stella MacBride, at the Council for some budget figures that needed to be submitted that day. Nesta believed that she had already submitted this information but as she was the only one who could retrieve the material from the computer she left the park early to email another copy. By the time she was able to return to the park the children had returned.

The next day Stella MacBride received a phone call from the chief executive asking if she had watched local television news the previous evening. When she said she had not, he told her that there had been a news item about a disabled four-year-old girl being found sitting on a park bench having not been taken back to the nursery after a visit to the park. A neighbour had recognized the child and taken her home. No one had called to collect the child because of a family mix up. The nursery in question was Nesta's.

Question:

How should Stella handle this situation?

Introduction

In this chapter attention is paid to the objectives of disciplinary policies. Preventative policies in the disciplinary area are important to try and ensure that disciplinary problems are kept to a minimum. When problems nevertheless arise it is important that they are dealt with effectively and fairly. Often the term 'discipline' is seen as synonymous with dismissal, but discipline is a generic term, and dismissal is simply the severest penalty that an employer may enforce. Also some dismissals, for example on grounds of redundancy or ill-health, are not for disciplinary reasons. Discipline is a term that relates to misconduct. Similar if separate procedures may exist, or need to exist to handle performance problems. Performance management was covered in Chapter 10. It is necessary, however, to cross-refer to the relevant material in the current chapter about the procedural and legal issues that may apply to performance problems. A poor performer may ultimately have to be dismissed even if they are trying their hardest and there is no question of indiscipline. However, in handling performance or capability issues there is still a need to follow procedure. Following procedure is not just to try and secure performance improvement but also to act within the law. In practice, disciplinary and performance issues do sometimes overlap.

A key concept is that of the **disciplinary pyramid**. This concept is explained in this chapter and demonstrates that the greatest volume of activity is likely to be at an informal level, at the base of the pyramid. It is crucial that line managers accept their responsibilities for maintaining discipline (and appropriate performance) on a day-to-day basis at an informal as well as a formal level. Reasons why line managers might not accept responsibility are explained, as are strategies for encouraging managers to act effectively in this area.

The skills involved in formal disciplinary and/or performance issues and appeal hearings are also examined in this chapter. The need for clear role identification and separation at hearings is explained. Key roles – those of the chair, case presenter and employee representative – are explained. Important issues include the need for a logical sequence of events at a hearing and for an open mind on the part of those who adjudicate on disciplinary and performance issues.

Some explanation of dismissal law in the UK is given. This is not just for the benefit of UK readers, but also because it may provide a framework for understanding the legal protections in other countries. A basic explanation is also given of European legal protections for redundancy. However, it has to be remembered that national law in individual EU member countries may exceed the European minimum requirements.

Two appendices are included in the chapter. Appendix 1 gives a model sequence of events at a formal disciplinary hearing. Appendix 2 provides a checklist of the items that should be considered when writing disciplinary letters.

The objectives of discipline

Key objectives

The primary objective of disciplinary handling in organizations is to prevent or, failing that, to deal with inappropriate behaviour by employees, particularly that which has an adverse effect on their work or the work of colleagues. The preventative aspect involves educating employees about the behaviour that is expected of them. Unless a person is dismissed, the aim needs to be to change their behaviour so that it becomes acceptable. Another important objective is to demonstrate that discipline and performance issues are handled fairly. It is necessary to try to do this, not only to the person who may be the subject of disciplinary or performance proceedings, but also to their colleagues, whose attitudes can be considerably influenced both by the action taken and by the way it is taken.

Areas that may need to be examined include:

- Levels of cost-effective performance in an organization
- Quality standards, including levels of customer service
- The extent to which important disciplinary and performance rules are observed, particularly in the area of health and safety
- Absence and timekeeping levels.

Weaknesses in disciplinary effectiveness may be a symptom of the wider issue of managerial effectiveness and control in an organization. A wide range of factors other than discipline can however also cause performance problems.

The responsibility of the individual manager

Determination of standards

There is a tendency for some managers to overestimate the extent to which work standards are decided externally. It can be very convenient to assume that the responsibility for establishing and maintaining work standards lies elsewhere – either within the organization or outside it. Organizations invariably have overall policies and procedures concerning work standards, but these provide a framework within which a manager should operate. However, it is only the manager in an individual department who can monitor and interpret the policies and procedures. If a person is not doing their job properly, it would seem to be a fundamental part of the manager's job to consider bringing the matter to the individual's attention.

Sometimes employees prefer a stricter discipline than actually exists and may resent seeing colleagues being able to behave in an inappropriate way. Inconsistencies in treatment, especially within a department, can create considerable resentment. Standards can vary widely from department to department, even within the same organization, according to the lead given by the managers concerned.

The political judgements that managers have to make may be particularly difficult when dealing with professional-level employees. Some of them may find any concept of external control unacceptable and develop their work in a way that does not fit with the needs of the organization. It is useful to distinguish between the professional's technical competence and their accountability for achieving objectives. It may be more effective, and acceptable, to make the point that discussion about accountability does not necessarily reflect on the professional employee's specialist competence.

The disciplinary pyramid

The existence of unfair dismissal law has tended to concentrate attention on dismissal. Discipline is a generic term, and dismissal is just one aspect of the disciplinary process. Ideally, policies and practices should be such that disciplinary (and performance) issues are contained, so that it is rare for a dismissal to be necessary. If there is effective supervisory and managerial control, disciplinary issues should be generally so handled. If this is not the case, too many issues may be allowed to spiral upwards before being dealt with. The main volume of activity should be in encouraging self-discipline, containment and low-level penalties (see Figure 13.1). However, there will be occasions when the nature of an employee's behaviour will require formal action.

Sometimes supervisors either see themselves as not having any disciplinary responsibility at all, or are extremely vague about just what those responsibilities are. It may be particularly important to clarify exactly what the disciplinary responsibilities and powers are of the various levels of management.

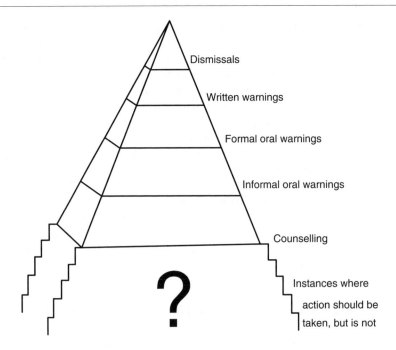

Dismissals

Written warnings

Formal oral warnings

Informal oral warnings

Counselling

Instances where action should be taken, but is not

?

Figure 13.1   The disciplinary pyramid

This is likely to be most needed with regard to the penalties that can be awarded at the base of the disciplinary pyramid where most action needs to take place and where the opportunity for confusion is greatest. The need to discipline staff is often an embarrassing and unpopular, if necessary, activity.

Clear procedures are necessary for the handling of disciplinary and performance issues, coupled with any necessary supervisory and management training. If these steps are not taken one is likely to have supervisors and managers intervening and getting it wrong, or getting away with the potentially disastrous attitude that disciplinary control of their own subordinates is nothing to do with them but is some other mystery person's responsibility.

Even when responsibilities are clarified, it is common for disciplinary and performance issues to be referred upwards. However, it is important that senior and middle managers do not get sucked into handling disciplinary issues that should be handled at a lower level. Instead they should coach those at the lower level in the managerial hierarchy in how to handle their responsibilities. This may be necessary so that junior managers can keep a diary note of informal warnings when appropriate. This may be useful if an employee later claims that they had not been told about a particular issue. However, such notes of informal warnings may be best kept in a general diary and not a diary or local file specifically about the person concerned. This is to avoid complications under the data protection legislation. To make such entries on a central file would also contradict the concept of an informal oral warning. The operation of discipline at this level is likely to overlap with general managerial control and the giving of work instructions.

A further reason for generally handling issues low down the pyramid is that any required change needs to be achieved with the minimum amount of pressure that will have the desired effect. If a quiet word will do the trick, there is little point in antagonizing employees by using more pressure than is necessary. The informal oral warning may be the most important sanction in the disciplinary process. It may be convenient for people to argue that the only penalty is dismissal, but the reality is that most people do not like being corrected and that, psychologically, the informal oral warning is a sanction that managers may find they can use effectively. Only if this does not lead to the required change in behaviour does a manager need to consider more formal measures. In some cases employees may not even need reprimanding to change their behaviour.

EXAMPLE: Is there a need for disciplinary action?

A technician wrecked an expensive piece of chemical equipment. His manager took no disciplinary action on the basis that the technician was so upset about it that the manager felt the technician would not make that mistake again.

Sometimes employees do though need to have the error of their ways pointed out to them – either because they do not realize that they are in error or because they think that they can behave in a particular way with impunity.

Procedural skills

Any form of action needs to be preceded by careful diagnosis. There can be many reasons for inappropriate behaviour, including an inaccurate definition of what is appropriate. It is only when the facts have been checked out that one can begin to consider if disciplinary action may be necessary. If an issue is sufficiently serious this may need to be done by a specially appointed investigating officer. When formal proceedings appear to be needed, managers need to refer to the appropriate rules and procedures which should already be established within their organizations, or they should point out the need for such rules. It may also help to refer to the ACAS Code of Practice (ACAS, 2009).

Suspension

A predicament that employers can face is behaviour by an employee which necessitates them leaving the employer's premises immediately. This could be for a variety of reasons, including fighting, apparent drunkenness or apparent theft. The appropriate course of action in such situations is to suspend the employee on pay pending an investigation. Even if it appears that the employee has committed gross misconduct that justifies summary dismissal, the decision should not be taken without there being a disciplinary hearing. If the case against an employee is established at a hearing, then dismissal may be given without notice from that point in time. If there is no such hearing, the employer will have fallen into the trap of prejudging the issue. Apart from giving an employee time to prepare their case, an interval between an incident and a decision can lead to a cooling of tempers all round and increase the prospects of a rational decision.

Suspension from duty is quite distinct from suspension without pay, which is sometimes used as a penalty after a hearing has been completed. The imposition of such a penalty would have to be provided for in the contract of employment. This distinction may need to be made to employees who are being suspended, together with an explanation that nothing is decided until the hearing is completed and that there is no loss of pay involved. The important point is that managers faced with the problem of needing to get somebody off the premises immediately should do this by paid suspension and not instant dismissal. A related point is that employees who are suspended with pay pending an investigation may nevertheless face embarrassment at being suspended and may not welcome the suspicions about their behaviour that may arise. If paid suspension is nevertheless necessary, it is up to management to see that the accompanying investigation and associated proceedings are conducted within a reasonable period of time.

Disciplinary hearings

Perhaps the most crucial of all the distinctions that need to be made is that between a 'disciplinary hearing' and 'disciplinary action'. The word 'hearing' is as important as the word 'disciplinary', and one cannot be sure that disciplinary action is appropriate until the hearing has been completed. A hearing enables the case against an employee to be heard and gives an opportunity for the employee to give their side of the story.

EXAMPLE: Potential costs of not having a hearing

Sharon Shoesmith, the former Head of Harringey Council's Children's Services (London), received an award £679,452 following a judgement by the Court of Appeal. This was after her dismissal in 2008 in relation to the death of a 17-month-old child who had been under the protection of the council. The award was because Ms Shoesmith had not been given the opportunity to put her case before the decision to dismiss her was made (*The Times*, 24.7.14).

A formal hearing may not be necessary if relatively minor disciplinary action is likely, but whatever the level of formality it is important that the employee is given the opportunity to state their case before any action is taken. At a formal hearing, it is usually appropriate for whoever is conducting the hearing to adjourn before communicating any decision. This gives the chair, or panel, time to consider the position carefully or, if a panel is involved, to consider any differences of view before a decision is taken. Even if an employee's conduct seems quite inexcusable, there will be occasions when it turns out that an issue was not as straightforward as it first appeared. In any case, justice needs to be seen to be done, not just for the benefit of the employee concerned, but for their colleagues as well. Although these points are obvious enough, unfortunately they are sometimes neglected. The same logic and procedure applies to performance issues.

EXAMPLE: The need to demonstrate that a decision has not been pre-judged

At one disciplinary hearing an employee was listened to carefully, only to be handed a letter of dismissal – which must have been typed before the hearing started!

On another occasion an employee was asked to sit outside the room to await the decision of a disciplinary panel and was then given a letter of dismissal that could have been typed during the recess – apart from the fact that it was dated a week earlier.

The role of the chair

When formal hearings are held, consideration should be given to one of the managers acting as chair. A manager obviously will not be viewed as a totally independent person, but proper chairing can help ensure that proceedings are conducted as impartially as possible. The chair should not have been directly involved in the case before a hearing; it may be appropriate therefore for the chair to be the boss's boss. One of the dangers of the senior manager present putting the case is that they may then be seen as judge, prosecutor, jury, executioner and possibly witness all rolled into one. A further problem is that if the senior manager gets involved in an argument, which would not be surprising given so many conflicting roles, then it will be difficult for anyone else to keep the proceedings in order. A more satisfactory procedure is for the senior manager to concentrate on chairing, leaving other people to present any case and evidence. This is necessary not only for form's sake, but also to see that the proceedings are conducted in a systematic manner, so that no decision is taken until all the arguments have been properly considered. Those who have been involved in presenting a case should not be included in discussions about what the outcome of a hearing should be. As with employment tribunals, the standard of proof, or the strictness of procedure, in disciplinary and performance cases does not have to match criminal proceedings. The parties are in fact considering a civil issue – concerning the degree to which an employee has fulfilled their contract of employment – and not a criminal trial.

For proceedings to be handled effectively, a clear and preferably agreed sequence of events needs to be established. This should include arrangements for the exchange of any written documents and explanations of when each side should state their case, produce witnesses, ask questions and sum up. The framework is essentially judicial, but sometimes the parties can mistakenly adopt a negotiating approach. If that happens, proceedings can degenerate into an unsystematic attempt by each side to browbeat the other, which can aggravate an already delicate situation instead of defusing it. The chair will also need to be aware of one or other party trying to take over the chair's role by, for example, giving procedural rulings (as opposed to raising points for the chair to rule on). Other dangers include the use of leading questions to the party's own witnesses, and attempts to intimidate witnesses produced by the other side. An example of a procedural sequence that will help a chair maintain control and facilitate a systematic hearing is given in Appendix 1 to this chapter. The general skills of chairing are explained in the final chapter of this book.

If the chair does give the decision orally, it is essential that there should not be any further argument. If the proceedings have been conducted properly all the relevant points should have been made and considered anyway. If an employee disagrees with a decision, the appropriate way of handling the situation is simply to explain the employee's right of appeal. Sometimes heated arguments break out at this stage simply because it is not made clear to an employee that there is an appeals procedure that they are entitled to use.

Presenting officer

Managerial representatives presenting a case need to prepare carefully beforehand. They may combine their role with that of investigating officer, or someone else may need to be appointed to fill that role. A person's guilt may be self-evident, but the whole point of a quasi-judicial hearing is to enable the person or people sitting in judgement to decide solely on the basis of the evidence and argument that is openly presented. Consequently, patient work has to be undertaken in developing logical arguments and collecting relevant evidence. Consideration also has to be given to the presentational skills involved. All this is particularly important, as the skills of advocacy are often much more part of the 'stock in trade' of union representatives than of managers. This means that if managers fail to do their homework they may needlessly lose cases, and their confidence.

The role of the representative

In practice the person who accompanies an employee is likely to act as a representative. It is difficult to see how a hearing can be fairly conducted otherwise. The representative can be a colleague or a union official of the employee's choice (even if the employer does not recognize unions). Employers may want, however, to consider restricting the rights of representation to work colleagues or trade union officials. If there is no restriction, the employer may find that an employee is accompanied by a lawyer who may introduce a greater level of formality and legalism into the proceedings than the employer wishes to have.

There is a need for employees to be represented regardless of any statutory rights. A representative's function is to help a person put their case so that any decision is taken only after all the relevant arguments have been considered. The representative may have heard only the employee's version of events beforehand. A formal hearing can provide an employer with the opportunity to put over their version of events. This may influence the representative, whose views may be crucial if an issue is sensitive and could lead to industrial action. If an employer has a good case, it is appropriate that it should be explained; if the case is weak, then perhaps it should be dropped. Often managers fail to realize that the really critical audience in disciplinary proceedings can be the employee's colleagues who will be interested in the outcome but will also want to be reassured that the process has been handled fairly.

The position of the representative also has to be considered. They may well feel that, whatever an employee has done, they have the right to have their case argued strongly, even if privately the representative does not condone the employee's behaviour. At the end of a hearing at least the representative can explain that they have done what they can for the employee concerned. If the representative does not agree with the action that an employer eventually takes, at least any subsequent disagreement need not be compounded by arguments about whether the person had a fair hearing. The crucial distinction is that, whatever an employee has or has not done, this should not affect their right to a fair hearing. Care should be taken to ensure that employees know their procedural rights and it is preferable that they have a copy of any relevant rules and procedures. They also need to have copies of any written evidence that is to be used.

Communicating the result

Before any decision is taken after a hearing, there needs to be a careful review of the options and of the need to communicate accurately what has been decided. The options include stating that the employee has been cleared. Care needs to be taken in deciding just what a person is to be warned about. If the grounds of the warning are too specific, 'lateness' for example, an employee may be able to maintain that their lateness record cannot be taken into account if they are subsequently disciplined for more general absence. Thus it may be appropriate to broaden the base of a warning from lateness to general attendance. Warnings about other matters may need to include a proviso that repetition of a particular action or related misconduct can result in further action.

Too narrow a definition of what the warning is about can lead to a person getting a number of 'final' warnings, all for different offences.

Consideration also needs to be given as to whether or not there should be time limits for any penalties imposed. However, one needs to be aware of the rigidities that specific time limits can create. Holidays, sickness, staff changes and other work commitments can cause procedural delays, causing a warning to be 'spent' before it can be used as a platform for further action. If general fixed expiry time limits are not used, for each warning given it will be necessary to decide at the time how long the should reasonably remain on an employee's record. It will also be necessary to consider which previous warnings can or need to be taken into account. The importance and number of points to be considered in drafting written warnings is such that a checklist of the potential issues is necessary. Such a checklist for disciplinary letters is produced as Appendix 2 to this chapter.

Appeals

Thought has to be given to the stage at which appeals can be lodged. It may not be necessary to provide for appeals against informal warnings, for example, especially as an employee can always use the grievance procedure if there is no formal procedure for handling appeals against minor penalties. It would seem appropriate, though, to build an appeals procedure into disciplinary and performance procedures when warnings get to the stage of indicating that dismissal is becoming a possibility. Appeals should be to managers not previously involved in the case, unless the organization is so small this is not practicable. The grounds for an appeal should be clarified – they need not involve a total rehearing of a case unless that is clearly appropriate. The time within which an appeal must be lodged also needs to be stated. It may be a mistake to keep people on the pay-roll pending any appeal against dismissal. This is to discourage people from taking appeals primarily, or simply, to extend the time they are on the pay-roll. If an appeal is, however, successful, any loss of pay can be made good.

The law relating to dismissal

General framework

The grounds on which an employer can establish that a dismissal was fair are quite broad. In the UK the three main grounds are:

1.   Capability (which is likely to encompass performance)
2.   Conduct
3.   Redundancy

Dismissal can also be for 'other substantial reasons'. This is when the employee has broken their contract of employment in a fundamental way that is not necessarily covered by the three main headings.

For dismissal to be fair the employer has to have behaved reasonably in the circumstances. Because this is a civil issue, judgement is on the balance of probabilities. Employers can no longer simply dismiss staff because they have reached the organization's normal retirement age. Such retirements, if challenged, will need to be objectively justified.

Exclusions

Not all dismissed employees in the UK can take a case alleging unfair dismissal to an employment tribunal. They have to have had two year's employment with the employer concerned (at present) unless they are claiming that they have been dismissed because of illegal discrimination, or for exercising a statutory right. An employee does not have to work a minimum number of hours to benefit from this protection.

Constructive dismissal

Normally the act of dismissal is not contested. However, there can be cases where it is unclear whether the employee resigned or was dismissed. If an employer breaches a basic element of the contract, the employee has the option of treating such action as a repudiation of the employment contract and therefore a dismissal. Such action can include severely unreasonable behaviour on the part of the employer. If the employee does not leave immediately, they need to make it clear that they regard the contract as having been broken. The longer an employee stays with their employer, the more difficult it is for them to succeed in a claim that their position had become intolerable. One way of maintaining their position might be though to institute an action for breach of contract whilst continuing in their job. It may also be possible for an employee to withdraw notice if it was given in the 'heat of the moment' and after provocation. Relevant issues may be the extent of any provocation and the mental state of the employee.

Capability

Dismissal on grounds of lack of capability may be justified because of a person's poor performance. There are, unfortunately, occasions when people can be trying their best but nevertheless still fail to meet minimum job standards. Such situations are not really disciplinary situations, although they may still result in dismissal. It is crucial that all reasonable help be given to enable people to improve their performance, including training where necessary. Medical cases might also be dealt with as 'capability' cases or under 'other substantial reasons'. Again, dismissal could result even though the person concerned may not be to blame. In some organizations separate procedures are established to deal with such cases. In the case of sickness absence it is important to check on the prospects of an early return to work and to consider seeking medical advice. It may also be necessary to warn employees of the consequences of their not being able to resume normal work, or appropriate alternative work. Another important issue is the impact of the Equality Act 2010, which includes protections for employees with physical and mental disabilities. Employers need to be careful in demonstrating that they have taken all reasonable steps to help an employee who may be classified as disabled before considering dismissal.

Conduct

Dismissal on grounds of misconduct may be either because of a single instance of gross misconduct, which can entitle an employer to summarily dismiss (without notice), or because of cumulative misconduct, in which case the appropriate notice, or money in lieu, has to be given. Gross misconduct is not easy to define but legally occurs when an employee's (mis)behaviour goes to the root of the contract. It is prudent for an employer to clarify the position by giving predictable and accessible written examples of what is considered to be gross misconduct. These might well include theft or fraud perpetrated against the organization and physical assault in the course of employment. This may have an educative effect and make it easier to establish that particular behaviour constitutes gross misconduct. However, lack of such advance publicity will not automatically prevent employers from treating other behaviour as gross misconduct if it is sufficiently serious.

The basic expectations the employer has of employees should also be an integral part of induction training for newcomers. Also, if new rules are introduced, or if there are other changes in the expectations that employers have of employees, these should be communicated in advance. It is important that employees do not learn of the existence of rules or new expectations by being disciplined. Employers also need to demonstrate that they have systematically and fairly sought to enforce any such rules. Their position at a tribunal would be weak if a former employee was able to demonstrate uneven application of any such rules. Erratic attendance and timekeeping are particularly common examples of cumulative misconduct, and in cases like this the employer needs to be able to demonstrate to a tribunal that they have tried to operate policies fairly and in such a way that the pressure on an employee was gradually stepped up before any consideration of dismissal.

Redundancy

Employers are able to fairly dismiss on grounds of redundancy, provided that it is genuine, that the selection is fair and that there is appropriate consultation.

Selection for redundancy

A crucial test in establishing a redundancy is whether or not the dismissed employee was replaced. Selection for redundancy may be in accordance with a previously established policy, which may also have been agreed with recognized trade unions. Length of service is an important criterion in deciding who should be retained and who should be dismissed, but other criteria, including capability, may need to be considered as well. Objective data may be necessary to demonstrate that selection criteria have been fairly applied.

It is necessary to ensure that redundancy selection does not unfairly disadvantage a particular group. This could happen, for example, if all part-timers were dismissed and the majority of part-timers were women. A problematic area can be determining the pool of people from whom those to be made redundant will be selected. Consideration may need to be given to 'bumping' some people from jobs that are to go into other jobs that will remain. This could involve staff accepting demotion to stay with an organization and other people being made redundant in their place. Employees are entitled to four weeks' trial in the alternative job without forfeiting any of their legal rights. An appeal procedure may be appropriate to consider appeals against redundancy and appeals against offers of alternative work within the organization. In the event of the redundancy selection being deemed unfair by an employment tribunal, the former employee would be entitled to compensation for unfair dismissal as well as their redundancy entitlement.

Consultation

Employees are entitled to be consulted about redundancy, if appropriate on an individual basis. This should be done as early as is practicable if they are likely to be made redundant. Such consultation should include ways of avoiding the redundancy and also examination of the opportunity for alternative work within the organization. Redundancy consultation is also affected by the European Collective Redundancies Directive. The minimum requirements are that an employer planning a redundancy of 20 or more employees is required to consult with relevant trade union representatives or, in the absence of a trade union, with elected employee representatives, with a view to reaching agreement.

Consultation is necessary even if the redundancies are all voluntary. Such consultation would also need to include ways of avoiding or minimizing proposed redundancy. The consultation has to take place 'in good time' – and start at least 30 days before the first notification of dismissal with redundancies of between 20 and 99 employees, and 45 days (in the UK) before dismissal if the redundancies are expected to number 100 or over. Dismissal notices cannot be issued until that consultation process has been completed.

There are also financial penalties for any breach of the provisions for collective redundancy consultation. A protective award of a normal week's pay for a maximum period of 90 days can be awarded if an employer is in breach of this requirement. The award can be in respect of every employee where it is held that there has been such a breach.

Employers acquiring new businesses, or even sometimes winning contracts for economic entities, must consult with employee representatives if the acquisition or the contract involves the potential or actual redundancy of acquired or existing employees. This is in addition to the European-wide legislation regarding the transfer of undertakings, which creates a further potential liability for employers. These regulations also necessitate collective consultation even if only one person is threatened with redundancy or if existing employees are likely to be significantly affected by the transfer.

Employers are also affected by the European Directive on Information and Consultation. This requires them to consult with employees about the current and future business economic situation, particularly developments that may affect employment arrangements. This Directive covers all businesses employing 50 or more people.

Redundancy compensation

The statutory minimum payments that employers have to make in the UK to employees with a minimum of two years' service with them are:

- For each year of service under the age of 22 – half a week's pay
- For each year of service at age 22 but under 41 – one week's pay
- For each year of service at age 41 or over – one and a half week's pay.

These limits are subject, however, to an earnings cap which is reviewed annually. In 2014 the cap was £464 per week. This means that the compensation is calculated on the basis of regular weekly earnings or the cap, whichever is the lower. The statutory entitlement is also limited to a maximum of 20 years' service. Redundant employees are also entitled to a week's notice, or money in lieu, for every year of service up to a maximum of 12 weeks. Employees faced with redundancy are also statutorily entitled to reasonable paid time off to look for another job and for training during the notice period. Employees may be entitled to higher payments under their contract of employment.

The arrangements for statutory minimum payments vary from country to country, even within the EU, and are significantly higher in some EU countries than others.

Procedural requirements

Whenever employees are facing disciplinary proceedings and/or are liable to dismissal particular care has to be taken of internal procedures and relevant law.

The weakness of employers at tribunals often turns out to be their failure to follow a systematic procedure, even though there may be a clearly defined procedure within the organization that the employer should follow.

Individual managers may fail to deal with a disciplinary issue and then, when their frustration builds up, dismiss an employee in a moment of anger. The legal requirements are not so much aimed at preventing dismissal but at ensuring that, when it does take place, it is done for appropriate reasons and in a manner that preserves the rights of the individual concerned to natural justice.

The observance of appropriate procedures is not just a technical matter but one which can affect the actual decision that is taken. The decision to dismiss a person before they have, for example, had the opportunity to state their case is wrong, not just because it is a breach of justice but also because the fact-finding process is incomplete. However, employers also need to beware of overcompensating in this area by having procedures that are unduly elaborate. In some organizations, especially with some public sector employers, this has led to the procedures being too complex for many of their managers to handle. This in turn may lead to managers opting out of discipline and/or the organization repeatedly losing tribunal cases because they have not kept to their self-imposed elaborate requirements.

The relationship between civil and criminal law

A further issue that has to be considered is if a person has apparently committed a criminal action. It is a fallacy to assume that such action can only be handled by the police. If, for example, someone has apparently stolen something, it may be appropriate for the employer to institute disciplinary proceedings about the employee's apparent unauthorized possession of property belonging to the employer. This will involve investigation and a hearing if necessary. Any decision about whether or not there should be a prosecution should be handled separately. This is assuming, of course, that evidence does not rely solely on that which is only held by the police.

The option of letting such an issue be handled just by the police may not be as easy as it seems. The burden of proof in criminal law has to be established 'beyond reasonable doubt', as opposed to the civil law requirement of proof 'on the balance of probabilities'. The procedural rules are also much stricter in the criminal courts and it may be necessary to establish that a felony was committed or attempted. Added to this is the problem that, if no action is taken pending a court hearing, an employee may have to be suspended on pay for several months, or in some cases even longer. In any case, the employer may find that, if the case is substantiated, the primary remedy they want is to be able to dismiss the person concerned. The point that needs to be stressed is that apparent criminal activity by an employee against their employer does not automatically remove the employer's rights to handle an issue as a disciplinary matter.

Provided there is no specific procedural requirement that a prosecution should be resolved before disciplinary proceedings are taken, it may be better for the employer to resolve the disciplinary issue in advance of a prosecution being resolved. Amongst other things, this avoids the dilemma of what to do if a person has already been acquitted in the criminal courts. Subsequent acquittal does not invalidate disciplinary action previously taken, because the disciplinary action should be based on the rather separate issue of the extent to which the employee, or ex-employee, fulfilled their employment contract. If the employee is not prepared to state their case because it may reveal issues they prefer were only raised at subsequent criminal proceedings, this does not of itself prevent the employer from going ahead with a disciplinary hearing. Documentation, including statements by those accused, may need to be prepared separately and to different standards in any subsequent criminal case. People may raise the issue of 'double jeopardy', arguing that a person cannot normally be tried twice for the same offence. However, this argument may be fallacious as the law may simply prevent people being tried twice under criminal law for the same offence.

Employers may want carefully to consider the timing of any disciplinary action so that they do not jeopardise any covert police surveillance that is in progress. They should also not automatically assume that conviction for a criminal offence justifies dismissal. Much will depend on the circumstances of a case, including the relevance of the conviction to a person's job. In the event of a custodial sentence being awarded by the courts, employers might decide to dismiss the employee concerned, if only because of their non-availability for work.

EXAMPLE: Example of the difference between criminal and civil law

The much higher standards needed to secure a criminal conviction, compared with success in a civil action were dramatically demonstrated by the O. J. Simpson case. O. J. Simpson had been a particularly famous American football star. In 1995 he was acquitted by a Californian court of the murder of his former wife, Nicole Simpson and her boyfriend, Ronald Goldman, both of whom had been killed the previous year. However, in 1997 in a civil action he was unanimously held to have caused both deaths. Initial damages were awarded against him of US $8.5 million, followed by punitive award of US $25 million.

Employment tribunals

Claims regarding unfair dismissal can be made in the UK to an employment tribunal. Tribunals can also hear claims regarding redundancy and a wide range of other statutory employment protection rights and related matters. Employment tribunals have three members – a judge and two lay members. In many circumstances, there is provision for the judge to sit alone.

Appellants are obliged to contact ACAS who will check whether a conciliated settlement can be made before a case proceeds to an employment tribunal. Appeals can be made against tribunal decisions, but only on points of law or where the decision is claimed to be perverse.

Employment tribunals in the UK have proved to be more formal and legalistic than was originally intended. This has been an almost inevitable development given the right of appeal through the legal system against the decisions of employment tribunals. The volume of case law has contributed to the increased use of lawyers. Legal aid is not normally available. Employees, but not the employer, will normally have to pay fees to the tribunal in order to take a case, the amount depending on the complexity of the case. Those on low incomes may be granted remission of this requirement. Applicants may have costs awarded against them if they lose. The introduction of 'up front' fees has so far had a dramatic effect reducing the number of all cases taken to tribunals. In the last quarter of 2013 there were 65% fewer unfair dismissal claims than a year previously. All employment claims were down by 79% (Ministry of Justice, 2014). It may also increase the attractiveness of the ACAS voluntary arbitration option which, at the time of writing, is free, has no provision for the award of costs and is confidential.

The main costs to an employer can be the time spent defending a case and any fees paid to professional representatives. Former employees can be deterred by the formality and legal complexity, although if they are a member of a trade union they may be able to access free representation. Even if evidence available after the dismissal (and after any internal appeal hearing) proves that the employer was wrong, the dismissal may still be judged to have been 'reasonable' on the basis of the information that was available to the employer at the time.

The freedom of action of the employer to dismiss is often greatly underestimated. This may be because of misunderstandings about the legal position or because it may be a convenient pretence to maintain that the employer has much less discretion than is really the case. In defining reasonable behaviour it is necessary to consider what a reasonable (not a perfect) employer might have done, the size and administrative resources of the employer, how genuine the belief was, the basis for the suspicion of wrongdoing and the norms in the particular industry. Tribunals are required to consider whether or not the employer's behaviour was within the range of reasonable options. Tribunal decisions should not be made on the basis of what they would have done in that situation themselves.

Any well-organized employer should, almost by definition, be more likely to successfully defend a case at a tribunal. Successful claims against the employer occur particularly in the less well-organized sectors of the economy where managerial resources are limited. A low success rate may indicate weaknesses that need attention. Every high success rate raises the possibility that the employer is being too cautious and only dismissing when they feel certain they will win. There will be some differences of opinion between employers and tribunals. Employers can always consider reinstating an employee if they lose a case at a tribunal. It is important to recognize that, if employers are seen to opt out of dismissing employees unless the reasons are overwhelming, this can create a climate where nobody tries to tell anybody what to do on the basis that nothing is likely to be done if the person refuses. The impact of decisions concerning dismissal needs to be seen in relation to the signals it is sending within an organization and not in isolation, or just in terms of the track record at tribunals.

Compromise agreements

As was explained earlier in this chapter in the context of financial compensation, employees who have made a claim to a tribunal for unfair dismissal often reach a conciliated settlement with the employer instead of proceeding to a tribunal hearing. However, there is also provision for compromise agreements to be made before an application is made to an employment tribunal under which claimants waive their right to take a case to a tribunal. For such an agreement to be valid, it is necessary for the former employee to receive independent advice from a lawyer or acceptable other specialist, who is covered by professional indemnity insurance. The other specialist could be a full-time trade union official.

Other implications of dismissals

Industrial

Employers also have to consider the industrial repercussions of a dismissal. Irrespective of whether a tribunal judges a dismissal to have been be fair or unfair or even whether a tribunal even hears a case, sanctions may be applied by the remaining workers to try to secure the reinstatement of a colleague. Changed economic circumstances and access to tribunals have, however, greatly reduced industrial action on dismissal. However, a dismissal may still have an effect on other employees and may have to be organizationally acceptable. This will particularly be the case where the employer is heavily dependent on employee goodwill.

Public relations

There may also be public relations implications involved in tribunal cases. Organizations with a high public profile might be particularly sensitive, for example, to discrimination cases. Even if they win a case at a tribunal, some of the publicity they receive may be unfavourable.

Personal

Tribunal cases can be stressful and time-consuming. There may also be a temptation on the part of employers to look for scapegoats if any fault is found with the way they handled a case. However, witch-hunts are likely to have the effect of discouraging managers from taking appropriate action when it may be needed in the future. The checks and balances in internal procedures, particularly of separating the chairing of a hearing from case presentation and the right of internal appeal, should in any case mean that responsibility for dismissal is shared.

Precedent

Some issues may involve important matters of principle and employers may feel that they need to defend a case to demonstrate that they have behaved correctly. Employers may also want to demonstrate to their managers that they will back them when they have behaved correctly.

Remedies for unfair dismissal

Employers have freedom to dismiss. Any action for unfair dismissal will normally be made only after the employee has been given notice of dismissal. However, the employer needs to be aware of the consequences of being judged to have dismissed an employee unfairly. If the decision is in favour of the former employee there are three potential legal remedies. These are: 1) reinstatement, 2) basic award, and 3) compensatory award.

Reinstatement

Employment tribunals are obliged to consider reinstatement (or re-engagement) as a remedy if an application alleging unfair dismissal is upheld, but this can only be recommended and not enforced. Although tribunals can award extra compensation if a recommendation to reinstate is resisted by the employer, the normal remedy is financial compensation and not reinstatement.

Basic award

The basic award is based on the employee's age, length of service and weekly pay. It can be reduced because of contributory fault by the employee, but not below a statutory minimum.

Compensatory award

The compensatory award is designed to cover any further loss suffered by the applicant. It will include loss of earnings suffered since the dismissal, loss of pension rights and an estimate of future earnings loss. The maximum award was £76,574 in 2014, or a year's salary, whichever is the lower. However, the median compensation awarded by tribunals for unfair dismissal claims (including basic awards) in 2012–2013 was £4,832. The weekly earnings cap in 2014 for basic and compensation awards was £464 (or actual earnings whichever is the lower).

In a range of cases involving illegal discrimination there is no limit on the compensatory award. In the UK illegal discrimination can be for a variety of reasons, including gender, race, age, religion and physical or mental disability. However, people who have been dismissed for whatever reason have a duty to mitigate their loss by looking for other work. Also, compensation can be reduced by the proportion by which people contributed to their own dismissal. Additionally, if the employee has not used the internal procedures, including any rights of appeal before proceeding to a tribunal, any compensation awarded would normally be reduced. However, in the case of a significant procedural breach by the employer, compensation would normally be increased and the employer may have to pay costs to their former employee.

Summary

The importance of effective disciplinary handling has been examined, as has the need for preventative policies and procedures. Separate but similar procedures are likely to be needed for performance issues. Sound management and education about what behaviour is expected of employees can do much to contain or prevent problems in this area. Most disciplinary handling needs to be at the lower level of the disciplinary pyramid in terms of the level of sanction. Unfortunately, those with managerial responsibility often opt out of their responsibilities in this area. This can be for a variety of reasons. These include a general reluctance to manage, a lack of clarity about who has responsibility for control and discipline and the unpopularity that managers can fear from taking disciplinary action. This can lead to a general loss of control and to issues having to be dealt with more seriously than would otherwise have been necessary. On-the-job coaching and formal training can do much to train people about their responsibilities in this area and how to handle them. The roles that managers may play in handling disciplinary and performance issues were identified as were the ways in which they may need to handle such roles.

Where appropriate law has been considered an explanation of the law regarding dismissal in the UK has also been given, including redundancies. This is of particular relevance to British readers. However, the main aspects of law in the UK may be of interest to readers from other countries. This is because there may be similarities with the law in other countries, and dismissal law incorporates much that is simply good management practice anyway. Finally the framework of disciplinary and performance handling and related employment protection rights may be useful if readers are in danger of having their own rights infringed.

Self-assessment questions

1. How would you assess whether or not disciplinary and performance policies in an organization were effective?
2. Explain the concept of the disciplinary pyramid.
3. How would you handle a disciplinary or performance issue at the informal level?
4. How would you set out to present a case at a disciplinary or performance hearing?
5. What are the basic requirements for seeing that a formal hearing is chaired properly?
6. What are the three main grounds for fair dismissal in the UK?
7. How would you see that your own basic rights were protected regarding discipline, performance or redundancy?

Case study notes – The Nursery Care Incident

This case can also be handled as a role-play, with a number of groups, simultaneously if necessary. The key issues are Nesta's priorities and accountability. There is also the issue of the unfavourable publicity. Whilst there were mitigating circumstances, a particularly vulnerable child was put at risk. Leaving eight children with one just member of staff is not acceptable. Nesta was accountable for the safety of the children. There is also the accountability of the junior member of staff who only brought seven children back. A formal investigation appears appropriate with the possibility of a formal penalty against both members of staff concerned. Child-checking procedures may also need to be reviewed.

A related factor is that the council has been brought into disrepute. It is likely that a formal hearing is necessary and thought will need to be given to the people who should attend a disciplinary hearing and in what capacity.

Appendix I

Example of procedural sequence at a disciplinary hearing

1. Introduction(s) by chair

   Explanation of allegation(s)
   Check that the parties have received any relevant documentation
   Explanation of sequence of events at hearing

2. Presentation of case against the employee by the appropriate line manager

   Management witnesses
   Questioning of management witnesses, via the chair

3. Response on behalf of the employee

    Witnesses on behalf of the employee

    Questioning of employee witnesses, via the chair

4. Further points by management

    Further points on behalf of the employee

    Questions by chair/panel

5. Management summing up

    Employee summing up

6. Recess

7. Decision – orally and/or in writing later.

Appendix 2

Check list for disciplinary letters

Item	Comments
1. *Requesting attendance at disciplinary hearing.* Specify allegations.	Allegations may or may not be proved as a result of a hearing.
Suggest the employee brings a representative if they wish and relevant witnesses, if appropriate.	If a representative comes it will enable them to see that the issues are properly examined.
Give appropriate information and time for the employee to prepare their defence adequately.	Failure to allow this may invalidate the proceedings.
Refer to the disciplinary procedure.	The employee should have a copy. If there is any doubt, send them one.
Indicate that disciplinary action could be imposed according to the outcome of the hearing.	
2. *Disciplinary letter (after the hearing).* State the nature of the offence(s). State what disciplinary action, if any, is to be taken.	You may wish to incorporate general terms, such as misconduct, in any warning letter. This may make it easier in the future to refer back to earlier offences.
Specify any conditions about future behaviour. This may include any help you are prepared to give.	You may warn an employee about future conduct and state that any repetition or related offence may/will render them liable to further action.
Specify any time limits.	Sometimes procedures provide for warnings to lapse after a specified period of good behaviour. You do not have to put in time limits though – they can be rather rigid.

(*continued*)

Continued

Item	Comments
Specify the appeal procedure and the time limit for using it.	The more serious the penalty the more important it is to specify the right of appeal.
State whether you want the employee to: Acknowledge receipt of the letter and register any dissent about any part of the letter they consider inaccurate.	
Send a copy of the letter to the employee's representative and to any managers concerned.	

References

NB: Works of particular interest are marked with an asterisk.

*Advisory Conciliation and Arbitration Service (ACAS) (2009), *Discipline and grievances at work, Code of Practice.*
    Particularly important for its treatment of disciplinary handling and related statutory rights in the UK – for web access, see http://www.acas.org.uk.
Ministry of Justice (2014) *Tribunal Statistics Quarterly: April to June, 2014* https://www.gov.uk/government/uploads/system/uploads/attachment_data/file/352914/tribunal-statistics-quarterly-april-june-2014.pdf [accessed 15th November, 2014].

Taking it further

*ACAS, *Redundancy and notice*, ACAS (an essential reference and comprehensive guide to redundancy handling in the UK – for web access, see http://www.acas.org.uk).
Evans, Keith (1992) *Advocacy at the Bar – A Beginner's Guide*, Blackstone Press.
    Despite its date of publication a really useful guide to presenting cases.

Negotiating Skills

14

Learning outcomes

By the end of this chapter you will be able to:

- Identify the range of negotiating situations in which you are likely to be involved, both formally and informally
- Assess key theories relevant to the negotiating process
- Create a framework within which negotiations can be conducted
- Identify the different roles that people need to play during negotiations
- Identify and assess realistic negotiating objectives
- Use tactical skills in conducting negotiations
- Take preventative action to reduce the chance of misunderstandings during and after negotiations
- Understand the processes of evaluation and implementation of agreements.

Case study

Availability or Activity?

Assume you are Derek Matthews, depot manager of a local road haulage company.

Six months ago you engaged a new, and much younger, permanent night worker, after the previous job holder retired. The duties of the night worker are to keep watch on the yard and book in the few lorries that have not been able to return during the day. The person doing the job, Norman Watson, is paid 8% less than the manual day workers based at the depot, which include the day gate workers. Norman has recently joined a trade union and they have made representations on his behalf for him to be paid the same as the day gate workers. They have to book lorries in and out of the depot relatively frequently. The slingers and crane drivers are also on the same rate of pay. The day gate workers alternate each week on an early and a late shift. The person doing the early shift works overtime on a Saturday morning. Norman's shift is from 10 pm to 6 am – Mondays to Fridays. He is not paid a night shift supplement and does not get the opportunity for overtime. The union representative claims that Norman needs and has the same skills as the day gate workers. The haulage market is very competitive and there is no shortage of labour.

Question:

How would you as Derek Matthews handle this situation?

Introduction

Negotiation is seen by many as a mystic art, with the corollary that negotiators are born with innate skills that are not easily transferable. However, whilst some people may have a natural aptitude for negotiation, the process of negotiation is capable of analysis. Once it has been analysed it is possible to consciously develop people's skills in the area just as it is possible to develop other skills. The accelerating pace of change means that this is an increasingly important part of a manager's job as commercial and working arrangements often have to be renegotiated to meet changed circumstances.

The range of formal and informal negotiating situations in which managers are likely to be involved is identified in this chapter. Relevant theories are examined to help with both the analysis of the negotiating process and with skills development. The need to create a framework for negotiations is explained. This framework will apply even in informal negotiations between two people. A key feature is the need for those involved in negotiations to understand the different roles that need to be played, sometimes by the same person. Often negotiations fail because people get so involved in the negotiations that they neglect to create a proper framework or allocate appropriate roles.

The various stages in the negotiating process are identified, including the concept of the **negotiating ritual**. The importance of effective chairing during negotiations is explained, as is the fact that this sometimes needs to be done on an informal and discreet basis. The process skills of the chair, in particular, can be crucial in determining whether there is a constructive outcome to negotiations or not. These skills are also necessary to avoid false agreements being reached, based on misunderstandings of the parties about what was agreed. This can all too easily happen because communications during negotiations are often very fragile. Often the parties obtain the best results by behaving assertively rather than aggressively. By adopting assertive behaviour, the potential for agreement can be explored and confrontations that threaten the process avoided.

The importance of preparation is explained, as is the need to set realistic objectives. This is likely to involve an examination of the power realities and consideration of what to do if negotiations fail. Sometimes it is better to have no agreement than a bad one. In group negotiations, a considerable amount of time may be needed to resolve internal differences. Often such internal differences are harder to resolve than differences between negotiating groups.

Finally, attention is paid in this chapter to the need for agreements to be evaluated, implemented and monitored. For the negotiating process to be effective, formal and informal training may be necessary. A Negotiating Skills Observers' Form is included as an appendix at the end of this chapter to help readers assess their own or other people's negotiating skills.

Range of activity and trends

Range of activity

Negotiating is not something that is just the province of specialist negotiators. All managers are likely to be involved in some level of negotiations. Whilst most negotiations will be small-scale, their cumulative effect can be considerable. Much of the negotiation managers are involved in is likely to be about operational matters, for example the implementation and monitoring of existing commercial contracts. They are likely also to be involved in a considerable amount of negotiation about how they meet other managers' needs and how other managers meet their needs. Organization of their own department may also involve managers in much informal negotiation. This is likely to include allocation of work, logistical working arrangements and the quality control of what is done.

Negotiations do not cease when managers finish work. They will inevitably be involved with negotiations about, for example, their living arrangements and purchases. Social trends have created a much more egalitarian society which involves continuous negotiations about domestic arrangements. Some of the hardest negotiations can be with children about such issues as bedtime, homework and contributions to domestic chores.

A particular need is for managers to develop the habit of reflecting on the way that they, and others, negotiate. The increasing amount of time spent in negotiations creates a considerable opportunity to learn from the skills that are used and the mistakes made.

The stereotype of the effective negotiator is the person who drives a very hard bargain. Whilst this can sometimes be appropriate, it is not always a helpful image. Negotiators need to get the best that they can out of a given situation and often this may involve coming to a mutually satisfactory agreement. To try and drive too hard a bargain can sometimes mean no agreement at all. The key to effective negotiation is developing procedural and process skills so that the framework and conduct of negotiations enables that which is potentially attainable to be achieved.

Trends

The amount of negotiations that managers have to do seems to be increasing significantly. Whilst negotiations with trade unions are often easier than they were when unions were generally more powerful, in many areas negotiations are becoming more difficult and more frequent. The increasing pace of change causes organizational arrangements to be reviewed more frequently. This can involve reviewing commercial contracts and negotiating with employees about what they do, when and where. Failure to do this can affect the very survival of an organization. A general excess of production capacity in the world, boosted by technological development and globalization, has turned many industries and services into a buyer's market. This has created chronic pressures for producers and providers of services simultaneously to increase quality and reduce costs. The mismatch between expectations and available resources in the public sector has also created increasing pressure to improve value for money.

Relevant theories

The process of negotiation is so complex that there neither is, nor can there be, one theory that embraces all its aspects. However, there are two particularly useful theories about negotiation that cover key aspects. These theories can create an analytical framework for examining and developing your own skills and examining the behaviour of others. As with all theories, they need to be applied in the right context. Unsurprisingly, the two theories are not recent. This is because the process of negotiation is so long established that writers have had plenty of time to study it.

Integrative and distributive bargaining

The seminal work on the theory of negotiation was written by Walton and McKersie (1965). They distinguish between **distributive bargaining** and **integrative bargaining**. In distributive bargaining one party can only gain at the expense of the other. This can be described as a fixed-sum game, such as in the sale of an item by one party and its purchase by the other. In integrative bargaining there is the potential to increase the amount that can be distributed. This can be described as a varying-sum game. An example of integrative bargaining from the employee relations area is productivity bargaining. Productivity bargaining can enable the value added by a group of people to be increased. In return they would expect to have some reward for their increased contribution. However, if the parties don't cooperate effectively not only could they fail to generate a mutual gain, but they could actually undermine existing arrangements. In that event, the potential for a win-win outcome may not be achieved and instead there may be a lose-lose result.

Whilst the concepts of integrative and distributive bargaining are very clear in theory, in practice they may overlap. A negotiation can involve elements of both types of bargaining. Although the sale of a house, for example, is essentially a fixed-sum game, there may be some potential for integrative bargaining. This could arise, for example, by agreeing a mutually advantageous completion date. In conducting negotiations it can be useful to identify what elements of integrative and distributive bargaining potentially exist.

Unitary and pluralistic frames of reference

A second relevant and important theory relates to the concepts of unitary frames of reference and pluralistic frames of reference (Fox, 1965). These concepts were examined previously, particularly in Chapter 2. However, these concepts are also basic to an understanding of negotiations. This is because conflicts of interest are not always obvious. In internal organization bargaining, those with a unitary frame of reference may be unable to recognize conflicts of interest between different parts of the organization. This is because they are likely to apply a team concept and assume that everyone will or should subordinate their own objectives to those of the organization overall. Those with a pluralistic frame of reference, however, will recognize that when sectional interests are threatened, people will not automatically cooperate for the common good. It is necessary to be able to recognize such conflicts of interest in order to develop a framework for dealing with them.

Conflicts of right and conflicts of interest

A further useful concept is the difference between **conflicts of right** and **conflicts of interest**. Conflicts of right occur when there is a dispute about the interpretation of an existing agreement. Conflicts of interest occur when the parties dispute what an agreement should be, as opposed to what it is.

The framework of negotiations

Whenever people negotiate there needs to be a framework, however informal it may be. The framework relates to how an issue is being negotiated. The parties can be so involved in the substance of the negotiations that they can neglect to pay sufficient attention to the way in which the negotiations are being handled. This can reduce the chances of a positive outcome. This is particularly the case when the negotiations are complicated and/or a number of parties are involved. In team negotiations there may need to be a clear division of labour so that the different aspects of negotiation are handled effectively. Particular attention may need to be paid to internal differences between team members. As well as needing to structure negotiations effectively, it is also necessary for those involved to be clear about their objectives and tactics.

Procedural and substantive issues

A basic distinction in negotiations is between the procedure that is used to negotiate and the actual substantive issues being negotiated about. If negotiations between the parties are part of an established pattern, the negotiations may have been formalized into a procedural agreement. If that is not the case, at least the historic pattern will probably represent the expectations of the parties as to the way they wish to proceed. Even in small informal negotiations the parties should consider the way in which they need to proceed and may also want to come to a joint understanding about that. There can be so much conflict and tension in negotiations about substantive issues that it can be in the interests of both parties to try and remove beforehand any misunderstandings about how the negotiations are to be conducted. There is a strong argument therefore for having a procedure agreed well in advance of negotiations. It can be difficult enough trying to resolve the substantive issues without having to agree the procedure as well, or having to make it up as you go along. To make an analogy with sport, the rules of the game are agreed well in advance of an actual game: great care is usually taken to ensure that the neutral parties in charge of sporting contests apply the rules in a consistent manner.

Objectives

Managers and others involved in negotiations need to carefully establish their objectives. Sometimes objectives are self-evident. On other occasions they involve patient diagnostic work. If a reactive style is taken, it may be automatic to respond to a demand by saying 'no', prevaricating or making an ungenerous counter-offer. However, on some occasions it may be in both the parties' interests if a demand is accepted. If, for example, there is a shortage of a particular category of staff, it may be in management's interests to agree to a demand for a wage increase rather than reactively resist it. In identifying objectives it can be crucial that the parties look forward and do not dwell on perceived historic injustices. Another important issue can be that demands may only be the symptom of a deeper underlying problem.

EXAMPLE: Identifying the real problem

In a former public utility there was high turnover of computer staff. When people left they said that they were leaving because they had been offered more money to work elsewhere. More money was given to the computer staff but the labour turnover remained high. The employer then asked people who were leaving what had caused them to look for another job. The clear pattern with the responses to his question was the poor interpersonal and management skills of their technical supervisors. The primary solution was clearly to do with the selection, development and monitoring of the supervisors of computer staff and not increasing wages.

Preparation

Once the negotiating objectives have been defined, it is then necessary to work out how those objectives might be achieved. One useful framework is as follows:

- Define objectives and rank them in order of importance
- Decide tactics to achieve objectives
- Identify the maximum concessions you will make (the bottom line)
- Decide on the action you will take if you do not achieve your objectives; This may cause you to rethink the concessions you are prepared to give.

It is particularly important to examine the power relationships. These may have far more impact on the outcome of negotiations than the intellectual or moral quality of a case. It involves asking such blunt questions as, 'Who can do what to whom and when?' A man with a knife at your throat may have a poor intellectual and moral case for robbing you but is likely to succeed.

EXAMPLE: Importance of understanding power realities

A local community leader in Britain was involved in negotiations about the closure of a rural railway line. He realized that he would not be able to stop the closure, so he concentrated his attention on getting the maximum concessions with a replacement bus service. This enabled him to get a better result than by simply protesting about the closure.

Negotiations can take place at two levels. The surface element may be the intellectual presentation of a case supported by apparently relevant information. However, this can have a large element of charade about it. The parties may in reality be concentrating on what pressure they can bring on the others involved and how they might do it. However, whilst it is important to recognize and take into account the power realities, careful case preparation and presentation do sometimes significantly affect the outcome. Issues to consider when constructing a case might be:

- Economic impact
- Legal impact
- Precedents and practice elsewhere
- The precedent effect of accepting a demand
- Ability of the parties to pay.

A further factor to consider is the nature of the relationship between the parties. Managers may be able to take much more on trust with a party if they have a long established relationship with them and if the other party has a good reputation. However, managers will need to be much more cautious in dealing with people they know little about, especially in a one-off negotiation. In a long-term relationship there is the factor of goodwill to be taken into account. It may also lead to the giving of face-saving compromises to the other side. If goodwill is not an issue there may be the temptation to use sharp practice to gain a better deal.

The confidentiality of information about bargaining positions can't always be taken for granted. Information can be leaked deliberately or accidentally. There is also often a grapevine by which people can gain information. However, care should be taken to try and avoid damaging leaks. Sometimes it is also necessary to beware of 'information' that is created or released to undermine the negotiating position of another party.

Internal differences

Attention is often concentrated on the differences between the two 'sides' or parties in a negotiation. However, often the 'sides' represent coalitions of interest groups. Members of a negotiating team can assume that because they are all on the same side they have a common position. However, as well as differing personalities, there can be quite different pressures on different members of the same side. Some team members may feel that other team members are being disloyal by not agreeing with their position. However, it is more profitable to try and understand the reasons why members of a team might disagree and explore what accommodations are possible. The worst thing to do is to not explore these issues beforehand and then to find that the internal differences only become obvious during negotiations with the other side.

The scale of the internal differences within a side can be greater and more difficult to resolve than the external differences between them and the other main party. This is not always obvious because of the much greater secrecy that may be involved in trying to resolve such differences. However, adequate time has to be given to establishing a 'party' line. Sides can split into 'hawks' and 'doves'. Moderates are sometimes called doves because of the term 'doves of peace'. This is in contrast to hard-liners, who are sometimes called hawks, hawks being birds of prey. It may be counterproductive to exclude hawks from the negotiating team. They may need to be exposed to the negotiating pressures and be involved in any proposals for settlement. They may cause far more trouble shouting their opposition from the sidelines.

There are many examples from the world of politics of the problems of reconciling internal differences. In Northern Ireland it became increasingly possible to get agreement between the moderates on both sides. The problem is getting their hawks to agree. Too many concessions to the other side, however, can destabilize the position of leaders and even lead to their death. An example is the assassination of the Israeli Prime Minister Yitzhak Rabin by an Israeli fundamentalist in 1995 following the Oslo Peace Accords. An earlier example is the assassination of Michael Collins by Irish nationalists in 1922. This followed his conclusion of a peace deal with the British

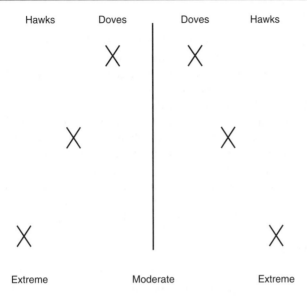

Figure 14.1   Handling internal differences

government, which involved independence for the south of Ireland but not the north. Sometimes deals are made secretly between the leaders who then try to persuade their own side to accept them.

The relationship between internal and external differences is illustrated in Figure 14.1.

Role allocations

Even in one-to-one negotiations there can be a number of different roles that the parties have to handle according to the stage they are at in the negotiating process. A procedural framework needs to be established. This needs to include the time and place for negotiations, an agenda, and the preparation and presentation of any relevant documents. The parties will need to spend time presenting their own arguments and listening to one another during the substantive negotiations. It may be necessary to organize adjournments and further meetings. If a deal is concluded, attention then has to be paid to how it is implemented. Failure to pay adequate attention to these issues can jeopardize the negotiations. It may be necessary for one of the parties, even if informally, to assume a chairing role in identifying and dealing with these issues.

In team negotiations the need for a division of labour between different members is more obvious than the need for one person to switch roles when they are bargaining on their own. However, even in team negotiations the need to arrange a sensible role allocation is often sadly neglected. This can lead to one person being quite unnecessarily overloaded, whilst their colleagues don't have enough to do. Key roles that have to be handled in team negotiations are described below.

Chairing

There can be three dimensions to the chairing role: 1) chairing a team in the negotiations with the other party, 2) chairing internal discussions and 3) chairing joint meetings. Sometimes there are formal arrangements for chairing joint meetings, for example by rotation or by having an independent chair handle it. Often there is no such provision and the chair of a team may need to handle this in such a way that an effective framework is provided without irritating the other side at this exercise of control. The chairing roles can be of great importance and require significant skill and attention, as explained in Chapter 15 on meetings, chairing and team building. It is up to the chair to see that negotiations stay on course and to intervene if there is a danger of the process breaking down. This is much more easily done if they are concentrating primarily on this aspect and are relatively detached from the substantive negotiations.

Case presentation

A common practice is for the most senior person on the management side to handle all the chairing roles and be the lead negotiator. However, given the danger of role overload and the damaging consequences this can have, it is often best to have a separate person act as the lead negotiator. The lead negotiator can then concentrate on just the negotiating issues and leave the procedural aspects to the chair. It also means that if there is a deadlock in discussions, or if the discussions get too heated, the chair can intervene. This may also create valuable thinking time for the lead negotiator.

Recording

Another way of easing the burden on the chair and lead negotiator of each side is to have someone else take notes. The case for someone doing this is even stronger if that person does not have any other formal responsibility in the negotiations. Verbatim notes of a whole meeting are not necessary, but great care may be necessary to get an accurate record of key issues. The person taking notes will normally need to sit next to the chair of their side so that they can liaise about note-taking. The chair may need to have their lead negotiator on their other side.

Observing

Much may be learnt about the other side's real intentions and internal differences by a careful study of their behaviour during negotiations. Points to watch can be:

- Who people defer to within a team
- Body language, including facial expressions
- Signs of tension, e.g. in rate of talking, language used and pitch of voice
- The issues on which negotiators seem to need to refer back to their principals

- Cross-talk within a side
- Contradictions in what is said.

It can be time well spent to have someone concentrate on observing. If appropriate, this can be combined with another role, for example recording.

Specialist representation

Sometimes managers need to consider the case for appointing a specialist to lead negotiations. This will be logical if the costs of such representation are less than the potential gain in the negotiations. The specialist may be internally or externally appointed. Human resource (HR) managers often lead in internal negotiations with employee representatives because they may have developed specialist skills and knowledge. However, there are dangers of the HR function taking over too much executive authority. One option is to have line managers lead negotiations with a HR representative present as an adviser.

Trade unions have long understood the need for specialist representation. The expertise of some employee representatives and of full-time union officials generally is such that they can often outmanoeuvre an inexperienced line manager. Also, union representatives may be appointed because of their negotiating ability, whilst this may not be such a key skill in the selection of line managers. It is for this reason that the issue of training managers in negotiating is addressed later in this chapter.

Sometimes organizations, groups or individuals need to consider the use of external negotiating specialists to represent them. On commercial issues it may be necessary to consider using a commercial agent. The advantages that specialist negotiators can bring include emotional detachment; knowledge of the substantive area, market trends and practice elsewhere; and contacts. Managers may be at a disadvantage if the person they are dealing with has specialist knowledge or specialist representation and they do not.

EXAMPLE: A need for specialist representation

Four young musicians, who had formed their own group, were offered a contract by a medium-sized recording studio. They told their accountant of this, and he advised them to take a lawyer with them. When the musicians entered the conference room they found that four printed standard contracts had been placed on the table for them to sign. The secretary, who had showed them into the room, asked the members of the group who the fifth person was. When they introduced their lawyer the secretary responded by saying 'you won't be needing these contracts then'. She returned with four different printed contracts. It emerged that the original contract forms contained an open-ended cost clause, which would have enabled the recording company to offset costs against the income generated by the contract, so that the musicians might never have received any money. The contract that the musicians eventually did sign had a fixed level of costs.

The negotiating process

The negotiating ritual

It is often best to try and agree the sequence of events with the other party before negotiations begin. If there is a procedural agreement, this may specify the sequence. Invariably there is a ritual to negotiations. This usually consists of a series of offers and counter-offers and eventual compromise agreement. This ritual can fulfil a necessary function. This is particularly so if the parties negotiating have interest groups to whom they are responsible. The negotiators will need to demonstrate that they have got the best offer available in order to 'sell' any deal to whomever they represent. Consequently it is important to avoid public displays of triumph if a good deal is obtained, as this can undermine the position of the negotiators for the other side. Even in cases in which the principals are negotiating directly with one another, they will also need to feel that they have achieved a good deal.

Thought needs to be given as to whether it is better to make the first offer yourself or to try and get the other party to make the first bid. The pitching of an initial offer can have a crucial effect on the ultimate outcome. In the case of trying to buy something, too low an offer may mean that you are not taken seriously. Too high an offer can create the expectation that you can be persuaded to improve your offer significantly.

Parties to negotiations may have a recognizable historic pattern in the way they handle the ritual. It may help a manager in handling the ritual to try and identify that pattern. It may be necessary to take account of the possibility that past patterns will alter if a new and important person joins a negotiating team. The **negotiating ritual** needs to be handled with some skill. Sometimes mistakes can be elementary.

EXAMPLE: The need for skill in handling the negotiating ritual

At the start of annual railway pay negotiations the lead management negotiator referred to management proposals as 'the first offer'. This drew a swift response from the union spokesperson: 'We don't like the first offer – what about the second one?'

There is also a need to consider who makes their case first. Often it makes sense for the person who is trying to change a situation to be allowed to go first. If one side is particularly emotional about an issue it may be best to let them present first so that they can dissipate some of their anger. Having done that they may be more able to listen to the response and also may even have moderated their position through being given the chance to be heard. It is particularly important for the chair of the opposing side to prevent retaliatory comment from hawks on their own side at this stage, as this could undo all the good work that may have already been accomplished. A further point is the need to consider what you should ask for in return whenever you make an offer. Opposing negotiators may be much more likely to make concessions if a trade-off is involved.

Keeping in role

The chair needs to ensure that parties keep to their allotted roles. It is all too easy for 'tennis matches' to develop whereby each side refutes what the other says and the discussions not only do not progress but get increasingly acrimonious (Rees and Porter, 1997, p. 67). Understandably, both sides will want to concentrate on the strong and not the weak points in their case. It is up to the chair to let both sides make their case and then move on. Sometimes it may be necessary to agree to differ on a particular point and agree to return to it later. To navigate through these difficulties it is essential that the chair stays in role and doesn't get unnecessarily involved in argument about the substantive issues. If the chair is for some reason involved in the substantive negotiations, possibly because the negotiations are conducted between just two people, they may each need to be adept at signalling when they are bargaining and when they are trying to manage the procedure and processes. This situation is akin to refereeing a sports match in which one is also playing and is a topic given further detailed attention in Chapter 15 on meetings, chairing and team building.

Tunnel vision

A further issue is the need for the parties to avoid **tunnel vision**. This can happen when the parties focus their attention on one aspect of negotiations and ignore other issues that may be far more important. Sometimes one or both of the parties may fail to see that the issue with which they are dealing is a symptom of something more fundamental. This reinforces the need to keep remembering one's objectives, as explained in the section on the framework of negotiations earlier in this chapter.

Communication issues

Communication processes can be fragile at the best of times. However, they can be particularly vulnerable during negotiations. This is because of the presence of factors such as conflict and emotion and the complexities that can arise during negotiations. Also, distortion is possible at each stage of the chain of communication. There is a need for people in chairing roles to pay particular attention to the potential for misunderstandings and to take preventative action to avoid them and the often very serious consequences that can flow from them. Key communication areas in negotiating will involve listening and observing, taking account of any cultural differences and avoiding ambiguity.

Listening

One of the dangers in negotiating meetings is that people get so involved in presenting their case that they do not listen carefully enough to what the other side has to say and then reflect on it. People in chairing roles need to give the other side adequate opportunity to present their case and ensure that it is listened to. A common problem is for people to use the time when the other side is presenting their case simply to rehearse the arguments they are going to use instead of listening to what is being said (this is called 'behaviour rehearsal'). If a person has been given particular responsibility for 'observing' this could be combined with a particular responsibility for listening.

The style used in the negotiations can also be very important. There can be complications enough without the differences being personalized. The parties should generally try and behave assertively and not aggressively. The distinction between these two styles of behaviour was explained in Chapter 4. If a person is nevertheless aggressive, it is best to remain assertive and not make matters worse by responding aggressively. The tactic of remaining assertive can have the effect of calming the other person down. If it doesn't, it may lead to the other person losing the thread of their argument, making mistakes and losing sympathy with their colleagues.

Particular attention may need to be paid to the language that is used. Sometimes coded messages are sent between lead negotiators to indicate whether they are taking a hard or a soft line on a particular issue. On other occasions parties may unintentionally reveal their intentions by the use of particular words or by carelessness. Words such as 'review', if used in the context of pay negotiations, are likely to be interpreted as meaning an increase.

Body language

Body language was covered in a general manner in Chapter 8 in the context of communication. The concept of body language can be of particular importance in negotiation. People can give away their intentions by accidental gestures. However, other gestures may be deliberate signals to indicate how well or badly a particular suggestion has been received.

Cultural differences

Attention will need to be paid to any potential cultural barriers to understanding during negotiations, especially given increasing cultural diversity within nations and globalization. It may be important to have a person to advise on how to handle the different negotiating conventions of those from other cultures. The impact of culture on communication was also considered in both Chapter 4 on managerial and leadership style and in Chapter 8 on communication.

The rituals that people from other countries are used to may be different and in some countries much more prolonged than in others. In countries such as the USA, communications are likely to be direct and often reinforced by written contracts. In some Asian countries, in contrast, much more attention will have to be paid to the context in which negotiations take place. More may have to be taken on trust, as to ask for too much written clarification could be taken as insulting, with the implication that the other party is not to be trusted. In such cultures there may also be a higher need to save the face of the weaker party. Deference to elders can vary from culture to culture. In dealing with the Japanese, for example, it may be important to recognize the deference shown to elder members on their team and to show politeness yourself. It may also be important to work out the effect that culture can have on power realities within a team.

The nature and importance of body language may also differ considerably from one culture to another. People from some cultures may be much more impassive than those from other cultural backgrounds. If a manager causes offence to people from some cultures, they may not realize it, however damaging it may be, because of the lack of visible reaction from those who have been offended. The meaning of gestures can vary critically from one culture to another.

EXAMPLE: Variation of the meaning of body gestures in another country

Negotiations in India involving an international organization were hampered at one stage by the habit of the people with whom the organization was trying to do business shaking their heads from side to side as if in disagreement. It then emerged that in this particular part of the country that gesture meant agreement and not disagreement!

Avoiding ambiguity

It is crucial for negotiators to avoid unintended ambiguity during negotiations, especially in any agreement that is reached. Unfortunately, this can all too easily happen. Negotiators may remember the concessions that they have gained during negotiations far more readily than the concessions they have made to the other party. Such selective perception may be compounded by the use of words that can have more than one meaning. Words such as 'may' can be interpreted as 'must', 'probably', or 'possibly'. Those involved in negotiating are apt to make the interpretation most convenient to them, unaware that the other party may be doing the same thing in reverse. To make matters worse, when the difference in interpretations emerges, the parties may think that there has been deliberate deceit rather than genuine misunderstanding. A related issue is the need to distinguish between a quote and an estimate. A quote, if accepted, may create a contractual arrangement. An estimate though may lead to variations in what exactly is to be done and for how much.

EXAMPLE: The frequency of ambiguity

In a series of experiments involving simulated negotiating exercises with managers it was found that it was more common than not to have significant misunderstandings about what the parties thought they had agreed. This emerged when, at the conclusion of negotiations, each individual was asked to record the main items of agreement. The people involved were not allowed to confer with one another when recording their perception of the outcome. The managers concerned tended to misperceive the outcomes in their favour, that is managers would all tend to think that they had conceded less than other managers playing the part of employee representatives, thought they had (Rees and Porter, 1997, pp. 68–69).

To avoid unintended ambiguity it is necessary for the chair and lead negotiator in particular to keep on checking during negotiations that misunderstanding has not occurred. Careful listening and observing is a way of helping to see if misunderstanding has developed or not. Frequent summarizing of what has or has not been agreed may be necessary during a meeting. It may be necessary to repeat the same point a number of times to make sure that there is genuine agreement and understanding. The following example shows how serious misunderstandings can easily and innocently arise.

EXAMPLE: An important but avoidable misunderstanding

The payroll computer at a factory crashed on pay day at a time when most manual employees were still paid in cash. Because of this employee representatives demanded that each employee affected be given a cash payment. The company refused to do this, and a three-day strike ensued. It was then discovered that the employees had simply wanted a cash advance which could later be deducted from whatever wages were due to them. The company had thought that the employees were asking for a cash payment to compensate for inconvenience as well as receiving their wages. The problem then arose as to whether the employees should receive any payment for the three days they had been on strike because of this misunderstanding. The nature of the confusion was only identified during talks convened to try and resolve the dispute when the two parties were asked to explain just what their differences were.

Recording the outcome of negotiations is a further way of preventing misunderstanding. However, the damage may be done by the time a written document is issued. It is necessary to ensure that ambiguity does not arise during negotiations so that a written record confirms what was really agreed, not just what the person writing the document thought was agreed.

Sometimes there is a need for deliberate ambiguity. This can be the case when neither party wants to concede a particular issue but nor do they want to contest it at that point in time. Providing there are no problems about implementing ambiguous wording, this can be a necessary device for getting agreement.

Reporting back

Particular problems can arise when negotiators report back to the groups they represent. This can be because of the pressure that negotiators may come under to say that they have obtained a better deal than they really have. If this is happening on both sides of a negotiation, the perceptions of those in the interest groups of what was really agreed upon can become even more distorted. It is therefore important that those who receive reports from negotiators coax out of them what really happened at the negotiations. If there is a danger of distortion in reporting back from employee representatives to employees, managers may need to distribute written details to employees on the outcome of negotiations.

Handling deadlock

Handling deadlock can be a key skill for negotiators. There are a number of ways of trying to prevent or resolve deadlock.

Agree on what can be agreed

It may be best to identify what can be agreed on and what cannot. Finding some areas of agreement can create an element of mutual trust and become a platform for later agreement on more difficult issues. If necessary, more difficult issues may have to be left for another occasion.

Dealing with conflicting principles

Particular difficulties can emerge if the parties are pursuing different and conflicting points of principle. This may appear to rule out room for manoeuvre. Ways of trying to resolve this are to:

■ Make value judgements about the respective importance of the principles involved. In some cases it is necessary to let one principle override another because of its greater importance. This may involve giving way or standing firm;

■ Consider whether the other party has simply run out of arguments and is clinging to a principle in order to save face. If so, it will then be necessary to try and find ways of saving the face of the other party to help them discreetly withdraw from the issue of principle;

■ Examine whether the principle involved has practical significance or is actually hampering the party that is clinging to it;

■ Devise a compromise deal that appears to leave conflicting principles intact, even though in practice that may not be the case.

Appointing a devil's advocate

It may help to have someone act as devil's advocate. This involves one of your team examining the negotiating position of your opponent, which may generate insights into the position of the other party. These may include an understanding of the concessions the other party may be able to make and the points that they will not be able to concede.

Identifying convergence and divergence

There is often a pattern in negotiations of the parties sometimes converging towards agreement and sometimes diverging. If the convergence is bringing the parties close to agreement, further small concessions may result in a deal. Once divergence sets in, the opportunity may be lost. There may be no point in making concessions when parties are moving apart – they may have to wait until there are prospects of convergence again before getting a constructive response to concessions.

Deadlines

Sometimes deadlines are set for agreement to be reached. If agreement is not reached, an offer may be withdrawn, change implemented or some other action taken. This can work provided that the party setting the deadline has a viable plan of what to implement if there is no agreement.

Adjournments

If negotiations become acrimonious or if fresh ideas are needed, it may be best to seek an adjournment. Adjournments may also be necessary if one or other party needs to consider a fresh point or to resolve internal differences within their team. It may also be necessary for one of the parties to report back to its interest group or groups to receive fresh instructions. Sometimes parties need time to come to terms with what concessions have to be made. Delicate issues of timing can be involved in judging when it can be productive or counterproductive to arrange an adjournment.

Keeping the parties together

If agreement seems possible, it may be best to try and keep the parties together and clinch a deal. In marginal situations, factors such as fatigue may help to encourage people to agree. If the negotiations are adjourned, people may have second thoughts or be urged to take a harder line by the interest groups they represent. Once the parties have separated it may be difficult to bring them back together. This why a former chief conciliation officer of ACAS (UK) said that it may be necessary to provide 'cold fish and chips and warm lager' to keep the parties together and encourage agreement. However, any deal has to be realistic and not one that will be repudiated afterwards. Sometimes there can be a problem of getting the parties together in the first place.

EXAMPLE: Problems of negotiating when one of the parties will not meet with the other

In the case of a six-week brewery strike in the UK, the management found that they were unable to negotiate with the people they desperately wanted to talk to because management themselves had previously stated that they would not 'negotiate under duress'. Management had to find a way around this.

Back channels

Deadlock can sometimes be resolved by the use of 'back channels'. These are secret contacts between some of the negotiators on each side. They may or may not involve the use of a third party. Back channels can be used to explore the possibility of agreement. If agreement is found to be possible, then the proposals can be presented to the respective negotiating teams. If the secret talks indicate that agreement is not possible, then the discussions remain secret to protect the respective positions of the parties involved.

Some issues may be so important and yet so sensitive that the parties may reach secret agreements about them. These may involve mutual understandings or formal secret protocols. There are dangers in this, particularly if a key negotiator is replaced or one party fails to honour their side of the bargain.

EXAMPLE: A secret deal

During the Cuban missile crisis in 1962, President Kennedy secretly agreed to withdraw nuclear missiles from Turkey. This was in exchange for the Russians' public withdrawal of nuclear missiles from Cuba. President Kennedy needed secrecy about his concession because of his greater dependence on public opinion than the Russian leader, Nikita Khrushchev.

Use of third parties

Sometimes third parties may be able to help resolve deadlock. Independent parties include lawyers and commercial arbitrators In the case of employment disputes in the UK the services of the Advisory, Conciliation and Arbitration Service (ACAS) are available. ACAS has considerable experience and expertise in providing conciliation, mediation and arbitration services in disputes between employers and trade unions. Many other countries have similar arrangements. Arbitration is often on a voluntary basis. This means that both parties need to agree to the process, unlike the case of compulsory arbitration. However, the party in the more powerful position in a dispute may be reluctant to accept arbitration if they think that this will give them a less favourable outcome than using their negotiating power. Arbitration awards in trade disputes in the UK are not legally binding, but are invariably accepted. If recourse is made to arbitration, it is essential to have clear terms of reference.

Accepting failure

Not all deadlocks can or even should be broken. Managers need to consider their bottom line, as explained in the section on objectives earlier in this Chapter. No deal may be better than a bad deal. However, the consequences of not having agreement may need to be fully considered before breaking off negotiations. If agreement is not reached there is always the possibility that the matter can be reconsidered in the future. In that respect, a 'no' is not as final as a 'yes'. Also, opportunities for progress may arise in other directions.

Even if a negotiator fails to achieve their objectives, it can be possible to put up markers for the future. This can be about issues to be raised at a later date. If negotiators make predictions that are ignored but which later turn out to have been correct, this is likely to enhance their personal reputation. They are also likely to enhance their reputation by the dignity with which they accept failure.

Negotiating outcomes

Communicating the result

Once an agreement is made it may need to be written up and communicated to all the parties concerned. Employers may want to see that each employee is given details of any agreements affecting them. Care needs to be taken to see that there are no misunderstandings about the content and interpretation of an agreement. In some cases it may also be appropriate to issue press releases or hold press conferences.

Evaluation

It may help to do a cost-benefit analysis of an agreement to see what lessons there are for the future. This can help decide whether there should be further negotiations in the area concerned or if it should be left alone.

Implementation

The terms of an agreement need to be achieved in practice. The practicability of being able to implement the terms of an agreement needs to be considered very early on in the negotiating process. Historically there are many cases in the UK of productivity deals between trade unions and employers at a national level which were not implemented locally. Consequently, employers were paying for productivity gains they were not getting. Attention needs to be paid to arrangements for monitoring and control and the need for safeguards if promised concessions are not implemented. Sometimes phased payments are made in accordance with progress made.

Interpretative disputes

It may be necessary to provide a mechanism for resolving disputes about the interpretation of an agreement between the parties who made it. This may be handled by internal organizational procedures. If internal procedures do not result in agreement there is sometimes provision for reference to an outside party. In the UK there is increasing use of an ombudsman, for example in national and local government and in the banking and travel industries. As previously explained, in the case of disputes between employers and trade unions there can be reference to ACAS for voluntary arbitration.

The way in which disputes about the interpretation of agreements are to be resolved needs to be taken into account when agreements are written. In collective employee relations agreements in the UK the tradition has been to abide by the spirit rather than the letter of the agreement. This is in contrast to the USA, where such documents are legally binding between the parties and interpreted according to the letter of the agreement. Agreements that are binding in spirit may be difficult for outsiders to interpret because of ambiguities and mutual unwritten understandings. However, there is always a case for expressing agreements as clearly as is practicable. The ease with which disputes can arise about what was agreed and the difficulties that can arise in settling such disputes underlines the need to ensure that negotiations are conducted and concluded in such a way that there is little or no room for subsequent disagreement.

Variation of agreements

Provision may need to be made for the variation of an agreement. The duration of an agreement may need to be specified, as well as the procedure for seeking to vary it. There may also need to be provision for inflation and escape clauses in the event of specified circumstances. Building and construction contracts usually allow for renegotiation of the price if extra work is requested. It is necessary to beware of open-ended commitments, especially if they can be manipulated by one of the parties.

Training

In evaluating negotiating outcomes attention may need to be paid to the skill with which the negotiations were handled. This may reveal training needs. Training needs may also be created by reorganization, particularly if that involves giving more responsibility for negotiation to line managers. The development of negotiating skills can be achieved by the gradual exposure of managers to negotiating situations. They may learn much by watching experienced negotiators in action. Skills can also be developed on formal training courses. Participants can develop their diagnostic skills by identifying objectives and tactics in a graded series of exercises. Simulation exercises involving role-playing can provide the opportunity for people to practice their negotiating skills and gain feedback on their performance in a risk-free environment. Feedback can be given by other participants, observers and, if appropriate, closed-circuit television replays of critical incidents. It can be particularly useful for participants to identify misunderstandings that arise during simulated negotiations and the causes of these misunderstandings. It can also be very useful for participants to experiment with different role allocations during team negotiations (Rees and Porter, 1997, pp. 65–68,153–157).

Summary

Managers spend much of their time in negotiation over a wide range of topics, and often such negotiations are informal. The pace of change is such that negotiation and renegotiation is becoming ever more important. A key theoretical distinction is between integrative bargaining and distributive bargaining. In integrative bargaining the parties may be able to co-operate in such a way that they make their objectives complementary to one another. In distributive bargaining one party can only gain at the expense of the other. The importance of the frames of reference of the negotiators was also considered in this chapter. Managers with a unitarist perspective may be handicapped by failing to understand the rationale of those with whom they are negotiating. Those with a pluralist perspective are more able to understand the rationale and even the legitimacy of the claims of other parties.

The need for managers to develop a framework for negotiation even in informal situations was explained. This involves preparation, identification of objectives and a rational sequence of events during the bargaining process. Often the internal differences within a team can be more difficult to resolve than differences with the external party with whom negotiations need to be conducted. Consequently, considerable time may need to be taken to try and resolve internal differences before negotiations can start. It is also important to examine the power relationships in a bargaining relationship. Power relationships are likely to have much more influence on the outcome of negotiations than the debating skills of the parties involved.

The need for clear roles to be allocated to those involved in team negotiations was stressed. The complexity and pressures involved in negotiations can be such that misunderstandings easily arise. It is important to anticipate communication problems to help ensure that real agreement is reached. Division of labour within negotiating teams is one way of avoiding such problems. Key roles are chairing, case presentation, recording and observing. In one-to-one negotiations these activities will all need to be covered by the same person. Sometimes the cost of hiring a specialist negotiator may be a sound investment. The skill with which a negotiating ritual is handled can also be very important.

Consideration was given to how deadlock may be handled. One way of doing this is by the involvement of a third party. However, no agreement may be better than a bad agreement. Consideration was also given to the effective implementation and monitoring of agreements. It may also be necessary to make arrangements for variations of agreements and for resolving disputes about the interpretation of agreements. The way in which negotiating skills can be developed was also covered.

Self-assessment questions

1. Identify issues you recently had to negotiate both at work and/or elsewhere.
2. Explain one theory relevant to negotiation.
3. Why is it necessary to have a procedural framework for negotiations?
4. What are the different roles that people may need to play during team negotiations?
5. Why is it necessary to identify the power realities of the parties involved in negotiations?
6. Explain the term 'negotiating ritual' and its potential importance.
7. Why are misunderstandings likely during negotiations?
8. How can you try and ensure that agreements are kept?

Case study notes – Availability or Activity?

The power realities are such that the company would seem to be against increasing the pay of the night worker – labour is not difficult to get, the work is not skilled and there are cost implications in a commercially competitive environment. There could also be repercussive effects of regrading the jobs of a day gate worker, slinger and crane driver which seem significantly more demanding. They may object to being graded the same as the night worker. The night worker does not get a night shift supplement but the job is not very demanding and it is not unknown for people to combine such jobs with day jobs. However, the company would want someone reliable doing the job. If there are other depots in the company, which appears not to be the case, one would need to consider the repercussive effect at any such other depots. The night worker may also not have much support from colleagues as he is not likely to see much of them. One can't see them easily agreeing to a three shift system, including the night worker, if that was suggested. One option may be in any case to contract out the security aspect of the job but that could mean lorries arriving at night would have to be left outside the depot.

One option is to handle the case as a role play. If this is done the Observer's Negotiating form, reproduced as an appendix to this chapter, may be particularly useful for some of the students to analyse the way the negotiation is handled.

Appendix

For negotiating skills exercises

Observers' Form

Before negotiations start:	*Points to consider*	*Notes*
Analysis of power realities	How thoroughly were these discussed?	
	How accurately were the power realities analyzed in your view?	
Resolution of conflict within the group	What areas of conflict existed within the group?	
	Were the conflict areas recognized by the group members?	
	Was any attempt made to resolve these areas of conflict?	
Organization of the group	Was any attempt made to allocate roles to the individual group members?	
	Was any attempt made to ensure that everybody was in agreement as to negotiating strategy?	

(continued)

Continued

During negotiations:

Organization of group	To what extent did negotiators keep to the briefs decided upon before the exercise began?
Chairing of the negotiations	To what extent did the chairing of the meeting rest with the person originally allocated to the role?
Further process skills to be observed	Did the negotiators *listen* to what the other group had to say?
	Was there any evidence of certain negotiators developing 'tunnel vision'?
	What effect did the use of *emotive words* have on the other group?
	Were there any examples of negotiators phrasing their sentences ambiguously? What effect did this have, if any?
	Was there any evidence of the use of the 'negotiating ritual'?
	Did either group give the other group the opportunity/possibility of 'backing down' without losing face?

After the negotiating exercise:

Evaluation	Did each group agree amongst themselves the exact nature of the conclusion that was reached at the end of the exercise?
	Similarly, were the groups in agreement with each other about the exact nature of the conclusion that was reached between the two groups at the end of the exercise?

References

NB: Works of particular interest are marked with an asterisk.

*Fox, Alan (1965), *Industrial Sociology and Industrial Relations*, Research paper no. 3, Royal Commission on Trade Unions and Employers Associations, HMSO.

It may be difficult to access the original paper. Fox's explanation of the concept of unitary and pluralistic frames of reference is a classic, however, and even summaries of his work are well worth reading.

*Rees, W. David and C. Porter (1997), Negotiation – Mystic Art or Identifiable Process?, Parts 1–2, *Industrial and Commercial Training*, Vol. 29, Nos. 3, 5.

Part 1 of the article gives a useful account of the value of running training workshops in negotiating skills and how they can be organized. Both articles received a highly commended award by the Emerald Literati club.

Walton, Richard E. and Robert B. McKersie (1965), *A Behavioral Theory of Labor Negotiations*, New York: McGraw-Hill.

Taking it further

*Fisher, Roger, William Ury and Bruce Patton (2011), *Getting to Yes: Negotiating an Agreement Without Giving In*, 3rd ed., Perfect Paperback Publishing, UK.

A popular, informative, easy to read and useful account of the negotiating process.

*Mead, Richard and Tim G. Andrews (2009), *International Management, Culture and Beyond*, 4th edn., Blackwell Business.

See Ch. 8 Dispute Resolution and Negotiation – Mead is invariably good value and Chapter 8 includes the cross-cultural dimension of negotiation.

Meetings, Chairing and Team Building

15

Learning Exercise

Instead of a case study for this chapter there is a learning exercise relevant to key issues. Details of this exercise are given at the end of the chapter.

Introduction

In this chapter the role of meetings in organizations and the associated skills of seeing that they are conducted effectively are examined. Meetings, whether formal or informal, are an integral part of organizational activity and attendance at them can occupy a considerable part of a manager's time. In addition, important decisions are taken at meetings and mistakes not always easily reversed. The different types of meetings are explained and the need stressed for those attending a meeting to be clear about their objectives and any decision-making arrangements involved. It is particularly important that the chair and secretary of formal meetings prepare beforehand to ensure that the time at meetings is used effectively. Other members may also need to prepare beforehand, particularly if they want to influence any outcomes. Prior preparation may also be necessary for informal meetings.

The differences between procedures, processes and tasks are explained. Attention is given to the way in which conflict at a meeting may need to be handled and the need for the chair to avoid getting over-involved in discussions. The importance of follow-up action, including implementation and monitoring, is covered. The term 'chair' is used throughout the chapter rather than the alternative expression 'chairman' to emphasize the point that the chair can be a man or a woman.

The skills involved in organizing meetings effectively lead naturally into the topic of team building. Meetings can be viewed as teams – whether temporary or arranged on a more continuous basis. Managers or leaders are almost by definition likely to be in charge of groups of people who need to be organized effectively. Key issues are the membership of such groups and the dynamics of their interaction. These issues are necessarily examined after a consideration of the skills involved in conducting meetings.

The need for meetings

Place in organization structure

Meetings can be an indispensable part of an organization's structure. In some organizations, such as local government, policy decisions must be taken by a committee-type structure with various committees or sub-committees reporting to the council as a whole. In commercial organizations the need for meetings below the level of shareholders' and directors' meetings may not be obligatory but will still be very necessary.

Meetings may be necessary as an aid to the running of departments. They can also be vital in promoting interdepartmental cooperation which otherwise might not be achieved. The growing complexity of decision-making, caused partly by the diffusion of knowledge within organizations, means that very often decisions can only be taken effectively by groups of people coming together and pooling their knowledge and expertise. Globalization and developments in information technology mean that some meetings involve simultaneous multilingual translation and/or electronic conferencing. If meetings are ineffective it can mean that a vital aspect of organizational structure is failing.

Consequences of ineffectiveness

There are many reasons why attention needs to be paid to the effective conduct of meetings. The decisions that are taken in meetings can be very important. The quality of decision-making may correlate with the skill with which meetings are conducted. Small improvements in the effectiveness of meetings can also lead to considerable savings in time because of the multiplication of the time saved by the number of people present. Meetings can also have functions other than decision-making, such as providing briefing for those present or ensuring that decisions are taken in an open way.

The quality of decision-making and the efficiency with which business is conducted can affect working relationships outside meetings and the credibility of the role of meetings for future occasions. Managers should also be aware that they are in the spotlight when chairing meetings and that the effectiveness of their performance is likely to enhance or damage their reputation, often before critical audiences. However, if others are responsible for the poor conduct of meetings, at least managers can learn by their mistakes. By contrast, effective chairing is not so obvious as bad chairing simply because things go so smoothly. It is for the same reason that the best sports referees are often the ones who are least noticed.

Activities in meetings

Level of formality

Meetings can vary in importance and formality, from the proceedings of Parliament or international bodies such as the United Nations to the informal discussion of a temporary problem between colleagues. Whatever the type of meeting, it is necessary for the participants to be aware of the methods by which the business is conducted. These activities fall broadly into the categories listed below.

Substantive content or task

The substantive content or task can be defined as the business of the meeting. For the business to be conducted effectively there needs to be a sound procedural and process framework.

Procedural arrangements

These are the rules that govern the conduct of the meeting. They may be formally embodied in the constitution or terms of reference of a committee, agreed by the parties present or, in some cases, imposed by one party on another.

Process control

This is the interpersonal interaction between those present. For meetings to be effectively handled there needs to be constructive management of these interactions. Even in very informal situations there is always a process aspect to the discussions, and the skill with which this is handled can affect the quality and acceptability of any outcome. It may be very necessary for someone to discreetly take the lead in managing the process in informal situations, thus creating a framework within which discussions can take place. Once the other people involved realize that the lead is being taken by someone simply to facilitate matters, rather than to impose their own decision, they may relax and welcome the lead that has been taken.

Purposes of meetings

Meetings can be for a variety of purposes. Important aims of meetings include:

- Decision-making (which may be part of a constitutional decision-making process)
- Negotiating
- Consultation
- Briefing
- Fact-finding
- Exchange of views (which sometimes may involve brainstorming)
- Problem-solving
- Bonding – this may be between individuals who are part of a group and/or between groups from different parts of an organization.

The above classification is a very broad one, and there can be subdivisions within the general headings. Also, some meetings may involve a number of the above activities or even all of them.

Decision-making

In the case of decision-making meetings, there are a number of ways in which decisions may be taken. Decisions can be taken by:

- The most senior person present
- Voting
- Consensus
- Negotiation
- Recommendation to another body.

It is important for people to be able to distinguish between the different decision-making arrangements of meetings. If the members of a meeting fail to see the distinctions it can lead to confusion; if the chair does not see the differences it can lead to chaos. This can happen if people have a stereotyped view of meetings and start applying the wrong conventions in a particular situation. Managers may assume that they have to operate by consensus or majority vote, when the reality may be that an organization has vested them ultimately with the sole decision-making responsibility within a particular area. Management chairs at joint consultative meetings can, and sometimes do, use voting procedures and short-circuit established management structures because the chair has not appreciated that a consultative meeting literally means just that. It is an aid to decision-making via established management procedures, not a substitute for those procedures. During formal negotiations there can be two different centres of decision-making: 1) at the pre-meetings of two separate groups, and 2) during a joint meeting. Both discussions require effective chairing.

Roles in meetings

Even in small informal meetings it may be necessary to identify the roles that members need to play and have an appropriate division of labour. In some cases people can change roles in a meeting, for example from presenting a case to acting as chair so that others in their turn can put their case. Particularly important roles are those of chair and secretary.

The role of the chair

A chair of a meeting needs to understand the substantive issue under discussion but also needs to devote some time to a consideration of how a meeting is to be handled effectively. An appropriate division of labour in formal meetings may be that the chair spends perhaps most of their time on procedural matters and process control, someone else takes the minutes and the other members concentrate on the substantive issues. A meeting where no one concentrates on or even bothers about the procedural and process aspects is the one most likely to be ineffective. The role of the chair is examined later in the chapter with particular regard to resolving conflict during meetings and the danger of the chair's over-involvement in discussion.

The need for process leadership may exist even in informal discussions between relatively few people. Sometimes the level of informality, the competitive nature of relationships or the sensitivity of the issues being discussed is such that it is inappropriate for a formal chair to be appointed. It may nevertheless be both useful and necessary if one person, perhaps quite informally, deals with the process aspects of discussion. This may involve taking a purely neutral role and asking such questions as 'What is the problem?' or 'What are everyone's views?'. The other parties may be quite prepared to let one person emerge as the informal chair, particularly if that person is seen to be confining themselves to a neutral role. It may later be possible for that person to enter into the substantive discussions – but only so long as they demonstrate that this is not going to endanger the process control arrangements that have evolved. Otherwise, the person may find that their substantive contributions are not welcome or that their process leadership is challenged.

The role of the secretary

If a meeting is of any size it may be necessary to have a secretary. This can be a very influential role. This may be a legal or other formal requirement. The secretary can share much of the work load with the chair. This may be particularly important if the chair has other extensive commitments. It will also enable the chair to concentrate on the important issues that need attention. Much of the preparatory, administrative and follow-up work may need to be handled by the secretary, including preparation of the draft agenda and distribution of relevant papers, including the agreed agenda. The chair and secretary should spend time together before a meeting to plan how it can be most effectively handled. This can increase the influence of the secretary, but one should beware of the business of a meeting being pre-empted by such discussions. A preliminary meeting should be to facilitate the smooth running of the main meeting, not to ensure that it acts as a rubber stamp for the chair and secretary. One recent development in some organizations is to have paperless meetings for environmental reasons. This involves members using tablets (e.g. iPads) or lap top computers to refer to documents, but accessing documents in this way can be less convenient than referring to paper documents.

The secretary will also take responsibility for keeping a record of a meeting. They may do this themselves or alternatively they may have another person operating under their control and taking notes. The minutes will need to be checked by both the secretary and chair. Even in small informal meetings it may be best if one of the parties identifies and carries on whatever secretarial activity is necessary. This may include a note of any significant outcomes, including what follow-up action is needed and by whom. This topic is considered further in the section on recording the outcome of meetings later in this chapter.

Preparation before meetings

The amount of preparation required before meetings will vary according to the type of meeting – its formality, importance, predictability and the role that the individual who is attending the meeting is going to take. There can be few meetings, however, to which people do not need to give some prior thought. Perhaps the most important issue to consider is what your own objectives are going to be at a meeting. It is only when these have been clarified that it is possible to establish what other preparation is required. It is also necessary to consider what is likely to be expected of you at a meeting. This may also indicate the preparations you need to make so that other people's needs can be taken into account.

Any procedural rules or constitutional statements about the powers of a meeting need to be to hand and also thoroughly understood, so that such issues can be dealt with immediately and reassuringly if they emerge during a meeting. One would not be reassured by a football referee who continually had to refer to a rule book whilst a game was being played. The more formal the meeting, the more a chair may rely on the secretary to handle procedural matters before a meeting and to be a source of information during it. It may be expected that the meeting will be run not just in accordance with its constitution but also by the normal conventions of committee procedure (Rees and Porter, 2008). The chair will also need to understand the substantive issues and their history sufficiently to guide the discussion effectively.

The agenda and its management

Clearly, meetings need a structure for the consideration of substantive items. This structure is normally provided by an agenda. However, it is necessary to be proactive in thinking about an agenda and not simply list the items in the order that they are received. Both the chair and the secretary may have to think carefully about what items need to be considered. They may also want to indicate how much time should be given for some items according to their priority. Operational issues that are more appropriately dealt with outside a meeting should not be put on the agenda. If decisions are to be taken at a meeting, the degrees of freedom available need to be identified and explained.

The frequency of meetings and their duration need to be related to the volume of business. The volume of business may also need to be managed by combining items. Thought should also be given to logical sequence of items. A further issue is the need to allocate time for discussion of individual items. It is all too easy to spend an inordinate amount of time on easy and relatively minor items with key issues being left to the end when people may be in a hurry, tired and a meeting may not even **quorate**. Approval may be needed from the meeting as a whole about issues such as sequence, time allocations and deferment of items. Exceptionally, the order of business may need to be varied because, for example, a key person has to leave. Other items may be introduced under 'any other business', but not if the items are controversial and should have been identified on the original agenda. The chair also needs to beware of the agenda being hijacked by a member or members raising items 'on the back of' other items instead of tabling these issues beforehand with written reports if necessary. Another issue for the chair to beware of is a meeting being used as a dumping ground for issues where responsibilities lie elsewhere or for problems that simply cannot be resolved.

Sometimes it is the practice to include agenda items under standard headings, such as reports from the heads of the various departments. However, there is a danger that this can descend into an unproductive ritual.

EXAMPLE: Reporting by exception

In a British manufacturing company most of the time in meetings was spent in receiving and considering reports from departments within the company. These tended to be both detailed and defensive and they led to little productive outcome. As a result it was decided to institute reporting by exception, that is reports were only received from individual departments if there was something exceptional that needed to be discussed. This had the advantage of freeing up considerable time for the issues that really did need discussion.

Who should attend meetings?

Thought may have to be given to who should be invited to a meeting. This may be totally prescribed by the constitution of a committee but, when the constitution is first established, the matter has to be examined. In any case, constitutions sometimes need amendment. People with specialist expertise relating to a specific item on the agenda may need to be specially invited to attend particular meetings and, on occasions, people may need to be excluded from meetings or part of the proceedings because of conflicts of interest. A balance usually has to be struck between having the interested parties present and not involving too many people because of the varying levels of interest and the costs involved, particularly in terms of time. A system of subcommittees can be a way of getting the optimum balance between differing interests and economy of time. Sometimes it will be appropriate to establish ad hoc subcommittees that can enable the detail of a particular issue to be examined without holding up the main business of a meeting.

It can be particularly dangerous to exclude a person from a meeting primarily because they are likely to take a controversial position, or at least one that is considered to be controversial as far as the chair is concerned. To exclude someone on this basis may lead to charges of unfair chairing, which may then mean that the chair is under procedural challenge as well as being challenged on a substantive issue. Controversial issues tend to surface anyway, and it may be best to see that this happens via the established machinery for resolving conflict rather than in another way, particularly if the chair would otherwise lose respect in the process.

Other preparation

Other issues that may require forethought include the exact nature of information that people attending meetings need to have beforehand so that they can contribute effectively and also the seating arrangements at a meeting. The type of room and layout can affect discussion, as can seating arrangements. Seating arrangements can be controlled by providing place names, which have the added advantage of identifying those present.

There may be pre-meetings before the main meeting. In national and local government it is customary for political parties to meet to agree on a party line before engaging in public debate at the formal decision-making body. It is usually the case that the real decisions are taken by the majority party in their pre-meeting. Other pre-meetings may be of groups of people forming a **caucus** to try to agree the line that they will take during a meeting. A small minority who prepare in this way can have a powerful influence on the outcome of any discussions. They will be primed and create a certain amount of momentum for the views that they express during a meeting. If they vote together at a meeting, they may find that the natural divisions amongst the other people present make it relatively easy to get a majority in favour of their point of view. This may lead other sub-groups to have pre-meetings as well, in an attempt to counter such tactics. One way of dealing with an attempt to force a minority point of view through a committee or other meeting is simply to alert other members as to what is happening beforehand. The chair or any member of a committee may wish to forestall a particular proposal. It may be a matter not so much of converting others, which may be difficult, but of alerting people as to what is happening so that they are on their guard as far as their own interests are concerned. This may also be necessary when there is an attempt to conceal information.

The importance of preparation before meetings was illustrated by the example given in Chapter 4 concerning the former Wales Gas Board. Those managers who prepared for the consultative committee meetings with employee representatives found that the committees played a constructive role. Those who did not prepare and who perhaps also did not take the committees seriously found that the employee representatives simply stopped attending, causing the committees to collapse.

Video-conferencing

Meetings can now take place by video link-up, which means that all members of a team do not have to be physically present. Whilst video-conferencing can have many advantages, saving the need to travel and therefore saving on time and money, it is also necessary to be aware of its limitations. Considerable technological resources are needed to set it up. Also, there is less interaction between members and the quality of such interaction as there is cannot be as great as it would be if members were physically together. Additionally, a key aspect of meetings can be the informal exchanges between members that often take place before, during and after meetings. These disadvantages have to be weighed against the advantages and perhaps consideration given to the utilization of a mix of methods – using video-conferencing alternately with meeting face- to-face meetings, for example.

Skype and other applications (such as Linux) using Voice over Internet Protocol (VoIP) could also be very usefully considered for one-to-one communication. These applications are much more cheaply set up than video-conferencing. While they have similar drawbacks such as occasional interruptions in connection quality, it is far easier to interact on a one-to-one basis using these applications than for a group of people speaking together, as in the video-conferencing situation described above.

Plenty of advice abounds on the Internet about how to maximize one's impact during such interactions. Such advice includes:

- Looking the part and dressing appropriately, even though the meeting may be taking place while you are at home
- Clearing any clutter from the background so as to give an impression of being well organized
- Ensuring that there are no distractions from other colleagues or members of your family during the 'conference' (including family pets)
- Giving consideration to making a practice video of your performance so you can improve self-presentation if necessary for the actual event.

Conduct by the chair during meetings

The chair as facilitator

Several problems can arise during a meeting. A key job of the chair is to see that they actually use the knowledge of the people who are present. It is up to the chair to see that appropriate issues are identified for discussion and then ensure that the collective knowledge and skills of the members are used to resolve the issues. If further information would help, the chair needs to consider releasing or obtaining it.

The chair may contribute to the substantive discussions, but should only do so when the issues have been properly identified. In practice chairs vary considerably in the skill with which they use the abilities of the people present. Good and bad examples are obvious on radio and television programmes, just as there will be good and bad examples of chairing in most organizations. It can be instructive to identify the differences between effective and ineffective chairs on public display in the media. Some chairs of radio and television programmes are very adept at drawing out the views of those who have been invited to speak and at controlling subsequent media discussion. Others lacking this skill, or just wishing to be the centre of attention themselves, may invite people to contribute to programmes and then use their procedural position and studio confidence to talk too much themselves, and in so doing wreck any discussion. However, observing such behaviour can be very instructive about how to handle discussions.

The chair's role in resolving conflict

One of the key roles of a meeting can be as a way of resolving conflict. Ironically, the role of a chair can be to identify what the conflict is in the first place. Unless this is done, agreement may be reached before the basic issues have been adequately considered. Another general problem is the need to handle conflict in such a way that the mechanism for resolving it is not destroyed in the process. Sometimes there is little or no conflict and the exchange of specialist information leads to a decision to which all contributors are equally committed. On other occasions the conflicts can be so bitter that the decision-making process collapses. The range of potential conflict within national government assemblies is such that members do not risk having a chair who is not neutral: the speaker, who chairs the proceedings, has a neutral procedural role. Non-executive mayors fulfil the same function in meetings of local government councils. Many trade unions appoint a president who fulfils a similar function. One of the advantages of having separate people as chair of the board of directors and chief executive, is that the chair can concentrate on the procedural and process issues, leaving the chief executive to take the lead on substantive matters.

In the absence of a specially appointed and generally neutral chair, it will normally be the most senior person present who will chair a meeting. If they are in conflict with other people at a meeting it will often be appropriate to simply try and talk the issue through. Often other members of a meeting may be able to challenge inappropriate ideas more strongly than the chair because they are not hampered by the need to control discussion in an equitable way at the same time. Members of a meeting may also find that it is more acceptable to have the flaws in their logic exposed by members other than the chair. Often the members will resolve controversial issues without the chair having to get involved. The group can be given an opportunity to discuss the issues without the chair needing to reveal their point of view. At the very least, some of the conflict may get resolved, leaving the chair only having to deal with residual issues. However, that does not mean that the chair should not, when appropriate, take the lead and explain why a particular course of discussion is likely to be unproductive. This may be particularly necessary because often the chair is also the person who may know most about the substantive issues that are being discussed.

What members of a meeting may take particular exception to is not being allowed to air their views when appropriate. It is one thing to have the reasons explained why one's own views are not acceptable, but quite another thing not to be given an opportunity to express them at all. In situations in which the final decision rests with the chair it may be quite appropriate and acceptable for the chair to say at the end of the discussion: 'I have heard all that you have had to say and this is what I am going to do.' If disagreement has to be resolved in some other way, for example, by a vote, that is the time when the chair should ask for one of the members to put the issue to a vote.

A further cause of irritation, particularly when the final decision rests with the chair, can be if members are invited to discuss issues that the chair has secretly already decided upon. It may then emerge that the members have complete freedom to come to the decision that the chair has already determined! A chair can avoid or reduce such irritation by saying that they are disposed to take a particular course of action but want to check if there are any objections that they had not anticipated. It may also be appropriate to say that a decision has been taken and the discussion is only about implementation. What a chair should avoid is the pretence that the members of a meeting can influence a decision that has already been made.

The ability of chairs to manage a discussion where they have an interest in the outcome varies considerably. It can be likened to trying to referee a football match in which you are also playing. Some people will be able to handle such potential conflict better than others. Sometimes it may be appropriate to have someone else chair discussion on an issue where the chair is particularly involved or where there is a conflict with the chair's personal interests. However, it is not always practicable or desirable to keep asking to have a neutral chair. This means that chairing skills are one of the key skills that managers need to develop.

Dangers of over-involvement by the chair

It is very easy for the person chairing a meeting to underestimate the extent to which they get involved in discussion and to overestimate the extent to which other people are involved. This is also a problem that can confront lecturers who have responsibility for leading discussions. One system for training lecturers in the technique of discussion-leading involves charting the pattern of contributions during a discussion. The resultant chart or 'sociogram' can reveal a pattern of which the discussion leader was unaware. A typical pattern is shown in Figure 15.1.

An examination of the flow of discussion in Figure 15.1 shows that most of the discussion was centred upon the chair or discussion leader. There was little cross-discussion, and one person did not contribute at all. If this was appropriate, and the chair was aware of what was really happening, it may have been perfectly satisfactory. However, it is very easy for a chair to assume that, because they are involved and interested, so is everyone else. This is not automatically the case. It is possible for a person to sit through a meeting, seething with frustration, but not contributing. Others may remain passively silent although able to contribute. Meanwhile, the chair may be quite unaware of all this. It can be instructive for a chair to be shown a flow chart (or sociogram) of a meeting they have chaired and then mentally try to build up a picture of the actual pattern of discussion during their next meeting. Regular checks on the body language of those present can provide important clues as to their feelings about particular topics and about the conduct of the meeting generally.

Involving members

Often the flow of discussion that is actually needed is more like that shown in Figure 15.2 In this second chart it is much less obvious who is the chair.

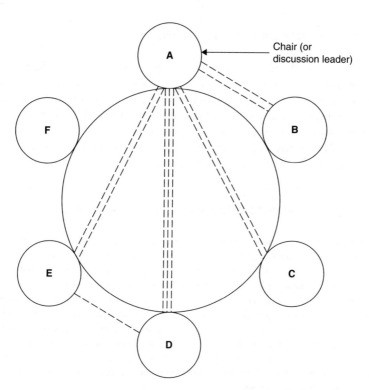

Figure 15.1 Chair-centred discussion

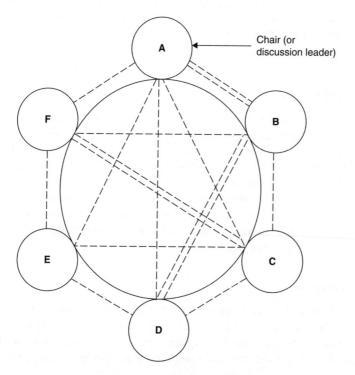

Figure 15.2 Group-centred discussion

Everyone has contributed and there is more cross-discussion than was the case in the previous chart. The flow of discussion may need to be routed more through the chair in large formal meetings, but even in that situation it may be appropriate to allow some cross-discussion provided it is not disruptive. In large formal meetings it may still be necessary for the chair to check out the attitudes of members to the way meetings are handled. There may be major misperceptions of the dynamics of meetings.

EXAMPLE: Involvement of members

The attitudes of the various members of a hospital board towards the way in which meetings were handled were established by observation of the meetings and interviews with key participants. There were some surprising differences in perception. The chair and secretary appeared convinced that everyone had ample opportunity to contribute. This was in marked contrast to the senior member of the nursing staff in particular, who was clearly of the opinion that she was only permitted to speak when invited to do so. In this particular case, open discussion was not helped by the fact that meetings were conducted in a long rectangular room. The higher the status of a person, the closer they sat to the head of the table. Discussion was confined to those sitting close to the Chair. The nursing representative sat at the far end of the table, away from the chair and secretary.

At another hospital in the same group as in the previous example, executive meetings were held in a room that permitted seating arrangements to be in the form of a semi-circle, which seemed to permit a more genuinely open discussion. The different seating arrangements, whether by accident or design, reflected the very different managerial styles of those organizing the meetings.

Control by the chair

There are other important points to note. These include the need for the chair to protect the position of a member if that person is being ridiculed, particularly if they have a potential contribution to make. The routing of all contributions through the chair may only be necessary when the group lacks the self-discipline to evolve a means of taking it in turns to speak. If the chair is ignored, or if people talk whilst the chair is speaking, a pointed silence may be a more appropriate way of re-establishing control than by the raising of one's voice. The use of humour may also be an effective way of relieving tension and progressing a meeting.

Pace of discussion

Chairs need to strike the right balance concerning the pace of discussion. People may be very concerned to state their own views but impatient of the right of others to do the same. Too quick a pace may leave many people with the feeling that they have not had adequate opportunity to state their views, whilst too slow a pace may leave many people with the view that their time has been unnecessarily wasted. The ease with which points at issue can simply be misunderstood should never be underestimated. It is important that the chair clarifies and summarizes whenever there appears to be any doubt or whenever decisions are taken.

Cultural issues

It is increasingly necessary to take account of any cultural diversity within meetings. This is more common because of globalization, ease of international travel, greater cultural diversity within countries and developments in technology. It is also more likely because of organizational developments such as multinational and transnational companies, joint ventures, greater inter-government cooperation on a regional and national basis and developments such as European Works Councils. Sometimes such developments necessitate simultaneous translation into a number of different languages.

Recording the outcome

The possibility of confusion about the content and outcome of a meeting will be reduced if there are adequate minutes or whatever other record is appropriate. However, for this to be undertaken effectively, meetings need to have been conducted properly in the first place. One does not, for example, want misunderstandings about what was really decided to be left to surface when the minutes are distributed. As was explained in Chapter 14 in the context of negotiation, there are many factors that can cause confusion. These include selective perception, poor listening skills and the use of ambiguous language.

Recording can take a variety of forms. A circulated minute is the most common type of record but, if this is inappropriate, as a minimum the chair should make an *aide-memoire* even in many informal situations. Other parties involved may also find it prudent to record an *aide-memoire* where there is no formal minute. A record of the whole course of discussion may be counterproductive. In the heat of discussion people may say things that it is in no-one's interest to record. Consequently, considerable tact may be needed in writing up minutes so that the outcomes are accurately recorded without rekindling arguments that have been settled. The responsibility for action also needs to be carefully identified to help ensure that action that is agreed is actually implemented. Where the scale and importance justifies it, one may need a note-taker who is separate from the person advising the chair on procedural matters.

Team building

Many of the issues already covered in this chapter are relevant to team building. The leaders of teams need to carefully consider the difference between process and task leadership. They also need to consider the related concept of distributive leadership – previously considered in Chapter 4 on managerial and leadership style.

The way in which groups operate was also discussed in Chapter 4, particularly in relation to the work of George Homans and the assessment of the effectiveness of managers and leaders. The way in which group members interact in meetings has been considered earlier in this chapter, with particular consideration having been given to the technique of examining group interaction by way of a sociogram. Chapter 8 on communication is relevant as is Chapter 14 (on negotiating skills) about the way in which internal differences between group members can be resolved. Some attention has been given in this current chapter to the division of labour in meetings but it is also necessary to consider the broad distribution of roles that may be necessary in teams.

Team mix

Meredith Belbin's work (2010a) focuses on the relationship between the membership of management teams and their effectiveness. He identifies the right 'mix' in a group as a key requirement for effectiveness. Belbin suggests that it is necessary for a management team to contain people prepared to play the various complementary roles. A group of talented individuals could fail because there could be too much competition to play some roles with no one prepared to play important but possibly less glamorous ones. The roles that Belbin (2010b) identifies as likely to be necessary are:

- Plant (who is creative and intelligent but may be introverted)
- Resource investigator
- Coordinator
- Shaper
- Monitor/evaluator
- Team worker
- Implementer
- Completer/finisher
- Specialist.

This list needs to be viewed as a set of guidelines for group membership, as not all groups will require the exact permutation identified by Belbin. Also, people may need and be able to play different roles according to the needs of a situation. People may also need and be able to switch from one role to another within a group. This is particularly important as managers may have to work with groups where they have little or no control over group membership. Training exercises are sometimes used so that participants can analyse the nature of the group they are in with a view to making the process more productive.

A key ingredient of effective groups is often the development of trust. The need to develop trust may be especially necessary if the membership is disparate and if there are significant conflicts of interest. Allowance may also need to be made for the time necessary for people of different cultural backgrounds to get to know and understand one another. Trust and confidence are likely to be developed by the successful accomplishment of tasks. This can be an argument for giving new groups relatively easy tasks initially.

A particularly important aspect of group activity is their potential creativity. Managers sometimes make the mistake of believing that they must be the ones who come up with the creative ideas and ignore the potential creativity of the rest of the team. This may be because such managers have a concept of managerial leadership that is old-fashioned and egocentric. It can actually be counterproductive to have a senior manager also trying to play the role of creative thinker as this may detract from the effective organization of the group. Groups also have to beware of unbalanced **groupthink**.

EXAMPLE: A consequence of poor team mix

The importance of having the right mix of people in a group and the potentially disastrous consequences of unbalanced groupthink were sadly illustrated by a climbing disaster in 1995. Six climbers were blown to their death while trying to descend from the summit of the second-highest peak in the world, K2 in the Himalayas. A seventh member of the team, who did not reach the top, died of pneumonia. The lack of a person who was prepared to play the role of monitor/evaluator may have been crucial. Peter Hillary (1995) – another mountaineer and the son of Sir Edmund Hillary, one of the pair who first scaled Mount Everest – had abandoned his simultaneous attempt to climb K2. He commented to the effect that no one in the other group seemed to have been prepared to voice concerns about the huge risk involved and that a 'blinkered … summit fever' had developed in the group.

Summary

Informal and formal meetings are an integral part of organizational activity. Consequently, managers need to know the various purposes of meetings and how they are or should be structured. As managers are often likely to chair meetings it is particularly important that they develop effective chairing skills. The effects of badly organized meetings were examined. These effects include poor communication and decision-making. Badly conducted meetings can also waste a lot of people's time and damage the reputation of those responsible for their organization. The need for preparation was explained, even with informal meetings. This affects all those involved in a meeting, but particularly the chair and any secretary. The preparation for formal meetings involves the drawing up of an agenda and arranging a division of labour at a meeting so that the chair in particular is not overloaded.

The role of conflict at meetings was examined, as was a strategy for handling it. Usually it is best for chairs to facilitate a fair discussion about the issues and then use whatever mechanism is appropriate (e.g. voting, negotiation, or unilateral decision-making) for resolving it. Members may be far more likely to be upset about not having had the chance to raise legitimate concerns than by having a decision go against them. Decisions are in any case likely to be more balanced if they are taken after a full examination of the issues.

The need for chairs not to get over-involved in substantive discussion at meetings was stressed, as this can damage the procedural framework within which discussions need to take place. The over-involvement of chairs can also lead to inadequate process control during a meeting. The need for effective recording was also considered. It is important that responsibility for any action is clearly identified and that implementation is monitored.

Consideration of the skills required to make meetings effective helps explain how to make work teams effective. The objectives and role allocation need to be clarified. Time may need to be allocated to build trust. Hopefully the potential creativity of teams can be realized but care may still be needed to ensure that unbalanced decisions are not taken.

Self-assessment questions

1. Identify the range of meetings in which you are likely to be involved in any one day or week, both formal and informal.
2. Identify the purpose of these meetings and any decision-making mechanisms.
3. Select a meeting that you have recently attended and consider whether roles were properly allocated and kept to or not.
4. Practise using chairing skills at an informal meeting you attend.
5. How might the chair of a meeting best handle conflict? If possible, answer with reference to a meeting you have attended.
6. What follow-up action may be necessary to ensure that meetings are effective? Answer with reference to a meeting you have attended.
7. Identify the key elements in effective team building.
8. Reflect on the quality of your relationship with any team that you are leading: what does your team need you for? Do you and the team share the same goals? What issues do you and the team avoid discussing? What could you do to turn your team into a 'dream team'?

Learning exercise

Chart a sociogram at a meeting you attend, as described in this chapter. Identify what you learn about the dynamics of the meeting and how you apply what you have learned in attending other meetings.

References

NB: Works of particular interest are marked with an asterisk.

*Belbin, R. Meredith (2010a), *Management Teams – Why They Succeed or Fail,* 3rd edn., Butterworth Heinemann.
   A very useful account about the roles and dynamics in managerial teams.
Belbin, Meredith (2010b), *Team Roles at Work*, 2nd edn., Butterworth Heinemann.
Hillary, Peter (1995), Comments reported in Evening Standard (London), 23 August.
Rees, W. David and Christine Porter (2008) *Skills of Management,* 6th edn., Cengage Learning.
   See appendix to Chapter 16 on Definitions and Explanations of Terms used in Formal Meetings *or any other final chapter in previous editions of the book.*

Taking it further

Hurn, Brian and Barry Tomalin (2013), 'Cross Cultural Communication, Theory and Practice', Ch. 8 in *International Team Building and Team Working*, Palgrave Macmillan.
Clutterbuck, David (2007), *Coaching the Team at Work,* London, Boston: Nicholas Brealey International.
Peberdy, Duncan and Jane Hammersley (2010), *Brilliant Meetings – What to Know, Say and Do to Have Fewer, Better Meetings,* Pearson Business.

Glossary

The terms below are printed in bold in the text the first time they are used in a chapter.

ACAS: Advisory, Conciliation and Arbitration and Service (UK).

Act down: undertaking tasks that are normally or more appropriately undertaken by subordinates.

Act up: undertaking tasks normally done by one's boss when the boss (or bosses) is unavailable.

Added value: the value added to a product or service by an organization.

Ad hoc: set up just for a particular purpose. This Latin phrase literally means 'for this' or 'for this situation'. Its meaning has been extended to 'set up to serve a particular purpose'. Thus, an *ad hoc* committee is one which has been set up to serve a particular purpose and which will cease to exist as soon as this purpose has been served.

Assertiveness: putting one's point politely but firmly while recognizing the right of others to do the same.

Assessment centres: mechanisms for measuring the potential that either external candidates or internal post-holders can add to an organization. They can be used for selection, promotions or staff development.

Balanced score card: a means of staff appraisal to assess the performance profile of a person in key areas.

Caucus: a sub-group of people who meet privately to try and influence the decision of a larger group or meeting.

Charisma: charm combined with force of personality.

Clinical governance: the system for maintaining and improving the quality of service, particularly with regard to health.

Comfort zone: an area of work activity where a person feels confident and capable, but which is not necessarily a priority area.

Conflicts of interest: differences about what an agreement should be, for example the amount of an annual pay award.

Conflicts of right: differences about the interpretation of an agreement.

Consensus: agreement of all the parties directly concerned.

Contingency approach: the adaptation of behaviour (or choice of management techniques) according to the needs of the situation.

Corporate governance: the system of policy-making, control and ethics in any organization, including governments.

Corporate social responsibility: acceptance by an organization of its wider responsibilities towards those affected by its decisions, such as customers, suppliers, the community and the environment, as well as to those who finance it and its employees.

Critical path analysis (CPA): a method for determining the most logical sequence of scheduling a project.

De-layering: removing at least one level of command in the organizational structure.

Digital divide: the division between those who are computer literate and those who are not.

Disciplinary pyramid: A triangular representation of disciplinary action indicating that most such action is for minor offences.

Discretionary content: that part of a job where the manner of execution is left to the job-holder, as long as the execution is conducted in a reasonable manner and the overall objectives are achieved.

Disposable workforce: the employment of staff so that they can be released with the minimum of notice and payment when the need for them has reduced or ended.

Distributive bargaining: a situation in which one person or group can only gain at the expense of another.

Distributive leadership: the dispersal of the leadership role between more than one person.

Diversity management: a way of managing that capitalizes on a diverse workforce by using the mix of talent, values and points of view to organizational advantage.

Dotted line organizational relationship: the relationship of a person who reports to, or gives advice to, another.

E-commerce: trade carried out by electronic means.

E-learning: the use of information technology to facilitate learning.

Emotional intelligence: being able, for example, to rein in an emotional impulse, to handle relationships smoothly, to motivate oneself and to persist in the face of conflict and frustrations.

Empowerment: the authority of a person or group to take decisions without prior authorization by a higher level.

Equal pay: equal payment for same or similar work. Generally there is a legal right to this between the sexes under European law.

Equal value: equal pay for work which although different is equally demanding. There is a general legal right to this between the sexes under European law.

Ethnocentric: attention, concern and values based around a particular national group.

Exit interviews: interviews with employees who are about to leave. A key objective may be to find out why they are leaving as well as wishing them well.

Explicit knowledge: important know-how in an organization that is clear and probably recorded (the converse of tacit knowledge).

Flexible organization: an organization with a smaller core group of workers but many peripheral ones, which may be very reliant on outsourcing as well. Where there are very few core workers, such an organization may be described as a virtual organization.

Fordism: mass production based on division of labour and strict control, as practised by Henry Ford and the Ford Motor Company.

Frames of reference: whether a person adopts a unitary or pluralistic perspective to conflicts of interest within an organization. See also *pluralistic* and/or *unitary.*

Functional control: where those in charge of functional areas of management have line authority over others in the same function, wherever they are located. Examples of the standard functions in organizations are production, finance, sales, human resources and quality control.

Functional flexibility: an organization that has a high capacity to switch human and other resources to alternative activities.

Globalization: the increasing internationalization of market forces, technology and social interaction.

Grapevine: an unofficial channel of communication of information and rumour within an organization and which can be faulty.

Greenwash: environmental policies that are introduced for the sake of appearance rather than to achieve significant results.

Group think: a norm developed by a group and which is not necessarily rational.

Halo effect: a perceived favoured aspect of an individual's behaviours or a favoured personal characteristic that is assumed to be representative of an individual's total ability or behaviour. The opposite is 'reverse halo effect' or 'horns effect'.

Human capital management: protecting, consolidating and developing the intellectual assets of an organization.

Human resource management (HRM)*:* the effective utilization of the human resources in an organization, facilitated but not directly controlled by an HRM department if there is one.

Integrative bargaining: where constructive bargaining can lead to gain on the part of both or all the parties involved.

Intellectual capital: the accumulation of intellectual assets of an organization.

Intellectual property: the legal rights to the intellectual assets of an organization or person e.g. patents and copyright.

Investors in People (IIP): a UK government accreditation scheme recognizing organizations that manage their training and development needs appropriately.

Inward investment: capital investment in a country by an organization or persons in other countries.

Job competences/competencies: defining job demands in terms of the outputs that are required; potentially useful in selection, training and pay.

Job distortion: when a job has been rearranged so that the appropriate objectives and activities are not being met either in full or in part; can particularly happen when a job is rearranged to meet individual rather than organizational needs.

Job instrumentality: taking a very calculating and material approach to one's job and carefully limiting what is given in return to the employer.

Kaizen: discussion groups designed to secure continuous improvements in quality and efficiency, used particularly in Japanese business organizations.

Key performance indicators (KPIs): measures of effectiveness in an organization, potentially particularly appropriate in the public and other not-for-profit sectors.

Knock-on effect: the repercussive consequences of decisions.

Knowledge management: systematic review of an organization's intellectual assets with a view to their maintenance, protection, development and utilization.

Learning contract: an agreement under which the trainer and the trainee specify their respective inputs and the desired learning outcomes they expect to be achieved.

Learning organization: an open type of organization that facilitates the exchange of ideas both internally and externally with a view to developing staff and the organization.

Line and staff relationship: organizational arrangement where authority is vested in line managers and advice given by functional staff.

Management by objectives (MBO): a formal scheme of management direction and control centred upon interlocking objectives.

Managerial escalator: the steady progression from specialist activity to a greater amount of managerial activity.

Managerial gap: the extent to which managerial activities are neglected in favour of specialist activities.

Managerial hybrid: a person with significant managerial and specialist responsibilities.

Managerialism: a managerial style associated in parts of the public sector with the close monitoring of objectives achieved by professional employees.

Matrix structure: an organizational arrangement under which people have both a line manager and a project leader.

Mechanistic structures: a clear if rigid set of arrangements for structuring an organization based in particular on hierarchy, specialization and unity of command.

Micromanagement: involvement in the detailed control of the activities in one's area of responsibility.

Mission statement: a statement of the overall aims, objectives and values of an organization.

Monochrone/Monochronic: a person (or preference for) concentrating on one task at a time.

Negotiating ritual: a series of offers and counter-offers made with a view to obtaining eventual agreement.

Non-government entity (NGE): a not-for-profit organization that is not controlled by the government, for example a charity. If international, for example OXFAM, it is known as an INGE.

Non-governmental organization (NGO): similar to NGE.

Numerical flexibility: an organization that is relatively easily able to increase or decrease the number of staff it employs.

Off-shoring: contracting out production or services to overseas suppliers.

Opportunity cost: the alternative use that could have been made of resources.

Organic structures: a fluid approach to organizational structure based on market needs with authority and reporting relationships arranged to fit those needs.

Outsourcing: contracting out of production or services, not necessarily overseas.

Peer audit: review of performance by colleagues.

Performance management: managing staff in such a way that their performance is maintained or increased, particularly with regard to achieving organizational objectives.

Performance related pay: a formal link between pay and performance. Usually dependent on the achievement of specified tasks and/or objectives.

Personal development plan (PDP): a programme for improving one's performance and capability.

Person specification: the main personal attributes, education and experience that a person needs in order to be able to do a particular job.

Pluralist/pluralistic: a recognition that whilst there will be common aims in an organization, there will also be competing sectional interests.

Polychrone/Polychronic: A person (or aptitude for) dealing with several tasks at once.

Positional power: The influence that derives directly or indirectly from the position a person holds in an organization.

Positive action: employment policies designed to improve the representation of minority groups within the workforce in general and/or specific grades for example by the provision of developmental training. It does not involve positive discrimination.

Positive discrimination: preferential treatment of minority groups within the workforce to improve their representation in general and/or specific grades.

Power distance: the hierarchical gap between people in an organization – may also involve the extent of the deference by one person to another.

Prescribed content: that part of a job that must be carried out in a particular way, for example to conform to organizational policies and the law.

Presenteeism: where a person tries to justify their contribution to an organization by being present rather than actually doing their job.

Psychological contract: the expectations that an employee will have of their employer and vice versa. These expectations will not necessarily be written down or enforceable in law, but will influence the state of the relationship between an employer and their employees.

Quorate: having the constitutional minimum number of people at a meeting to make it valid.

Re-shoring: bringing work back to the 'parent' country.

Role behaviour: behaviour that occurs more because of requirements of the situation a person is in rather than because of their personality.

Role set analysis (RSA): a technique for prioritizing work.

Rubber desk: desk of a person who is in the habit of passing on or back work to others as quickly as possible.

Sapiential authority: influence by virtue of one's job expertise and facilitation skills.

Serial entrepreneur: an entrepreneur who starts up a series of successful businesses.

Shadowing: learning by observing the behaviour of a senior manager or colleague.

Shock absorbers: staff who can 'soak up' pressure and/or stress and in so doing protect colleagues.

Silo mentality: pre-occupation with the interests and/or achievements of just a section of an organization.

Sociogram: a chart of the pattern of discussion at a meeting.

Socio-technical systems: an organization structure or substructure caused by the interaction between technical and social factors.

Span of control: the number of people reporting directly to a particular manager.

Stakeholders: individuals or groups who contribute to the performance of an organization and/or who have an interest in its success. Examples are shareholders, financial backers, employees, suppliers and customers.

Status quo: arrangements as they are before an actual or planned change.

Subsidiarity: allowing decisions to be taken at the lowest appropriate level

Swot analysis: examination of an organization's strengths, weaknesses, opportunities and threats.

Synergy: where the whole is greater than the sum of the parts.

Systems theory: a view of organizations as a dynamic set of interconnecting activities which also interact with the external environment.

Tacit knowledge: implicit 'know-how' in organizations that may be held by groups and/or individuals which, though important, may not be recorded (the converse of explicit knowledge).

Talent management: nuturing of the people who hopefully will ensure future organizational success.

Transnational corporation: an international commercial organization with its roots in no particular country.

Tunnel vision: over-concentration on a particular task or job.

Uncertainty avoidance: the desire to avoid ambiguity.

Unitary/unitarist: viewing an organization as having common aims to which all should or do subscribe.

Unity of command: an organizational structure in which each member of staff has only one boss.

Universal inclusion: an employer that takes a positive approach to all sections of the workforce and their potential contribution.

Upward appraisal: assessment from below, particularly by subordinates.

Virtual organization: an organization that is essentially a network of inter-connected external facilities, with no significant geographic core and usually linkages that are computer based.

Zero-hours contracts: an arrangement by an employer to provide work but without actually guaranteeing any.

360-degree appraisal: performance assessment of a person by the key people or groups with whom they interact. May include external people or groups such as customers.

Index